The Enneagram

Thorsons First Directions

The Enneagram
Karen Webb

Thorsons
An imprint of HarperCollinsPublishers
77-85 Fulham Palace Road
Hammersmith, London W6 8JB

The Thorsons website address is:
www.thorsons.com

Published by Thorsons 2001

Text derived from *Principles of the Enneagram*,
published by Thorsons 1996

10 9 8 7 6 5 4 3 2 1

Editor: Jo Kyle
Design: Wheelhouse Creative Ltd
Production: Melanie Vandevelde
Photographs from PhotoDisc Europe

A catalogue record for this book is available from the British Library

ISBN 0 00711036 7

Printed and bound in Hong Kong

Contents

What the Enneagram is 3

How the Enneagram Works...7

The Nine Personality Types 21
    Type One: The Perfectionist 22
    Type Two: The Giver 30
    Type Three: The Performer 38
    Type Four: The Romantic 45
    Type Five: The Observer...52
    Type Six: The Questioner 59
    Type Seven: The Epicure 66
    Type Eight: The Boss 73
    Type Nine: The Mediator 81

What Do I Do Now? 89

The Enneagram

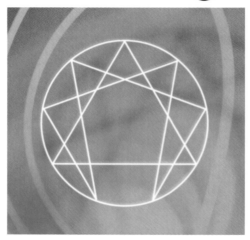

is the ancient system of personality types

linking personality to spirit

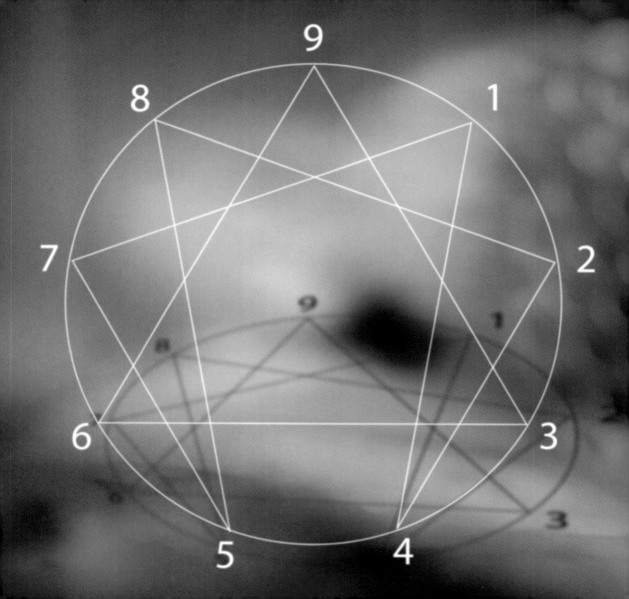

What the Enneagram is

The Enneagram (from the Greek *enneas* nine, *gramma* something written) is an ancient and beautifully accurate description of human personality in all its diversity, and of how personality is directly linked to each person's spiritual self.

Not a religion, it encapsulates and unites apparently different principles found in all major faiths. Now psychologists of various schools have found it corresponds uncannily closely to modern personality descriptions. Simple, accurate and profound, it links, explains and puts in context disparate elements of myself, and how I (and others) work, which otherwise have taken years to understand.

The Enneagram describes nine personality types, none better or worse than another, yet recognizably and radically different in their way of responding to the world. There are five billion of us on the planet:

probably at least half a billion of each type; yet we *are* unique, and the Enneagram allows us to be so. Our personality *type* is recognizable, but our personality – the experiences, memories, dreams and aspirations, and what we do with them – is our own.

Whether beginner or experienced self-explorer, the Enneagram has a unique role to play in the life of anyone seeking psychological or spiritual development, or looking to bridge the gap between them.

For anyone, at any stage of their journey, the Enneagram fosters:
• Deeper insight into who we are, our potential, and how to attain it.
• Self-directed growth from whatever level to whatever level we wish.
• More harmonious and creative daily lives.
• Deeper empathy, compassion and more creative relationships, through seeing ourselves as others see us and seeing others as they see themselves rather than through our projections and beliefs.
• The realization that we do not need to 'conquer' our personality, but befriend it, understand it and use it to help our growth.
• Understanding how our personality is the key to our personal spiritual path, whatever our religious beliefs.

History of the Enneagram

The Enneagram's nine-pointed star is an ancient diagram, and not an arbitrary device, though no-one knows its origin. It encapsulates the esoteric Laws of Three and Seven (also called Octaves), is very like Pythagoras's ninth seal symbolizing humanity, and some researchers link ancient stone circles with the mathematics of the Enneagram.

However, this book concerns the Enneagram of Personality, a modern name for an ancient wisdom of which this much is known for certain: Christian mystics of the Desert Father tradition, in the third and fourth centuries, worked with the concept of converting vice to virtue, using personality traits named in the Enneagram. A conversion concept including the diagram and nine personality types has also been a cornerstone of Sufi ethical training for 1400 years.

In the 1920s it was brought to Europe by G. I. Gurdjieff, a mystic and spiritual teacher. He claimed to have learnt it from Sufis in Afghanistan, and used it as an esoteric wisdom known only to spiritual teachers to determine practices for their pupils.

It remained a secret teaching until the late 1960s, when Oscar Ichazo initiated an intense psycho-spiritual training at Arica in Chile, incorporating much of the esoteric wisdom of the Enneagram. It was he who assigned the correct key words or 'passions' to each of the nine points. Many now famous people attended this training and subsequently wrote about it, including Claudio Naranjo, a transpersonal psychologist. He then took the still fairly rudimentary knowledge to California where he started a series of workshops to explore and extend understanding of the personality types described by the diagram, using discussion with people who recognized their type.

Helen Palmer, also a transpersonal psychologist, and Bob Ochs, a Jesuit priest, built upon the insights they gained there in 1970–71 and continued to expand our understanding and teach it in their own fields. From these sources the Enneagram has spread rapidly around the world as others learnt and then started to teach it.

How the Enneagram Works

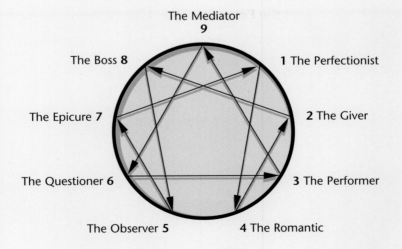

The Mediator
9

The Boss 8

1 The Perfectionist

The Epicure 7

2 The Giver

The Questioner 6

3 The Performer

The Observer 5

4 The Romantic

The shape of the diagram is central to the Enneagram model. Each person inhabits one basic type, which does not change. However, the lines connecting the points show how each type changes in extreme stress and in security (and allow us to predict how the nine personality types interact), whilst the external circle indicates the types on either side that can influence our behaviour. Each type also has three distinct variants.

   All of this, together with our environment as children and our individual level of self-knowledge, means that two people may be of the same Enneagram type and yet appear very different as personalities.

Basic personality type

It is now common knowledge that everyone filters and interprets what they perceive. The basic principle of the Enneagram is that:

- each of us has one of nine possible 'filters' which sets the tenor of our whole lives, a habitual focus of attention so deep it is usually hidden from conscious awareness; *and* ...
- this filter was not developed at random, but to protect a specific aspect of our essence (higher, or divine, self) which was particularly vulnerable in the infant.

Though our personality developed as a strategy to help us cope with the outer world as infants, by the time we are adult it is an automatic biased perspective. The way we view others and interpret events is coloured by it; our choices and actions are often based on it.

The unique and heartening aspect of the Enneagram theory is that our 'false' personality reflects, as in a mirror image, our highest self. It is not an enemy to be conquered but our best friend, showing us which lessons we need to learn and how to learn them.

Head, heart and belly

Human beings have three main ways of experiencing the world: thinking, feeling and sensing. Everyone uses all three, but each type favours one of them as their main channel for perceiving and responding to events. In addition, the Enneagram model, and every mystical tradition, recognizes three spiritual centres of perception and intelligence, located in the head, the heart and the belly.

The diagram divides into three triads, each corresponding to one of the centres. Each centre has its particular way of experiencing life, as

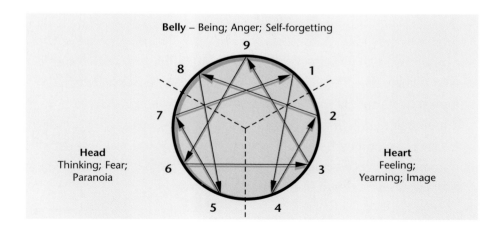

Belly – Being; Anger; Self-forgetting

Head
Thinking; Fear;
Paranoia

Heart
Feeling;
Yearning; Image

well as the 'negative' emotion and concerns associated with it. The three types within each triad are the ones which favour that centre.

The head centre is where we do our thinking: analyzing, remembering, projecting ideas about other people and events and planning future actions. This area corresponds to the 'third eye' or visualization centre used in, for example, Tibetan Buddhist meditations.

Head-based types (5, 6, 7) tend to respond to life through their thoughts. They have vivid imaginations and a strong ability to analyze and correlate ideas. For these types thinking is (usually unconsciously) a way of pre-empting fear in a potentially threatening world.

The heart centre is where we experience emotions: the wordless sensations which tell us how we feel rather than what we think about something. Emotions of the heart range from the strong and dramatic to the most subtle, almost muted feelings. We feel connected to others in this centre, but also a yearning for love and fulfilment. This is the heart centre opened in Sufi, and many Christian, practices.

Heart-based types (2, 3, 4) operate in the world through relationships, and are sometimes called 'image types' as they are concerned with how others see and relate to them. They are quick to sense another's needs or moods and respond to them, consciously or unconsciously. Successful relationships keep at bay the sense of emptiness and yearning that mark this centre.

The belly centre (sometimes called the body centre) is the focus of our instinctual intelligence, or sense of being, as contrasted with thinking and feeling. We experience ourselves physically in relation to people and the environment through this centre. It is the source of our energy and power to act in the physical world. This centre corresponds to the area known as Hara in Japan and Dan Tian in China, and is the focus of Zen practices.

Belly-based types (8, 9, 1), whose focus is on being, tend to 'be' in the world through action. Their instinct is to do, and they may speak of basing decisions and actions on a gut-feeling even when they have thought them through in detail. They are known as 'self-forgetting' types as they may be unaware of their own truest priorities. Being active in the world is fuelled by and mitigates the anger which, for Type Ones and Type Nines, only occasionally surfaces in direct expression.

As already mentioned, although everyone favours one centre, everybody contains and is affected by the head, heart and belly centres in themselves. The Enneagram model describes specific spiritual and psychological aspects of the centres in each person, regardless of type.

The head and heart centres both have a personality-based aspect and a 'holy opposite', which is a particular aspect of essence lost sight of as personality developed. The personality protects and masks the essential self but also mimics it, like a mirror reflecting its opposite, by looking for the forgotten aspects in the outside world instead of within. The belly centre can be a source of energy for growth, but also has three elements which relate to personality and help to mask essence.

These aspects of the centres are given names for convenience. Additionally, each type has its own key words for the aspects of the centres, descriptive of that type's personality preoccupations and essential states of being. The diagrams which follow give a summary of words which are explained in the relevant chapters on type.

The head centre: Fixation and Holy Idea

The names for aspects of the head centre are: Fixation, meaning the personality's habitual mental preoccupation or focus of attention, and Holy Idea, the state of being which is experienced, rather than thought of, by the head centre when it is free of the fixation.

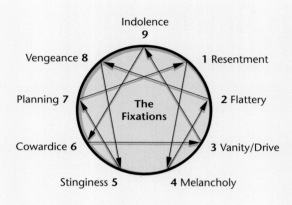

Indolence
9

Vengeance 8

1 Resentment

Planning 7

The
Fixations

2 Flattery

Cowardice 6

3 Vanity/Drive

Stinginess 5

4 Melancholy

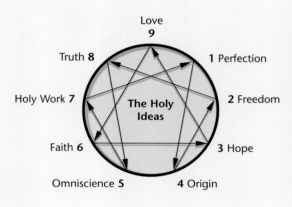

Love
9

Truth 8

1 Perfection

Holy Work 7

The Holy
Ideas

2 Freedom

Faith 6

3 Hope

Omniscience 5

4 Origin

The heart centre: Passion and Holy Virtue

The habitual preoccupation or focus of the heart centre is called its Passion. Christianity's founders were well aware of this aspect, and the passions correspond to the seven capital tendencies or 'deadly sins', plus Fear and Deceit. The essential state of being experienced in the heart is called the Holy Virtue.

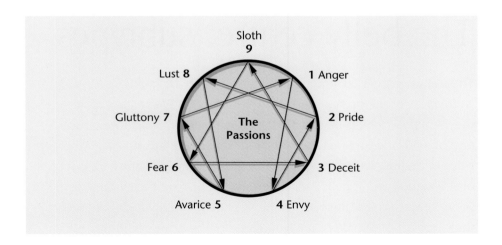

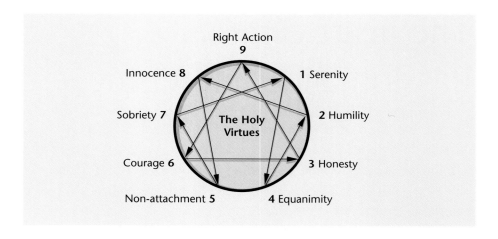

The diagram shows an enneagram circle labeled with "The Holy Virtues" in the centre:

- Right Action 9 (top)
- Innocence 8
- Serenity 1
- Sobriety 7
- Humility 2
- Courage 6
- Honesty 3
- Non-attachment 5
- Equanimity 4

The belly centre: subtypes

The belly centre contributes to our personality by giving us three 'subtypes', or instinctual patterns of behaviour. These are survival mechanisms to help us cope with *Self-preservation*, *Social* interaction, and one-to-one or *Sexual* relationship. Each type has its own different ways of dealing with these, and it is one of the ways in which people of the same type appear very different, as subtype behaviour overrides some of the 'typical' responses. Most people usually focus on one of these areas of life unless survival in one of the others is threatened.

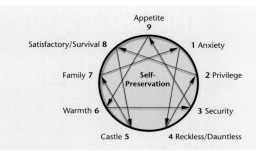

Self-Preservation

- Appetite **9**
- **1** Anxiety
- Satisfactory/Survival **8**
- **2** Privilege
- Family **7**
- **3** Security
- Warmth **6**
- Castle **5**
- **4** Reckless/Dauntless

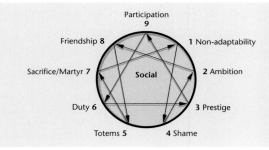

Social

- Participation **9**
- **1** Non-adaptability
- Friendship **8**
- **2** Ambition
- Sacrifice/Martyr **7**
- **3** Prestige
- Duty **6**
- Totems **5**
- **4** Shame

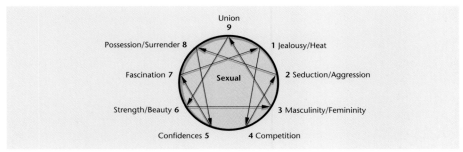

Sexual

- Union **9**
- **1** Jealousy/Heat
- Possession/Surrender **8**
- **2** Seduction/Aggression
- Fascination **7**
- **3** Masculinity/Femininity
- Strength/Beauty **6**
- Confidences **5**
- **4** Competition

Factors influencing type

Stress and security

Everybody's feelings and behaviour alter somewhat when they are under stress, and again when they are in an emotionally secure life situation. The lines on the diagram show the shift in mental and emotional strategy that we experience in these circumstances. The direction of arrow indicates the change: for each type the arrow points *towards* the stress point and *away from* the security point.

   People do not 'become' another type in stress or security: they take on characteristics of that type, but retain the concerns and issues of their own. If someone has been stressed or secure for a long time they can appear very like their stress or security type.

Wings

Each type has two 'wings' – the types on either side of it on the circle – and these may influence the way an individual manifests type. For example, a Type Six may at times lean towards Type Five, and become more withdrawn, or towards Type Seven and become more playful.

There are a number of theories as to how the wings function in relation to type. In my experience, wing influences seem to be particular to the individual – that is, they cannot be predicted. Looking at your own personality, you may find you 'lean' towards one wing or the other all the time, or towards neither, or to each at different times.

Personal growth

The Enneagram is an instrument of great subtlety, yet the central premise it is based on is very simple: that our personality was developed to protect our higher self, and is inseparably linked to it.

There is also one simple observation that allows us to use this knowledge, and it is not unique to the Enneagram. This is that we are two 'people' inside. One is the personality, which identifies itself with our thoughts, feelings and sensations; the other is the inner witness, sometimes called the observer. This is not the part of our personality which watches and comments on our lives, but an awareness which is neither thought, feeling nor sensation, yet *is* us in a way the personality is not. This difference between our psychological and spiritual natures is only apparent. Both are integral to who we are.

While we are alive we need a personality to mediate between our higher self and the world, and to help us get things done, but we also need to recognize its nature. The observer differentiates between personality (built of memories, ideas, plans, dreams) and essence, and this is the key to growth.

To transform something, first you have to know what is so; and this is a major part of the Enneagram's value. Gurdjieff said that if we can identify our chief feature, much of the work has already been accomplished; and the Enneagram provides the key to this. Then, through self-observation, we can recognize the personality's automatic reactions and use them as reminders of our essential qualities. In this way we regain the ability to respond to life from an unbiased perspective in tune with our true selves. It is not a question of transcending or subduing the personality, but of befriending it and learning which way it points us.

Finally, whether we approach the work of personal growth as primarily psychological, spiritual, or both, the 'proof of the pudding' is in the personal world. Unless it increases our humane-ness and loving-kindness; unless our daily actions, thoughts and relationships are more harmonious and lovingly creative, it is not growth.

The Nine Personality Types

The following chapter contains descriptions of the nine personality types. Through reading it, some people may be able to uncover their personnality type, though this requires deep soul-searching, and others may need more help.

It may be hard to decide which type you are. Maybe two or even more of the types seem familiar. The only sure way of knowing your type is through self-observation, and from the unmistakable affinity with others of your type when you hear them talk about themselves – and the surprising contrast with other types. For this reason I recommend Oral Tradition Workshops (*see page* 90) as the next step in working with the Enneagram.

Note: A book like this can only contain 'thumbnail sketches', and I have had to omit many subtleties of type.

Type One:
The Perfectionist

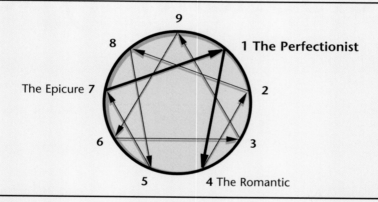

9

8   1 **The Perfectionist**

The Epicure 7

2

6   3

5   **4** The Romantic

Critical of themselves and others, Type Ones have an internal list of shoulds and should nots. They take responsibility seriously and wish whatever they do to be done absolutely correctly. They find it difficult to allow themselves pleasure for its own sake, as they monitor their behaviour against very high standards, and feel there is always more to do. They may procrastinate for fear of not 'getting it perfect'. Feeling morally superior, Type Ones may also be resentful of others who don't follow the rules, held in the One's mind, especially if they get away with it. Excellent organizers, they can spot just what's wrong and what needs to be done to get it right.

Ones became aware in infancy that they were not considered perfect, and their attention focused on becoming worthy of love. They felt themselves continually under a critical gaze, never acknowledged for doing anything good but told to do better. They became preoccupied with trying to be 'good'; internalizing the critical gaze and monitoring themselves in an attempt to pre-empt criticism by doing nothing 'wrong'. Emotions became dangerous. They learned to see them as bad, and even pleasant emotions could trigger an incorrect action.

As Ones continued to 'fail', their set of rules expanded. Self-forgetting consisted of replacing intuitive truth and real priorities with adopted correct behaviour, and focusing on what was wrong in themselves, their actions, and the outside world.

- **Unaware Ones** can be cynical, judgemental, self-righteous, cold, bigoted, controlling, anxious or angry, obsessive-compulsive, sarcastic and dogmatic.
- **Aware Ones** can be inspiring, caring, wise and ethical, self-disciplined, productive, discriminating and serene.

Passion and Fixation: anger and resentment

Ones are belly types who suppress their 'gut' reactions, and emotions, in favour of rationality. *Anger*, which in its cleanest form is a freeing cathartic energy which can fuel growth, is Ones' emotional preoccupation. Yet they report that they are rarely if ever angry, even when others can feel it. Their initial anger at being unrecognized was suppressed and displaced into anger at themselves, through which it validates self-forgetting and the censoring of all emotions.

Occasionally real anger will erupt, usually after months or years of suppression. This can be frightening as it has all the force of its accumulation, and is often misdirected.

Resentment is rationalized anger, and more easily recognized by the One. Unacceptable rage is transmuted into acceptable thoughts, from frustration to irritability and resentment. These, together with the righteous wrath which they sometimes express, can be justified because they are 'caused by' external faults.

Stress and security

Under stress, Ones take on the emotional idealism of Type Fours, emphasizing their belief that perfection is unattainable, and that somehow they are unworthy. Their focus shifts to relationships or emotions, and their feeling of being unlovable. They can become depressed, feeling that they are worthless and will never get it right – so life is pointless. On the positive side, taking on Type Four qualities can enhance Ones' appreciation of and longing for perfection, and opens up their feelings.

Some Ones barely recognize Type Seven in their make-up, even when in a secure relationship. Others delight in the respite it gives from the critic, and seek out Sevens as friends. When Ones do allow themselves to relax into security they can have fun for a while.

Subtypes

In the area of self-preservation, Type Ones divert the energy of anger into anxiety about personal security: getting things right, having exactly what one needs, keeping the job, looking after the family, and so on. It may look like fear but is more of a permanent resentful worrying.

When it comes to social interaction, Type Ones' tendency to ally themselves with the worthy group and support the politically, socially or spiritually correct cause, can lead to them experiencing confusion, frustration or outright anger at the group and/or at themselves. They criticize the group for not being perfect, and themselves for not being able to adapt themselves to the group's mores.

Sexual subtype Ones, idealizing the perfect connection to the one person (friend or spouse), fear that other people will be seen as more

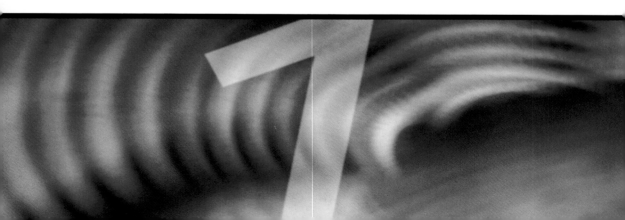

attractive, intelligent and desirable than themselves. Anger is channelled into a jealous scanning to make sure they are still wanted, and any imagined rejection produces a physical rush of 'heat'.

Relationships

Though Ones desire relationships they find it hard to trust the world because it often seems people do not mean what they say. They also feel they may be unworthy of friendship because they are not perfect.

Perfectionism in intimate relationships can cause problems and misunderstandings unless the ground rules are well established. Ones long for the perfect relationship, and when flaws appear, as they inevitably will, they look to see if they are doing anything wrong. If not, it is easy for them to resent and blame their partner.

Holy Virtue and Idea: serenity and perfection

Serenity is not the cessation of emotion, but a state of awareness that allows all feelings to come and go in the body and heart, and be fully experienced as they do, without judging some as good or pleasant and others as bad or unpleasant. Ones who learn to release their anger, once the backlog of suppressed feeling has been cleared, experience a sense of being fully energized and yet light of heart and body, a joyful acceptance of all facets of being, and an ability to engage with life and feelings fully and serenely.

When fully engaged with life, Ones realize everything, including themselves, is already perfect even in its imperfection. The habit of resentment can be hard to let go of. If the mind is not the correct source of criteria for perfection, and if it may not assign blame, how can perfection be attained? When Ones allow themselves to accept that the mind, which is partial and imperfect, cannot produce perfection, they experience and celebrate the *perfection* in everything around them.

Things Ones can do to help themselves grow:

- Find a friend or therapist who can help you depersonalize issues for which you are blaming yourself or others.
- Join a group which encourages expression of immediate emotions, including anger, in a safe environment.
- Notice your thinking in terms of either/or, right/wrong and include more sides to the story.
- Notice that resentment at others who break the rules may mask a wish to do what they are doing.
- Take time to observe the critical mind in action, and dis-identify with it – use it to remind yourself of your achievements and skills.
- Put play and pleasure in your list of oughts, until you can allow them for their own sakes.

Type Two:
The Giver

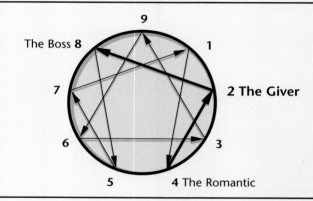

Type Twos are active, helpful, generally optimistic and generous with time, energy and things. Since they do not find it easy to recognize their own needs or ask for help, they are unconsciously drawn to having their needs met through relationships, and are happiest when indispensable. Very sensitive to others' needs and feelings, they are able to show just that part of their personality which will draw a person to them. Better at giving than receiving, they can at times be manipulative, giving to get, and at others genuinely caring and supportive. With their natural empathy, Type Twos are able to give what is truly needed for another's success and well-being.

Twos believed in childhood that to be loved they must meet the needs of others, and so have discounted their personal needs, and in a sense themselves, in favour of giving what will gain attention and approval. They may remember a needy parent, demanding to be looked after; or they may have needed to disarm a domineering or critical figure; or their parent(s) may have been distant and absorbed in other things.

As heart types, Twos are naturally sensitive to others' feelings. In early childhood they learned to become acutely aware of the emotional and physical cues of important adults, and respond in a way that would gain the adult's attention and approval.

- *Unaware Twos* can be hysterical, manipulative, smothering or ambitious give-to-get personalities. The archetype is the self-sacrificing intrusive mother, who complains that her family never appreciate her.
- *Aware Twos* are loving and empathic, truly supportive, and appropriate in their giving. They are perceptive, adaptable, loyal and selfless helpers.

Passion and Fixation: pride and flattery

Pride for Twos is the inner certainty that, because of their deep sensitivity and ability to tune in accurately to others, they can fulfil other people's needs better than anyone else. This is coupled with the belief that they have very few, if any, needs of their own. They believe they are independent whilst others depend on them, and find it hard to realize that, in fact, they are dependent on others not only for approval but for their sense of who they are from moment to moment.

Flattery as a habit of mind may or may not be a conscious flattering of others. It relates to Twos' ability to make others feel good by appealing to their inner preferences, and recognizing and supporting their highest potential. They can see other's abilities, but have difficulty acknowledging and developing their own abilities for themselves.

Stress and security

While hysteria is a sign of stress rising in Twos, when real stress hits they take on the characteristics of Type Eight (the Boss), and can become domineering, irritable and finally angry. This does not fit well with their normal charming persona, and some Twos find anger in themselves or others very frightening, avoiding it almost at all costs.

Under stress, too, the Type Eight-ish desire not to be controlled magnifies Twos' desire for freedom, and they will fight for their own position and resist other people's demands in a way they normally would not.

Twos move towards Type Four (the Romantic) in security. For some the increased emotionality, especially the romantic yearning of the Four personality is very painful. Others find a release into the self-nurturing and artistic side of themselves very energizing.

Ironically, the Four's push-pull way of relating may emphasize Twos' tendency to pull back from intimacy, even in security, while their yearning for true connection is deeper than ever.

Subtypes

Twos express pride in the area of basic survival by making sure they are at the head of the queue, not sharing certain personal things, and securing the survival of pride itself by not asking for help until survival is definitely threatened. Insecurity about meeting one's own needs is suppressed in favour of meeting the needs of others who can ensure survival.

Social Twos seek out and attach themselves to important people in the group. Ambition is expressed through being the power behind the throne and meeting the needs of the most prestigious people present. It may also take the form of belonging to groups with status and taking pride in social position.

Twos who focus on one-to-one relationships take pride in being able to make anyone want to be their friend or lover. It's a very selective and seductive approach, and aggressive in that once Twos have chosen a person they will keep going until that person is 'caught'.

Relationships

Friendship and relationships are the heart of Twos' lives but, in the long term, putting other people's needs first has a variety of negative effects. Beneath the generally happy and confident public face, Twos suffer painful emotions and personal dilemmas: 'People's expectations can push me into sadness and anger. They get used to what I give, and take it for granted and in the end there's no appreciation. I'm not understood. And if I get angry they might leave.'

Holy Virtue and Idea: humility and will/freedom

The virtue of *humility* is mimicked by the pride which puts Twos at the service of others and denies their own needs. A person who experiences humility as a state of being knows and accepts their own nature, both strengths and weaknesses, and their real value to each person they encounter whether fleetingly or in a long relationship. They can embrace the fact that they are not always needed, and that they have needs of their own, without feeling diminished or unlovable; they can celebrate what they have to offer to the world.

Focusing their attention on the necessity, and ability, to flatter means that Twos surrender their will, and therefore their *freedom*, to others' agendas. Taking pride in their independence and emphasizing freedom, they are, in fact, dependent. Real freedom is experienced by Twos when they follow their own highest will, which is born of essence and their true needs rather than an idea of 'I want' or 'I can give ...'

Things Twos can do to help themselves grow:

- Develop interests and activities that are meaningful to you on your own, and do them on your own.
- Make time to be alone and bring your attention back inside, for example meditating; notice the anxiety and desire to focus out again.
- Notice your own achievements and their worth.
- Consciously do things well for their own and your own sake alone.
- Notice flattery and the tendency to be helpless or second to others, and that dependency is manipulation.
- Tell people what you need, and allow them to give it to you: learn to enjoy receiving.

Type Three:
The Performer

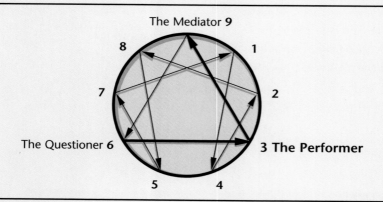

The Mediator **9**

8   1

7   2

The Questioner **6**   **3 The Performer**

5   4

High energy workaholics, Type Threes strive for success to gain status and approval. They are competitive, though view it more as a love of challenge than a desire to beat others. Aiming to succeed in whatever arena they are in – the successful parent, spouse, business person, playmate, hippy, therapist – they change their image to suit the people they are with. Though out of touch with their real feelings, as these interfere with achievement, they can display appropriate feelings if called for. Type Threes are tireless and single-minded in pursuit of a goal. They make excellent team leaders, motivating others to believe anything is possible.

Beneath the striving for success and recognition, Threes are in reality striving for love and acceptance for who they are. It seemed to them in childhood that only successful producers are loved, and therefore who they are, by itself, is not enough.

As children, Threes felt they had to do a lot, and do it well, to be loved or to feel worthy. Most remember being asked what they had achieved today, and what they were going to achieve tomorrow, next week, next month. For some Threes the desire to succeed was driven by the need to escape from, be better than, an 'unlovable' family or social group.

- *Unaware Threes* can be contemptuous hard-nosed go-getters, dominating others for their own ends, with no access to feeling or human intimacy.
- *Aware Threes* can be empathic, socially conscious leaders, able to enliven others with their own enthusiasm and hope, and capable of deep connection to people and worthy goals.

Passion and Fixation: deceit and vanity

The passion of *deceit* does not mean Threes wilfully deceive others. First and foremost they deceive themselves by identifying with the role(s) they have taken on. Since the need to be loved and accepted underpins the drive to succeed, Threes select arenas, both professional and social, which will gain the approval of the types of people they want to be accepted by. They identify with their chosen roles, deceiving themselves that this is 'who they are', and may not even notice if these identities change over time.

Vanity lies in Threes' knowledge that they have the energy, the motivation, and the skills (or the determination to acquire the skills) to succeed where others don't. This is supported by their drive to keep 'doing'. They bring all their energy and motivation to an enterprise, and respond instantaneously to a challenge. Because of this Threes can work themselves into the ground. Energetically there is no middle ground, and they only stop doing when they run out.

Stress and security

Threes thrive under what most of the rest of the world would call stress, but they can experience it: public failure, taking on far too much, illness which forces them to stop, inactivity – these are examples of stress for a Three. They take on qualities of Type Nine, and start to lose their focus, and with it their confidence. There may be a tendency to over-indulge with things like 'football, drink, drugs', and they become easily swayed or distracted, and upset that they can't seem to promote themselves well.

When Threes feel secure, for example in a committed relationship, they may begin to get in touch with their own feelings. This can feel frightening as they go to Six, the central fear type, in security. This is one of the reasons Threes find it so hard to relax and do nothing.

Subtypes

In the area of self-preservation, Threes' attention focuses on material security. Success means having enough and to spare; and from this point of view there is never enough. The ultimate success is always in the future, with the achievement of yet another goal.

Threes who focus on social survival are concerned with their status in the group. Each goal is targeted for the potential prestige it will give them in their workplace and their community, and membership of a certain club may be as important a goal as success at work.

For the sexual subtype the constant focus on image in general is overlaid and augmented by a need to appear absolutely masculine or feminine, depending on gender. These Threes are successful at being 'men' or 'women', at least in the eyes of the world.

Relationships

Relationships are a difficult area for Threes. Friendship in itself has no goal, and the prospect of just 'being' together, maybe for ever, can make them anxious and restless.

Personal relationships can be instrumental in backing up image for Threes, so for some it is worth working hard at doing it right. This doesn't always work, however, if their partner wants more feeling and more 'being together'. Partners can feel disregarded in a social setting when their Three's attention is on the crowd and the image they are creating, and can feel they are not seen and valued for themselves, merely as an adjunct to the image.

Holy Virtue and Idea: honesty and hope

Honesty is an inner state in which there is no need to find a role to identify with. Rather than look to others to have their being validated, a person experiencing honesty knows that 'this is who and what I am, and this is enough.' They do not need to look outside and convince others, and so themselves, that they are lovable: they know it already.

Hope in essence is not, as it often is in its day-to-day meaning, a sort of wishing. The mental focus of vanity can be stated as 'I am the one who can – and therefore has to – do it.' When Threes reach a state of awareness in which they know that essence takes care of what needs to happen, there is holy hope. They are able to let go and allow things to be done through them rather than by them.

Threes who experience hope and honesty can turn their leading, achieving and motivating skills to the service of other people, and experience the unconditional love they have always longed for.

Things Threes can do to help themselves grow:

- Stop from time to time and ask 'What am I feeling?'
- Take time out to stop and be: go for walks (but without a goal!), stare at the sunset, learn to meditate for its own sake rather than as a task.
- Ask trusted friends to tell you when they feel you're not being real, or you're fudging an issue, and listen even if they seem wrong.
- Notice yourself changing image to please, and ask yourself: 'Is this who I am, or am I going for the image?'
- Work on valuing empathy and connection as highly as status.
- Ask yourself what really matters to you, in your work and leisure, and make time to pursue it.

Type Four:
The Romantic

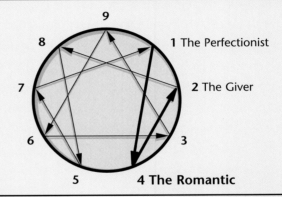

9

8

1 The Perfectionist

7

2 The Giver

6

3

5

4 The Romantic

Artistic, passionate, searching for the ideal partner or life's work, Type Fours live with a sense of something essential missing in their lives. Feeling they would be complete if they could find true partnership, they tend to relate in a push-pull way; the more distant, the more perfect someone looks, whereas once they are close their imperfections become obvious and they are pushed away, whereupon distance makes them attractive again. This creates a self-fulfilling prophecy of relationships not working.

Fours are drawn to the heights and depths of emotional experience, and to expressing themselves as unique. In whatever field, their lives reflect a search for the significant and meaningful. Though easily caught up in their own emotions, they can be supremely empathic with and supportive of others in emotionally painful situations.

The Fours' underlying feeling is that they were abandoned, or somehow separated from the original source of unconditional love, and their attention focuses on seeking out the perfect love which will make them complete again. This has a complementary belief that, to have been abandoned, they must have been unworthy. Their unconscious premise is 'I must be special to attract and deserve the perfect love, but secretly I know I cannot deserve or keep it.'

- *Unaware Fours* can be moralistic, guilt-ridden, self-obsessed emotional manipulators, demanding attention for their pain, and unwilling to admit either help or the idea that their emotions might be over-blown.
- *Aware Fours* can be creative, charismatic and empathic people, combining love of the spiritual in life with acceptance of the here and now.

Passion and Fixation: envy and melancholy

The passion of *envy* underlies Fours' sense of being inferior. Envy is not jealousy, but a constant sensation in the heart of something missing, and a yearning to fill the emptiness. Fours look around them and feel that if only they could have that particular thing, they would be all right. It can range from envying someone an unusual item of clothing or a character trait, to imagining everyone else has the perfect relationship they can never have themselves.

Melancholy is a mental focus which gives life a bitter-sweet flavour. Life is not about anything as trivial as happiness: when Fours experience joy it is passionate and deep, but includes the knowledge that its opposite is never far away. They recognize that the 'dark' side of life is meaningful, and embrace the idea that true creativity and perfect love must be suffered for — in fact are born of suffering.

Stress and security

The further Fours are from the ideal, the more they feel they need to change themselves, whether in their work or in relationships, the more stressful life becomes. As they take on characteristics of Type Two, there is a dovetail with their characteristic push-pull way of relating, as they feel the need to attract people and be approved of.

Fours are idealists in the realm of feelings. When a relationship or their work goes well, and they start to feel secure in themselves, they add another aspect of perfectionism to their personality, taking on qualities of Type One and becoming critical of themselves and others.

Subtypes

In the realm of self-preservation envy is kept at bay by taking risks and living life recklessly. To really be alive means to experience life to the full, to be willing to take whatever comes along and ride with it.

In the social arena envy expresses itself as a sense of shame, of not being good enough, and a fear that people will notice this and reject the Four. They deal with this by applying creativity to their involvement in the group, for instance being wonderful hosts. In one-to-one relationships Fours can become competitive, both with a third party, and with the friend or partner. Envy is displaced into hatred of whatever threatens to show up their own shortcomings. It can sometimes take the form of competing with themselves against their inner ideal, and knowing they are bound to lose.

Relationships

Even though relationships are central in Fours' lives, friends and particularly partners may find it hard to know exactly how to relate to them. Fours' emotional experience can vary so widely and so intensely that, coupled with their push-pull habit, it may be hard for them and others to know where they stand.

Fours appreciate friends who will match their intensity and share their awareness of the meaningful and romantic. When they feel they have found a real friend they are loyal and generous.

In intimate relationships, partners can feel they are trying to measure up to what is expected, and often failing. Fours project their original abandonment on to all relationships, and can push their partner away if the going gets even a little tough or they foresee rejection.

Holy Virtue and Idea: equanimity and origin

Equanimity is the experience of being harmonious and complete in oneself in the midst of any experience. The habit of envy places the source of completion outside the self. Fours who re-attain equanimity realize they already have everything they need, and have a genuinely important place in life by virtue of who they innately are. They are able

to stay balanced, not needing to lose themselves in intense experiences as a way of proving their worth.

Along with this is the realization that they have never lost connection with essence. Melancholy because they feel abandoned, Fours feel they must seek out perfect or divine love, the creative source. Once they look inside they find they are part of the *holy origin*, and are able to celebrate and let that creative source express itself through them in their lives.

Things Fours can do to help themselves grow:

- Take up a body-based activity to learn to ground yourself.
- When your emotions become very strong about something, question them by tracking back to the first feeling which triggered them: it may be different from what you feel now.
- Notice your attention going to what is missing, and learn to value the positive aspects of what is here and now.
- Remind yourself 'abandonment' was in the past and is not inevitable.
- Recognize specialness and self-absorption as a way of masking fears of abandonment: focus on what is important to someone else.
- Discover in yourself the qualities which you envy in others.

Type Five:
The Observer

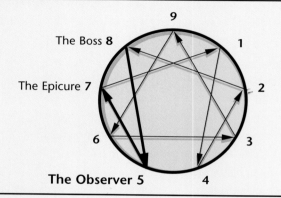

The Boss **8**

The Epicure **7**

9

1

2

6

3

The Observer 5

4

Avoiding emotional involvement, Type Fives experience life from a distance, observing rather than engaging. They are very private people, and feel drained and anxious if not allowed sufficient time to themselves, which they use to review events and to experience in safety emotions they do not feel whilst in the thick of things. The life of the mind is very important to them, and they have a love of knowledge and information, often quite specialized. Type Fives compartmentalize their lives and, though they do not like predictable routine, like to know in advance what is expected of them both in work and leisure. They can be excellent decision-makers and creative intellectuals.

In childhood Fives learnt that it was possible to be safe in an intrusive world where their very survival felt threatened, by withdrawing into their minds and becoming self-sufficient. They minimized hurt by distancing from sensations and emotions and, unable to escape physically, they could become untouchable by being a spectator of events in their own lives.

As children they may have had intrusive, domineering, violent or smothering parents. Some Fives, rather than feeling threatened by people, felt their survival threatened because they were left to fend for themselves.

- *Unaware Fives* can be withdrawn, distrustful, critical, intellectually arrogant, unable to commit to anything, very controlled, and out of touch with feelings and the world.
- *Aware Fives* can be sensitive, perceptive, dedicated, objective and creative thinkers, who can combine their sensitivity and analytical skills to be wise rather than knowing.

Passion and Fixation: avarice and stinginess

Avarice is an emotional preoccupation, in which Fives feel they are always potentially lacking the means for safe survival, and so are avaricious of whatever enables them to feel secure and independent. This is not usually anything material, but information which enriches their inner world and helps them feel prepared for the onslaughts of the outer world.

Stinginess with necessities is natural when at any moment they might be taken away. For Fives, the greatest necessities are time, energy and personal space. Alert and observant, like all head types, they are particularly responsive to nuances in another's presentation. If other people make demands on them they respond calmly, but just enough so they go away again.

Stress and security

Anything that forces Fives to deal with feelings, or be immediate, can be stressful. As the fear of being overwhelmed increases (and fear itself is a feeling they normally block out) they become more like Type Seven (the Epicure). Scanning for all possible escape strategies, they are unwilling to commit themselves to any, and may appear scattered.

When they feel secure, Fives become more Eight-like. They can take charge, be definite and forthcoming, and access their anger. Protective of family members, they can also seem bossy. Normally they find it easiest to express feelings through touch, and this is enhanced in security with a release of physical enjoyment.

Subtypes

In the area of survival Fives experience avarice as 'my home is my castle'. Attention is focused on the home, and creating a warm, secure place where they have everything they could possibly need. Its expression can range from solitary living to being the dedicated home-maker in a relationship.

Social avarice in Fives is reflected in the 'collection' of totem figures or totemic information: that is, knowing people who have symbolic importance in society or the chosen social group. In this way Fives feel safe in the group because they have direct access to the key source of information and control.

For the sexual subtype the exchange of confidences in one-to-one relationships enables Fives to feel safe. Sharing secrets keeps the world at bay, and means people trust each other, so Fives need not fear intrusion or loss. There is also a confidentiality in the physical expression of friendship or love which feels safer than verbal expression.

Relationships

Fives know they are distanced from the world and crave emotional connection, but since it means making themselves vulnerable to feelings, and carries the risk of intrusion, it can be difficult for them. However much they may like another person, anything experienced as invasive or demanding will make them back off, whereas they will be attracted towards a person who allows them their own space.

Successful intimate relations depend on partners respecting Fives' need for privacy and their dislike of being at the centre of attention.

Holy Virtue and Idea: non-attachment and omniscience

A possible pitfall for Fives in their personal growth is confusing detachment, which comes easily to them, with the higher awareness of non-attachment. *Non-attachment* allows feelings, experiences and things to come and go, knowing that the universe is abundant. Conversely, Fives try to re-create the feeling of sufficiency by pulling in and holding on to the necessities for survival. Detachment is a way of holding back, and enables them to deny that they care about things and are attached to them. As they start to allow their energy to flow more freely and share it with other people, they discover that it is self-renewing. They also discover how much they have been attached to their necessities. The inner knowing that they will be taken care of by life itself gives a simultaneous ability to be involved and yet to let go.

Omniscience is the experience of essential mind in which all knowing is available without the need to think or accumulate knowledge. Fives pacify their unacknowledged fears by acquiring information. As their personal growth takes them more into the realm of immediate experience and non-attachment to their personality, they discover they have access to wisdoms other than that of the intellect. Safety is found in an inner experience of already knowing all they need to know.

Things Fives can do to help themselves grow:

- Take up a physical practice which helps you ground in your body.
- Join a group which encourages self-disclosure, e.g. gestalt, oral tradition Enneagram workshops.
- Let yourself feel physical sensations and emotions as they happen.
- Notice how your mind detaches from feelings and sorts things into compartments, and how secrecy and superiority create separation.
- Cultivate here-and-now behaviour, particularly allowing yourself luxuries.
- Notice when you are controlling your space/time/energy and manipulating others through restricting what and when you will give: start to allow the control to drop.

Type Six:
The Questioner

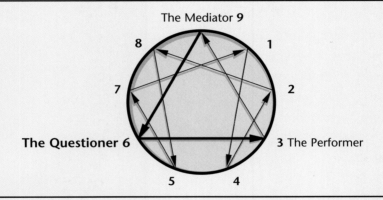

The Mediator **9**

8   **1**

7   **2**

The Questioner 6   **3** The Performer

5   **4**

Though possibly unaware of being fearful, Type Sixes view the world as threatening. They scan for sources of threat, and imagine worst possible outcomes in order to be forearmed. Their doubting frame of mind may produce procrastination and suspicion of others' motives. They dislike or fear authority, align themselves with underdog causes, and are not at ease in authority or with continued success. Some Type

Sixes tend to withdraw and protect themselves from threat; others pre-empt it by going forward to confront it, and may appear quite aggressive. Having given their trust, Type Sixes are loyal and committed friends and team members.

Sixes decided early in life that the world is threatening and potentially damaging. Often, Sixes report a genuinely threatening environment as children, such as violence in the family. Wanting to be safe, their focus turned to scanning for clues to potential threat, vigilance, doubting the obvious and a strong imagination.

- *Unaware Sixes* can be paranoid, ineffective, inflexible, unable to relate and have difficulty getting started or completing things.
- *Aware Sixes* can be productive and imaginative with a fine discriminating mind, and committed and protective friends and co-workers.

Passion and Fixation: fear/doubt and cowardice

Doubt, rather than overt fear, is what defines Sixes. It is natural to feel doubtful of the trustworthiness of anything when there is a constant feeling of imminent threat. Doubt also masks fear by allowing Sixes to feel that, since everything is doubtful, the probability of negative outcomes is real. The two classic responses to fear – fight or flight – result in two types of Sixes. Some use both responses, depending on circumstances, but many lean to one or the other. 'Counter-phobic' Sixes pre-empt fear by confronting danger and going toward it. These people can be aggressive, independent, and seem afraid of nothing.

'Phobic' Sixes prefer 'flight'. Unassertive, even timid, these people are usually aware of their fear and avoid potentially harmful situations.

Cowardice is a facet of the imagination, rather than unwillingness to face things. Sixes' behaviour is rarely 'cowardly', but they anticipate a negative outcome and this focus underlies procrastination, projection of imagined feelings on to others, intense curiosity and the need to control their environment.

Stress and security

Under stress Sixes take on Type Three-like qualities. Many enjoy the feeling of 'kicking into gear'. They can deal with success more easily, stop procrastinating, and apply their imagination to getting the job done. They also become more image-conscious and able to promote themselves. However, like Threes, they may work themselves into illness, and this stance reinforces their distance from emotion.

Once Sixes allow themselves to feel secure for a while, they become soft, warm and loving, or long to make connection. Like Type Nine they are able to just be with friends and loved ones, and enjoy the respite from vigilance and questioning. Paradoxically, it is not comfortable for long since fear is re-aroused by the unsafety of not doubting. Since Nine is a non-initiating type, long periods of security can reinforce Sixes' tendency to inaction.

Subtypes

In the area of survival Sixes handle fear by disarming potential hostility, being warm, giving, affectionate and personally loyal. Although this is enacted in the social arena, it is a way of dealing with concern for security and personal survival.

In the social sphere duty is important to the Six. This manifests as loyalty to the group, and desire to ally with a socially worthy group and actively support it. Usually the focus is upon under-privileged or otherwise deserving groups. Family ties are also important, even when maintaining them is not always easy or pleasant.

Sexual subtype Sixes affect others so as not to be affected. They do this through strength and/or attractiveness and love of beauty. Strength may be in the unswerving service to a cause, or in personal 'courageous' behaviour – sky-diving, motorcycle racing and so on.

Relationships

In friendship as well as intimate relationships, Sixes look for someone they can trust and with whom they can feel united against the (threatening) world. They need to feel they 'know' friends and partners, so they may ask questions without saying much about themselves, until they are sure they can trust. They express love and friendship through actions, working alongside and supporting the other person.

Holy Virtue and Idea: courage and faith

Courage is trusting the body's and heart's intuition enough to act on them. Many Sixes have a taste of the heart state of courage, when in the midst of calamitous danger they have simply known what to do, and done it. Sixes who achieve this awareness as part of their daily existence allow the immediate experience of life to affect them, and respond appropriately.

Faith is not belief, nor can it be created by proof. Sixes look to the world to provide evidence that they can place faith in it, and one negative can cancel years' worth of positive signals. When a projection has the kind of force engendered by a fearful mind, it is hard for Sixes to realize they are looking for something outside to explain the sense of threat which may only exist within, a result of their habit of mind.

By practising trust, initially as an act of will, Sixes reach the inner state of faith where they simply focus on a positive experience without questioning its truth or looking for the hidden negative or 'thousand deaths'. They, like Shakespeare's valiant, 'taste of death but once.'

Things Sixes can do to help themselves grow:

- Take up a physical practice to help bring your awareness into your body and out of your head; notice being braced to face the worse, and relax.
- Ask yourself from time to time 'Am I imagining this? Is it a genuine intuition or a projection?' Ask friends for feedback and a reality check.
- Take time to remember and enjoy past successes and skills, and congratulate yourself on present ones.
- Notice how doubt shuts out relationships ('Can I trust them?'), and practise trusting and having faith.
- Use your imagination: to create pleasant options; also to project threatening scenarios to the improbable limit so you can defuse and laugh at them.
- Counter-phobic Sixes: before going into action, ask yourself if it is appropriate, and whether you have anything to prove.

Type Seven:
The Epicure

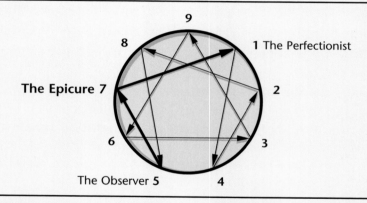

Type Sevens are optimistic, energetic, charming and elusive. They have a Peter Pan quality, hating to feel trapped or coerced, and keep as many pleasant options open as possible. In an unpleasant situation they can mentally escape to pleasant fantasies. Type Sevens are future-oriented, and have an internal plan that includes everything they want to achieve, and they update it as new options arise. Their need to keep life pleasant leads to 're-framing' reality to exclude negative emotions and potential blows to their self-image. They enjoy new experiences, new people and new ideas, and can be creative networkers, synthesizers and theoreticians.

In childhood, Sevens kept hurt at bay in a frightening world by using their imagination to create pleasant options which distanced them from pain. When a situation became painful, they learnt to pay just enough attention not to get in trouble, while focusing almost entirely on inner vistas of wonderful possibilities. They also learnt to glamorize the present when it was good, and remember the past selectively. Sevens do not usually report an unhappy childhood: 'My memory of the past is a re-run of all the happy family films my father took though talking to people, I know that's not true.'

Narcissism and pleasure became unconscious camouflage for their fear of being judged, rejected or humiliated and, as adults, of having their self-image punctured.

- **Unaware Sevens** can be self-centred, grabbing, mendacious and hypocritical seekers of pleasure, easily bored and ruthless in their quest for experiences.
- **Aware Sevens** can be enthusiastic, perceptive, generous, creative and caring, able to put their vivid and far-ranging imagination, powers of synthesis and love of people to good use.

Passion and Fixation: gluttony and planning

Gluttony is the emotional habit that keeps fear at bay by focusing on the myriad enjoyable possibilities. Sevens do not pick one good thing and experience it in all its depth, but sample a little of all the best available. Often gluttony masks anxiety about deep-felt emotion. Sevens want to move on, get out of the situation, and not feel it.

Planning as a mental preoccupation is not a matter of to-do lists, though they are included. Sevens' attention is on how they will experience everything they want. They say it is fun to plan whether or not the plans are carried out, often more fun planning than doing. It is a way of being open to all possibilities.

Planning is a way of avoiding pain, and is intensified as soon as anything threatening happens. 'Any projected anxiety about the future and then the mind starts racing . . .'

Stress and security

Sevens encounter stress when firm boundaries appear – for example inescapable deadlines at work, or emotional confrontations. The fear of criticism and of making mistakes, that are normal, if unconscious, aspects of the Seven, become intensified and conscious as they take on aspects of Type One. They become irritable, nit-picking, angry at anything that seems to interfere or censure them, self-critical, and their standards become very high.

In security, Sevens take on aspects of the Observer (Type Five). They are happy to spend time alone with a good book, and withdraw somewhat from relationships. They may not seek time alone, but are satisfied to take a more background role than usual. In intimate relationships this stance can cause problems, since withdrawal may be read as rejection, and Sevens' discomfort with deep feelings is accentuated in security.

Subtypes

In the area of self-preservation gluttony can be expressed by the Seven forming a 'family' of like-minded people, who provide varied and exciting input, and who can be trusted to back up the Seven if their safety is threatened, and vice versa.

Social subtype Sevens often appear more serious than other Sevens. Their attention goes to the happiness of the group, and in the short term they are able to sacrifice their own enjoyment for the group's well-being, whether that is their family or the world.

In one-to-one relating, gluttony manifests as intense and immediate fascination with new people and the possibilities they represent. Sevens' attention focuses minutely on the new person or idea, to the exclusion of anything else. They glamorize people, and their interest is so intense the person may be deeply shocked when they become fascinated by something else and move on.

Relationships

Sevens place a lot of value on friendships and family. Although the life of the mind is stimulating, real experiences with real people are much more satisfying. Unconsciously, having many and varied relationships confirms their idea of themselves as exciting people.

Sevens can be loyal, supportive and stimulating partners, offering access to things others might not ordinarily experience, once they have sorted out their own priorities. Their feeling of entitlement makes it hard for them to believe one person could be enough for them.

Holy Virtue and Idea: sobriety and holy work

Sobriety is a state of being in which the emotions are focused and single-pointed. Sevens look for fullness by sampling as much as possible of what the world offers. As they grow they realize that a complete experience is only available within themselves, with the deep

and committed focus of the heart on what is truly worthwhile and what is actually present.

Their internal plan, covering all possible routes to satisfaction, masks the fact that a sense of purpose, and willingness to go deep and complete that purpose, are what bring satisfaction. H*oly work* is the equivalent in the mental realm of sobriety, allowing Sevens to transcend their fear of pain and enter deeply into the state that T.S. Eliot called 'the condition of complete simplicity costing not less than everything.' It is not an idealization, or a mental choice of a worthwhile job, but an experience of joyful necessity.

Things Sevens can do to help themselves grow:

- Take up a meditation practice; notice the boredom factor in personal growth (been there, done that) and stay steady with it.
- Realize that pleasure is only half the story: remind yourself you may be missing something, and include painful experiences.
- Notice your mind racing and reaching for options: slow down and focus on the present moment whether pleasant or painful; ask yourself what you are avoiding.
- Let go of some of the options: a deeper focus on fewer things may bring you more valuable experiences.
- Notice yourself rationalizing and re-framing, particularly when criticized or pinned down – ask yourself: 'What are the facts?'
- Learn to include criticism and conflict.

Type Eight:

The Boss

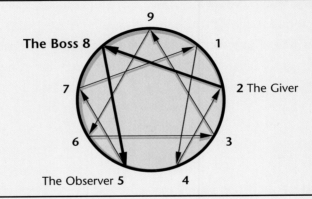

Assertive, sometimes aggressive, Type Eights have an all-or-nothing approach to life. Often the leader, or fiercely independent, they can be very protective of friends and people in their care. They know what they think, are concerned about justice and fairness, and are willing to fight for them. Type Eights can be excessive in the pursuit of pleasure, which may involve anything from drinking with friends to intellectual discussion. Aware of where power lies, they will not let themselves be controlled by others, and can be dominating. Type Eights can use their power in loyal and tireless support of a worthy cause.

Eights decided at an early age that to survive in an unjust, threatening and often violent world they needed to be stronger than anyone else. It seemed that the strong were valued, got what they wanted and remained unhurt, while the weak were despised and damaged. To stay strong, Eights adopted a habit of internal denial which protected them from awareness of their own vulnerability. It also protects Eights from the devastating knowledge that their focus of attention produces in them the very behaviour they hate in others: domination, insensitivity and injustice.

Although Eights are self-referencing – they act on their own rather than others' opinions – they are also 'self-forgetters'. Denial is a facet of self-forgetting, in which Eights replace their true goals with the pursuit of enjoyment, helping friends, or goals which are not their own.

- **Unaware Eights** can be cynics, bullies, law-breakers, strong-arm people, unaware of others' feelings and using force, lies, manipulation or violence to get their own way.
- **Aware Eights** can be deeply loving, protective and empowering, using their great energy and natural authority to combat injustice.

Passion and Fixation: lust and vengeance

The Eights' emotional focus of *lust* is not sexual (though they do like sex) but an urgent impulsive reaching out to grasp life fully: lust for life. Focusing on whatever makes them feel fully alive, they may bring as much gusto to intellectual pursuits as to 'bed, booze and board'. Their great capacity for sensate experience also defuses their energy and releases the strain of constant control, and is one of the ways of self-forgetting.

Vengeance focuses on injustice and redressing the balance. Seeing the world in black and white, believing themselves right, Eights assign blame and direct the force of their anger towards righting the wrong. They will ensure the punishment fits the crime, and can go to great lengths to do so. Even with friends, 'I want them to admit they were wrong and make them change their ways.' If anger is conscious and expressed, issues can be resolved and forgotten, whereas if unconscious or suppressed it can become obsessive.

Stress and security

When not in control, weak, or in self-vengeance, Eights take on aspects of Type Five, withdrawing mentally or physically to think things through and regain balance. Some disappear into compulsive activities like reading or playing Patience. In extreme situations this can last months, and they become depressed, inactive, incommunicative and unable to decide what they think and how to act on it.

   In the security of a trusted relationship Eights become more Type Two-like. Much more compliant, giving, easily affected, they admit things matter to them. Their protective and empowering instincts are magnified, and they enjoy their increased openness. However, it brings insecurities, including fear that it won't work out, and they may retreat into the aggressive approach after a while, with the feeling, 'What about my needs? Get off my back . . .'

Subtypes

In the area of personal survival, Eights will ensure they have what they need to survive in a satisfactory way. They may buy things in bulk, or hoard, or be compulsive about having enough of the right kind of food available at the right time.

Eights manifest lust in the social arena by having many friends, often a network of friends who work and/or play together. They like to introduce friends to each other, make sure everyone enjoys life, and provide mutual support and protection in times of need.

Eights who prefer relating one-to-one have 'their' special friends, felt to be lifetime relationships. Possessiveness may not be obvious, but they need to know they are central to a person's life. They look for someone whom they can trust enough to surrender to and let go of control, and with the surrender they become very vulnerable to betrayal.

Relationships

Although Eights value friendship deeply, a few find it hard to achieve because of their need for control, and their dogmatism. Independent and pleasure-loving, they may see commitment as a trap, but once

committed in friendship or love they are loyal for life, though it may not be conventional since they have their own rules. Usually Eights are unaware of trying to have things their way.

Holy Virtue and Idea: innocence and truth

Innocence is a state of being in which the world is experienced as safe, without hidden intent, and in which an Eight, too, is innocent of agendas or defences. In innocence it is possible to respond to life appropriately in each moment through the bodily 'knowing' of what is right, without the need to judge or consciously evaluate. Eights realize that their grasping for experiences is an attempt to recreate the essential experience of life force flowing through them fully and rightly at every moment.

Allowing and welcoming life as it is leads Eights to realize that *truth* is not either/or but the totality of existence as it is. Any set of facts, or any concept, however right, is not necessarily true. In essence, there is only one truth, which cannot be arrived at or re-created by seeking justice, and truth changes continually without ever changing its nature.

Things Eights can do to help themselves grow:

- Take up a meditation practice, and stay with it when your impulse is to get up and go.
- Use anger to remind you to relax and breathe deeply several times a day.
- Check out your impact with your friends and colleagues: are you being too much?
- In confrontations, make sure you listen to the other side, and use it as an opportunity to recognize the validity of other points of view.
- Start to question whether excessive behaviours (socializing and so on) are a way of concealing and forgetting your real priorities.
- Write down and review insights about yourself daily as a way of opposing self-forgetfulness and denial.

Type Nine:
The Mediator

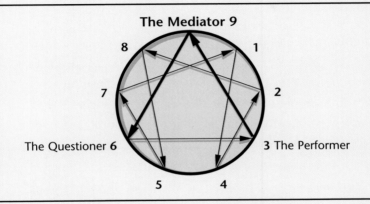

The Mediator 9

8   1

7   2

The Questioner 6   3 The Performer

5   4

Type Nines are peace-makers. Excellent at understanding everyone else's point of view, they are not so good at knowing what they themselves think or want. They like life to be harmonious and comfortable, and will go along with others' agendas rather than create a conflict. However, if pressurized, they can express anger passively in stubbornness or inaction, or in outbursts so distant from their original source that even they are not sure what it's about. They are usually very active, with many interests, but put off their highest priorities till the last minute. Type Nines make good arbitrators, negotiators and can focus a team project.

In childhood Nines wished to retain their intuitive feeling of connection and belonging in a world that seemed to be one of separation and lovelessness. They learnt to submerge themselves, put their attention outward, and merge with others. They report that as children they were not heard, their family seeming to overlook them. To take a stance, positive or negative, and so draw attention to themselves would have been to risk further separation. It seemed preferable to forget themselves and be what other people seemed to expect. They also learnt to 'forget' their anger at not being seen, and to displace their considerable natural energy into inessentials lest it force them to act. Their anger was expressed in ways that seemed not to involve a stance on their part.

- **Unaware Nines** can be needy, indecisive, judgemental, apathetic and obsessive, craving relationships yet blaming the world for their situation and expressing it through complaint and passive-aggressive behaviour.
- **Aware Nines** can be empathic and generous, peaceful to be with, open-minded, forgiving and able to create harmony in a group.

Passion and Fixation: sloth and indolance

Sloth and indolence are inwardly focused, not outwardly, and support self-forgetting. The emotional focus of *sloth* keeps Nines disconnected from their own emotions, particularly the physical impulse of anger. They replace them with a gut-level awareness of others' moods and feelings which is so immediate it is as though they 'become' the other person whilst in their presence.

Inertia is also part of the mental preoccupation of *indolence*. It is a form of self-neglect in which, caught between things that have to be done or unable to decide which of their many personal priorities to pursue, they cannot motivate themselves to choose and act on their choice. Nines avoid acknowledging indolence, and cut off the enormous physical energy which threatens to overwhelm them, by 'narcotizing' – numbing themselves with repetitive and almost compulsive inessential activities such as reading, hanging out with friends, watching videos or even meditation.

Stress and security

Under stress, when being pushed or forced by circumstance to take a position, Nines take on aspects of Type Six. They become fearful, aware of all potential threats, and become either withdrawn and even more compliant, or obdurate, more stubborn and belligerent. Procrastination increases as their indecision turns to doubt, and it can seem that the only safety lies in refusing to act at all.

When secure, feeling at home, included and appreciated, Nines become more Type Three-like. Their energy becomes directed and they can achieve many things excellently in a short time. The Three tendency to seek approval adds to their natural wish to do what others want, and a supportive relationship with a partner or a boss brings out their enthusiasm and abilities.

Subtypes

By compulsively immersing themselves in some form of numbing behaviour, Nines avoid having to take action. This 'appetite' feels safe, minimizing the dual risks of separation (through having to take a stance) and of losing identity (by having to merge with people).

Social Nines channel self-forgetting and physical energy into merging with the group. Participation may mean joining teams, or setting up activity groups for others to participate in, or networking. Nines act on behalf of the group to the extent that they lose themselves.

Sexual subtype Nines have a passionate drive to find the person with whom they can merge completely, feeling thereby they will find themselves. It can also be channelled into religion and the desire to be at one with God. In this case there may be a conflict between merging with the partner or with God, or they look for the divine in the partner and merge with that.

Relationships

Supportive relationships are very important to Nines, allowing them to relax and just 'be', without having to take responsibility, and giving them their motivation to act.

Though Nines seek union in intimacy, they may avoid both commitment and disengaging once a relationship is over, because either would mean taking a position and getting off the fence. Some move from relationship to relationship as they merge with the wishes of each new partner. However, once in a partnership Nines do not think of leaving, and are committed to a settled and inseparable relationship.

Holy Virtue and Idea: right action and love

As Nines bring their attention back inside they find a source of great energy and intuitive wisdom in their belly-based awareness. Instead of looking for the motivation for action outside themselves they understand that it lies within. They realize they are innately connected, and from that springs the ability to know, and carry out, the *right action* in any moment.

   This goes hand in hand with the awareness of *love*. In the grip of their fixation, Nines believe that to be an 'I' means to be separate, and to merge with another is to achieve the supreme one-ness. They must be indolent towards their true selves to achieve merger. This is a spiritual trap, since to be at one is actually to experience the underlying unity of two (or more) separate entities. Love is a state in which the awareness opens to include all others, and in this experience Nines realize they do not need to deny or suppress themselves since they are already fundamentally inseparable and loved in return.

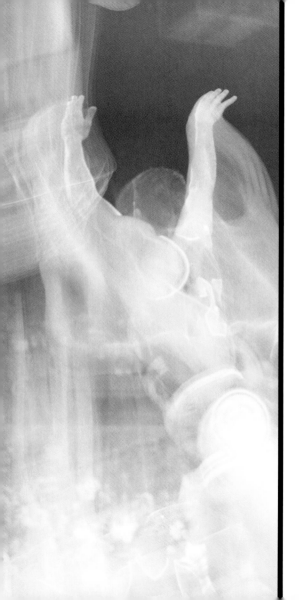

Things Nines can do to help themselves grow:

- Start a daily practice of previewing what is important for you today, and reviewing how well you did with this.
- Start a practice or join a group which encourages you to contact and express your gut feelings in the moment, including anger.
- Notice when you get distracted or obsessive, what the accompanying feelings were/are, and start to let yourself feel them through.
- Avoid belittling yourself and making others more important or more intelligent.
- Decide on goals, make action plans with clear time frames, and enlist support in sticking to them.
- Notice your stubbornness and passive resistance, and start to state what you disagree with.

What Do I Do Now?

The Enneagram is not a panacea, though simply knowing the material can bring about change in your day-to-day life. With this in mind, and the fact that this is only an introductory book, I make the following suggestions:

Basic awareness

Follow the pointers in the chapter on your type. You may find it useful to copy them and keep them somewhere handy; in any case, look at them from time to time.

Self-observation

Practise self-observation, or as Gurdjieff called it, self-remembering. You might purposely stop several times a day to review what you are doing, thinking and feeling. Simplest of all is to start catching yourself in the act when you are doing or about to do something automatic and reactive. Expect first to notice it after the event, then during, and then before you start.

Oral Tradition learning
Attend classes in the Oral Tradition. This is the very best way of learning about type. For workshops in the Oral Tradition contact: Karen Webb, 66 Cowleigh Bank, Malvern, Worcestershire. WR14 1PH.
Tel: 01684 561258. Fax: 01684 576995.

Friends
It is very useful to have friends who know the Enneagram, to discuss what you are learning about your own and their types, experience the interaction between types in practice, and give and receive feedback.

Belly-based meditation
Attend classes in breathing meditation, for example Zen or Vipassana. This is a basic practice which helps you find the neutral ground of your being and strengthens the inner observer.

A
Suitable
Match

A Suitable Match

Joy Freemen

ST. MARTIN'S PRESS / New York

Design by SHERRY BROWN

Library of Congress Cataloging in Publication Data

Freemen, Joy.
A suitable match.
I. Title.
PZ4.F8556Su   [PS3556.R3914] 813'.54   80-14195
ISBN 0-312-77537-7

c. 2

To Betty Glenn White with affection and gratitude

A
Suitable
Match

August
1813

1

THE CLATTERING WHEELS of Lord Sherworth's smart sporting carriage blended with the endless night sounds of London as he swept over moon-bathed cobbles into Green Street. The match-pair of high-stepping blacks were eased in, and Sherworth drew to a halt before an elegant town house of moderate size.

"Take 'em to Berkeley Square, Wiley. They'll want their beds," he said, gripping the nape of his neck and stretching his back. "You may have what's left of the night. I'll walk home."

Wiley's grateful nod fell on a vacant seat, for his master, with characteristic precipitancy, had already sprung down and was applying himself to the brass knocker belonging to his stepmother, the dowager Lady Sherworth.

The door was opened with patent disapproval, but, at sight of the late caller, the countess's elderly butler abandoned his chilling resolve to draw attention to the hour and took on an aspect of fond resignation. Longly had been with the Sherworth family since his mistress had married the young man's widowed father well over twenty years ago. It was then that he had encountered the young heir for the first time, a lonely little boy, untrusting, but holding his own against the spiteful tricks of a jealous elder sister. He had watched him respond to the warmth and affection of the first mother he had ever known and learn, under the countess's loving guidance, to laugh and enjoy the world to which he had been born. Under Longly's interested eyes, sturdy young limbs had developed into the strong, supple arms and legs of an accomplished athlete, and the engaging boy into the ruggedly attractive man of eight and

3

twenty that he was today. There were some, he fancied, who might say that his lordship had managed to escape from his gentleman's education a trifle untamed, but, to Longly's way of thinking, at least he was a man and not one of them twiddlepoops who minced about with shirt points up to their eyebrows.

With all this in mind, Longly was able to view the irregularity of Sherworth's calling at midnight, improperly dressed in top boots, with the same tolerance with which he accepted the fact that the young earl's patience would be sorely tried if it came to being led up the stairs at a decorous pace. The butler received the low-crowned hat thrust unceremoniously into his hand and stepped aside to make way for what, to one of his years, would seem an all-out gallop up to the first floor.

Sherworth grasped the implication with amusement. He harbored few illusions about himself. He was often inclined to be careless of the graces that distinguished the finely polished gentlemen about town, and his manners were apt to be far too abrupt if he was preoccupied or impatient to get on with something. He came under criticism for these qualities a good deal and cared not a rap, but, contrarily, he was always moved to a sense of gratitude when those he liked made allowances for his ways. He drew the old man's smile with his own and headed for the stairway where, though by no means galloping, he defied his skintight, leather breeches by mounting the steps two at a time. He swung open the door of the drawing room and found his stepmother and stepsister each reposed in a red damask wing chair on opposite sides of an empty fireplace.

They had both been lost in separate volumes of the same novel, but the instant the countess, an unusually lovely woman in her midsixties, spied her stepson's tall figure framed in the doorway, she thrust her book from her and smiled, a little surprised and more than a little touched that he should have responded so quickly to her note begging him to wait upon her at his earliest convenience.

But theirs was a teasing relationship, so she merely said, with a hint of mischief in her humorous gray eyes, "My dear. Indeed, I hadn't looked for you to arrive in the wake of my message. Can it be that things weren't as interesting as expected there at Brighton?"

Sherworth was prepared for her raillery. Few of his amorous adventures escaped her notice. Nodding a greeting to his stepsister, he laughed as he dropped an affectionate kiss onto the countess's upturned face. "I wonder if it's even possible for me to break a fingernail, and you not be aware of it."

"Oh yes. I'm sure no one would think to run to me with news of your fingernails," she replied, smiling an affirmation to her butler, who had reached the room and was waiting to see if refreshments would be desired. "Wine, I think, Longly. Thank you."

Sherworth carried over a straight-backed chair and placed it between the two ladies. Rocking it back on its two hind legs, he settled himself with an arm looped behind and said, with his engaging smile, "Well, end my suspense. What has you so fired up?"

The sound of rustling skirts emanated from the wing chair on his left, as the countess's daughter, a handsome army widow in her late forties, rose to go. Sherworth raised a curious brow, thinking that things must be in the devil of a stew if the matter was too delicate for his stepsister's mature and worldly ears. But the thought was dismissed almost as it was formed, because the countess urged her to remain. She paused then, however, weighing the situation. She had seen in a trice that to allow her daughter to go would set up a train of unhelpful questions in her stepson's mind. Yet, his late call had taken her by surprise, and she dared not risk having Chloe draw her into more than she wished to say.

She caught her daughter's hand, as she was resuming her seat, and squeezed it meaningfully. "You will naturally have questions, Chloe, my dear, but I beg you will keep them until we are alone." Again there was a slight hesitation before she continued smoothly: "Or Adrian's patience will not hold."

Sherworth said idly that he was seldom impatient in good company, a statement that contained a deal more goodwill than truth, but which neither lady took the trouble to contradict.

The countess seldom troubled herself about him. She was entirely too familiar with her world to suppose that a young man of birth and good-looks, who had come into rank and considerable wealth before even reaching his majority, could have helped becoming a little spoiled and disillusioned. But she knew him as no one else did and was perfectly content that his character was sound and that his responsibilities to his dependents and loved ones would never be found wanting.

"We'll wait for the wine," she announced cheerfully, "and then I shall explain. The matter concerns my granddaughter—you know, Bancroft's girl."

Sherworth frowned thoughtfully, wondering what this unknown product of his stepmother's first marriage could possibly have to do with him. He wouldn't have dreamed of refusing anything the countess had asked of him, but her message had managed to reach him at an inopportune moment, and learning now that a silly chit was at the bottom of the disturbance made it seem nothing but a confounded nuisance. As he waited for Longly to arrange glasses and a decanter on the table beside him, Sherworth's brow furrowed even deeper, as the suspicion crept into his thoughts that his beloved stepmama had matchmaking in her eye. But, although his wariness in this regard was acutely developed, after years of finding himself the unwilling object of a dozen and sundry marriage plots, even as he unconsciously swept his fingers through his fashionably arranged, dark chestnut hair, he was already reassuring himself that the countess, of all people, would surely have realized that, if he could be induced to marry at all, it would be to a more suitable female than a daughter of Lord Bancroft's could possibly be.

It was well for his peace of mind, and the countess's carefully worked plans, that he had been so easily able to lay his fears to rest, because that was exactly what she did have on her mind, and much depended on catching him off his guard. She felt a twinge of conscience at having to hoax him, but she was convinced that marriage to the right girl was a destiny very much required by his particular nature, and she could think of no better way of bringing him to realize it.

It had been sometime before he'd even come down from Oxford that her young stepson had first informed her of his resolve to remain single, explaining, when she'd asked after his reasons, that one of them stemmed from the discovery that there were at least half again as many husbands as bachelors competing for the fashionable impures who graced the opera boxes and select saloons about town. To her mild suggestion that perhaps those roving husbands were insatiates or the products of unfortunate alliances, he had replied with a teasing gleam that, while he had no way of knowing, of course, he had it on good authority that most *ladies* conduct their bedchambers as they do their drawing rooms—with cold, boring formality! Through the years the countess had had great fun roasting him with that remark, and, though Sherworth, who possessed the ready laughter that often accompanies a quick temper, was perfectly able to see the humor in his youthful absurdities, he had nonetheless taken advantage of those opportunities to remind her that there had been no alteration in his determination not (as he had so dampeningly phrased it) to become leg-shackled.

The countess was not so foolish as to have attempted to argue him out of his notions. Besides, she was a great proponent of the theory that a man should be encouraged to sow his wild oats in his youth, so that he would be less tempted to do it at a time when he might reasonably be expected to know better. So she had let him go his own way, with no lectures or homilies, being careful only to see that he received a full measure of the disadvantages of a bachelor's existence along with its pleasures. But now the time was right, and she was determined to have at least one go at trying to unite what she privately thought would make a most suitable and delightful couple.

The countess pulled herself from these musings as the door closed behind her butler and smiled spontaneously at Sherworth, who had become lost in a brown study and evidently took it that she was expecting him to comment on her granddaughter.

"I collect you mean the girl you're always running off to Wiltshire to visit," he said. "Tricilla or something."

"Yes, dear. Her name is Vescinda, and I fear I haven't been able to run to Dorsetshire for over a twelvemonth. As it happens, such a journey has become necessary now, because I feel Vescinda's eyes must be opened to a sad fact of life."

His thoughts still somewhat abstracted by his grievances, Sherworth murmured that he should have expected a daughter of Bancroft's to be awake to every suit, then added with a quick look of apology: "But, of course, she's no doubt escaped his influence. I shouldn't think he's what one could call an *attentive* parent." His deep-blue eyes filled with sudden laughter. "Have you heard of his latest folly?"

"Can you ask, when you know Chloe contrives to be aware of every scandal scarce moments after it occurs?" Glancing at her daughter, she chuckled softly. "Chloe is now itching to tell you that I never demur to listen. It is the sad truth, I fear. Yes, and Bancroft's start was no exception. Dueling over a light skirt at his age! It passes all bounds!"

"And making a cake of himself into the bargain," interjected Chloe, whose favorite pastime was pointing the finger of scorn at her former brother-in-law.

"Also the sad truth," the countess sighed. "Now, where was I? Oh, yes. Vescinda has not entirely escaped her father's influence. Though you are perfectly correct, Adrian—he is far from an attentive parent. It is one of the reasons I require your services."

This statement caused Sherworth's sense of wariness to come bounding back, as it occurred to him that, if the countess was in fact trying to promote this highly unsuitable match, it could only be that she had found herself at point non plus in a matter of extreme urgency—that she was intending to beg him to offer the chit the protection of his name.

"Perhaps you'd like to tell me how it comes about that I have never met this granddaughter," he said, bringing his chair down on all fours and folding his arms across his broad chest. "I should be fascinated to learn why she's been kept hidden in Dorsetshire all these years."

"Do recall, Adrian, that you are sometimes prone to leap to conclusions," the countess laughed, warming to her game. "I promise you, Vescinda is not kept locked in a tower or tended by servants sworn to secrecy. Really, there is no mystery at all. Her mother—my second daughter, Louisa—died when Vescinda was only five. Naturally I couldn't like a mere child to travel such a distance without a parent. So I formed the habit of going to her for our visits." Sensing his next question, she added, "I should, of course, have liked to raise her myself at Whitowers with the rest of you, but I couldn't bring myself to expose another child to Katherine."

The reference to his spiteful sister instantly satisfied Sherworth on that point, but he closed in again. "Understandable. But why doesn't she at least visit you now—here—in London? It must be some time now since she's figured as a 'mere child.'"

"Oh, indeed! And she has. A few years back she came to me for a month or two—I believe you must have been in Ireland, looking over horses, at the time. And she was here again last Season twelvemonth. Most certainly you'd have made her acquaintance then, but, before I could present her, we received word that her Aunt Eudora had died. The poor woman had been standing in place of a mother to Vescinda. So naturally we could consider nothing less than a twelvemonth's mourning. And, naturally, I returned to Blakely with Vescinda, to see her through her grief. But, unfortunately, it was then I learned the sea air had become an enemy to me—a slight rheumatic complaint."

She waved away Sherworth's sudden look of solicitude. "Oh, it doesn't trouble me worth the mentioning in town, but I was forced to abandon Dorsetshire for good and all. And even *that* seemed no great matter at the time, for I fully expected Vescinda would shortly be finished with Dorsetshire herself. But what should occur? Last January, her cousin fell in the American war! The unhappy result," she sighed, "is that Vescinda, who will turn twenty the sixteenth of this month, has spent nearly the whole of her time, since emerging from the schoolroom, in mourning."

Sherworth rocked back in his seat once more, comfortable in the knowledge that at least the girl hadn't succeeded in ruining herself. With that much settled, there seemed no reason why he should be expected to sacrifice himself in her cause. So he was able to smile affectionately at what he considered a great parcel of female nonsense.

"Well, at last the problem is clear!" he teased. "With Bancroft's side of the family perishing in this thoughtless way, you're naturally all a twitter, thinking the girl will end her days on the shelf. Only tell me, do we gather to lend prayers that she manages to catch some poor Tony before the next demise, or to arrive at a suitable consolation for her spinsterhood?"

Chloe gave a hoot, and the countess said with her delightful laugh, "Idiot!"

"I must be," he laughed back, "because I haven't grasped yet what part I am to play in this piece. Six months is ample mourning for a cousin. Surely she's free to come to you now—oh, I'll be bound Bancroft won't find it possible to sit a horse for some time. Is it to escort her to town for the Little Season that you want me?"

"Perhaps. But, first, there is a problem I should like you to solve. She won't come for the Little Season, nor any other."

"Won't come? Why the deuce not?"

The countess rummaged through a drawer in the table between them and produced a letter. Handing it to him, she said, "I shall leave you to draw your own conclusions."

Sherworth accepted what appeared to be the last sheet of a missive laid out in a fine flowing hand and read: "—strongest love for Freddy. But, of course, he must first complete his education, unhampered by such a responsibility. At all events, since he will certainly wish to make Blakely his home when he comes down from Oxford, I feel in honor bound to remain living here until then. Pray, understand, dearest Grandmama, that, while I should like nothing more than to *visit* you, I will not have you put to the pointless task of introducing me into society when I cannot accept, nor consider, offers of marriage."

Sherworth glanced up from the letter, a pained, questioning look in his eyes. At length he dropped them again and read aloud, "The 'strongest love for *Freddy?*' I collect she refers to Freddy Bancroft—another cousin. Unfortunately, *this* one lives." He heaved a despairing sigh. "Well, she surely will dwindle into an ape leader if she means to wait for that loose screw to marry her."

"Dear me, is that what you think?" asked the countess, casting a quelling look at Chloe, whose mouth had dropped open.

"Of course!" Sherworth returned irritably. "Even you must hear enough of his exploits to know he's got in now with the peep o' day boys . . . I don't know what sort of education this—Vescinda, is it?—thinks he's getting, but he isn't getting it at Oxford!"

"No, he was sent down, and the worst of it," said the countess sadly, "is that the shocking pranks that caused his expulsion took place during the mourning periods I've already mentioned—or perhaps you don't realize that Vescinda's Aunt Eudora was Freddy's mother?"

Since Sherworth merely indicated that he found nothing to wonder at, she went on: "Well, my dear, it is to Freddy's new ways that I wish to open Vescinda's eyes. The boy, besides being cut of the same cloth, is Bancroft's ward, and, as you may well imagine, he has received little or no guidance. I fear he is setting the same ruinous course as his guardian—but, more to the point, I fear Vescinda is deluding herself when she supposes that a mere three years will see him ready *or* willing to settle down to the sort of life she is trying to make for him."

"Most likely. Well, what of me? Am I to post down and abduct her?"

"I shouldn't cavil," the countess smiled, retrieving her letter. "But Vescinda has stated herself most firmly. Until the problem is solved, she would simply post herself back."

After a brief inner struggle, Sherworth said, with more patience than he was feeling, "You know, Mama, perhaps you're wasting your concern on this girl. After all, *she's* cut from the same cloth, too. Perhaps it would be a kindness to the world if this pair of obstinate woolly crowns were to keep to the confines of their own family."

"No, no, my dear," the countess laughed. "You mustn't be so hard on my poor granddaughter. Naturally blood will tell, but Vescinda cannot be blamed for that."

Anticipating that he was soon to be put to considerable inconvenience because one idiotic Bancroft loved another and the head of the Bancroft family kept himself too steeped in debauchery to attend to his own responsibilities, Sherworth could not forgive Vescinda her blood—nor anything else. Still, he could see that his stepmother was fond of her senseless relative, so he refrained from comment.

He refilled his glass and Chloe's, which she had drained and proffered urgently. She was almost beside herself with the wish to be given further details of the astounding news that had come to light through Vescinda's letter, but she had twice now been reminded, by extremely speaking looks, that she was to hold her questions until after Sherworth had taken his leave. So she sat and stewed in silence, over what she could only think a perfectly incredible turn of events. Her niece!—the last girl in the world she should have expected to form such an alliance! And Sherworth—well, she couldn't help but laugh, thinking of him having to deal with the girl. Not, however, because she was anything like what he was so obviously envisioning—an uncomely and brainless baggage!

Chloe knew her niece only from the two brief visits she had made to London, but the girl had seemed to epitomize everything Sherworth most disliked in a female—full as could hold with proprieties, and a cool, untouchable quality about her. In fact, Chloe had found it almost awesome to see such controlled, flawless conduct in one so young, and she had taken the countess aside at the first opportunity, to learn how a child sprung from her own vaporish sister and the lawless Lord Bancroft could have emerged with such perfect poise and nicety of manners. Not once had she seen her niece at a loss—not even on morning calls to the most formidable of dowagers. And, what was more, not one of the old tabbies had referred to Vescinda as a nice little puss or a very prettily behaved chit, but had treated her to a respectful manner usually reserved only for their peers!

Chloe was forced to feign a cough, as it occurred to her that just knowing *that* would doubtless set Sherworth on the run back to Brighton. What was more, she decided, as she banged each eye with her handkerchief, by the time he came to know it, odds were, he'd be sped on his way by the girl herself. For no less incredible than that such a fastidious miss should elect to marry her wild rascal of a cousin was the likelihood that she would have anything at all to say to such a lusty, ill-conducted fellow as Sherworth.

He, Chloe knew, made it an object to avoid gently bred young ladies, but, when "inescapable" invitations forced him into association with them, he generally managed to cause some sort of stir. Chloe had often wondered if he did it deliberately, in order to frighten them off, or if he simply didn't trouble to adjust his manners to his company. In any event, his effect upon these unfledged damsels, though varied, was seldom beneficial. Some were left tongue-tied; some were sent into fits of nervous giggling by the disconcerting things he would say; and others were intrigued in a way that was suspected to be inconsistent with their youth and innocence.

Chloe abandoned her entertaining reflections to concentrate on the conversation, for Sherworth had just asked what the countess wished him to do.

"I collect you have something in mind," he said.

"Oh yes. I wish to arrange a house party to be held in Dorsetshire—and, for that, I need both of you. Vescinda's governess, though perfectly capable, is not a relation and therefore ineligible to be hostess. That must be Chloe's role. On the other hand, Bancroft, though certainly a relation, is not at all capable, so that must be yours. . . . Oh, naturally, Vescinda may not have a house party unless her father is in residence. I shall see that he is present, but I should like you, my love, to be a sort of host incognito. Now, what more? Oh, yes, I shall also prod young

Freddy into attending our little affair, and, of course, I shall provide the lady guests."

"I shudder to think what pressures you'll bring to bear," Sherworth laughed, "but I'll back you to get the thing done."

The countess acknowledged the compliment with a mischievous gleam, saying, "And I am equally confident of your ability to supply, in addition to yourself, four interesting gentlemen." Laughing merrily as he dropped his head into his hand, she added, "Yes, yes, I daresay you, too, will have to bring some pressures to bear. However, you have always possessed more than your share of ingenuity. I shall be depending upon that quality as well, to assist me in solving this little problem with my granddaughter. Should she fail to see for herself that Freddy's—ah—new interests promise little hope for her plans, perhaps you can contrive another means of dealing with the situation. But mind, you mustn't bully her, my dear. Vescinda's sentiments, however misguided, are not only sincere, but far more complex than you imagine. I suggest you discuss the matter with her before taking action of any kind. Now, Chloe, my dear, you must go down for three weeks, in order to prepare the house. Adrian, I shall desire only two weeks of you, one for planning the entertainments with Vescinda, and one for the party itself. May I depend upon you both for this?"

Naturally, they both pledged their aid.

It could scarcely have been otherwise, thought Sherworth, as he pushed aside the last dish of an unsatisfactory breakfast on the following morning. Yet it couldn't have come at a more devilishly inconvenient time. For one thing, he didn't much relish passing a se'enight in Berkeley Square. It hadn't occurred to him until he was actually mounting the steps of his imposing town house, but, with his staff supposing him to be fixed in Brighton for the summer, he could almost depend upon finding things in more than their usual disorder. And so it had proved. The furniture was shrouded in Holland covers; the beds had not been aired; and those servants not in a nervous fret were in a state of imperfectly concealed dudgeon.

But there was nothing new in this sort of confusion. Things had been going on in much the same way since the countess had inexplicably insisted upon setting up her own establishment in Green Street. Sherworth, with no knowledge of domestic arrangements, and uninspired by the smallest desire to learn, had found himself the sole possessor of a place designed for large families and grand entertainments, and soon lost interest in the home he had once loved as a boy. But for the fact that his elder sister would have seized on the opportunity to ensconce herself, he would have closed it indefinitely and taken lodgings in St. James. As it was, he spent most of his time out of town or, when he had a mistress in keeping, at the snug little place he maintained at Kensington for that purpose.

But there was no hope of his taking refuge at Kensington just now, because he'd closed the place several months ago—a circumstance that had all but set the town on its ear. At first, word had spread feverishly among hopeful mamas that the earl meant to mend his ways and take a wife; then, when it was seen that his interest in "unfortunate women" had become even more pronounced, it was suggested that he had fallen victim to an impossible love and was seeking consolation in excess. The true case, known only to Sherworth, was simply that, a few weeks after installing a most promising little beauty in his Kensington retreat, he had made the depressing discovery that she was a dead bore. And so, not unnaturally, he was being cautious in the selection of her successor.

Despite waggish comments to the contrary, however, long before he'd sifted through the entire muslin company, he had all but settled on a beautiful young actress. But, because this dazzling redhead was engaged for the season at a theatre in Brighton, and Sherworth had no wish to interfere with her career until he'd had ample opportunity to appraise her less obvious attributes, he had closed his house at Kensington and instead hired one for the season at Brighton.

More than all else, it was this circumstance that was fomenting Sherworth's growing dislike for the unknown Vescinda Bancroft. In his view, but for this rustic ninnyhammer in Dorsetshire, he would not be in the position of having to leave his rather delicate affairs at Brighton in so unsettled a state.

2

THE COUNTESS, COMING down to her more orderly breakfast parlor, found her daughter waiting in evident impatience.

"Dear Chloe," she laughed, "I doubt you've ever passed so much time in silence as I imposed upon you last night. But, never mind, you shall have your reward—only permit me one mouthful of coffee."

Despite her nagging curiosity, Chloe had found herself unable to outsit Sherworth, who had lingered on for hours, chatting companionably with the countess and finally accepting her suggestion of a late supper. She was by now thoroughly disgruntled, and, though she nodded a grudging agreement to her mother, she couldn't help remarking that she knew for a fact that not one letter had arrived from Dorsetshire in over a se'enight, and yet the news of that outrageous marriage plan had been kept from the girl's *only* living aunt.

As the countess took that first luxurious sip of coffee, she thought with interest that, if Sherworth occasionally leaped without looking, Chloe had the more amazing faculty of looking thoroughly into everything, yet seeing remarkably little. Smiling at her daughter's look of mumpishness, she slipped her hand into her reticule and produced her granddaughter's complete letter, consisting of several sheets, and offered it with a chuckle.

"Here. You may come out of your sulks, my dear. This will shed light, while I take a little more coffee."

Chloe scanned the sheets with a series of frowns, gasps, and chortles, then cried, "Convenient!—the pages separating just there."

"Yes," agreed the countess, "the idea came to me as I was reading the thing over for the hundredth time, trying to decide what might be done to take advantage of this pretty kettle of fish Vescinda has stirred up. Naturally, regardless of all else, I cannot permit her to waste three years of her young life, watching over Freddy's future inheritance, simply because her father is too slipshod to attend to his own estates."

"No. And it makes sense to involve Sherworth in a problem concerning estate management, but what I can't see is *why*, if he is to deal with the matter, you didn't show him the entire letter— why you wished to bamboozle him into thinking it was the girl, rather than Eudora, who had the 'strongest love for Freddy.'" She shook her head, the area around her gray eyes crinkling with amusement. "Of course, he'd do anything for you, but you've deliberately let him think the girl is past praying for."

"Yes. Yes, I did," the countess sighed. "But if he hadn't formed that conclusion, without a doubt, he'd have leaped to the correct one."

"A match!" exclaimed Chloe, at once startled and enlightened.

"Why, yes," the countess agreed placidly. "And though I've been sadly delayed by all this mourning, possibly it is for the best. They are both of a better age now."

Chloe's eyes were big with wonder. "But he's apt to strangle the girl once he learns he's been hoaxed."

"Nothing so drastic, I think," replied the countess calmly. "Certainly he will be extremely vexed. I hope he may be, indeed. He is too much accustomed to viewing the loveliest of gently bred girls with indifference. However, you will own that one can scarcely keep aloof and be in a passion at the same time."

Chloe was not only prevented from owning this, but from making her own gloomy observations, because just then Longly entered with the countess's baked egg.

"Your countenance leaves little doubt as to your opinion of my scheme," said the countess, when they were alone again.

"You don't need me to tell you that Sherworth don't care for proper young ladies," Chloe shrugged. "Says they lack pluck, spirit, and wit. Lord, if he's bored by girls who are just *barely* acceptable by ton standards, how can you expect him to take a fancy to my niece, who you've had drilled like a crack trooper?"

"I have had Vescinda 'drilled,' as you call it, to enable her to properly fill a position suited to her birth—if not as my successor, then another. I trust you realize that I should have continued your training to the same extent, except that you showed no aptitude, and I am not one to cast stones against the wind."

"Thanks be!" Chloe gasped. "I have no hankering for such a stiff-rumped existence!"

"It is well," the countess replied with a twinkle.

That made Chloe laugh. "Roast me if you've a mind to, but field officers need wives the same as earls! I'd like to know what use I should have made of all that fancy training while following the drum and presiding over makeshift billets." She paused to drink her coffee, then went on, "And what of Miss Propriety? Strikes me, she'd prefer a man with a cooler disposition—and certainly one who won't strip her to the skin with one of his looks, or fall into downright profanity when he loses his temper. How do you imagine such a prim miss shall deal with the likes of Sherworth?"

"I haven't a notion," the countess smiled. "Perhaps you will be good enough to write of it. I have been to every sort of nuisance, these past years, keeping them separated until the right moment, and now I shant even be by to witness their first meeting . . . Well, that, too, is for the best," she sighed wistfully. "They are both too used to being guided by my opinions. This is a situation which they must conduct in whatever manner they think best." Glancing down at the gold watch she wore pinned to her lavender morning gown, she said, "Just now, I shall require you to lend me countenance, for I mean to drive out and visit Bancroft in his lodgings. When we have returned, we shall have to spend the balance of the day going over plans, because, if you don't dislike it, I shall ask you to start for Dorsetshire in the morning."

Jumping to her feet, Chloe exclaimed, "Good Lord! No, no, I don't *dislike* it, but, if that's the way of it, I must set Millie to packing and not a minute to waste!"

Lord Bancroft's mood, already darkened by the necessity to spend his hours lying on his belly in a weakened condition, was in no way improved when, an hour later, an amused servant informed him that the countess was below, demanding to see him, and not the least bit daunted by the necessity of conducting her visit in his lordship's bedchamber.

"Damn!" he ejaculated, then muttered, "Oh, hell and the devil, show the tedious woman up. She'll come anyway. Might as well preserve the *appearance* of being master under my own roof."

His already florid countenance deepened alarmingly when he spied Chloe following her mother into the room. He heaved himself up on one elbow to protest, but fell prone again with a grunt of pain.

Staring down into his one visible eye, Chloe said, by way of a greeting, "We've all been wondering how you came to be wounded in the rump. Were you loping off?"

Lord Bancroft's mouth worked furiously, until he could manage to sputter, "You—you know nothing of these things, woman! The curst book on dueling advises one to make the smallest possible target by standing sideways!"

This sent Chloe into whoops. Finally she gasped, "Gad, Bancroft, that might have served twenty years ago, but you're too wide in the bow by half to put any faith in it now. What you did was supply the largest possible target—and one impossible to resist. I'm told Barnsby's a crack shot."

"Well, don't credit it!" he roared, adding in horrified tones, "And don't be spreading it abroad either. If it gets about that it was a deliberate aim, I'll be expected to demand satisfaction for *that* insult!"

The countess, though amused, cut off the exchange between the two old combatants and set about the business that had brought her. At the end of an hour, during which she had wrung a reluctant promise from Lord Bancroft to assist in the matter concerning his daughter and had imparted careful instructions as to what would be expected of him, she set forth in her landaulet to attend to one or two small errands before returning home.

As they were driving in Piccadilly, she suddenly exclaimed to Chloe, "Oh, dear, I have just seen young Freddy—on the strut, I believe it is called. Unhappily, *he* is in the way to expose my little deception, and I have neglected to warn Adrian not to mention that absurd marriage should he encounter the young rascal."

She signaled her coachman as he was about to turn into Bond Street and directed him to drive instead to Berkeley Square. When the carriage was again in motion, she said to Chloe, "There is little hope of finding Adrian at home, but I shall leave a note for him. I pray I may yet be beforehand."

Her prayers would likely have been answered had she permitted her coachman to follow his original instructions and drive to

Hookham's Library in Bond Street. At much the same time, Sherworth was stepping out of number thirteen where he had been working off his morning irritations in several rounds of sparring at Jackson's school of boxing. As it turned out, however, instead of meeting the countess, Sherworth came upon the prime article who, only after a close race, had finished second to Miss Stratton. But now, with Miss Stratton situated inconveniently in Brighton, Sherworth was able to reevaluate the charms of the lady standing before him more favorably. He expressed a regret that he was undoubtedly too late to find Miss Kelly free for dinner, yet showed not the smallest surprise when Miss Kelly, as clever as she was beautiful, assured him that, by the greatest coincidence, she was unengaged for the entire evening. Still, her cleverness did not go unrewarded, for Sherworth sent Wiley off immediately to bespeak a private dining parlor at the Clarendon, a shockingly expensive establishment, but the only public hotel in London where a genuine French dinner might be had.

Miss Kelly, understandably pleased with this handsome form of entertainment, was no less impressed when she found a pretty garnet brooch under the lid of a dish served to her during the second course. She exclaimed with delight that she couldn't think how his lordship had found time to arrange so enchanting a means of bestowing a gift. She prudently refrained, however, from asking how he (never out of her sight since they'd met in Bond Street) had contrived to negotiate its purchase. And Sherworth, with a kindness to match her discretion, did not explain that the arrangement was common enough to require little more than a flick of his wrist.

When they left the Clarendon, they passed several hours in the Eastern splendor and frolicsome atmosphere of the Royal Saloon, after which Sherworth returned a very gratified Miss Kelly to her home in Golden Square.

Several hours after that, as he set out for home, he came face to face with Freddy Bancroft.

He had been preparing to turn left into Silver Street when a disturbance, coming from the opposite direction, caused him to draw in his horses. There was shouting mixed with the urgent sound of boots slapping hard upon the cobbles. Soon he was able to see that the noise was coming from a group of young bloods, running toward him at full cry.

Two of their number halted several yards from where Sherworth worked to reassure his horses. His disgust turned to fury when he recognized one of the dandified louts, weaving on unsteady legs before him, as young Mr. Bancroft. Then he realized that what he had at first assumed to be a second batch of rowdies was actually a group of watchmen in pursuit of them and that Freddy was acting as accomplice to one who'd purposefully provided himself with a length of cord in anticipation of this event. At the moment, the pair of them were drawing the cord taut, at about two feet from the cobbles, with the object of felling the unsuspecting Charlies, who were running toward the trap as fast as their old legs would permit. Sherworth cursed the ill-conceived policy of staffing London's watch with elderly men, who were seldom able to outrun or outfight the athletic young blackguards who, out of boredom, menaced the town until dawn.

As the last of the "gentlemen" scoundrels shot past, Sherworth urged his horses forward, crossing to the corner of Garnaby Street, and reined in near the place where Freddy was crouched. Several yards still separated them, but driving enthusiasts, who described Sherworth as capable of removing a fly from his leader's ear without the slightest discomfort to the horse, spoke only simple truth. Flourishing his driving whip, he sent its point stinging smartly across the back of Freddy's hand, encouraging him on easy terms to release his end of the cord. Seconds later, the squad of puffing old watchmen trotted safely over the impotent line, unaware of their near fate.

Sherworth passed the reins to Wiley and in the next minute had the dazed Freddy pulled up short by the lapels of his wasp-waisted coat. "You damned little thatchgallows," he hissed. "You might have killed one of those old scouts."

"What the——? Who——? Sherworth?" slurred Freddy, who was examining the welt across the back of his hand with uncomprehending fascination. All at once, allowing for a somewhat slack mouth, his expression became intelligent. "You——! Was *you* tipped me the lash!" Struggling unsuccessfully to free himself of Sherworth's grasp, he shouted for his friend, who had, however, prudently disappeared into the shadows. Left to deal with his tormentor by himself, he snarled, ineffectually flailing fists at Sherworth's ribs, "Take your curst mawlies off me, or I'll lend you a clout! Will, anyway! I'll stave in your damned crazy timbers for this piece of work, you confounded, meddling bull huff!"

"You must try that sometime when you're not shot in the neck," invited Sherworth through clenched teeth. Releasing his hold on Freddy's oversized lapels, he added, "Just now, let's see if you can stand."

Since Freddy's balance had been precarious in a calm state, the thrust of his own struggles sent him soundly down, slap into the kennel. Sherworth looked at him in disgust. "What in the name of the devil can this cousin of yours be?"

"Cousin?" repeated Freddy, his attention drawn from the unhappy state of his lemon-colored pantaloons. "Must mean Ves. Devilish fond of Ves. A grea-t gun, Ves," he panted, trying to get to his feet.

"A tomrig or a noddy to want you for a husband," Sherworth sneered. "But you may forget that. I'll see she gets some sense, if I have to shake it into her."

"Tap your claret, if you come the ugly with Ves," Freddy warned, gaining his knees. But, after peering intently at the swaying ground, he looked up, an idiotic grin on his face. "Wants me for a husband?" he giggled, flopping back on one hip. "She's bubbled you properly, my lad—!"

However, Freddy's jovial words were heard only by a businesslike cat making her nocturnal rounds, for Sherworth was already climbing back into his curricle.

Arriving home a short while later, Sherworth groaned as he read the countess's note desiring him to refrain from discussing Vescinda with Freddy until they were established together at Blakely.

However, when he described his early morning encounter to her the next day, she heard him with no sign of distress. She knew, if from nothing else, that her quick-tempered stepson would not have entered her breakfast parlor so calmly had young Mr. Bancroft said anything to give the game away. After assuring him that no harm had been done, she approved warmly of his timely intervention, not only for the sake of the watchmen, but because he had stopped Freddy doing something, she was sure, he would have regretted on sober reflection.

Sherworth expressed strong doubts on that, but then, dismissing the episode from his mind, asked, "Have you dispatched Chloe, then?"

"Oh, indeed, yes. She drew away early this morning, with enough baggage to stay the year out. Tell me, can you report any success in securing our gentlemen for the party?"

"Hardly," Sherworth replied, drumming his long fingers on the table. His thoughts drifted automatically to his oldest friend, Sir Richard Thale, who, because of absentee parents serving in India, had been almost a second son to the countess, and he said, "Richard, when I can locate him, may be depended upon, of course—and I'll want him to assist me in pressing the other three. No point in wrapping it up in clean linen. No one worth having can be expected to accept an invitation from Bancroft willingly."

"Well, perhaps I can assist you and dear Richard with your task. Vescinda writes that Sir Harold and Lady Wildborne have been in residence since July. They have a place quite near to Blakely, and, if I recall correctly, it is their daughter whom some of the gentlemen styled 'the Incomparable' last season."

Sherworth's brows rose speculatively, but he did not comment. After leaving him to digest this information for a moment, the countess remarked with a chuckle, "Chloe claims that this same Miss Wildborne drew a deal of *your* interest last spring."

Sherworth met her words with a comical grimace. "For once Chloe's intelligence is at fault. It was Miss Wildborne's superb black stallion that had won my interest. . . . Nothing will persuade her to part with him, however."

The countess caused Sherworth's deep-blue eyes to gleam appreciatively, when she remarked drily that she rather thought there were terms Miss Wildborne would consider.

"You've hit it squarely," he laughed. "Together with the rest of her sorority, she has her cap aimed smack at my coronet. But, much as I hanker after her horse, not for a thousand such stallions would I suffer Miss Wildborne under my roof. Oh—a beauty to be sure, but a regular jaw-me-dead." He seemed for a moment to be entertaining an unpleasant memory, then said, "I pray she doesn't live *too* near your granddaughter!"

After another brief period of reflection, he sighed irritably on the conclusion that Miss Wildborne was precisely the sort of female likely to be the bosom-friend of someone who would choose to marry Freddy Bancroft. But soon his thinking became more constructive, and he nodded slowly, "Still, you're right again. The Wildborne's presence in Dorsetshire might well prove useful in recruiting one or two less discriminating fellows."

3

THE COAST OF West Dorsetshire rises from the sea in a line of sheer cliffs that continue inland as a series of green hills. Atop one of these hills, a lone rider paused to watch the progress of a coach and four moving at a dashing pace along a valley lane below. Evidently thinking to interest a neatish gray mare, she exclaimed: "Why, it's turning into the Blakely gate!"

The carriage disappeared behind the lodge, only to come into view again, as it passed through a short clearing in the parklands. It was impossible to discern the nature of the arms emblazoned on the door panel, but it could be seen that, instead of a shield, they were set out on a lozenge, and the mare—informed in some excitement that it must be Grandmama—was sent in full career down the steep hillside.

This spectacular descent was being viewed from within the coach by Chloe, who startled her dozing maid by demanding, "Never tell me it is my niece racing down that hill like a cavalryman at full charge!"

In another minute the coach came to a halt in front of a broad stone stairway. The door was flung open and the coach steps let down by a young giant in footman's livery. Chloe accepted the powerful arm, eyeing its owner appreciatively, then raised her brows as a second goliath came out of the great rambling stone house. As she stepped from the carriage onto the sweep, she craned her neck toward the hill, exclaiming: "Heaven send she isn't in splints for the party!"

As the footman's eyes followed the direction of her gaze, a grin broke out on his pleasant face. "Nay, ma'am! Not Miss Vescinda on her Twilight. They ride as one, they do."

A groom was running from the stableyard at the far side of the house, but, long before he arrived, the mare stiffened her forelegs and halted a few yards from the accumulating audience. Vescinda kicked her foot free of the stirrup, sprang lightly to the ground, and left the mare with instructions to, "Await Archer." She swept up the long skirts of her gray riding habit and hurried toward the coach. But she drew up short and exclaimed, "Why, Aunt Chloe! Goodness, this is certainly a surprise!"

"Surprises me to see you off that hill in one piece," returned Chloe. "No, no, girl, there's no use peering into the coach. Your grandmother ain't along."

Disappointment flickered in a pair of unusually beautiful green eyes, but was gone in an instant. "Of course, she wouldn't be. Silly of me—and selfish too—when I know perfectly well that the damp air is harmful to her." Vescinda's gaze traveled over the extraordinary amount of baggage piled high on the roof of the coach. She mused in a tone mixed of wonder and relief, "I know she must be well, or you wouldn't have come to—" She broke off, a laugh escaping her. "Is it a visit, or have you come to stay?"

That made Chloe laugh too. "I collect you're referring to the few little comforts I've carried along. No, it's strictly a visit."

Vescinda was naturally anxious to learn the reason for this sudden and unprecedented event, so undertook immediately to guide her aunt up the stairs to the privacy of the house. During this short trek, she found herself subjected to several quick, appraising glances and wondered, with dancing eyes, if she was measuring up favorably for whatever was planned for her. She was given no clue, for, as Chloe stepped past the butler into the house, she promptly lost interest in everything but the impressive collection of ancient armaments hanging about the timbered walls.

Vescinda tossed her riding crop onto a table, pulled off her gloves, and removed an attractive gray hat, revealing an abundance of shimmering, dark hair. With her thoughts focused on the mountain of baggage she had seen strapped to the coach, she said to her butler, "Rigsby, my Aunt Standish will be making a long stay with us. Will you find Mrs. Redding for—Millie, isn't it?" she asked, smiling in her friendly way at Chloe's abigail.

Millie, awed by the young lady's memory, dipped a curtsey. "Why, yes, miss, it is!"

"Mrs. Redding is our housekeeper, Millie. She will see you settled and prepare a chamber for Mrs. Standish," explained Vescinda pleasantly before turning to take Chloe's arm again. "And we, Aunt, shall wait in the yellow saloon, just here——" She looked for her butler's answering nod before continuing, "where Rigsby has had the foresight to place wine for us."

Chloe tore her eyes from the inspection she was making of the room and exclaimed, "Gad, what a great barn of a place this is! Yes, yes, just coming."

Vescinda stepped aside to permit her aunt to preceed her into a bright, cheerful room giving onto the terrace. Begging her to be seated, she went to a table where Rigsby had placed wine and glasses.

After taking in her surroundings with approval, Chloe said in a resigned tone, "I daresay it's an interrogation you have in mind."

"As well you may!" Vescinda laughed, selecting a decanter. "I recall your once saying that you thought the country too slow by half. So we needn't trouble to pretend you've come by choice." She conveyed a crystal glass filled with a light amber liquid to her aunt. "I suspect in fact that Grandmama has sent you to try if you can bullock me into giving over my plans."

"It was Mama who sent me, of course, but not for that—nor anything you should dislike."

Vescinda perched gracefully on the edge of a chair and listened in growing astonishment to the complicated plans for her entertainment, asking, when Chloe finally paused, "But *why,* for heaven's sake? Oh, I don't mean that it isn't just what I should like, but . . . so much fuss and bother for everyone! And you say that most of the guests are yet unknown?"

"My mother shall write to tell us of them," returned Chloe, waving away this reasonable point. "As to why, it's just she don't want you to get out of the way of being in company—nothing odd in that!"

But whatever hope Chloe might have harbored, of brushing through with a high hand, dissolved into a feeling of acute discomfort when her niece agreed, with a musical laugh, that forcing upward of a dozen people to attend the house party of a complete stranger was, of course, the merest commonplace. Chloe had forgotten, or perhaps had never noticed, the quick intelligence that lay behind the engaging twinkle in those green eyes. Their exciting color might be traced directly to Bancroft's mother, but the expression in them was disturbingly reminiscent of the countess when she was getting ready to devil one to death. Chloe had prepared no better excuse, supposing that, like most girls, Vescinda would be too excited by the news of a party to interest herself deeply in the reason for it. And now, she thought irritably, the girl obviously intended to cut up all her peace with a great siege of cross-questioning.

There could be no doubting that Vescinda was, indeed, full of questions. She was quite enough like most girls to welcome the news of a party, particularly coming as it did after the restrictions of a prolonged period of mourning. And she couldn't be more delighted that she was at last to make the acquaintance of the stepson who, for as long as she could remember, had figured so intriguingly in her grandmother's conversation, but who, by the most disappointing mischance, had been absent during her only two visits to the metropolis. By the same token, she could scarcely fail to realize that such an unconventional party was being got up for a more complex purpose than to keep her in the way of company, and that Lord Sherworth, or indeed her own father, would not journey such a distance merely to accommodate her in this way. What struck her as most puzzling was that she was sure, if her grandmother hadn't wished her to spy the cloven hoof in the business, it would have been much, much more difficult to do so. And so the mystery was rendered even more fascinating by her aunt's obvious wish that she accept such a thin excuse.

However, Chloe had misjudged her niece in this regard, as well. Vescinda's manners were far too good to permit her curiosity to discomfit anyone, and the instant she'd caught Chloe's flash of agitation, she turned the subject politely to her governess. "Oh, I have just realized that Elena shall be as delighted as I by this happy surprise. Her sister, Lady Sarah, you know, is soon to be brought to bed of a child, and she has been wishing of all things that she might go to her. I fancy I needn't tell you that I have been at fiddlestick's end, trying to persuade her that I should go on perfectly well for a few weeks without her. Well—this *quite* solves the problem. Now that I have you to bear me company, she may set forth immediately and without a qualm." Seeing that her aunt was still looking a trifle guarded, she rose, asking, "Shall I take you up to your chamber now?"

Chloe came to her feet with alacrity, grateful that the matter of Lady Elena's sister's forthcoming confinement had intruded so opportunely into her niece's thoughts. To be on the safe side, she kept the conversation flowing along these lines, only digressing now and then to comment on various aspects of the house, as Vescinda led her up two flights of stairs and through the long gallery. She remained in the safety of her chamber for a little over an hour, not rejoining her niece in the drawing room until she was armed with half a dozen improbable explanations for the party. When, however, it began to seem she would not be called upon to impart any of these inventive flams, she settled herself comfortably and set about bringing Vescinda up to date on events concerning her grandmother, her hapless father, and a great many other people quite unknown to her.

They were chatting along these lines when Rigsby entered and announced dully that Miss Wildborne had called and was insisting upon waiting, even though she'd been most firmly assured that Miss Vescinda would be occupied until the dinner hour. He added, in a tone which hinted his opinion that she should be left there to rot, that she was presently in the blue saloon.

"That one!" Chloe hissed, when the butler had left them, "Is she by often?"

"Very often. Owing mostly to a restless nature—though I'm tolerably certain this call comes of word having spread that a foreign coach has entered the premises."

"Oh, Lord," Chloe groaned. "Is that all the gossip they have down here? Well, I think I'll beg off from meeting the Wildborne chit. Don't like her above half. Do you?"

"Not even so well, but it's a moot point. I couldn't refuse her—not without having my character cut up." She laughed. "Why, in no time at all, you would be hearing—oh, that my jealousy of Liza's beauty and popularity made it too painful for me to endure the sight of her. You may be sure that neither Liza nor her mother would allow the world to draw its own conclusions."

"Do you care so much for that? What a parcel of rustics may think?"

Vescinda looked a little surprised as she rose. "Why, yes, I shouldn't like anyone to believe such a humiliating thing of me—

to be thought capable of such a stupidish jealousy. Indeed, yes, I'm afraid I should dislike it excessively. Besides," she went on in a lighter tone, "surely there is a rule that one may not be uncivil to one's neighbors simply because they are annoying. Oh, I'm persuaded there must be. Think of the shocking decline in country social life if it were otherwise!"

Left again to herself, Chloe sat in pursed-lipped cogitation. Things, to her way of thinking, were not progressing at all well. She'd made it a point to warn the countess of Sherworth's interest in the Wildborne girl, but she'd had no notion that country people, separated by several miles, hobbed and nobbed together on a daily basis—or that that blond hoyden stood so ready to make mischief for Vescinda! Well, there it was! Chloe had no doubt that Sherworth would rather be in Brighton with his light skirt than waste time on either young lady, but he'd be stuck here; and, now that a rambunctious female was available, it was ten to one he'd prefer her.

Not, thought Chloe, with a martial gleam, that her niece had cause to be jealous of this so-called "Incomparable" in the ordinary way. She might lack the Wildborne's classically perfect features, but there was an alluring quality in Vescinda's beauty that made it hard to keep from looking at her over and over again. Those lively and indisputably green eyes, set off by long dark lashes, were largely responsible, but considerable fascination was also aroused by a wayward muscle at one side of her mouth, which made her smile appear almost seductive and intriguingly at variance with her cool, well-bred manners. What was more, Chloe decided with a nod of approval, she rigged herself out with better taste than that yellar-haired creature. She couldn't know if her niece had ordered that gray habit during her recent mourning, or merely to indulge a fancy to match her mare, but, either way, the most exacting critic among the sprigs of London could be depended upon to hail it as all the crack. The well-cut Georgian cloth conformed to a fashion that was merciless to those with less than a perfect figure, falling softly from a high waist to touch lightly on each and every curve. And happily, Chloe thought, the girl possessed enough of *them* to suit Sherworth to a turn.

Vescinda arrived at the blue saloon and found her neighbor pacing like a lioness on the fret and, like a jungle creature, almost invisible in her surroundings. A little amused by the notion, she wondered if, in choosing to place Miss Wildborne in a room dominated by hangings of much the same shade as her velvet riding habit, Rigsby had indulged an unconscious wish to make her disappear. Certainly the yellow saloon had been nearer to hand.

Miss Wildborne spun dramatically to a halt, exclaiming, "Vescinda! I pray I haven't taken you from company . . ." When this hopeful gambit won only the shadow of a smile, Miss Wildborne resumed her rapid perambulation, saying in a tone that made no pretense at apology, "Well, I didn't *wish* to interrupt you! Oh, but, after the excitement of a London Season, country life is so vexaciously flat. It is all I can do to keep from running mad! And— and remaining cooped up at home is past all bearing—"

"I perfectly understand, Liza. It was my Aunt Standish," Vescinda said calmly, scanning the room for a vantage point that would spare her neck during conversation with her restless visitor.

"You needn't think *that* is why I have called— Standish? Isn't she that brash daughter of Lady Sherworth's?"

"She is my grandmother's daughter, and, as I have already said, she is *my* aunt," returned Vescinda, choosing a window seat. Her tone had been perfectly level, but there was a decided sparkle in her eyes.

Miss Wildborne, who was for the most part impervious to subtle snubs, merely replied thoughtfully: "Oh, yes, I place her now. One sees her *everywhere*, though she will often talk as if she had just stepped out of a military camp or some such place."

A lively sense of the ridiculous extinguished the fire in Vescinda's expressive eyes. "If I'd had the least notion that your sensibilities were so easily ruffled by brusque speech, I should have warned you instantly that my father will soon be with us as well."

Though conceit and a strong self-interest kept Miss Wildborne well insulated against the opinions and actions of others, she was by no means lacking a shrewd and active mind. The irony of Vescinda's comment was lost upon her, but not its significance. The infrequency with which Lord Bancroft graced his estates was well known to the neighborhood. That he was about to do so, coupled with the arrival of a female relative, hinted that some form of entertainment was in the offing. Miss Wildborne questioned Vescinda excitedly, going into raptures when it emerged that there was to be a house party, with guests actually coming down from London to attend. A depressing thought occurred, however, and she pointed out, "You know, Vescinda, the only entertaining your father has ever done was to fill the house with that set of middle-aged rakes he goes about with." After a moment's consideration, she observed in a more optimistic tone, "Still, it isn't likely that Lady Sherworth would have sent her daughter to act as hostess to such an affair as *that*!"

Vescinda agreed drily that it was not.

On the move again, Miss Wildborne became lost in a reverie. Soon her steps slackened, and she began abstractedly to finger various ornaments along her route. Finally she paused, her eyes narrowed with suspicion. "Vescinda, surely, if this party is to be no more than a fortnight from now, you *must* know who is coming for it."

"I assure you, I do not," replied Vescinda, determined not to betray that she found the arrangement at all out of the way. "The invitations were sent out from London, and we must await a letter from my grandmother to tell us who has accepted."

After a moment's consideration, Miss Wildborne appeared to be satisfied and took her leave, assuring Lady Sherworth's granddaughter self-importantly that, if Lady Sherworth were arranging the party, they need expect none but the highest ton.

By the next morning, Chloe had persuaded Lady Elena to make her journey in comfort, by availing herself of the countess's luxuriously appointed and well-sprung coach. "No point in having it sit idle here for three weeks," she'd said. Then, taking Vescinda's highborn companion aside, she added in a conspiratorial tone, "And, if all goes as my mother hopes, there'll be no need for you to come back to this godforsaken place at all."

Lady Elena wasn't in the least distressed to learn that she might soon find herself bereft of her posts. With such a beautiful and charming charge as Vescinda, she had scarcely expected to remain employed so long. Her salary had been handsome—far beyond that of an ordinary governess—and a generous pension, added to what she'd been able to put by, would make her mistress of a respectable competence for the remainder of her days. Like Vescinda, she had instantly suspected that the bizarre arrangements outlined by Chloe were only a cog in a scheme of the countess's hatching. They'd laughed together over it, each putting forward a variety of outrageous conjectures. When, however, she'd learned that Lord Sherworth was to make one of the party, Lady Elena had no longer to wonder. She had been in the countess's confidence, on that head, for many years. Moreover, she had realized at once that removing her restrictive influence from the proceedings would be just what the countess would wish—perhaps had even anticipated! The more she thought about it, the more convinced Lady Elena became that, if her sister hadn't conveniently been in an "interesting condition," she would undoubtedly have received a message from the countess, instructing her to partake of a much-needed holiday.

Once Vescinda had bid a fond farewell to her governess and dear friend, she joined her aunt in a second cup of coffee. Chloe, learning that she had been so unwise as to inform Miss Wildborne of the party, immediately expressed her disapproval.

Vescinda's eyes brimmed with amusement. "Dear ma'am, *your* arrival, alone, has inspired no less than five people to contrive the flimsiest excuses for calling. I promise you there would have been no hope of concealing such a stirring event as a house party. I'm afraid we shall have to face the fact that Liza must very definitely be invited to some of the entertainments and that she will somehow contrive to intrude herself upon most of the others."

"But why do you put up with her?" demanded Chloe.

"Because she leaves one no means, within the bounds of civility, to exclude her. And, as I have already mentioned, her reprisals can be quite hair-raising."

Chloe remarked hotly that it would be past her powers to allow such a snip to corner her in that way.

Forbearing to point out that a widowed lady would not be so vulnerable to an attack upon her reputation, Vescinda merely smiled and said, "I daresay I'm inured after all these years." She sipped her coffee thoughtfully and added, "Still, I own that I wish she hadn't learned of it until *after* I had been able to supply her with a guest list. Foolishly, I allowed myself to be goaded into mentioning that Papa was coming down. That enabled her to all but guess what was afoot, and, of course, I have quite unintentionally provided her with reason to positively haunt us until she can discover whom we shall be entertaining. Oh, well, at least I had the presence of mind not to mention Lord Sherworth, or we should not be rid of her yet. She talks of little else since her return from London."

"What does she say of him?" asked Chloe, her ears pricking up.

"All she knows or cares for—that he is wealthy, an earl, and has thus far escaped the matrimonial net. Odd, isn't it? I mean that she should know him and I should not. What is he like, Aunt Chloe?"

Chloe would have liked nothing better than to gossip on this fruitful subject, but the countess's instructions rang in her ears. ("Pray, say nothing that will spoil the spontaneity of this first meeting, which I have so carefully preserved for them.")

Observing her aunt's reluctance, Vescinda tilted her head a little to one side, a curious humor showing between her brows. "Do you think him too shocking to discuss with me? Surely Grandmama wouldn't send someone who is even more shocking than Papa."

"She'd be hard put to find someone if she would," returned Chloe. Then, laying to rest the last tug of temptation, she said, "No, it's merely that he has always stood a younger brother to me, and one doesn't notice them, you know."

A speculative gleam flickered in Vescinda's eyes, but she laughed and turned the subject. "Very well, dear Aunt, there is something *else* I have been meaning to discuss with you. Wouldn't you rather I take on the project of readying the house for the party, while you act more as an advisor? I don't think you have a guess as to the work involved, and I cannot like your being put to such trouble for my party."

Having seen the size of the place, Chloe had a fair notion of the work involved, but the countess had been most explicit: ("You, Chloe, must keep full charge of the house as it relates to the party, for I wish Vescinda to remain free to entertain Adrian. On the other hand, I should like her to continue as mistress of the day-to-day affairs.") So, Chloe disclaimed hastily, "Oh, no, no, I don't mind the work, but I've never had a home of my own, so I expect it will be you advising me."

"Very well, if you are determined, I shall instruct the troops to stand ready for your orders."

In referring to the servants as troops, Vescinda had spoken facetiously, hoping to make her aunt feel more at home, but it soon became apparent that the term had been amazingly apt. Chloe took command with a slight trepidity, but, by the end of the day, she was so zealously engrossed in her campaign that Vescinda was forced to remind her several times that the next day was a Sunday, lest she scandalize the servants by assigning improper work projects.

And, indeed, on the following morning, it took all the discipline at Chloe's command for her to march past the chores she had already ticked off in her mind in order to join Vescinda in the carriage that waited to convey them to services at Charmouth. The small church there was of ancient origin, the only date of record being that it had been rebuilt in 1503. It contained a screen and some of the Miserere carved with grotesque figures. Chloe, always interested in new surroundings, ran her eye over these, but, try though she would, the sermon had not the power to forestall the lists that her mind continued to make, as she slipped in a mental progression through Lord Bancroft's great, rambling house.

Her thoughts were wholly diverted from this labor, however, when, after the service, she watched the ritual that evidently took place every Sunday, as her niece, greatly hampered by a swarm of more than a half dozen hopeful gentlemen, slowly made her way from the church steps to her carriage. Although she was friendly to them all, there was nothing in her manner that even the most optimistic of her suitors could have called encouraging. She accorded each a pleasant smile, congratulated any new accomplishment that was described to her, and sent civil messages to their several mothers, all the while moving steadily toward her objective.

When the carriage was again rolling along on its way back to Blakely, Chloe said tentatively, "You don't appear to favor any amongst your squad of admirers."

"That business at the church?" Vescinda smiled. "It means nothing. They have merely made it a fashion to try and flirt with me."

"Well, no harm in that! Don't you enjoy a little flirtation?"

Vescinda drew her brows together. "I've never really considered the matter, but, even if Elena wouldn't box my ears for behaving so improperly, I rather think it would be a trifle boring to flirt with gentlemen who, only a short while ago, were enacting the role of knights on fat ponies."

"You're saying that you couldn't care for any of them?"

"None. Well, not to the degree that I collect you mean. And if I could, it would still be wrong in me to encourage such attentions. But why do you stare? Can you believe that Grandmama would be pleased to receive an express from me, informing her that I have decided to wed a local swain?"

"No, dare say she wouldn't like it above half," agreed Chloe readily. "But I can promise you this—my mother would never wish you to marry *against* your inclination, or—or someone you couldn't hold in affection."

"No, no, indeed! But I am sure that she expects me to marry a man of fashion, and, though I am not acquainted with many at present, it seems reasonable that there should be one amongst them whom I could hold in affection . . . Are you afraid I should dislike the life I have been prepared for? No, no, I'm sure I should like it excessively. Already I am performing the duties that should fall to me on a gentleman's estate—apart, of course, from entertaining, and that I know I should enjoy. And, though I shouldn't like to fix permanently in Town, I am certain I should love everything to do with London in the Season. Well, naturally, I haven't seen much of *London,* but Grandmama thought it advisable to *ease* me into society before bringing me out and has taken me to Weymouth and to Bath, where I have been to several private parties—oh, and to concerts, plays, gala nights, and a great many fashionable lounges." She chuckled, "Ah, and, of course, to all those wonderful shops. I'm afraid *they* please me very much indeed!"

Once back in the house, Chloe, itching to set about her tasks, was happily kept in check for the remainder of Sunday by a series of callers. She found that country ladies were every bit as fond of gossip as town-dwellers and that, although only a few of them could claim a personal knowledge of the doings among London's upper ten thousand, all of them devoured the society journals with as much fervor as herself. Her ability to impart first-hand information and to correct omissions or exaggerations made by the press was received with an awe and interest that could scarcely fail to gratify, and, for the most part, she enjoyed the day very much, the only discordant notes coming in endless reminders of the hopelessness of her mission. She had never cherished much faith that there could be a happy conclusion to the countess's scheme, but no campaigner, worthy of the name, liked to enter battle, *knowing* he should be beaten all hollow. Throughout the day, she had been favored with praise of her niece's exquisite refinement, the delicacy of her principles, the fine tone of her mind—all of which would give her dear aunt nothing to fear in her temporary chaperonage of so exemplary a charge. Dear Mrs. Standish might rest assured that Miss Bancroft could be depended upon to know just how to depress attempts at improper familiarity or disrespectful conversation, which, alas, gentlemen in these sad times were only too prone to inflict on girls of gentle birth. Oh, yes, there had been Town Beaux in the district before! But the smoothest of them had been sent to the rightabout, smarting with the memory that they had dared suppose that Miss Bancroft of Blakely could be trifled with as though she were a serving wench from a common inn!

Generally Vescinda remained politely at her aunt's side, bearing these fulsome compliments with unimpaired composure, but, when these matrons were accompanied by sons or daughters, she drew the younger members to the far end of the drawing room and undertook the entertaining of them herself. This left the older ladies unhampered by considerations of "innocent" ears, while, at the same time, spared herself the tedium of what she considered were kindly meant, but sadly superficial, descriptions of her character.

As the accepted hours for callers drew to a close, Vescinda noted that her aunt's restlessness had been greatly assuaged by the company, and she invited the Davises to return for a potluck dinner. Mr. Davis, a tall, handsome young man, who, despite warnings dropped in his ear by a wise and loving mother, had long since set his mind on winning Vescinda, and his younger sister, a shy girl of seventeen, who looked upon her as the model for all the heroines in all the romances she had ever read, were both quite naturally delighted by the suggestion, so the widowed Mrs. Davis, content with her company, mentally condemned the noble turkey presently roasting in her own oven to reappear upon the following evening in the humbler guise of a haricot, and accepted with no discernable hesitation.

"There, now," said Vescinda, when the dinner guests had taken their leave and the tea tray was being removed, "country life is not so sadly flat as you'd imagined."

Snapping up one last pastry as the tray was whisked away, Chloe agreed to this. "I can't think where they all come from, but I'll warrant we had more callers today than my mother would on a summer day in London."

"Certainly, because most everyone comes to the country for the summer."

Chloe nibbled thoughtfully on the small delicate cake, then said, "But what of these Town Beaux I hear of? Why have you been dealing so harshly with them?"

"Why, can you possibly suppose I would permit them 'to trifle with Miss Bancroft of Blakely as though she were a serving wench from a common inn'?" exclaimed Vescinda, giving way to a gurgle of mirth.

Chloe couldn't help returning Vescinda's infectious laugh, but she accused, "Yet only this morning, you told me that you thought you could fancy a man of fashion."

"Dear me, I shall withdraw the remark if *those* were a fair sampling. Besides, you must see that these same ladies, who so carefully noted that I did *not* respond to their effrontery, would be speaking of the events quite as freely if I had!"

"Well—of course, I don't know what sort of mischief they were getting up to," said Chloe lamely.

She had noticed, however, that the Davis fellow had behaved as though Vescinda were made of fine china, and she thought despondently that it seemed highly probable, since he had known her all her life, that the poor young man was well-versed in how her perplexing niece liked to be treated.

4

THE FOLLOWING MORNING Chloe plunged into her venture, and there she remained, thoroughly immersed, for the next fortnight. Vescinda, wishing to be of help, accepted the role of captain to Chloe's general with her usual good nature and was deployed to the supervision of tasks ranging from the removal, cleaning, and replacement of the chandeliers in the great hall, to arranging for enough lobsters to feed Lord Wellington's army in Spain.

On Thursday morning, as she was coming up the few steps from the great hall to the entrance way, she found her aunt demanding news of the morning post, as she searched about the table where the mail pouch was usually kept. Vescinda smiled. "Have you been so long in the country you've forgotten the mail doesn't leave London until eight in the evening?"

"Oh, drat, yes—*no!* Just forgot how far *I* am from civilization! Very well, then, when does the mail stop here?"

"Stop here? Oh, it doesn't," replied Vescinda, a gleam of fun in her eyes. "You see, it only stops for fresh horses, and, after changing at Bridport, it goes straight through to Axminster."

"Do you say you must go there to fetch it?" demanded Chloe, suspicious of that gleam.

"Not at all, because they very thoughtfully leave it for us at Charmouth in their way." An enchanting ripple of laughter broke from her. "No, no, don't eat me. Truly, I'm not hoaxing you. It's the most exciting thing! The man at our receiving office goes up to the first floor window, at one of the clock, where he stands ready until he hears the mailguard's horn. In good weather, one can set his watch by it—always at six minutes past the hour. Then, as the mailcoach comes through at full speed, the guard tosses up the bag for Charmouth precisely at the same instant Mr. Arn throws down the outgoing bag for the guard to catch."

"Now, tell me your Mr. Arn has never knocked that guard right off his perch," said Chloe, her eyes crinkling with laughter.

"Indeed, he hasn't! And they never fail to catch their respective bags either. I go often just to watch."

"I'm relieved to learn you haven't been altogether without entertainment," Chloe remarked drily. Then jabbing the table with her finger, she said: "And now tell me how it gets here—and when."

"Well, that too is very interesting," returned Vescinda, beginning to laugh again. "Archer was used to send an undergroom to fetch it, but that has proved quite unnecessary of late because Liza is so very obliging as to ride down for it each day—where I'll warrant she heckles poor Mr. Arn all the while he is sorting. Then, as I understand it, she delivers it to our door as fast as her stallion can carry her. She has even been so good as to pay our postage—all of it—because, of course, the mail pouch is locked, and she can't know if *the* letter is amongst the batch."

By that afternoon, however, Miss Wildborne's patience had worn so thin from day after day of disappointment that she clutched the mail bag possessively to her breast when Rigsby attempted to relieve her of it and flatly spurned his efforts to install her in a saloon. She demanded, instead, in a voice threatening hysteria, to be told instantly where Vescinda might be found. With his own voice barely concealing the outrage he felt at such a request, Rigsby explained that Miss Vescinda was partaking of a late luncheon and a *much needed rest* and could not be disturbed.

But Miss Wildborne shared not a whit of Rigsby's reverence for his mistress's right to rest and burst past him, flung open the door of the dining hall and commanded shrilly, "Vescinda, come and open this bag at once!"

Vescinda's head jerked up in surprise, but she couldn't help being amused by the study of pure exasperation she beheld in the doorway. She said calmly, "Yes, but fetch it to me here."

She laid down her fork to unclip the ring of keys she carried throughout the day. The bag, when unlocked, revealed three letters, two of which were discarded in favor of a gilt-edged vellum bearing the word *free* stamped within a crowned circle and with Sherworth's name and style scrawled in the corner.

Miss Wildborne, dropping weakly into a chair beside Vescinda, squeaked, "It's from Sherworth!"

"Unlikely," replied Vescinda, breaking the seal. "They often come this way from my grandmother—once franked by the sixth earl, now by the seventh."

Miss Wildborne's expression was a ludicrous mixture of disappointment and relief. "Yes, I forgot your grandmother's connection to him for a moment. Well, never mind that. What does she say?"

After a swift perusal of the single sheet, Vescinda was prompted by her evil genius to reply, "That she will write in more detail later." But before Miss Wildborne could unleash the vociferous outpourings that trembled on her lip, Vescinda continued placidly, "Then there follows a list of those to attend the party, and—let me see—"

"Oh, never mind *and,* read the list!" directed Miss Wildborne impatiently.

"Very well," Vescinda agreed dulcetly, fully aware that Miss Wildborne would have found the *and* of far more interest than all the rest. She began the list of names: "Lady Oxbrook, Lady Milissa Milton, Lady Charlotte St. Paul, Miss Milton, Miss Katherine Milton—"

"*Not* the ladies!" wailed Miss Wildborne.

"That's the lot at all events. The gentlemen are: Lord Edward Renslow, Lord Caversham, Sir Richard Thale, and—dear me, one quite distinguished by being neither Lord, Lady nor Sir—not even an honorable."

"*I* am not an honorable," accused Miss Wildborne.

Vescinda surveyed her incensed countenance with interest for a moment, then said: "No. Well, it was the merest quip, inspired by that list of lofty titles. It can't signify, after all, since no one *says* honorable."

"But they write it, in order to make seating charts."

Vescinda made a slight gesture of indifference and returned to her unfinished meal.

"Do you say that you shan't observe precedence during the party?" persisted Miss Wildborne, who, because she frequently found it more expedient to respond to her own questions, went on with no appreciable pause. "You will doubtless have a dinner ball. Surely you must do so *then!* People expect it." She twisted her mouth angrily. "And I shall likely be escorted down to dinner last—and by a positive nobody! But, no, perhaps it won't be as bad as that. You will no doubt invite many locals—and weren't there a few misses in that list of ladies?" she asked, already extending a hand for the letter.

"Liza," remarked Vescinda, placing it out of her reach. "You will find yourself without the problem if you go on like this, for your mother will send you back to the schoolroom."

"Oh, well, I'm sorry, but who *were* they?"

"They were the Misses Milton," replied Vescinda, adding, with a satisfaction she knew to be unreasonable, *"Lord* Milton's daughters."

"Honorables!" recoiled Miss Wildborne. Then, rummaging in her mind for a misplaced thought, she said, "Most everyone seems to be a friend or a relative of Lord Sherworth's. If only he were coming, too."

"He is."

Miss Wildborne, speechless for a moment, almost shrieked, "And you have not *told* me?"

"I have just done so."

Miss Wildborne teetered on the edge of a scathing speech, but the agreeable aspects of this new situation took possession of her mind. "Lord Sherworth—here!" she breathed. "Oh, *nothing* could be better! When I am Lady Sherworth, I shall go before you all— even Lady Oxbrook. Oxbrook is only a second earl, you know. I have told you, have I not, that the betting at White's gives me excellent odds? And now that he will be where one can get at him, you may look for my betrothal any day."

Seeing that her neighbor was well launched on the topic of her own prowess and popularity and would soon be lost in flowing periods, Vescinda selected a peach from a basket on the table and turned her mind to the more interesting subject of what changes to make in her dinner menu. She'd learned from her grandmother's letter that she must lay an extra cover for her father that very night, and yet another for Lord Sherworth on the morrow.

During this time, Miss Wildborne's voice bored on, "Oh, to think of having him fixed in a house that one may visit with perfect propriety—*and* no other ladies invited but sisters and nieces! Well, *you* will be here, but you are not at all in his style. Time without number, I've been told that I am unique, in having received an attention that Sherworth never pays to marriageable girls. Why, it was so marked that one of my other suitors threatened to put a period to his existence, and another composed a poem called 'The Surrender of Perfection to One Worthier than I.'"

Miss Wildborne recited the poem, then continued with further examples, her flow only interrupted when Rigsby came in to advise Vescinda that her father's man of business had called.

Vescinda pushed back her chair. "You must hold me excused, Liza, but Mr. Tilsdale has driven down from Bridport and must not be kept waiting."

"Vescinda! Have you been listening?" demanded Miss Wildborne, incensed at having the description of her conquests dismissed so lightly.

"I have heard much of what you've said," replied Vescinda scrupulously. "Mainly, I collect that Lord Sherworth may bid farewell to his bachelordom, now that he is being so imprudent as to go where you can get at him. Oh, yes, and you have recited your poem for me again. I must go, Liza."

Taking up her letter, Vescinda hurried away to the estate room at the extreme rear of the house.

Miss Wildborne remained seated there after Vescinda had gone, continuing to enjoy her own vision of things to come, when suddenly her attention was wrested from these agreeable musings by a blood chilling sound on the other side of the door. "Dear God," she gasped aloud, "it sounds like one of the beasts they keep at the Royal Exchange!"

She slipped out of her chair, gathering up the folds of her habit, and stole over to open the door a crack. Her eyes widened in astonishment, and she flung the door wide, rushing into the hall. "Lord Bancroft! What is it? What has occurred?"

The master of the establishment, face down on a litter, was being borne through the hall by John and Joseph. The two sturdy footmen, almost weakened to collapse by mirth, instantly took advantage of Miss Wildborne's wish to converse with his lordship, by carefully lowering their burden onto a settle and escaping out onto the front steps to vent their emotion.

Lord Bancroft took a moment to assimilate his new surroundings, then, fixing a slightly unfocused eye on Miss Wildborne, roared in a thickened voice, "Tortured, that's what! Bounced and tortured all the way from London—and for what? A parcel of slum! Curst woman!—forcing us all out here with her damned cracked-skulled notion. *Wants Freddy for a husband!* Rubbish!"

Miss Wildborne knew, of course, that she oughtn't to counte-nance such language, but such considerations never weighed with her when she sensed intrigue. She could think of only one woman who could force Lord Bancroft to come to his estates, and that was Lady Sherworth. "Freddy, sir? Who wants Freddy for a husband?"

"*Nobody* wants Freddy for a husband, damn it!" he boomed, making groping motions toward his pocket. "Why should they?"

"But you have just said—"

"I *said* that the plaguey woman *thinks* she wants Freddy for a husband," he growled, dragging a flask to his lips.

Miss Wildborne's eyes almost started from their sockets. "Lady Sherworth? Oh, no! She cannot possible think that *Vescinda* means to marry Freddy!"

Lord Bancroft took the time to tear the cork, with his teeth, from the flask. "Damn it, don't tell me she can't, when she does. Tell me why her young rake of a stepson cut up stiff with Freddy, why she's sending him to draw Freddy off—forcing *me* to play propriety while he's about it! The devil!" He raised onto one elbow to take a long pull from his bottle, then rolled his gaze back to Miss Wildborne. "And tell me why in hell I'm talking to you! Have they carted me into the wrong damned house?"

Miss Wildborne was not put to the necessity of explaining, for Chloe's entrance into the hall, at just that moment, convinced the sufferer that he was indeed under his own roof.

"Still on your belly after nine days?" she asked, looking him over critically.

"Damn it, woman! Have you no natural pity? Bouncing along in such a condition, my curst wound opened before I reached Staines!"

"You'd have done better to travel in that position and *walk* into the house."

"*What?* How? Strapped to the confounded roof?"

At the sound of footsteps, Chloe glanced behind her and said, "Now your daughter may see what a fine figure you cut."

"You mean she may see what the damned clankers she's put about have cost me. Her fault I'm in this case!"

Vescinda, coming up beside her aunt, said, "Hello, Papa.

Indeed, I'm sorry to see you still so out of frame after all this time." Turning to her aunt, she asked with a twinkle, "I didn't quite catch it. How is it that I am to blame?"

Chloe, moving to the opened door, said over her shoulder, "If you know no better than to heed anything he may utter, you've failed to take your brain from *our* side of the family." Leaning out, she called to the footmen waiting outside, "Come, lads, you've left something lying in the hall."

Miss Wildborne took this moment to slip away. She hurried along the path leading to the Bancroft stables in a state mixed of confusion and fury. She had always considered Vescinda Bancroft (who cared for nothing but her dignity and reputation) to be so poor-spirited as to make a most unworthy opponent. Seldom did she rise to a challenge, and *never* had she come out into open competition where the attentions of a gentleman were concerned. But hoaxing her grandmother into sending Sherworth down to woo her out of a nonexistent plan to marry Freddy was a master stroke. With Sherworth so occupied, what hope would there be for anyone else to command his notice? *Very little!* And the most vexing aspect of Vescinda's shrewd plan was that Miss Wildborne was barred from making use of her gift of information. Oh, indeed, she could inform Sherworth that the business about Freddy was a hum, but, if that were his sole purpose in coming down, he would simply thank her and return instantly to London. She was powerless to foil Vescinda's game without depriving herself of the opportunity afforded by his presence.

Reaching the stableyard on the tide of this frustrating realization, Miss Wildborne lashed out at the greenery that lined the path, viciously severing a newly formed bud from its stem with her riding crop.

By early afternoon of the next day, however, Miss Wildborne had calmed considerably, having soothed herself with the recollection that Sherworth's last mistress had been fair and that Vescinda, besides being dark, lacked experience in the arts of attaching a man. Furthermore, Miss Wildborne had decided cheerfully that, hampered as Vescinda would be by her namby-pamby ways and missish airs, she could be no *real* threat in a competition for Lord Sherworth.

In fact, as Miss Wildborne climbed the steps to Blakely, she was more in charity with Vescinda than she had ever been. Although it would be too much to say that Miss Wildborne was moved by a sense of fairness, she was not unaware that, if it hadn't been for Vescinda's overreaching ambition, Lord Sherworth would not be shortly within her own grasp.

The house being in its typical whirl of activity, Rigsby was slightly distracted when he responded to the imperative summons of the front door bell, a circumstance that was in no way lessened at finding the outrageous Wildborne girl, who was maddeningly unconscious that her call could in any way be inconvenient. As all the saloons on the ground floor were presently being turned inside out, he was forced to lead her directly to the drawing room, and to leave her there, while he searched the house over for his mistress.

Meanwhile, Miss Wildborne unconcernedly began her characteristic pacing, her mind busily formulating plans to overcome Vescinda's advantage of actually having the quarry under her own roof. Halfway round the room, her path took her past a table where Chloe, hurrying off to inspect a problem that had arisen in one of her many assignments, had left Vescinda's letter from the countess.

Miss Wildborne furtively turned back a fold with one finger and arched her neck in order to study its contents. But, by the time Vescinda, rehearsing herself into a semblance of patient civility, entered the room, Miss Wildborne had abandoned all pretense of good breeding. Waving the letter wildly as evidence, she accused hoarsely, "Vescinda, this says that Sherworth is leaving London on Thursday, the twelfth, and will break his journey in Salisbury in order to arrive late afternoon, Friday! *Today!*"

Vescinda's eyes rested coldly on the sheet Miss Wildborne held. "Very true, and how kind in my aunt to have shown you my letter."

"You know perfectly well that your aunt didn't show it to me. I—I couldn't help but see what it said. And it is well that I did," she added defiantly, repeating with strong reproach, "*today!*"

"Yes, yes, today. But what has thrown you into this frenzy? Is it because it is Friday, the thirteenth? Are you superstitious?"

"Oh! *Oh!*" Miss Wildborne sputtered. "I didn't even *know* it is the thirteenth!"

"Well, console yourself that you knew instantly that it is Friday," replied Vescinda, walking to the sofa and slipping her letter from Miss Wildborne's fingers in her way.

"Oh, *why* must you always be so stupid?" shrieked Miss

Wildborne. "The only thing to the point—as well you know—is that Sherworth is due to arrive at any moment, and you have deliberately kept it from me."

Vescinda sat down, brushing a wisp of hair that had escaped from the striped ribbon holding it loosely back from her face. "I should rather say that I hadn't made it an object to inform you. No doubt you will be shocked to learn that I have a great many visitors of whom you are not advised."

"But that is different! You know that it is."

"No, Liza, I do not. I quite understand that you have aspirations in that direction, but it is no business of mine to maneuver in your behalf."

"But it *is* your business to maneuver against me, is that it?"

"Indeed, it is not," replied Vescinda with a sudden laugh. "I shall leave Lord Sherworth to manage for himself in whatever way he wishes."

Miss Wildborne looked through narrowed eyes. "Is that a promise?"

Vescinda gasped on another laugh. "A promise? Well, I daresay you may take it as one. Believe me, Liza, if you can capture—what is it he is called? The Elusive Earl?—I am sure you will deserve him."

"Very well," said Miss Wildborne, insensibly mollified. "But— oh, this is most oversetting! I thought he was coming for the party, a se'enight hence! I am not prepared! How am I to manage?" She broke off, to demand, "Why do you smile in that odious way?"

"Because, if I ask what it is you must prepare, you will no doubt fly into a grand fuss. Surely you didn't plan to hold him up on the road."

"What I must prepare?" repeated Miss Wildborne, ignoring Vescinda's levity. "Why, I must prepare for dinner, of course!"

"Dinner?" It was Vescinda's turn to be alarmed. "Oh, but, Liza, no, no, you quite mistake the matter. I've only just learned myself of his intention to arrive today. Indeed, I've had no opportunity to plan a celebration of the event! And, besides, there will be enough of that once the party begins. You must know that we are all at sixes and sevens here; I assure you, we dine quite simply—merely *en famille*—tonight."

Miss Wildborne's eyes narrowed again. "Vescinda, are you saying that you don't *wish* me to join you for dinner tonight?"

"I'm sure I could never say anything so uncivil," returned Vescinda, not without a sense of regret. "What I am attempting to impress upon you is that I haven't planned a dinner *party,* and I cannot alter my arrangements at this late hour. Certainly, your mother will not permit you to be out alone after dark, nor would she like you to attend a dinner unchaperoned. And, pray *believe* me, there is not the least possibility that I could accommodate your entire family at this stage."

Miss Wildborne weighed this point for a moment, then said that she believed she might be able to persuade her mother to permit her to come alone.

Vescinda required only the barest reflection on the type of persuasion that would befall Lady Wildborne to see the wisdom of making immediate preparations to include Miss Wildborne at her board.

5

By the time Sherworth drew up before Lord Bancroft's imposing mansion, the hour was near to seven, and his notable temper was smoldering beneath an apprehensive frown. Even if the countess hadn't mentioned it, he was well aware that it was customary for country establishments to dine no later than six. He sat for a moment, almost dreading to go in. He was tired and hungry and in no mood for further aggravation. By the same token, he had no reason to suppose that more was not in store for him. He was convinced by now that every evil that could possibly attend a short journey had marshaled together to launch him befittingly into a thoroughly irritating project.

If he had not been given the worst nags available each time it had become necessary to change horses, then he could only shudder to imagine what must be cluttering up the highways of England. And, although his overnight stay with his stepmother's friends at Longford Castle had been far from boring, he had been regaled with far too much French brandy. Sherworth's athletic pursuits had taught him the unwisdom of overimbibing, and it was his usual practice not to exceed one bottle of wine in a day and to steer clear of strong spirits altogether. Consequently, the lively hospitality of his host's several sons had caused him to resume his journey short of sleep and suffering all the agony that might be expected to enfeeble one unaccustomed to excessive potations.

After covering no more than three miles, his offside horse had gone lame. He had scanned the route laid out in *Paterson's Roads* with searing eyeballs and discovered that there was no posting house ahead for a full seven miles. So the curricle had been turned in one expert sweep and the exasperating project of returning the indisposed animal to the White Hart in Salisbury begun. However, a hobbledegee pace was in no way compatible with Sherworth's short supply of patience. A bare five minutes saw the reins thrust into his groom's hands and Sherworth jumping off the moving vehicle, declaring his intention to wait out the time at the Fox and Goose, a small house he'd noticed about a mile distant. Wiley nodded and advised a bit of the hair, advice which Sherworth was determined to try, though the very thought caused the delicate state of his stomach to run riot.

Unfortunately, whatever comfort he had hoped to gain in the cool atmosphere of a quiet little inn was not to be found at the Fox and Goose. Added to the agony caused by the tapster's seeming inability to make his tiresome observations without dealing the bar a resounding slap was the more daunting circumstance of finding himself in the midst of a major project of restoration. The incessant hammering transformed the buzzing in his head into erratic spasms of pain, and the sickening fumes of paint soon drove him back out into the hot sun. As a result, Wiley returned over an hour later to find his master pacing angrily over the cobbles and looking more downpin than ever.

A last-ditch hope that he might at least arrive in time to effect a scrambling change of dress and sit down to dinner, as close to six as could cause no serious inconvenience, was endangered by the necessity to have a broken harness repaired a few miles out of Dorchester and finally dashed into the ground by the misinformation of a kindly farmer as to the correct lane leading out of Charmouth.

Now, as he climbed resolutely down from his curricle, his weary brain paraded a galaxy of grim visions of the hungry group awaiting him inside: Bancroft, ranting and raging for his dinner; Chloe and the granddaughter, in various degrees of the vapors. He could remember once being less than an hour late to a country house party and arriving to find half the ladies wielding vinaigrettes.

Vescinda heard his arrival from her bedchamber, which was situated at the front of the house. She gave her exquisite gown of white India muslin a final check in the mirror and permitted her abigail to fuss one last time over her curls, before starting down to greet her guest. As she approached the large double doors of the drawing room, she could hear her aunt exclaim, "Sherworth, what maggot has got into your brain? Nobody that I know of is in danger of starving! And I can think of no reason why you must needs be *thrown* into your clothes."

Vescinda winced and quickened her step. It required no effort to reconstruct the scene that had inspired those artless words. Poor Lord Sherworth could have no way of knowing that his stepsister had converted the household to the town fashion of dining at eight. She found it all too easy to enter into the feelings of one who had passed an hour believing himself to be setting an entire household on its ears, easier still to imagine the chagrin of having one's anxieties made to sound baselessly foolish. She hurried into the room, hoping to intervene before her aunt had succeeded in driving his lordship into a towering passion.

Had there still been such a hope, it would have been given the final deathblow, as Chloe leaned forward and called out, "Oh, girl. Come in. Sherworth is in an unaccountable rush to dress. I want to make him known to you before he dances off."

Vescinda's first view of Sherworth was of a broad back tapering into a trim waist. As her gaze traveled upward, it fell on a head of chestnut brown hair, cropped short and giving every appearance of having begun the day neatly arranged in a fashionable style. Her mind was automatically forming phrases of a soothing nature when the head turned sharply round, and, for the first time in her life, Vescinda's unerring social presence completely deserted her. For a moment, she could only stare, yet found it impossible to see anything but his eyes. They were so startlingly blue and so *wild*. At length, the rest of his face came into focus. It had none of the refined handsomeness of a gentleman of fashion; it was the sort of face one might imagine for a highwayman or a pirate—romantically handsome, and a little frightening, particularly when its owner was giving every indication that he meant to behave in perfect accord with his appearance.

The alarming rage, which had been present when he turned, had been banished by a brief look of astonishment, followed in less than a heartbeat by one of warmest approval, an approval that did nothing to dispel the climate of danger he seemed to have brought into the room. Those deep-blue eyes had lost their fiery passion, only to become disturbingly sensuous, as they met hers after a lingering appraisal of her entire person. Vescinda had not blushed or flinched under his improper examination. For a time she was held fast by an ancient instinct, alert but motionless, like a doe newly aware of a wild creature in the forest. Then, without knowing why, she smiled—not the gracious smile of a hostess greeting a guest, but a slow questioning smile, which brought that alluring quirk at the side of her mouth into being, unconsciously exciting Sherworth to deeper interest and even bolder scrutiny.

Suddenly, however, those wild, blue eyes filled with suspicion. The fury, laying just below the surface of his attraction, flared up again, and he hissed, *"You,* I take it are Miss Bancroft—another of Mama's little jokes!"

Perhaps it was the sudden release from tension; perhaps it was the complete absurdity of the situation; but, after a praiseworthy effort toward trying to decide whether to confirm or deny or qualify this accusation, Vescinda went off helplessly into a fit of laughing.

At another time Sherworth might have appreciated Vescinda's reaction, noticed what a rich, musical laugh she had, admired her good nature or her lively sense of humor, all qualities he particularly liked. But Sherworth was in no mood to be amused. It had come forcibly home to him that the intriguing female who had so thoroughly caught his eye was as unlikely to throw herself away on Freddy Bancroft as she was apt to hurl herself into the sea. He knew his world. And even allowing for the poor breeding that made her think nothing of bestowing her siren's smile so freely, or the total lack of manners which enabled her to laugh in one's face without a qualm, there could be no doubting that such a piece of perfection would fare very well in London's marriage mart. In fact, he thought bitterly, as he glared down at her, such a prime article would most assuredly have her sights set on nothing less than *an earl with thirty thousand a year!*

The annoyances of his journey were as nothing compared to the violence of feeling that welled up in him. He had been sold a bargain and brought into line like a perfect flat. Naturally he could not fail to see that the countess and Chloe were hand in glove in the shuffling game that had rooked him in. Yet the main force of his resentment settled directly on Vescinda (or, as he thought of her, on "Bancroft's hoyden of a daughter"). Why he chose to distribute the blame so unjustly remained uncertain even in his own mind. He only knew that it was due in part to the extreme amusement she was deriving from the situation. And, as she struggled to control her hilarity, he soothed himself with the promise that she would find herself laughing on the wrong side of her face before he was finished with her.

Chloe had been looking from one to the other, attempting to commit to memory every detail of this first meeting, which the countess had been at such pains to arrange, so that it might be described to her in a letter. Had it not been so deuced amusing, she might have regretted what was very plainly an inauspicious beginning.

When at last Vescinda managed to choke back her mirth, she gasped, "Oh, *do* forgive me! I—I *am* Miss Bancroft—" Valiantly overcoming the temptation to laugh again, she went on, "—and evidently I have proved as much of a surprise to you as you have to me."

Chloe found that Vescinda's gaze had drifted accusingly in her direction and decided that it would be well to absent herself. Heading out of the room, she said: "Oh, don't heed him. I think he must have had a touch of the sun. Asked after my vinaigrette first thing in the door."

Sherworth's look, which positively dared Vescinda to laugh again, might have made it impossible for her to refrain, had she not been cast into temporary confusion by the sight of her chaperone blithely shutting her up alone in the room with a strange—a *very* strange—young man. She returned her attention from the firmly-closed door to meet his eyes again and found him regarding her with mocking contempt. She felt the color already tinging her usually cool white cheeks heighten. His thoughts might as well have been spoken aloud. To be sure, he had every right to look askance upon her aunt's precipitant departure, but that was no reason for him to suppose that she—. Fighting off a strong temptation to lower her eyes, she tried for a recovery, saying as lightly as she could manage, "I daresay my aunt has bethought herself of something she must add to her lists. S-she has been quite caught up in her project."

"Yes, it's plain that you have *all* been quite caught up in your project—consisting mainly of coming Tip Street over me."

Vescinda stiffened. It was most improper in him to use a cant expression in her presence, just as improper as it would be for her to betray that she had the least conception of its meaning. In the end she decided to ignore it. He was plainly holding his temper with an effort, and it was no time to ruffle him further. Instead, she said, with her friendly smile, "Come now, pray don't be out of reason cross. Surely you can see how very amusing this is."

"Is it? I fancy it's a trifle more difficult to perceive the humor in a joke when one is its butt."

"Oh, no! No, truly—but I think perhaps the fun has been spoiled for you by a harassing day. You are so much later than you'd intended. Pray, won't you sit a while and tell me of it?"

"No, Miss Bancroft. I will not. I should like to forget my harassing day."

"Oh! Yes—yes, of course! No doubt that would be best," she agreed, turning hastily to conceal a dangerously trembling lip. "Then, may I order wine for you?" she asked, moving toward the bellpull.

"I should prefer to be shown to my chamber. And then, if a few scraps of cold meat could be conveyed to me there, I should be most grateful."

"I—well, *yes,* if that is what you would like," she said, turning gracefully to face him. "Have we put you so out of charity with us that you would rather do that than dine at table? I wish you will reconsider. If for no other reason than a hot meal would be more fortifying after your journey."

"*Dine* with you? It was my impression that you had gone ahead without me."

"Ah! Then it is not surprising that you should be so vexed. Indeed we have not." She smiled. "You must know that we dine at the very fashionable hour of eight."

Vescinda had spoken facetiously, but taking it for affectation, Sherworth sneered. "Miss Bancroft, I think it only fair to tell you that you'll catch cold at these efforts. Changing your customary dinner hour to one quite out of place in the country, far from impressing me with your air of fashion, merely serves to betray your ignorance."

Vescinda's eyes flew open, not in indignation, but curiosity. She was more interested in the reason for his attack than the injustice of it. "Why do you say this to me, my lord?"

"Because I thought you ought to know that I'm up to all the rigs, and that I'm not about to be caught by stupid devices."

"I have collected as much, but—"

"But you supposed that I needed only to catch sight of that tantalizing body, to gaze once or twice into those bewitching green eyes, and my resolution would melt clean away! Well, you were dead wrong! I'll tell you willingly enough that you're about as tempting a tidbit as I've ever clapped eyes on, but there's not a hope in hell that I'll marry you! There's no cause to take offense, however, for I'll make myself plainer, and tell you that I haven't the smallest intention of marrying anyone!"

No cause to take offense? thought Vescinda, speechless with fascination. What had he said or done that *wasn't* offensive? Even that portion of his speech that had been complimentary had been couched in language that might be expected to shock all but a courtesan! On the other hand, she allowed, with an inward chuckle, he very kindly removed all doubt that one was being fobbed off with commonplace flattery.

She was at a loss as to how to deal with the situation. He was a guest in her home, the beloved stepson of her grandmother, and he had come, or so she'd been told, to lend his assistance with her party. She didn't know if he were drunk or mad or merely unbelievably conceited, but to treat him with incivility or to spare any effort to make his stay as agreeable as possible was unthinkable. Yet, apart from violating every canon of propriety, he had insulted her in so many ways that she had lost count. To permit such conduct to go unchecked was to condone it, and that was equally unthinkable. Finding herself squarely on the horns of dilemma, she decided that a period of calm reflection was wanted before she committed herself to either action. Perhaps, she told herself, the same might prove beneficial to his lordship. Very possibly his experiences had been even more distressing than she had supposed. Once he had recovered the tone of his mind, he might recall his manners—if, indeed, he had any—and simplify the entire matter by offering her an apology.

She walked without a word to the bellpull. Having rung for her butler, she said calmly, "My father is not yet returned from the village, or he would certainly wish to escort you to your chamber himself. I shall have our butler take you in his place. Then, if you prefer, a tray will be brought to you there. I hope very much, however, that you will give us the pleasure of your company at dinner."

Sherworth shook his head wearily and seemed on the verge of

making a scathing comment, but Rigsby, who had kept himself near to hand, entered almost on the heels of Vescinda's words, effectively forestalling further conversation.

When Chloe returned to the drawing room in half an hour, Vescinda was still trying to decide just how to deal with her strange guest, and wondering if he simply assumed that every female wished to marry him, or if he had been given cause to suspect her specifically.

At sight of her aunt, she abandoned these thoughts and exclaimed, "Good heavens! Such a fiasco! I will allow, dear Aunt, that one may remain unconscious, to some extent, of a younger brother, but surely you will have noticed that *yours*—to put it no higher—is something of an original! *Why* could you not have put me a little on my guard?"

"You may pluck that crow with your grandmother. She wanted you two to meet for the first time without—er—prejudgment."

"Did she? Well, that little plan went quite awry because I doubt she could have wanted me to behave like an unpracticed ninnyhammer, with no more notion of how to go on than a goose!"

"Don't let it trouble you. No one knows how to go on with Sherworth at first. The Lord knows," Chloe chuckled delightedly, "he made rather sad work of it himself. What do you think of him?"

"What do I think of him? What *could* I think of him? But—but that he is like a wild, undisciplined—*stallion!*"

"Never heard him described in just that way before, but there's no denying it's apt."

The discussion had to be dropped then because its subject reentered the room, presenting quite another picture of himself. He was exquisitely attired in black coat and satin knee-breeches, his snowy neckcloth folded carefully into the difficult style known as the mathematical and his Brutus crop painstakingly arranged. He lacked only the chapeau bras to be welcomed into an Almack's assembly. And, although his countenance made it plain that he had no intention of permitting himself to be coaxed into contentment, his temper had abated, and most of the wildness had died out of his deep-blue eyes.

Vescinda invited him to be seated and excused herself, explaining that she wished to check whether her father had returned to the house. "If he has not, I must send someone to—to remind him that we have guests for dinner."

When she had gone, Sherworth turned to Chloe. "Did she say *guests?* Who, beside me, has been snared to the Bancroft board?"

"I daresay she means the Wildborne chit."

Sherworth straightened in his chair. "Do you tell me that she actually invited the Wildborne?"

"No one invites her—prosing little bagpipe. She thrusts her way in," declared Chloe, uncomfortably aware of his sudden interest.

He leaned back. "Ah, for a moment there, you had me teetering on the fear that I might have been guilty of a gross injustice. No female on the catch would *invite* the competition of Miss Wildborne's beauty!" He waved away Chloe's bristling protestation. "You may forget the mummery. Do you take me for a flat? If that diamond is in love with Freddy Bancroft, I'm the tzar of Russia. The moment I realized who she was, I knew I was in the midst of a matchmaker's plot."

Chloe, finding herself on perilous ground, was spared having to reply because the door swung open. Vescinda poised there for a moment, her hand on the knob as she made a laughing comment to one of the servants. She rejoined them then, but no sooner had she seated herself than the door opened again, this time to admit Miss Wildborne, resplendent in gold gauzes, jewelry, and coiffure. Ignoring her hostess, who had risen to greet her, she sailed a direct course to Sherworth, who had not yet resumed his seat.

"Lord Sherworth!" she exclaimed. "I was so very delighted to learn that you would be making one of our number."

Vescinda sat down again, not daring to meet her aunt's eyes, and began a careful examination of a small sapphire ring she was wearing. She was able to make thorough work of this, for a lively monologue ensued, as Miss Wildborne held sway until her host limped in.

Lord Bancroft, who had just had two brimming glasses of porter forced upon him by his valet, in an effort to offset the effects of an afternoon spent drinking too many tots of brandy, bowed creditably to Miss Wildborne, nodded affably to Sherworth, and said, "Well, well, you two look as if you'd come from the opera." Casually attired himself, in pantaloons and hessian boots, he informed Sherworth, in an aside audible to the entire company, that for his part he didn't care to stand on ceremony.

Vescinda afforded Chloe's comical reaction to this a slight smile and was surprised to find Sherworth bearing down on her, with a look of burning reproach in his eyes. He took a place beside her on the sofa and asked in a harsh undertone, "Do you mean me to understand that this was a slippery form of retaliation?"

She regarded him in astonishment. "I'm afraid you credit me with too lively an imagination. You will have to tell me what you mean."

"Perhaps you will tell *me* why you didn't trouble to mention that it was unnecessary for me to truss up like a turkey for dinner."

Vescinda studied him for a moment, then said apologetically, "You are thinking, of course, that I ought to have seen right away how like Papa you are."

She rose, happy in the knowledge that even Lord Sherworth's atrocious manners knew some bounds. If one overlooked the fact that he had become a trifle white about the mouth, it was really quite impossible to guess just how insulting he had found this comparison to her father. Evidently deciding that he should be rewarded for his forbearance, she added kindly, as she moved off to join the others, "You look very elegant, my lord—not a bit like a turkey."

Sherworth had risen too, but he stayed behind, thinking grimly that the trap had indeed been well laid. The little granddaughter was not only a beauty, but clever as well. Moreover, he found it difficult not to admire how really well she contrived to ape the conduct of a well-bred young lady when she put her mind to it, and he was obliged to confess that, if he hadn't just happened to catch her off her guard, she might well have fooled him completely. Yes, he thought, very clever! But, unless he knew nothing of females, he'd back himself to have Lord Bancroft's daughter showing her true colors again before the night was out. He had the grace to remind himself that his efforts really ought to be confined to convincing her of the futility of her ambitions, but he was not accustomed to having young ladies roll him up so neatly with their set-downs. Besides, if he must pass a fortnight in her company, he was damned if he was going to spend it in the totally boring occupation of watching her play off the airs and manners of a fine lady.

When the dinner bell sounded and Sherworth very properly offered his arm to Vescinda and led her down to dinner, she began to hope that a truce might now be called between them. But, once installed in the dining hall, she saw that it was his fixed intention to make it the most uncomfortable meal of her life.

She had not meant it when she had likened Lord Sherworth to her father, but, by the time she was able to give the signal for the ladies to withdraw, she had begun to consider it in earnest. Lord Bancroft, after tenderly lowering himself onto the cushion which Rigsby placed in his chair, had entered into an unrelieved round of bickering with Chloe, and Lord Sherworth, with an equal disregard for table etiquette and the partner on his left, had been assiduous in his attentions to Miss Wildborne. It had naturally been embarrassing, for the servants could scarcely have failed to notice that she had passed the entire meal in silence. Vescinda felt she might have borne with that, had it not been for the blatant looks of triumph which Miss Wildborne had cast her way at every opportunity. Apart from their insulting implication, they made it appear that she had set herself up in competition for his lordship's hand. That it should be believed that she had done so at all was quite bad enough, but that it should be thought that she was making such poor work of it was particularly rankling.

She knew it was very bad to have laughed in his face when he was so upset, but his punishment surely seemed excessive. However, no one observing the cool poise with which Vescinda created the illusion of a contented young lady dining in the most ordinary of circumstances could have guessed how extremely difficult that punishment had been.

Once in the drawing room, Vescinda and Chloe exchanged weary glances, as Miss Wildborne paced and fidgeted in undisguised impatience for the gentlemen's return. Apparently their port held more allure than the feminine company awaiting them, for they did not appear until a short time before the arrival of the tea tray.

Lord Bancroft, following Sherworth into the room, was heard to grumble something about rubbishing parties, and Miss Wildborne, poised like a hungry yellow cat, pounced on his words. "Oh, how can you say so? Without parties, what should any of us find to do?"

Vescinda glanced up and caught Sherworth studying her covertly. She could see that he was a little curious and far from satisfied with the results of his deliberate rudeness. She decided, with brittle generosity, that anyone who had passed over an hour positively hanging on Liza Wildborne's insipid conversation was in need of some compassion and schooled the look she gave him accordingly. She then settled herself in a posture of polite attention, as Miss Wildborne went on to elaborate in an affected manner that her greatest regret was in having been *torn* from London before the end of June, thereby missing Lady Heathcote's waltzing party.

Chloe considered it a deal more than unlikely that an unmarried chit, in her first Season, had been invited to *any* party got up primarily for waltzing, but the thought was lost in her eagerness to comment on Lady Heathcote's latest peccadillo. "That one!" she exclaimed, thrusting herself into the brief pause Miss Wildborne had allowed only for emphasis. "She'd have landed herself in a pretty scrape a few months back if Sam Rogers hadn't sent an urgent message to the Duchess of St. Albans, saying to come instantly if she valued her sister, because she was alone in his house with four gentlemen—and in great danger of getting up to mischief with one of them—! We suspect Byron. Can't be sure. The affair was hushed up."

"Imperfectly, if you know so much," said Sherworth drily.

Vescinda afforded his comment a perfunctory smile and turned back to the discussion getting under way, between Chloe and Miss Wildborne, as to whether Lady Caroline Lamb had in fact made an attempt on her life with a jagged glass, as reported by the press, or, according to Miss Wildborne's information, she had used first a dessert knife and then a pair of scissors.

The argument had been raging for some time, Chloe contending throughout that the entire story was a pack of lies, when Miss Wildborne turned sharply to Sherworth and demanded, "What is your opinion, my lord?"

He was by this time bored to distraction and convinced that Vescinda could not be baited by jealousy. So he gave in to his irritation with Miss Wildborne for her affectations and grating voice, by saying dampeningly that the circumstance of any female having systematically stabbed herself with three separate weapons in the midst of a supper party was too staggering for his poor powers.

He met Vescinda's appraising glance with a shrug and made a face indicating that she might take the trick. It was the first overture, however slight, toward peace. She took it as evidence that he possessed a sense of good sportsmanship and felt there was a compliment in his change of tactics as well. So she acknowledged his gesture with a look of good-natured reproach.

Rigsby came in and set the tea tray before her, and Vescinda began to pour. Sherworth took the first two cups she passed to him and distributed them to the ladies, but, when she handed over the third cup, she said, with her engaging twinkle, "Unless you are tired, too, my lord, this one is for you. I don't think my father cares for tea just now."

Sherworth glanced over his shoulder and saw that Lord Bancroft was peacefully asleep in his chair, his legs outstretched before him, his hands folded neatly on his stomach.

He kept the cup and settled back with a smile, however reluctant, warming his rugged features.

And a sense of humor, too, thought Vescinda, stirring cream into her cup.

6

Miss Wildborne might have continued talking until the early hours of the morning, but social dictates demanded that she take her leave shortly after the removal of the tea tray. When she had gone, Chloe commended her niece, "Lord, you deserve a prize for thinking to have tea brought up two hours early."

Sherworth's head snapped round, and a slow, knowing smile formed, as his eyes fell on Vescinda. She was furious with herself, as she felt an unaccustomed heat rise to her face again. For, as quickly as she had realized he would now be convinced that she had responded to his goading after all, did she see the futility of attempting to explain that the tea arrangements had been made early in the day.

Fortunately, a sudden snorting sound diverted everyone's attention. Chloe leaned forward and spied Lord Bancroft. "Gad, will you look at him! Well, I don't say we mightn't have all been better entertained to have napped through the evening." This lenient view of the matter was in no way communicated to his lordship, as she barked, "Bancroft, wake up!"

When he bolted upright, he was treated to a lecture on the inevitable results of drinking oneself into a stupor hours before the dinner wine had even been poured. His eyes were red and glazed with sleep, but he rattled in as game as a pebble, countering with a pithy criticism of the chuckleheaded notion of keeping a man from his dinner until the middle of the night, just to suit a hoity-toity notion of fashion.

Sherworth looked up sharply. "Your innovation, Chloe?"

60

"I thought we ought be getting in the way of it before your high stickler of a sister arrives," she replied defensively. "You won't tell me *she's* used to dine at six!"

The color deepened beneath his tan, as Sherworth threw a look of apology in Vescinda's direction, but she had once again become interested in her ring and seemed unaware that anything untoward had occurred.

Taking advantage of the silence, Chloe recommended Lord Bancroft to seek his bed, so that the rest of them would be able to hear their own conversation. He rose, snatching up the pillow he carried from chair to chair, and retorted hotly that, so long as *he* didn't have to hear it, he would be as well pleased to seek a dungeon.

When he had gone, Chloe, hoping to ease the constraint between her niece and Sherworth, began to talk of inconsequential matters, eventually leading to a description of her experiences abroad, which she drew to a close by saying, "And then we were transferred for a year or two to Naples."

"Where, no doubt," Sherworth smiled, "you kept yourself busy, exchanging gossip with Lady Hamilton."

This comment had a startling effect on Chloe, who had been drowsily winding down as a prelude to taking herself off to bed. "*Oh,*" she all but shouted, "that poor, poor, ill-used woman! How—only tell me *how*—our country can make this sham of honoring Nelson, when they turn a deaf ear to his dying request that they look after his poor Emma? He didn't say, 'See to my brother!' Yet they make *him* an earl!—giving him a few thousand a year into the bargain! But *there,*" Chloe gestured wildly in what she supposed to be the direction of Southwark, "there is Nelson's dearest love languishing in a sponging house—or whatever hateful thing they call that extension of the debtor's prison!"

"My dear Chloe," said Sherworth, on the verge of laughing, "you can scarcely expect the government to honor a man's mistress in place of his wife. Particularly when she had achieved the position by making a cuckold of her husband under his own roof and setting up a ménage à trois to entertain the gossips of two continents."

"No such thing!" protested Chloe. "It was Sir William who encouraged Nelson to live with them."

"And did he encourage his wife to make a fool of him by leaping into Nelson's bed? I think not! If Sir William had been as complacent as you would have me believe, why, pray, did he leave the bulk of his fortune away from her?"

"I might have expected *you* to view things in that light," Chloe returned hotly.

"So you might," agreed Sherworth, who had been watching Vescinda out of the corner of his eye. "But, no doubt, I am outweighed in this circle. Miss Bancroft, do you, too, consider her a blameless heroine?"

Vescinda, though maintaining an outward calm, had been becoming more and more distressed. The subject was one that ought not even to have been mentioned in her presence. It was beyond thinking that she should be expected to discuss it with a gentleman! For some moments, she had been aware of Sherworth's sidelong glances. She had hoped he was awaiting an opportunity to give the conversation a more proper direction. But evidently there was to be no gallant rescue from that quarter. On the contrary, it seemed he had been delighting in her discomfort and now planned to go his length.

She addressed her aunt, in a carefully modulated voice. "I think, Aunt Chloe, that, before the time slips away from us, we ought consider whether we wish wine or some other refreshment brought up. I have instructed the servants to retire early, since most of them have been on the run since early this morning."

This prosaic message recalled Chloe to a sense of the impropriety she had been encouraging. She said, flushing, "Oh, ah, no, no. I don't care for anything. But I've been thinking, why don't you entertain Sherworth with a few hands of piquet?"

Though it was a trifle odd for her aunt to suggest a two-handed game, it was certainly more decorous than a lively discussion on adulterous relationships, so Vescinda, once again forced to hide her surprise, said pleasantly, "Why, yes, if he would like it."

Sherworth bowed an acceptance that was singularly lacking in enthusiasm, and Vescinda rose to fetch a pack of playing cards, a pad and a pencil. She carried them to a table where Sherworth was already waiting to seat himself. Taking a place opposite, she passed him the cards, asking, "Shall I keep the tally or should you prefer to do it?"

Sherworth made a gesture denoting indifference.

No sooner had he sat down and picked up the cards than Chloe stepped over to the table, saying, "Well, now that you two are settled comfortably, I'll say goodnight. I've been on the run myself since early this morning."

Sherworth watched her go with a time-weary expression, then, giving a disgusted shake of his head, began to deal.

Ignoring the cards tossed carelessly before her, Vescinda stared across at him, trying to decide how best to cope with the awkwardness of her situation. She supposed it was possible—not that *he* would believe it—that her aunt was simply unfamiliar with the responsibilities of a chaperone. She was forced to own, however, that it did *look* as though she were deliberately trying to throw them together. On more than one occasion, Vescinda had suspected that Chloe might have decided to try her hand at a little matchmaking. She would have thought it a matter to be laughed off, if only the disagreeable creature opposite weren't determined to believe it was being done at *her* instigation! But regardless of what he believed, to remain alone with him after the rest of the household had retired was out of the question.

She was about to excuse herself, when Sherworth said defiantly, "Miss Bancroft, you haven't yet given me your views on Lady Hamilton and her career."

She met his eyes coldly. "My lord, you *must* realize that that isn't a fit subject for me to discuss."

"Oh, confound it!" he snapped. "Miss Bancroft, this situation is going to be intolerable if we don't reach an understanding."

"Indeed, sir, I was thinking so myself."

"Yet my words have rolled off you like water from the back of a duck! Or why else would you persist in playing off missish airs, which we *both* know are impossibly ridiculous? If you think it's pleasing to me, you couldn't be more wrong! I was called away from a pleasurable engagement in Brighton to have my ears filled with a Banbury tale as to why I must rush down here and rescue you from your own folly. I was obliged to beg and connive, in order to accumulate the required number of men for this stupid party and then to face the hideous prospect of being buried down here for a fortnight—during which, not the least unpleasant of my duties would be to see that your father has some notion of how to go on in polite company and that *you* are brought sufficiently up to snuff not to ruin yourself! Through it all, my only consolation has been that, at least, while in the company of Lord Bancroft's daughter, I needn't be suffocated with restrictions and proprieties! I say this so that you will understand why I am not precisely killed with delight over these efforts of yours. And, while we're about it, my girl, I'll take leave to tell you that you're trying it on too rare and too thick. Good God, I'm enough acquainted with your father and your cousin to know that nothing *I* am likely to do or say could hope to shock you."

Could he but know it, no one had ever succeeded in shocking Vescinda so much. At first she could only stare as she fitted together the bits and pieces of what he had said. Then several emotions collided, one with the other. Insensibly, one thought predominated—his "only consolation"? Unable to refrain, she asked with equal parts of incredulity and fascination, "Can you possibly be saying that you would feel yourself compensated for all that inconvenience if I dispensed with—with my efforts to conduct myself proprietously?"

"Yes, somewhat. Of course it stirs the blood a trifle to realize that I was *put* to all that inconvenience only to set myself up to be hunted like a stag in the forest. But, in some respects, that makes it all the more important. I mean, since it's plain that I am going to be closeted up alone with you at every opportunity, it would be a great relief if I could at least enjoy a few of the benefits of your unconventional upbringing—" He broke off on an involuntary laugh as he caught her expression. "No, no, Miss Bancroft, I don't mean that I wish to *ravish* you. On the contrary, I'm not such a greenhorn as to get myself caught in parson's mousetrap by such folly as that. No, you may rest assured that I shall do nothing that might oblige me to marry you. But, if you'll put such plans from your mind and give over your sham prudery, I will try to make the best of the situation."

Vescinda sat in contemplative silence. His first speech had caused her considerable distress. She had, of course, realized that the type of gentlemen likely to respond to an invitation from her father would not be considered suitable, but she had supposed that her grandmother was gathering together a congenial group who enjoyed one another's company sufficiently that it would be no less satisfactory to be convened at Blakely than anywhere else. Learning that the guests she would shortly be receiving had been tricked and coerced into coming had filled her with mortification. No less had she been affected by Sherworth's reference to the "hideous prospect" of spending a fortnight in her home. But then she had become too intrigued by his notion of consolation to think of anything else. And during his last words, her lively sense of the ridiculous had become fully engaged. She wondered if *everyone* were coming down with the expectation of finding a hurly-burly female without conduct or shame. She was tickled further by recalling that, no, they were to be spared that fate by Lord Sherworth's efforts to bring her "up to snuff"! How vastly amusing. And no wonder he had been shocked at their first meeting. Undoubtedly he had expected to find her bedecked and bedizened and looking like a Covent Garden harlot. Yes, and his immediate reference to "Mama's little joke" had given an excellent clue as to how he had come by such a notion. She was delighted. Of course, it clearly behooved her to disabuse him of his misapprehension and explain that, far from having been reared in her father's wild and abandoned image, she had been schooled and guarded by an elegant and loving grand-mother, a dear but fastidious governess, and a staunchly matter-of-fact aunt. But, together with a full measure of the countess's elegance, Vescinda had inherited the Bancroft love of kicking up a lark. She was beginning to think it would be great fun to enact the role of a sad romp for a few days. Besides, her poor guest had been lured away from a pleasurable engagement in Brighton (easy to imagine what *that* had been), and it seemed sorely unkind to deprive him of his "only consolation"!

The slightest of smiles formed at the corner of her mouth, as her finger toyed with the hand of cards he had dealt her. Then she looked up and said briskly: "Good enough, my lord. Ah, but you must tell me, since it is settled that I am not to be ravished, how *should* you like to benefit from my unconventional upbringing?"

Sherworth, not immune to the humor of the situation, replied, his own lip quivering, "Oh, merely to relax the social code governing *ladies* and *gentlemen,* which limits one to uncomfortable postures, banal discussions and a thousand other bothersome restrictions. As an example—earlier, in the heat of the moment, I said something—I forget what precisely—a slang expression, a mild profanity—and right off, you were ready to poker up as though your shelllike ear had never before been exposed to such language. Now, I'll wager that there is little of either that you haven't heard all your life. Is that not true?"

"That is true."

"And I'd be more than astonished to learn that you've reached your present age, in *this* household, innocent of the knowledge that men keep mistresses, females take lovers, and bastards are sometimes born. Am I correct in assuming that such facts are known to you, Miss Bancroft?"

"Perfectly."

"Therefore, simply because Lady Hamilton's career has encompassed these things, I find it a dead bore that rational conversation must draw to a halt because 'it is not a fit subject for you to discuss'! You're not a child, and, if you're aware of the circumstances, you are quite as capable of discussing it as Chloe or myself. Are you not?"

"Quite."

"Very well," he said, making immediate use of his freedom to lounge in the presence of a lady, by turning his chair sideways, laying his arm along the table, and stretching his long legs out before him. "Then do so."

"I will," she said. Actually she had been positively burning with the wish to make one or two comments of her own. "But first, let me understand. Am I to share the privilege of dispensing with civility, as well?"

"Yes, yes, speak your mind, by all means," he said with an appreciative gleam.

"Then, if we are to speak of *prudery,* sir, I must wonder at yours in judging poor Lady Hamilton as I have heard you do tonight. And, more so, at the *unforgivable* degree of narrow-mindedness that enables you to condemn her to her fate! It's all very well to censure her faults and follies, but what of her good qualities and her worth? She has a warm and generous heart and has, time and again, extended herself to ease the suffering and want of people who could in no way serve her interests. Not to mention many poor beasts, which could in no way add to her consequence. But perhaps you, too, are of the opinion that her interest in the well-being of her servants—her sympathy for a hunted boar—her kindness to a stray cat or dog—are merely eccentricities carrying over from her low birth?"

She paused, but as he showed no inclination to reply, she went on. "And I should think, since you have been good enough to make allowances for *my* unconventional upbringing, that, before casting stones at Lady Hamilton's morals, you would spare a thought for what it must be like to be the uneducated, orphaned daughter of a blacksmith—endowed with the dubious blessing of bearing one of the most beautiful faces in England! Oh, it's easy enough to say that she ought to have preserved her virtue by taking a post as a scullery servant. But, if you're honest, sir, you'll own that upon finding just such a 'tempting tidbit' employed in your kitchens, you—or one of your noble peers—would have lost no time in robbing her of that virtue, and—and expected her to scrub up in her spare time! How many women, I wonder, *knowing* they would lose their virtue in any event, wouldn't elect to become a man's mistress rather than his maid? Not that in her case, poor thing, it proved to be an *enviable* position. Why, even women with far less to recommend them enjoy the privilege of *choosing* their protectors. But it's my understanding that Lady Hamilton was deceived into thinking that her visit to Sir William in Naples was in the nature of a holiday! Quite a predicament, wouldn't you say? To find oneself in a foreign land—without friend or fare—and to learn that one's former protector had never the least intention of fetching one back? What in heaven's name *was* she to do, but become the mistress of his uncle? A man many, many times older than herself! Why, your poor cuckolded Sir William got her with a shabby trick! And it wasn't with the *intention* of marrying her! No, *that* he condescended to do much later—and—and then only to further his own career! I—"

"Good God," Sherworth interrupted, his eyes bright with amusement. "I said to speak freely, not indefinitely! Is it too much to expect that *I* be given an opportunity to utter a comment now and then? I've been waiting for some time to mention that never, in all my life, have I raped one of my scullery maids—nor, for that matter, any other servant in my employ."

Vescinda responded with a brief smile, but she was too much stimulated by this unprecedented chance of speaking her mind to a gentleman to let the opportunity slip by. She lifted her hand disparagingly. "When a lower servant and the master of the house are involved, the distinction between rape and seduction becomes mere quibbling."

"Then I shall put the debate upon firmer ground and inform you that neither have I ever seduced one! And, while we're about it, my girl, if I had, I shouldn't have expected her to 'scrub up in her spare time'!"

This time she couldn't help laughing. "No? Well, if ever I come across a girl in a similar predicament, I shall certainly recommend her to your establishment." With the mood lightened between them, she added with her friendly smile, "However, since *you* were just an infant in arms at the time, I think you'll agree that in all probability Lady Hamilton's virtue was doomed from the outset."

"Oh, yes, but then, I'm no staunch supporter of virtue in that respect anyway, *nor* have I criticized her conduct up that juncture. My point is that Sir William did marry her—for whatever reason! Surely you can't blame a man for fighting shy of a marriage that must forever be an embarrassment to himself and his position— Do you know the notorious Emma?"

The smile still lingering on her lips, Vescinda shook her head, and, lacing her fingers together, made a support for her chin as she settled herself to hear him out.

"Oh, very beautiful, of course—and very winning. Her mind is quick. She has made a great success of educating herself, but there are things that can't be got from a primer. Her manners are by far too familiar. At a party she'll converse with the staunchest matron or the fustiest gentleman without a care that she hasn't been introduced to them. Her laugh will turn every head in a crowded ballroom, and whatever she is feeling at the moment is an open book. She has a temper she can't always control, and she displays her affections lavishly, regardless of where she happens to be. I mean any affection—for a child, an animal, a man, a woman. What is more," he laughed, "she treats everyone alike—a servant, a field hand—*royalty!* You can imagine for yourself just how unsuited she is to the uppercrust of English society."

"Yes, but you sound as though you like her."

"I do. At an informal gathering, I find her charming. And, at a formal affair, I think her amusing, but, at such times, I'm cow-hearted enough to be devilishly glad that *I* don't have a wife like her. It isn't that I care all that much for formal affairs—most are crashing bores—but my position requires me to attend a great many, and it would be more than I could bear to watch my wife receiving the cut-direct at every turning."

Vescinda murmured sympathetically, "Yes, that would be hard." But then she frowned. "Naturally I can understand why she wouldn't be received just anywhere, but that is not to say she should be in a *sponging house!*"

"Miss Bancroft, she is in a sponging house because she's very expensive and doesn't pay her debts. I think it's a coach builder has her clapped up this time. Do you expect him to provide elegant coaches to women, however charming, at his own expense?"

"No, of course I do not. But it's wrong that she should suddenly find herself forced to live without the means she has become accustomed to—particularly when Admiral Nelson begged with his dying breath that she should not! He virtually saved England from a French invasion!"

"Yes, yes, but it has never been a question of the *worth* of honoring his wishes. Unfortunately, the government found itself in the devil's own hobble over the matter. The opposition was naturally crying out against an official recognition of an improper relationship, a circumstance made all the more awkward by Nelson's wife being alive and blameless. Still, the fact remains that Emma mightn't be in her situation—her husband might well have provided more handsomely for her—had she not proved such an extravagant and faithless wife. You can't be expected to view it from Sir William's position," he said generously, "but I can. And, when a man gives his name to a woman, he has a right to expect that she won't make a byword of it—or a fool of him!"

"Fudge."

Sherworth almost jumped. "Well, I'll be damned!"

"Yes, very likely, if you persist in such uncharitable notions. It's positively outrageous the way you are heaping the full responsibility for that shocking affair on the shoulders of one young and ill-prepared girl! Have you no criticism for either of those two older and worldlier men? Good heavens, do you imagine that she *leaped* into Admiral Nelson's bed against his advice and wishes? I'll wager she was subjected to a determined pursuit, that she was invited—wooed and won and *invited*—into that bed! And, you are perfectly right, I cannot view it from Sir William's position, because if he was *not* complacent, then he was already a fool! He knew well how he had won his wife, and he must have known that her attraction to him would have understandable limits! Why did he encourage, and go on encouraging, Admiral Nelson to live with them? And why did he then take his young wife to live in Admiral Nelson's home? Someone ought to remind you, sir, that it takes *three* to make a ménage à trois—*and* that Lady Hamilton was the *only* one among them without power in the arrangement! *She* couldn't turn guests out of her husband's house. *And* she couldn't refuse to share the roof he chose! Sir William might have put an end to it. Admiral Nelson might have kept away. Why is Lady Hamilton the only one to be censured over that *abominable* situation? It is— It is—"

"The very devil?" offered Sherworth.

Vescinda accepted without thought. "*Yes!* The *very* devil!"

Sherworth threw back his head and laughed. "There, now," he asked, "isn't it much more comfortable just to be yourself?"

Vescinda stared at him blankly for a minute, then gasping under her breath, "Oh, dear God," she went off into a peal of laughter. At last she raised eyes, glistening with tears of mirth, and said, "Oh, indeed, yes, my dear sir, you can have no idea how truly good it *is*." She held his studying gaze for a moment. "Ah, but now that I have thrown off all disguise, and it is agreed that we shan't trouble ourselves with civility, I needn't scruple to tell you that I haven't the smallest wish to play piquet." She rose, adding, "I breakfast at ten, Aunt Chloe, much earlier, and Papa, much later. You may choose whichever hour suits you best. Goodnight, my lord. It has been most enjoyable."

In one graceful motion, she turned, catching up the demitrain of her gown, and swept from the room. Sherworth frowned after her. He wasn't used to being dismissed in quite that style. It was particularly annoying because he had planned to reopen another and more important discussion. He found it a trifle disturbing that, despite several opportunities and much provocation, she had neither refuted nor renounced her hope that marriage would be the outcome of his visit. He was, after all, only flesh and blood, and he would be locked away in the wilderness with those green eyes for a fortnight. Unless *that* matter was accepted and understood, he'd have to tread warily—and that would be a great pity, for he wasn't at all averse to indulging in a round of dalliance with such an enchanting creature.

7

EARLY DAY CONDITIONS at Blakely weren't calculated to mellow a
bad morning disposition. The low ridge of hills, sheltering Lord
Bancroft's home from the East wind, cost the occupants the cheery
warmth of an early sun. This, combined with a prevailing dampness
created by the not distant sea, caused the rooms of the ancient
mansion to begin even a fine August day shrouded in a penetrating
chill.

Sherworth, shown into the empty breakfast room, stalked over to
plant himself before the small fire which was laid routinely
throughout the year. Vescinda entered fifteen minutes later,
looking bright and cheerful in a jonquil morning dress. She bid him
a good day. He relaxed his position and placed an elbow on the
mantel with the air of one prepared to meet intrusion with
forbearance.

Vescinda's eyes danced as she came across the room. "Early
morning crotchets, my lord? Have no fear. I am accustomed. Papa,
you know, often suffers the same complaint."

Slipping into her place at the table, she said, "Actually, since
you are unlikely to interrupt, it is a famous opportunity to have a
word with you. I have been thinking over all you said last night and
have come to the conclusion that you have been grossly ill-used. It's
my opinion that you should return instantly to your pleasurable
engagement in Brighton. Now, I know what you will say, and, of
course, there's no denying, that *will* deprive us of your guidance
during the party, and I can see that it wouldn't do for you to simply

leave us to make a shabby mull of things on our own. But, you must consider, it is, after all, perfectly possible for us to engage someone—ah, perhaps a dancing master—to serve in your place."

Turning to rest his shoulders against the mantel, Sherworth asked, "Now, how long, I wonder, have you been planning this little revenge?" His tone had had a slight edge, but as a gurgle of laughter rose from the table, a reluctant smile tugged at his lips. "Oh, well, I daresay I was a trifle harsh."

"Nonsense! This is no time to be overcome with modesty. You were unflinchingly abominable!"

That made him laugh. "As you will. At least I'll apologize for laying the folly of the dining hour at your door."

"Ah, yes—well, no matter. Papa too has the habit of ripping up at me for things I could not possibly have caused."

"And *you* have the habit of comparing me with every unfavorable quality your father possesses," he returned sharply.

The green eyes began to dance again, but Vescinda afforded this observation no reply, asking instead if she was to take it that he meant to see his ordeal through. He nodded with an air of exaggerated resignation. She twinkled appreciatively and went on. "Well, then, we must do what we can to make you as comfortable as may be. To begin with, you must by all means wear your boots to dinner, and, further, you have my solemn promise that I shan't be missish or subject you to tiresome restrictions until the party begins. At that time, I shall try if I can overcome my background and be a credit to you."

"That's all very well," said Sherworth, "but there is something else I should like you to promise."

"Oh? Yes, of course. You want my word that I shan't fall in love with you," she replied, her countenance clouding over with worry. "Dear me, I don't know if I dare risk a *promise*. How will it be if I just agree not to force unwelcomed attentions upon you?"

Sherworth was left with a hot retort hovering on his lips because, just then, Rigsby came in, bearing a large coffee pot, which he placed before his mistress, advising her as he withdrew that breakfast would be along shortly.

Vescinda filled a cup and smiled up at Sherworth. "Come now, don't look so grim. I was only funning you a little. Can I not tempt you with this excellent coffee to join me at table?"

Sherworth walked over to take a chair opposite her. "Yes, you've been having a deal of fun, making me out a complete coxcomb."

Vescinda passed him the cup. "Indeed, I have, but you mustn't think it was at all difficult."

Sherworth's eyes flew open. Then he gave a shout of laughter. "By God, you're as bad as Mama!" he exclaimed, taking the cup and saucer from her and setting it before him. "Now, my girl, you will stop roasting me long enough to listen to what *I* have to say. Contrary to your belief, I am perfectly aware that few, if any, among the dozens of females who set their caps at me, hold me in the slightest affection. I wish to be assured that you—"

"Yes, yes," Vescinda interrupted. "You wish to be assured that I quite understand that you are not hanging out for a wife; that, if you were, you would not choose Lord Bancroft's daughter, who, like Lady Hamilton, could be depended upon to put you to the blush at these formal affairs you must attend; and that, although you are perfectly willing to amuse yourself while you are stuck here, I must on no account construe anything you may say or do as a sign that you have relented toward me—or that you have weakened in your resolve to remain a bachelor. I *do* assure you! I do not, however, quite understand your skittishness where I am concerned. Last night you told me that you had been sent here to rescue me from my own folly. If you have been apprised of my plans, you should realize that I am not at *liberty* to hunt you 'like a stag in the forest.' Or is it that you are afraid to effect this rescue until you can be assured that I won't instantly throw myself at your head? You may be easy on that score, as well. I am quite determined in my course. I don't *wish* you to rescue me!"

"Now, just a damned minute! Are you telling me that that parcel of slum I read in your letter is *true?*"

"I didn't know you *had* read a letter of mine. If it was the one explaining to Grandmama why I couldn't go to her in London, then, yes, of course, it is true. And, if *you* will put all plans to alter my decision from your mind, and give over your morbid fear that I am on the catch for you, I will do all in my power to make it up to you that you have been sent here on a sleeveless errand."

"But— Well, it's damned difficult to— Why, in the name of— *Why?*"

"Why would I throw myself away like that? Mainly because I

don't view it in that light. I owe far more than that to my Aunt Eudora."

"Your—? *Who?*"

Vescinda halted her cup halfway to her lips to look over at him. "You cannot have been attending when you were given this assignment. My Aunt Eudora—Freddy's mother. She had the care of me after my own mother died, and, as you might expect, she held Freddy's interests closely."

Sherworth dropped his head into his hands, in an effort to assimilate this startling development. A reference made by the countess to such a person stirred in his memory. He recalled that it had been because of this woman's death that the girl's debut had come to fiddlestick's end. At last he looked up. "Yes, I was told. I beg your pardon. The name had slipped my mind. So it is mostly for young Bancroft's mother that you are determined in this course."

"It is *entirely* for Freddy's mother that I am determined in this course," amended Vescinda. "I am extremely fond of Freddy, but I fear I shouldn't feel myself quite *that* beholden to him."

"I see," said Sherworth with some chagrin. The countess had warned him that the girl's sentiments were more complex than he had supposed, and, of course, this view of the situation—the fact that she had not *chosen* to marry her ramshackled cousin—was conceivable. Lord, was it any wonder that she found herself in sympathy with Lady Hamilton's earlier circumstances? In her case, she would be tied to a foolish young puppy. No doubt she had long since realized that her only hope for happiness would be in taking a lover. Well, it was a common-enough practice among the married ladies of the ton. Lord Oxford's numerous progeny were irreverently referred to as "Harleian's miscellany," because it was believed that there were not two among them fathered by the same man. And, although William Lamb, his brother George, and his sister, Lady Cowper, were recorded as the sons and daughters of Lord Melbourne, it was generally accepted that William owed his existence to Lord Egremont, George to the regent, and Emily to an unidentified buck about town.

Taking a long drink of coffee, Sherworth reflected thoughtfully that an odd set of rules goverened his world. Lady Holland was not received, because she had presented her husband with his *own* son slightly in advance of the wedding, yet other ladies, simply because they had married first, could frivolously produce false heirs by the dozen without fear of censure. He drew a weary breath. He had never approved of it, nor had he ever chosen his own mistresses from among the wives of other men, but he could see that in this instance Miss Bancroft must be forgiven. He made a mental note, however, to remind the countess to speak to her granddaughter, for it wouldn't do for her to emulate Lady Hamilton and bring her lover into the house or, in any other way, make it impossible for the world to turn its very willing blind eye.

Vescinda interrupted his musings. "What is it, my lord? You are still looking grim, and you should be relieved. Don't you apprehend that this quite ends your fears where I am concerned? I couldn't marry you if you were mad for the notion."

"Yes, I had mistook the situation, and I'm damnably sorry— sorry that circumstances oblige you to sacrifice yourself in this way, and sorrier still for my conduct toward you. I've insulted you dreadfully. I don't even know how you can forgive me."

"Yes, well, I don't know either. But I am determined to do so," she said with a rueful smile. "Nor do I know why you found it so difficult to believe Grandmama or the facts set out in my letter— but—well, you have been put to a deal of trouble in my behalf. So, let us simply cry friends and begin anew."

She extended her hand and was surprised to have him take it and raise it to his lips. Giving a little laugh, she said softly, "*Such* an odd creature," then turned the conversation away from matters related to their recent contention. Soon the door swung open and Rigsby reentered, followed by John and Joseph, each bearing a well-laden tray, which they set out on the sideboard. Vescinda waved away Sherworth's offer to fetch a plate over to her and joined him before the array of silver-lidded dishes where she helped herself to curried eggs and a slice of toast. Sherworth returned to the table a moment later, his plate heaped with slices of red sirloin and a slab of fresh ham.

She continued to direct their talk along sensible lines until bethinking herself of something quite irresistible. "I've been burning to know. Why did you call me 'Mama's little joke'? Did she describe me in a funning way?"

Sherworth waited to swallow a mouthful of beef before answering. "No, but she deliberately encouraged my natural assumption that the granddaughter lingering in Dorsetshire would be an antidote, a dowd, and a simpering rustic."

Vescinda was forced to catch her lip between her teeth. "Oh, my, a compliment turned inside out. Th—Thank you," she said, then added with a total disregard for truth, "but you must know that it came as a great shock to me as well that my Uncle Adrian wasn't a kindly old gentleman who would dandle me on his knee. Oh!—do forgive me. I daresay I ought not have said that just when you were drinking your coffee. Are you quite all right? Yes? Ah, well, I can see that you were somewhat taken aback, but, regardless of how oddly it comes about through remarriage that *is* our relationship."

"Good God! Yes, I see now that you're right. But don't take it into your head that I'm going to permit you to call me 'Uncle.'"

"Of course, I shan't, if you dislike it. What do your other nieces call you?"

"The devil, but you're a saucy baggage!" he choked again. "I begin to think that the firm hand of a stern uncle is precisely what is wanted here." He placed both hands on the edge of the table and looked very much as though he planned to go straight to work.

This surprised something between a laugh and a gasp from Vescinda, as she instinctively returned her cup to its saucer and straightened in her chair. Sherworth, a gleam of triumph in his dark-blue eyes, leaned back again, leaving her feeling a little foolish over her obvious alarm. Really it wasn't possible that he could have charged over to use her roughly in the breakfast room. At least, it was most unlikely, she modified, recalling his other altogether unusual behavior. As her eyes lifted to meet his, she was forced to laugh, for it was plain that he was following her thought processes quite as easily as if she'd been speaking them aloud.

The episode served to banish the lingering constraint between them, and they were chatting comfortably when Chloe, swathed in shawls, came bustling in. "Gad," she complained, taking her seat beside Vescinda, "it might as well be winter here. Have to stay busy to keep from freezing to death!"

Vescinda had just handed her aunt a cup of coffee when Rigsby looked in to advise his mistress that Heacham awaited her in the estate room. She pushed back her chair, explaining to Sherworth, who was looking slightly perplexed, "It is Papa's bailiff. I must see him this morning, but I shall have the balance of the day free— But why do you stare? Oh, I see. Evidently you don't realize that, even when Papa is here, he prefers to leave these matters to me." Meeting Sherworth's look of shocked disapproval with a little laugh, she hurried away.

Sherworth demanded of his stepsister, in revolted accents, "How in the name of the devil can a man *prefer* to leave the affairs of his estate to a female?"

"Bancroft prefers to leave everything to anybody else," Chloe replied absently. After a few minutes of mutual silence, she said, "Glad to see you ain't still ripping up at my poor niece. Daresay you've discovered by now that your artillery was aimed the wrong way."

"Yes," he retorted accusingly. "But she needn't have suffered at all, had I understood that her plans don't emanate from *love* for her abominable cousin!"

"Learned that, have you?" asked Chloe, surprised to find him so complacent.

"I have. It was all the doing of Aunt Euphoria, or something. Apparently, at some point before getting her notice to quit, she'd begged a promise from the girl to marry her idiot son."

Chloe mopped furiously at the coffee which had jolted out of her cup onto the cloth. Lord, she didn't know whether to laugh or cry. The countess had expected them to get the business straight between them in the first conversation, but somehow they'd managed to discuss the entire thing at cross purposes. *Or,* Chloe thought with a mental groan, her sportive niece had discovered the sham and was now embarked upon a game of her own. She was teased by the thought that no good would come of permitting Sherworth to continue in his misapprehension, yet the countess had wished him to learn the truth only from Vescinda. Actually she'd been a deal more explicit. ("Don't be tempted to help, Chloe," she'd warned. "I don't know how it can be, but your good intentions always manage to create the most shocking coils.") So, wishing at least to avoid becoming further implicated in the lie, Chloe rose to wander over to the sideboard. As she examined the succulent ham brought to the kitchen from the Bancroft's own smokehouse, she soothed herself that, surely, Sherworth couldn't remain hoaxed long enough to ruin the party, which she was coming to consider as peculiarly her own.

It was almost an hour before Vescinda was free to leave the estate room and seek out Sherworth again. With no experience and only an obligatory interest in estate affairs, Vescinda had been struggling on a trial-and-error basis since first discovering the necessary part her aunt had played in the management of Lord Bancroft's holdings. This knowledge had not come to her immediately, because the staff and tenants, respectful of the early weeks of her mourning, had kept back their questions and complaints until they could be kept back no longer. When the dam of their restraint had burst, Vescinda, after a brief confusion at being pelted with matters more properly her father's concern, saw what had escaped her hitherto carefree notice. Her Aunt Eudora had not merely been indulging an eccentric interest in the land but had been filling a position that would otherwise have gone by the boards. And so Vescinda had risen reluctantly to the demand, realizing that even her decisions, owing perforce more to logic than to knowledge, were superior to those of an aging and often befuddled bailiff or the absolute silence of her hedonistic father.

Today, the time had seemed to drag for her, and she'd found it even more arduous than usual to apply herself to Heacham's droning reports and questions. More than once she'd been forced to call her wandering thoughts to order, knowing that what was often difficult would be impossible without proper concentration. At last, having settled Heacham's mind on a matter concerning the Bancroft dairy, Vescinda dismissed him and set out, finding Sherworth and her aunt in the great hall. Sherworth had once more taken up a position at the fire, but this time, when she came into the room, he strolled forward to greet her. She met him with a brilliant smile and apologized for being so long away, adding, "Aunt Chloe tells me I'm not to assist her any longer—that my project is to entertain you. I— Well, I'm afraid I haven't planned anything in particular. But I am quite willing and open to suggestions."

Chloe intervened, suggesting drily that she should take him to see the mail delivered.

"Did I hear correctly?" Sherworth asked, looking at Vescinda in some amusement.

"Why, yes, and it's an excellent notion. Have you ever seen it?"

"Not since I was in short coats," he replied civilly. Then a slow smile of reminiscence crept over his features. "It used to be a favorite thing. You see, the mail didn't stop in our village—"

"Ah! That is what I enjoy so particularly," interrupted Vescinda, flashing a saucy smile at her aunt. "We have it the same in Charmouth. We can have luncheon at the Coach and Horse and watch it from there. Shall we?"

"Done!" he agreed, guiding her toward the stairs.

They parted then to change into their riding dress, Vescinda first taking time to order the horses brought round. It had been agreed that they would meet again in thirty minutes, and Sherworth rejoined her at the foot of the stairs in good time, beautifully attired in highly polished top boots, buckskin breeches, and a coat of deep russet.

Vescinda smiled. "Oh, I'm most impressed! I'd always heard that fashionable gentlemen required *hours* to dress. I was in the liveliest dread that the mail would be in Exeter before you reappeared."

A smile was his only reply. Vescinda gathered up the long skirt of her elegant gray habit, and, placing her free hand lightly on his arm, allowed him to lead her to the entrance doors, where Rigsby handed her her gauntlets and crop.

Both their grooms awaited them in the carriageway. Casting an appreciative eye over the sleek, little gray mare and the large chestnut which was evidently meant for him, Sherworth asked, "Does your father also prefer to leave the management of the stables to you?"

"Oh, yes. Papa never rides where he can drive, nor drives when he can be driven. Which," she added, tossing her head to laugh up at him, "is altogether for the best, because he's not much of a dab at either."

Sherworth handed Vescinda over to her groom, smiling at the affectionate exchange between mistress and mare, then turned to take the chestnut from Wiley, who said, "You'll like this mettlesome bit of blood and bone, sir."

Vescinda, already in the saddle and adjusting her reins and crop, called down, "I do pray you will. He's fresh and full of fidgets, but I made sure you wouldn't care for that."

Throwing his leg over the dancing chestnut, Sherworth assured her that she had judged his taste to a nicety.

"That reminds me, sir," said Wiley. "You ain't meaning to keep that pair of slugs we drove in last night, are you?"

Vescinda, admiring Sherworth's easy mastery over an animal she knew required the strong hands of an expert, noticed the expression he returned to Wiley and hastened to reassure him. "There is no need to put yourself in a pelter, trying to use job horses while you are here. I have a pair that I think you'll like."

Sherworth brought his large mount over to stand quietly beside the mare. "Are you one of those notable lady whips who drive a fiery team poled up to a high-perch phaeton?"

"No, oh, no," Vescinda laughed. "I'm the merest whipster, and I drive only a very ordinary phaeton—and never more than a pair. However, my bays are sound and well-mannered, thanks to Archer."

Sherworth accepted her offer graciously and said to Wiley, "While we are gone, then, you may join forces with the postilions and rid the stables of not only that pair but the team that drew my chaise as well." Addressing Vescinda, he added, "I doubt the chaise will be wanted before my valet is to return to town. There's no point in cluttering up your stables with six useless beasts."

"But it is not in the least necessary to send them back," returned Vescinda urgently. "In fact, I wish you will not. We have ample space and fodder—" Coloring slightly, she added, "You see, I share a fault with Lady Hamilton. I waste my sympathy on animals. I know they aren't fine horses, but they work so hard most of the time. It's an opportunity for them to rest and have all they want to eat and to run free for a few hours a day."

After submitting her to a long appraising gaze, Sherworth asked, "Are you aware that, all the while these animals are languishing in the luxury of your beneficence, I shall be obliged to pay post charges?"

Vescinda merely compressed her lips in a reproachful smile and indicated the direction they would take with her crop.

They moved out, with Archer following at a discreet distance, and connected with a trail leading cross-country to Charmouth. Wiley, released from his orders to return the post horses, went directly to the carriage house, grateful for the opportunity to get an extra coat of wax on his master's curricle, if it was to withstand the rigors of the sea air.

AFTER TESTING A few of Charger's paces, Sherworth came up to Vescinda on the path and commended her on her judgment of horseflesh.

"Thank you. But it is Archer who deserves the credit. He knows—oh, just everything, and has been instructing me since setting me upon my first pony. I'm particularly proud of Twilight, here," she said, giving the glossy neck a pat. Receiving a responsive nicker, Vescinda smiled. "I raised her from a filly, and she seems to value my companionship even above that of other horses. I daresay you will think it odd, but, because of it, I feel I belong to her as much as she does to me."

Sherworth did not appear to think it odd, but he said nothing. They both fell silent until emerging atop the fringe of hills separating the Bancroft estates from the charming little coastal village. Here they drew up to enjoy the prospect. Sherworth's gaze scanned the surrounding hills, overgrown with heath, furze and fern, then dropped to the green, fruitful valleys below, but Vescinda directed his attention to the higher hills, rising abruptly from the lofty coastline, saying, "Those are sometimes used for telegraphic signals. Freddy became acquainted with a retired naval officer living at Lyme, who claimed that with the use of these stations intelligence was transmitted, from Plymouth to the grand telegraph on top the Admiralty and back, in only fifteen minutes. Isn't that amazing? I mean, if one considers that the whole space penetrated by the telescopes was twice two hundred and fourteen miles— Oh," she exclaimed, laughing, "I can see that I'm giving you a tinker's budget."

Sherworth smiled. "It chances that I *do* know of it, but only because my brother-in-law was involved in the initial experiment." He added apologetically, "I daresay you were also meaning to tell me that, during the invasion threat, large stackings were piled atop those same hills and kept in readiness to be fired as a warning to the populace if one of your telegraphic lookouts spied Boney's grand flotilla on the horizon."

"Yes, oh, yes," Vescinda said, with a little laughing wince of memory. "It required all my powers of persuasion to keep Freddy from heading out for them with his tinder box."

Sherworth's lip curled into a sneer. "I can well imagine that he would think it high gig to send the entire population off in a frenzied evacuation."

"For goodness' sake, why do you look so—so *contemptuous?*" she asked, her smile fading. "He was a very young boy at the time, and, once I made it plain what should be the result, he *did* refrain!"

Sherworth acknowledged her words with a nod, but there was a slight pall attending their descent to the cobbled road leading through the center of Charmouth.

By the time they drew rein before the Coach and Horse Inn, Vescinda's buoyant mood had returned, and she told Sherworth, "I often stop here. The landlord is very kind and serves me at that table on the porch, which affords an excellent view of both the receiving office and the bay."

Vescinda allowed Archer, riding up alongside, to take Twilight's reins, but she waited in her saddle for Sherworth to dismount and give his horse into her groom's charge. There she remained, patiently watching him, as he surveyed all aspects of the village and the sea beyond. When he turned to glance up at her, his expression, although pleasant, was frankly inquisitive. Vescinda chuckled and waved her groom on to the stabling area, saying to Sherworth, "Pray do not trouble yourself with me." She kicked free of the stirrup and slipped gracefully to the ground.

Sherworth frowned defensively. "If you required assistance, I should think you might have said something—and *that* to your groom, who was the obvious one to lend it."

"Well, obviously I *didn't* require it," she said, adding mischievously, "which is indeed fortunate because I cannot conceive how poor Archer might have lent it while holding *three* horses. Now don't fly into a pet. I daresay it is an old-fashioned notion. Or perhaps it is that very consequential gentlemen don't assist ladies to dismount?"

"It's not my practice to do so," said Sherworth between vexation and amusement, "but I promise you, I'm not governed by a regard for my consequence!"

"No? Oh, *I* see! Of course. You would naturally be afraid that it might be thought you were becoming particular in your attentions! Very proper. It would be most unkind to raise false hopes," Vescinda laughed, waving to the portly landlord, who appeared briefly at the door of the inn.

Sherworth, accustomed by now to her bantering way, merely shook his head and followed her up onto the porch. They settled themselves on the roughhewn benches on opposite sides of a seaweathered table and fell into comfortable conversation. Vescinda, enjoying herself immensely, interspersed her talk with as many slang expressions as she could bring to mind and calmly disregarded it when her companion damned this or confounded that. Sherworth had been quite right. Between her father's careless ways and Freddy's fascination with everything, from thieves' cant to sporting slang, Vescinda was no stranger to improper language and warm topics. Of course, she had never had a gentleman demand, as his right, the license so casually taken by her male relatives, nor had anyone ever assumed that she must necessarily be as lax in her conduct as they. On the contrary, she was far more used to being treated with an almost oppressive degree of respect and deference. She knew, of course, that she could not grant the privileges that Sherworth was so smoothly taking for granted to the other gentlemen of her acquaintance, but she wondered somewhat wistfully why they must suppose that proprietous conduct was a natural bar to joking, or that their conversation must be confined to the milkiest commonplaces.

Conversation with Sherworth was far from that. After falling into warm and fervent agreement· that something must be done to eliminate the cruel amusements which forced various animals into combat with one another, Sherworth gave her a laughing description of a contest held between female pugilists—a pair of promising contenders, "with excellent bottom and a fair degree of science," called Nan and Sally. Next, he satisfied her curiosity concerning a murder that had taken place near his sister's home in Chislehurst. Vescinda had overheard Chloe recounting the tale of a footman who had murdered his employers with a poker as they lay sleeping, but had not liked to ask for details. Oddly, she felt no qualm in asking Sherworth, nor he in responding. The motive had been neither revenge nor a desire for plunder. The culprit had claimed to have acted solely upon an "irresistible impulse."

Their talk then fell to Sherworth's sister, who he said had been in such a quiver over the affair that she'd put her home at Chislehurst on the market forthwith and was now busy spreading it abroad that his refusal to let her take up residency at Whitowers was tantamount to proof that he would delight in seeing her murdered in her bed. "Really," he said, shaking his head with asperity, "if Milissa weren't so depressingly commonplace, I'd be forced to suspect that a strain of insanity had crept into our line."

"No, but unreasoning jealousy *does* often give the appearance of madness. I have sometimes thought the same of—of someone else. Grandmama has told me of Lady Oxbrook's treatment of you when you were a boy. But you mustn't think we were gossiping. She felt she must explain why she couldn't take me to live with her when my mother died. Had she done so, I daresay by now I should figure as one more tiresome sister in your life."

Sherworth reached across the table and gripped Vescinda by the wrist. "Thank God, she didn't!"

Vescinda was startled, not by his words, but at the thoroughly unusual experience of being handled in that way. To cover her confusion, she murmured, "But how unhandsome of you to say so."

He relaxed his expression and withdrew his hand. "No, I'm sure I should have found you a delightful sister—far more to my taste than the two I have. Except you wouldn't be as you are. Had you been reared under the same roof as Katherine, you'd be as spiritless as Milissa or Katherine's own daughter Charlotte—or, if not that, untrusting and entirely too hot at hand."

"Like you?" she quizzed.

"Like me," he agreed, in a way that made Vescinda wish she could say something further.

However, she was able only to give him a quick, reassuring smile before the landlord arrived, bearing a great earthenware pitcher, two mugs, a large wedge of cheese and two loaves of warm, freshly baked bread. Vescinda smiled at the jovial innkeeper and thanked him warmly, but the moment he was out of tongueshot, she said in a stricken tone, "Oh, I *am* sorry. He is just so in the habit of always bringing these things whenever I ride up. I know you must be accustomed to a more elaborate luncheon!"

"No, really, it all looks excellent," Sherworth assured.

"It's our Dorset cheese. And the cider is pressed just the other side of those hills," she gestured. "You may have noticed the orchards and presses on the way here. But—oh, I am persuaded you would at least prefer wine and meat."

"No, I should prefer you to busy yourself with cutting that cheese while I tackle the bread."

"If you are quite sure that you don't mind it," she said gratefully. "I own it would sink me to ask for something else. He was so *pleased* to be serving this. The moment we are home, I shall have Mrs. Rigsby, our cook, send up something to sustain you until dinner, something special because you— Oh, listen! That is it—the mail guard's horn! Come quickly!"

As Sherworth arrived to stand beside her at the porch rail, the thundering of sixteen hooves, beating over the cobbles, obscured all other sound. "There," Vescinda pointed, "is Mr. Arn, ready for the catch."

No sooner had she said this than the great red coach came rattling into view, the guard in his red coat standing up behind, with the leather bag poised for the toss. Both bags sailed out, crossed in the air and came safely home. The coachman saluted Vescinda with his whip, as he guided his speeding team past the inn, and the guard favored her with a broad wink as he held up the leather trophy for her approval. Aware that Sherworth was observing her closely, Vescinda did something she had yearned for years to do. She waved back to them both.

Her excited smile caused Sherworth to break out laughing as he helped her to her seat. Straddling his bench and dropping down onto it, he said, "I shouldn't wonder if there is a law against flirting so outrageously with His Majesty's servants."

"Then I shall trust you not to cry rope on me," said Vescinda, taking up the cheese knife again.

When they had completed the exchange of bread for cheese, Sherworth filled their mugs with the cool, rough cider and asked, "Is it a coincidence that you call your mare Twilight, or is there a relationship to Miss Wildborne's Midnight?"

"There is a relationship," replied Vescinda slowly. "Knowing, as I expect you do by now, how much I care for horses, you will understand what I must have felt when first setting eyes on Midnight. Since Liza couldn't be brought to sell him, I conceived the notion to locate just the right mare—to try my hand at a little matchmaking, you see."

"Yes, but I don't see Miss Wildborne's agreeing to your scheme. She doesn't care a fig for that animal, but he brings her a good deal of attention. And I have noticed that she doesn't like to share her attention. Or did you and Freddy plan a clandestine meeting between the two animals?"

This made Vescinda laugh. "No, but I might have considered even that, if Liza hadn't finally come to terms." She looked up sharply. "I was not sixteen at the time, if you mean to give me another of your disapproving looks."

"Disapproving looks? Oh, you're referring to Freddy and the bonfires. Not at all the same thing. Pray, go on. I'm all agog. What were the terms?"

"That I must give up the mare to her after the foaling."

Sherworth effected a soft whistle. "Then I'll go bail you paid dearly."

"Yes, Archer found a beautiful black—a perfect match—and, as you have guessed, at a handsome price. But I didn't care for that. I was so convinced that I should end by having a magnificent black stallion of my own."

"And, instead, you received a gray mare for your pains." He frowned. After a moment he went on, "My interest springs from having been also to some efforts over Miss Wildborne's Midnight. I'm partial to blacks, and, after spotting him last season, I probed into his background—" He paused to take a long drink. Setting down his mug, he said, "It's very good, your Dorset cider—er—I'll wager Archer didn't assist with the marriage you arranged for your black mare."

"No!" Vescinda agreed, betrayed into strong feeling. "Liza *would* have it that strangers would cause Midnight to be nervous, which is a great piece of nonsense because Midnight is forever— Well, never mind that," she broke off with a blush of color.

Sherworth, laughing, taunted, "And after giving your word not to be missish."

But Vescinda would only shake her head. She had meant to play his game to some extent, but that particular lapse had been unintentional. She thought, with an inward smile, that evidently Lord Sherworth's laxity of conduct must be contagious. She was a trifle surprised at herself, but not alarmed. Her life had been filled with grave warnings of the dangers of lowering one's standards, and, although she had no quarrel with the wisdom of this advice, she had considered all that and had decided that the present situation was as safe as it was irresistible. Even if Sherworth were the most shocking rake in London—or the saddest rattle—his relationship to her grandmother would bar his taking any serious liberties, just as it would insure against his spreading tales of her antics about town.

Sherworth's voice broke in upon her thoughts. "I know you must have been disappointed over the business, and I don't wish to distress you further, but I think perhaps you should know that the main reason *I* had wished to purchase Miss Wildborne's stallion is that he has an early record for breeding *true*."

Vescinda hesitated, then, making up her mind, said, "Well, if you know that, I trust I needn't scruple to tell you that there is a gray stallion in the Wildborne stables who boasts a similar reputation."

After weighing this disclosure and subjecting Vescinda to one of his measuring looks, Sherworth said, "So, you know that she played you foul. Is she aware that you know?"

Vescinda shook her head. "I have never mentioned it."

"You have a tighter rein on your temper than I should ever hope to have."

She laughed. "Scarcely a remarkable accomplishment since you appear to have so little. I certainly enjoyed a private rage over it, but, in the end, I preferred to take my losses silently rather than to advertise to the world that I'd been— What is it that Freddy says?—that I'd been such a rum bite."

"That you'd been taken in by such a rum bite," he corrected without a trace of humor.

Her smile wavered. She was touched by his sympathetic anger and found herself placing the tips of her fingers on his hand for an instant. "You mustn't look so, you know. I can no longer think of it as a loss, because I have my dear Twilight. And there has been a valuable lesson as well. I let my desire for the unobtainable override my good sense. You may be sure it has taught me to keep my wits about me. Consequently, I am much wiser and not at all unhappy—truly."

"No, not now! But I can't help thinking of an extremely disappointed girl of fifteen."

"I was that," she admitted, thinking back.

Sherworth poured out more cider, and they began to exchange anecdotes of their earlier lives, lingering long after they'd completed their luncheon, sometimes merely sharing a companionable silence as they gazed out over the peaceful bay.

It was nearly four in the afternoon when Vescinda glanced up at the sky in dismay. "Oh, I had intended to show you over Papa's estates. There is barely time to see half of them now."

"Then we shall see half," said Sherworth, rising to seek out the landlord and settle the reckoning. Before entering the inn, he tossed a penny to an urchin playing near the porch and gave him a message to carry to the stable.

"I'm afraid you've wasted your penny," called Vescinda. "You will find Archer in the tap room."

Sherworth acknowledged the enormity of his loss with a pained expression and disappeared into the inn. When he returned to the porch, Vescinda rose to join him, and they stepped down onto the cobbles to await their horses. In just a moment, they were confronted by the urchin, returning from his unsuccessful assignment. He scoffed slowly over to them, his fists clenched in reluctant resolution. He confessed his failure to find "thot laydee's groom" and made a brave offer to return "the guv'nor's blunt."

Vescinda stooped gracefully to take the extended hand in both of hers, and, closing the chubby little fingers over the coin, said, "But you have earned the penny by running the errand and reporting back." As the small boy, restored to spirits, scampered off, she looked up over her shoulder. "Now, guv'nor, I expect you'll tell me that I'm uncommonly free with your blunt."

"There is already a long homily on the evils of extravagance forming in my mind. I shall postpone it, however, for a less public place."

Once in the saddle again, Vescinda was stimulated by Twilight's playful capering into suggesting that they return by the road in order to enjoy a gallop. When Sherworth reminded her that she had only a few minutes ago promised to show him over her father's estates, she said, shrugging it off, "Oh, having so many estates of your own, I doubt these can hold any fascination for you."

"You're out there, my girl. It's because I have estates of my own that I am always interested in seeing others."

Her eyes flew to his, but found them perfectly serious. She murmured thoughtfully, "Yes, I can see how that would be so."

She continued to subject him to such an appraising stare that a twisted grin formed on his face, and he raised his hand in mock surrender, saying that he would release her from the promise. "Provided, of course, you make good your word directly after breakfast tomorrow."

"Yes," she replied, still distracted by her thoughts. The discovery that he was actually interested in other estates was tickling at her mind. He was someone who would actually know what was best to do, in many areas, where she could only hope to guess. She was trying to decide if it would be imposing too much to attempt to embroil him in such a tedious business. Then she recalled that, by his own words, his main purpose in coming down had been to rescue her from her own folly. Well, what better way?

She came out of her reverie. "Yes, we shall go over them all tomorrow, and I should greatly appreciate your advice on a few matters. It will have to be directly after *church,* however. You town people never seem to know when it is Sunday! Come, I'll race you to the lodge gates."

Vescinda whispered something to Twilight, and they were off in a streak of gray. Archer lagged behind, but Sherworth, holding the long-legged chestnut to a pace compatible with the mare, watched Vescinda closely as they sped along the lane. Reaching the lodge gates, they drew up and, after being admitted, walked the horses, to cool them, over the last stage to the stables. Sherworth complimented Vescinda on her skill in the saddle.

"Thank you, but it was kind in you to be concerned for me."

When they arrived at the carriageway in front of the large mansion, Sherworth swung from his saddle and led his mount over to Vescinda. Then, passing her reins as well as his own to Archer, he reached up and encircled Vescinda's trim waist with both hands.

She was cast into temporary confusion. She was accustomed to beind *handed* down by a gentleman, but never had one presumed to take hold of her in such a way. It was unnecessarily familiar, but she supposed he would consider it pure missishness if she demurred. She tried to deter him by assuring that she could manage, that, *truly,* she had only been jesting earlier.

"Come now," he said, lifting her effortlessly from the back of her mare. He held for an instant, her eyes on a level with his, giving her a full measure of his most provocative smile before setting her carefully down.

"Thank you," she murmured, suddenly feeling absurdly shy.

There was an interested witness to this activity in the person of Miss Wildborne, who had been pacing before the large, mullioned windows of the Bancroft drawing room. The sight of Sherworth performing this unprecedented act set the final torch to her inflammable mood. She called vengeance down upon everyone, particularly her own mother, whose strictures regarding the impropriety of dropping in on Vescinda at odd hours during Lord Sherworth's visit had launched her thoroughly unsatisfactory day.

Miss Wildborne had been quick to dispute with her mother, saying that Lord Sherworth did not care for such stuff. Nevertheless, she had finally conceded to Lady Wildborne's urgent entreaty. ("Still, my love, it is only prudent. Despite his lordship's willingness to countenance an informality of manners, you must not let it be thought that you lack the delicacy of principle that he will certainly demand in the future Lady Sherworth.")

Miss Wildborne had been regretting the concession to her mother's advice ever since the proprietous hour of her call, when she'd been informed (a trifle too exuberantly, in her opinion) that Miss Vescinda and his lordship had gone off together earlier in the day. Upon learning that they had ordered horses and conceiving the notion of overtaking them, Miss Wildborne had asked to be received by Mrs. Standish, whom Rigsby reluctantly supposed might know their direction. But only after she'd been left to fume and fidget for nearly half an hour, had she been shown up to a small room off the gallery, where Chloe was seated at a table, sorting and recopying her lists. Miss Wildborne could only conclude that this occupation had thoroughly cluttered her mind, for it took Vescinda's exasperating aunt several minutes to fully understand a perfectly simple question, and a great deal longer to recall that her niece had once mentioned Axminster. By that time, Miss Wildborne was near fever pitch and would have mortified her mother had that lady been privileged to witness her daughter's abrupt, if not wholly uncivil, departure. Miss Wildborne, however, was by then so desperate for action and so relieved by the gratification of a definite response that she didn't even take time to wonder what distempered freak had caused Vescinda to choose Axminster until she, herself, was halfway there.

However, when she failed to corner her quarry either on the road or in that town, her mind began to dwell heavily upon the subject. As she turned her stallion to retrace the five miles back to Blakely, it came forcibly home to Miss Wildborne that the tale of Axminster had been a hum from the outset. At this point, she chose to imbue Vescinda with a thought process more suited to herself and became easily convinced that Vescinda had supplied her shatterbrained aunt with false information in anticipation of its being passed on. Miss Wildborne didn't waste her time wondering what had been at the root of this treachery. *That* was perfectly plain: Vescinda had seen for herself, at dinner last night, which way Sherworth's preferences were running.

Moving along at a brisk trot, the blond beauty glanced up at the sky to calculate the time and then shocked her groom by spurring her mighty stallion into a dangerous gallop. The groom, mounted on a serviceable cobb, couldn't begin to keep pace and soon diminished into a tiny figure in the distance. Miss Wildborne's thoughts pounded violently, in rhythm with the powerful animal's beating strides, as she sped incautiously down the steep and curving grade. Her return to Blakely created all manner of confusion, because the identity of the person, or persons, at the apex of the cloud of dust thundering into the stableyard, could not be discerned. Consequently, Miss Wildborne was attended by every stablehand and groom at Blakely, including Sherworth's Wiley.

She gave neither thanks nor explanation to any of them, leaving behind her only a steaming black horse and a good deal of interested conjecture as to the nature of the emergency.

Upon learning from Rigsby that the errant pair were not yet returned, Miss Wildborne's agitation grew, and, by the time her pacing vigil was rewarded by the first glimpse of Vescinda and Sherworth approaching the house, she was trembling with frustration. It needed only for her to be forced to watch Vescinda, whom everyone *knew* was not in the least bashful, smiling shyly at Sherworth as he set her on the ground, for Miss Wildborne to swear an oath to send her to grass and no matter the cost!

Miss Wildborne knew from long experience, however, that to confront her cool-mannered adversary while she herself was in an uncontrollable rage would be to place herself at a grievous disadvantage. She therefore used the time it took Vescinda to enter the house to escape down a back stair, so that, when Vescinda came in, resigned to having another dinner invitation wrested from her, she found the room unoccupied.

She found as well, that the evening, free of Miss Wildborne's disruptive influence, was grandly improved. At dinner Sherworth more than atoned for his rudeness of the night before by keeping her well entertained and laughing throughout a leisurely meal. And, when they were reunited in the drawing room, he immediately drew her over to the little table they had shared for their abortive game of piquet, explaining that part of his assignment had been to assist her in planning the entertainment of the forthcoming guests.

She gathered up pencil and paper and joined him willingly, then listened in high amusement to a spate of offerings, none of which was fit to commit to writing. Finally, taking matters into her own hands, she listed several places of interest that could be visited by a riding party and suggested a carriage excursion to the seaside resort of Lyme Regis, adding that, if they waited until near the end of the party when her coachman promised a full moon, they could remain for a benefit ball, which was to be held at the assembly rooms, and which would boast the presence of as many as two hundred fashionable persons. Next, she compiled a list of the local people to be invited to her own ball and assigned it also to an evening when the moon could be depended upon to aid night travel. Far from helping with this endeavor, Sherworth did his best to distract her, either by besieging her with gallantries or teasing her by applying improbable histories and characters to the people on her list, guided solely by their various names and an outrageous imagination.

Vescinda smiled to herself as she jotted down another name. It was becoming plain that his lordship, convinced now that she was unavailable for marriage, had decided to embark upon a flirtation. Since it was equally plain that her chaperone meant to leave her to her own devices, Vescinda entered willingly into the spirit of this and would have been able to assure her, had her aunt posed the question again, that, indeed, flirting was a most agreeable pastime.

Vescinda suspected, however, that this was largely due to Sherworth's long practice in the art. Although, she thought, with an inward chuckle, he left no doubt that this practice had *not* been gained through dalliance with females moving in the first circles. More than once Vescinda had been forced to remind herself that she had promised not to "suffocate" the shocking creature with restrictions and proprieties, for he seemed to know nothing of keeping the line. This had been apparent at the outset. The lingering examination he had made of her, when she came down dressed for dinner, might have led her to suppose he was a devout fancier of fashion, except that she was left in considerable doubt as to whether he had noticed that she was wearing *clothes* at all. The provocative comments with which he laced his conversation had, on several occasions, come close to putting her out of countenance. And that smile—clearly a most useful tool for one bent on seduction. Not that she suspected him of planning that. Oh, no—merely of attempting to make her wish that he had!

In some ways, however, she found him even more disturbing when he became serious—the way he would catch her hand, or lay his own over hers, pressing home his understanding of something she had said, or the intense way he would look at her as he read beneath her words. He seemed always to guess when a light remark covered a deeper feeling. But, whatever else she thought of him, Vescinda thought him a stimulating companion in every way. They talked steadily until the arrival of the tea tray, their conversation drifting as it had that afternoon into all manner of subjects, some of which, a week earlier, Vescinda should have been surprised to think she would discuss with anyone, far less a gentleman with whom she had been acquainted for no more than a day.

Lord Bancroft retired directly after the removal of the tea tray, and Chloe, evidently well-pleased by an evening spent brangling with the master of the house, picked up her workbox contentedly and suggested that Vescinda and Sherworth might wish to continue their project at the table.

Sherworth rose, his eyes quizzing Vescinda as he admonished, "Yes, Miss Bancroft, we really mustn't idle away our time in conversation."

She allowed him to guide her back to the privacy of the far end of the room and said as they were seated, "What a fund of contradictions you are. Suddenly so formal and calling me Miss Bancroft, after addressing me the day long in such improper terms as 'my girl' and 'delightful goose.'"

"Well, there's no rule that decrees I must have your permission to call you delightful goose; your name is another matter. Did I call you delightful goose?"

"Twice."

"It must be the sea air. But I agree that we should dispose of Miss Bancroft. Vescinda," he said, testing the sound of it. "An unusual name. I don't think I've heard it before."

"Most unlikely. You would have to know two such other silly persons as my parents. My mother had wished to call me Lucinda after Grandmama, but Papa, besides disliking Grandmama cordially, had fixed on the name Vespatia. Mama, as I've told you, was not a spirited woman, but she stood out against that, on the grounds that not only was Vespatia the name of a man, but of one who had bloodied the beaches of Dorset while fighting *against* England! And, since Papa dislikes being teased even more than he dislikes giving over, he finally agreed to permit Vespatia and Lucinda to be merged."

Sherworth laughed and said with approval, "Ah, fitting! Then there is only one Vescinda in the entire world."

"I trust so."

"And certainly no other eyes so green—"

"I have been meaning to ask," she interrupted. "As concerned as you are that I might ruin myself at the party, oughtn't you to be teaching me how to go on instead of encouraging me to flirt in this way. These habits, you know, are sometimes the very devil to break."

He frowned thoughtfully. "Possibly you're right. I haven't mentioned it, but you should know, Vescinda, that some of the men coming for this party can't be trusted to keep the line."

"Oh?" she said faintly, as she struggled to keep her features in order. "T-then what must I do?"

"For one thing," he said, amused by the recollection, "when your father says something outrageous, as he did several times during dinner, you shouldn't go off into a fit of laughing."

"And, if you say something outrageous, should I not laugh then either?"

"I shall endeavor not to do so in public."

"I see. Then it is only when outrageous things are said to me in private that I may laugh."

"I think you're quizzing me, but I'll tell you in no uncertain terms that you must put an immediate stop to it if they attempt to say improper things to you at *any* time."

"Ah, tell them to stow their whidds," she nodded wisely.

He smiled. "I think it might be well if you culled the cant out of your conversation as much as possible."

"Just tell them in a more refined way to stubble it?" she asked.

Laughing, he said, "Perhaps it would be best if you took the position of refusing to dignify such attempts with any comment at all."

"Oh, that's a good notion," she approved. "For, I daresay it wouldn't be the thing to swear at them either."

"Decidedly not—even though I have no doubt now that you're quizzing me, minx."

She laughed. "Yes, I do know better than to swear. Though," she smiled reflectively, "the clearest memory I have of my mother is her pained expression as she tried to teach me not to borrow from Papa's vocabulary when I flew into a temper."

"I didn't know you *could* fly into a temper," he laughed.

"Oh, yes, before I learned to control my anger, I was used to do so quite often. But that was some time ago; so you needn't fear I shall embarrass you at the party."

"Well, I'd rather you flew into a temper than allow someone to cozen you into a compromising situation. That's another thing: you must never stay below, as you do, after Chloe and the other ladies go up to bed. Actually, you should take care not to be drawn away from the group at any time."

Vescinda promised that she would bear that in mind, and they began to talk of other things. But, when Chloe yawned and stood up, and Vescinda rose to follow her from the room, Sherworth demanded to know what the devil she meant by deserting him so early.

"But you have just said that I must on no account stay below after Aunt Chloe goes up," she protested.

"Oh, confound it, this is not the same thing," he returned irritably. "I meant once the party has begun. Now, sit down and finish telling your story."

9

ON THE FOLLOWING morning, Miss Wildborne ordered her stallion at an unusually early hour. She satisfied her mother's enquiry as to her direction with an ungrudging lie and rode directly over to Blakely, her beautiful features set in rigid determination. She was not surprised to be coolly informed by Rigsby that his mistress was not yet down; she was familiar with Vescinda's habits. Her plan hung precariously on the hope that Sherworth would precede his hostess into the breakfast room. She pushed past the weary butler, saying that she would await Vescinda there, and, after thirty minutes of rapid pacing, she was rewarded by the sight of Sherworth entering alone.

There was little beyond his mere presence to encourage her satisfaction, however. At sight of her, his hand groped instinctively to reclaim the door handle, and his countenance registered an expression that would normally accompany a groan. These signs were not entirely lost upon Miss Wildborne, but they were eclipsed by the single-mindedness with which she invariably pursued her goals. Time was her only concern at the moment, and she set right to work, saying mendaciously in return to Sherworth's curt bow, "Good morning, my lord. Mama sent me to beg the pleasure of your company at dinner this evening, though you may be sure I explained that you would most likely be too occupied with your mission to spare the time to us."

Sherworth had stridden over to the mantel and was on the point of uttering an automatic refusal, to an invitation he felt sure represented only the thin excuse for her call, when her closing words penetrated his brain. He studied her a moment, then replied stiffly, "Unless you mean that I'm here to assist with the party, you're barking up the wrong tree. Beyond that, I have no 'mission,' as you call it."

"Oh? But naturally I thought— Oh, *I* see, and I must say that I'm relieved to hear it. You mean, of course, that Vescinda has thought better of her little joke, that she has released you from the notion that you must try and make her fall in love with you."

Sherworth's bored gaze had drifted to the fire, but he brought it abruptly to bear on Miss Wildborne for a frowning moment, then said, in tones tinged with accusation, "One of us is mad."

Miss Wildborne naturally did not confess to this condition, but she fell into a creditable state of confusion and remorse. Turning away and throwing her hands up to cover her face, she exclaimed, "Oh—! Oh, dear, this is most awkward! Then you *didn't* know it was all a fudge about Vescinda's marrying Freddy!"

She glanced back to observe him from under her lashes, but Sherworth, on his guard since her opening gambit, had schooled his expression into one of mocking incredulity. She was disappointed and a trifle nettled, but by no means ready to accept defeat. Under the guise of excusing her accidental betrayal of Vescinda, she pressed home her point, making frequent use of the phrases "as Lord Bancroft said to me," and "as Lord Bancroft would tell you, if you cared to ask."

Had she been able to see beneath the snowy folds of Sherworth's neckcloth, Miss Wildborne would have been greatly encouraged by the vein that had begun to pulsate at her first disclosure. Her strategy had lost nothing in its transparency, and white rage was boiling beneath Sherworth's frozen features. He knew, of course, that she was making him a gift of the source of her information, volunteering Vescinda's own father as an indisputable corroborator of her veiled accusations. But that didn't alter the fact that Vescinda had been making sport of him from the outset, first conspiring in the tale that she was in love with her cousin, and then, when she saw that he couldn't be made to swallow that, hatching up the touching story of a dying aunt. He cursed himself for a fool, as his mind flew back to the protestations of love for Freddy he had read in Vescinda's letter. The jade had used all that effecting charm and those damnable green eyes to mesmerize him into forgetting what he had clearly seen in black and white! Evidently the game was to lull him into indiscretion, but there was no time to sort it all out—not if he was to keep from leaving the bodies of *both* tricking females strewn about the breakfast room! Only two things mattered for the time being: the Wildborne's underhanded ploy must not afford her the satisfaction she so obviously desired, and a confrontation with the countess's "little granddaughter" must be avoided until he could deal with her with far less violence than would be possible at the moment. He must somehow rid the house of the blond harpy and escape himself, before the perpetrator of this pretty coil came waltzing in to get herself hopelessly embroiled in the discussion. Sorely pressed by time, only one thought occurred to him.

He interrupted Miss Wildborne's unceasing flow. "Yes, yes, this is all very entertaining, but has it not occurred to you that your amiable mother would wish to know, as soon as possible, that there is to be an addition to her table tonight?"

Miss Wildborne's ludicrous expression confirmed his earlier suspicion that she had not seriously expected him to accept her preposterous invitation. No doubt Lady Wildborne knew nothing of it, and her daughter would now find herself in the devil of a hobble, but neither was there time to savor this pleasurable reflection. Taking advantage of her confusion, he ushered her to the door and said, in a confiding tone, "Such a clever girl must surely know that Lord Bancroft's drunken utterances are not to be heeded. At least *I* have no reason to suppose that Miss Bancroft ever intended to marry her cousin." Before thrusting her into the hall and closing the breakfast room door firmly after her, he recommended, "Now, I would lose no time in assuring Lady Wildborne that I am most honored by her kind invitation and shall present myself—shall we say shortly before six?"

Returning to the mantel, he waited, with fists clenched into white-knuckled fury, until he heard the front door shutting behind Miss Wildborne and then, as a release for his pent-up anger, smashed an exquisitely booted foot into the center of the neatly stacked log fire and stormed out of the room.

If his valet was surprised to have his master back, demanding top boots and breeches so soon after going down, he made no mention of it. For one thing, it was not Fairfield's practice to encourage unnecessary conversation before his lordship had had his breakfast; for another, anyone with half an eye could see that his lordship was not merely indulging his early morning crustiness; he was in a towering rage. The change of raiment was accomplished in absolute silence, and, in less than ten minutes, Sherworth was able to charge out again, leaving Fairfield to shake his head over the once magnificent Hessian boot, now sadly charred and scuffed.

Moments later, the earl, mounted on the same large chestnut he had ridden the day before, was heading toward the home wood at a spanking pace.

At near the same time, Vescinda was seated at her dressing table, completing her morning toilet. Dorcas, occupied with arranging her mistress's rich, deep brown locks in a simple but elegant style, was conscious of an edge of excitement. She glanced at her mistress in the gilt-framed glass, but found nothing in her placid expression to indicate that she considered the day in any way particular.

Still there was something. Dorcas was sure. So she ventured, "I reckon it's a regular treat for you to have your young gentleman to greet you at breakfast."

Not daring to move her head at such a crucial point in the hairdressing, Vescinda looked up under her lashes to meet her maid's eyes in the mirror. The corners of her mouth lifted. "Now, Dorcas, you mustn't let your romantical turn run off with you. I daresay it's not unreasonable to refer to Lord Sherworth's visit as a treat for me, but it is truly no more than that—a visit. He is quite as eager to return to his town pleasures at the end of the fortnight as I am determined to fulfill my plan to remain here until Master Freddy comes down from the university."

"Well," grumbled Dorcas, who did not approve of her mistress's plan, "there's no harm in taking pleasure in things natural to a young lady in the meanwhile."

"None at all. I have been doing precisely that. And if you can contrive to be finished before my young man grows old, I mean to continue doing so—in the most frivolous fashion imaginable."

Dorcas, as usual, could not hold out against Vescinda's teasing. She chuckled and gave the glossy head a final pat and said, "Out with you, then."

Vescinda entered the breakfast room a few minutes later, but there was no young man—no one at all—to greet her. Even the little fire, usually so welcoming, could only render up a dying gasp. Rigsby followed her into the room, giving a groan as he set down the coffee pot, and rushed over to the hearth.

"Has Lord Sherworth not come down to breakfast?" asked Vescinda.

"Ay, come down, and already gone out."

"Out? Do you mean for a walk?"

"No, Miss Vescinda, he ordered a horse."

"I see," said Vescinda, though it was plain that she didn't.

Rigsby turned toward her, his nostrils signaling his opinion of the information he was about to impart. "The Wildborne girl called at barely nine of the clock. Insisted on awaiting you in here," he said, allowing his gaze to pass meaningfully over the vacant chairs. Having done his duty in that regard, he turned to the shocking state of affairs in the grate. After restacking the scattered logs into a smoky little pile, he gave the remaining few embers a bracing stir, but things had gone too far. Straightening up, he apologized for the negligence of persons as yet unknown, but soon to be sorry, for making such shabby work of the fire.

Vescinda walked to the table and sank into a chair. "Never mind it, Rigsby, I'm not cold," she murmured abstractedly, the flesh beneath the short puffed sleeves of her gown belying her words. Glancing up, she caught her butler's expression and was forced to laugh at herself. "Well, it *is* a trifle chilly, but some hot coffee and I shall do."

"Ay, Miss Vescinda, that you will," he agreed, with just enough relief to leave no doubt that his concern hadn't been confined to her physical well-being.

She felt a little foolish. It occurred to her that Lord Sherworth had the distinction of having placed her in that position twice in as many days—and, in each instance, the cause of his defection had been Liza Wildborne. On the one hand, it would appear that he was smitten with her to the exclusion of all other considerations, yet, when they had discussed her yesterday, he had seemed to hold her almost in aversion. Vescinda was forced to wonder if she had only *wished* to think so. No! What nonsense! Why should it signify in the least? It didn't. It was just extremely odd. He had made his views on marriage more than plain, and what else could possibly make him pursue Liza with such single-mindedness? Finding herself host to an uncharitable thought, Vescinda gave herself a scold. Besides, however rackety Liza might be at times, she was not a fool! She decided it was pointless to speculate in so nonsensical a way. Sherworth must return soon, to accompany them to church, and would doubtless present her with an explanation then.

But he did not return. Vescinda lingered over her coffee until the last possible minute, then rose with a studied calm. By the time she joined Chloe in the carriage, her calm was a trifle impaired. There had been no mistaking several looks of sympathy she had encountered while going up to collect her bonnet and gloves.

As the carriage began to roll along the lane, Chloe demanded, "What has happened to Sherworth?"

"Perhaps, like Papa, he doesn't care for church."

"As to that, I can't say. The point is, he usually goes."

"Then I haven't a notion," returned Vescinda, interesting herself in the landscape.

Chloe eyed her speculatively, but said no more until they were once more seated in the carriage and heading home. "I didn't notice the Wildborne chit. Don't she care for church either?"

"Lady Wildborne keeps a chaplain at the manor house."

"Oh?" said Chloe, her interest diverted. "For consequence, or is she so religious?"

Vescinda laughed. "Well, you know, I have never asked her."

Her irritation waned during the time they were away. Possibly it was the beneficial effect of the service, but more likely it was because she expected to find Sherworth waiting with a reasonable explanation and ready to fulfill their engagement to ride over her father's acres.

But only Archer, standing with Twilight, was waiting for her when they drew up before the broad stone steps. He asked uncomfortably if he should have a fresh horse saddled for his lordship, owing that Charger would likely be properly done up when he got back.

Instructing him to return her mare to the stables and to wait for further orders, Vescinda went directly up to her bedchamber. There she found Dorcas, still in her Sunday best, but prepared to assist her mistress into her riding habit. Vescinda glanced at the outfit laid out on the bed and noticed that it was neither of the gray habits, which had been made up during her mourning and which she had decided would do perfectly well for riding over the countryside of Dorset. Instead it was the dazzling emerald green creation trimmed with black military frogging that had been purchased, before the sad news of her Aunt Eudora, for rides in Hyde Park. She curbed her annoyance, knowing that her maid had meant it for the best. But, even if Sherworth had troubled to keep their appointment, it would have been the height of folly to wear such a thing in the company of a man who looked upon *everything* as a plot to fix his interest.

She put off her bonnet and gloves and dismissed her abigail. Since there was every likelihood that Sherworth had no intention of returning, it needed only for her to pass the day outfitted in riding clothes to appear even more ridiculous than she already did.

It was nearly four in the afternoon when Vescinda, seated alone in the drawing room, stiffened at the sound of footsteps approaching the large double doors. It was not her errant guest, however, but Rigsby, to announce Lady Wildborne. Before she could venture a guess as to the cause of this unusual development, her ladyship had swept into the room, her troubled gaze fixed on Vescinda, who had risen to greet her.

"My dear," exclaimed Lady Wildborne in a hushed tone, "I could not be easy until I had assured myself that no difficulty had befallen you. Naturally, I should be delighted to have Lord Sherworth take dinner with us tonight, but, although Elizabeth would assure me all was well, I could not but wonder at the—at the odd circumstances of his *requesting* to dine with us! I trust Mrs. Rigsby has come to no harm. If there is any way in which I can be of assistance to you—"

Under cover of guiding Lady Wildborne to a chair, Vescinda recovered her countenance. Her whirling brain sought to make sense of what she had just heard. How *could* he? Obviously, however, he had—and the only thing to account for it, unless he had taken leave of his senses, was that his lordship was doing his best to make an utter fool of her.

Taking a seat opposite her guest, Vescinda said calmly. "No, no, ma'am, you mustn't distress yourself. Mrs. Rigsby enjoys her usual robust health, and I am in no more difficulty than one might expect from a house that is topsy-turvy with activity. Lord Sherworth has naturally wished to renew his acquaintance with you. I think he has chosen this moment in order to spare us the necessity of entertaining him in the midst of our confusion. I only pray that his consideration for *our* convenience hasn't robbed you of yours."

Vescinda thought it sounded a lame and nonsensical explanation, but Lady Wildborne, relieved of the fear that her daughter might have done something outrageous in order to secure Lord Sherworth's presence, was able now to give full rein to the hopes that had begun to rise in her breast. She was entirely too excited to probe further into the good fortune that would place the biggest matrimonial prize in England at her table that evening. She assured, in a series of disjointed sentences, that she was most happy to be able to ease the situation for dear Miss Bancroft, and that it entailed no inconvenience—none whatsoever! She then took her leave, with the contradictory utterance that she must fly, because Miss Bancroft would understand that the news that they must prepare to receive so exalted a personage, at such short notice, would naturally cast her household all on end.

Vescinda was not surprised that Lady Wildborne's delight had overborne her curiosity, but she knew as well that calmer reflection would reanimate that curiosity, and that a good deal of unflattering conjecture would result. As she closed the door behind her caller, she compressed her lips and stood there for a moment, refusing to hear the militant drumbeat in her ear. Then, moving coolly over to the small writing table near the window, she dashed out a terse, though perfectly civil, note to the Right Honorable, The Earl of Sherworth. Affixing a seal, she walked briskly to the bellrope, only to hesitate there as she gathered up the necessary resolution to inform her butler that his lordship, for whom several special dishes had been ordered, would not be dining with them after all. Finally, she gave a determined tug, and, when Rigsby presented himself, delivered her message, adding, "You will explain to those concerned that his lordship had informed me of his plans, but that it had slipped my mind until now." Her eyes met his for a speaking moment. "No, Rigsby, I don't mean to try and hoax *you*. But I should be very much in your debt if you could manage to convey that impression to the others." She smiled with a little effort. "Odd though it may seem, I feel it infinitely more dignified to be thought hen-witted than ill-used."

Indeed, it did seem odd to Rigsby, extremely odd, and he was tempted to argue the point, until it occurred to him that no one *he* knew of would be the least bit likely to believe that Miss Vescinda was hen-witted. He nodded grimly and received her letter, along with the information that she was going to remain in her bedchamber until dinner.

Just as he reached the door, Vescinda called after him, "Oh, and

Rigsby, you do understand that I am not to be disturbed for anything short of fire in the main wing."

"Right, Miss Vescinda," he promised, allowing his stern expression to relax as he bowed himself out.

Sherworth returned to Blakely close onto five o'clock and was handed Vescinda's letter as he stepped over the threshold. He glanced at it indifferently, demanding to know her direction. He had spent seven hours cooling his temper and deciding how best to deal with the perfidious Miss Bancroft. He had returned prepared to give her the thorough trimming she so richly deserved, and then (for the sake of the countess) to accept her apology. This temperate view of the matter was severely threatened by the news that she had apparently barricaded herself in her bedchamber. A civil, but chilly, request that a message be taken to her bounced off Rigsby with no effect whatsoever, and a heated order that he summon his mistress at once was countered by the firm statement that he could take no order that ran contrary to those of his mistress.

Sherworth was toying with the notion of dragging Vescinda bodily from her feminine fortress when the butler's cool reminder that Lady Wildborne sat down to dinner at six, and in full dress, brought home the hideous memory that he had actually promised to dine there. At the same time, the look of reproach in Rigsby's eyes effectively recalled him to the offense he had committed against his hostess—first, in accepting an invitation to dine out so soon after his arrival and, second, in failing to so much as mention it to her. "Oh, damn!" he growled, as he pushed angrily past the butler. "Order my chaise put to and send my man to me." Halfway up the stairs he turned, adding, "And have something to drink brought up to me immediately."

Sherworth entered his chamber an equal prey to disgust and fury. He had planned to settle the issue with Vescinda with at least an hour to spare before dinner, and then to spend another pleasant evening casually attired. Instead he would be forced to scramble into full dress and to jolt over country lanes merely for the privilege of becoming a captive audience to the biggest bores in England—no doubt to sit for hours on end, in a torturous chair, carefully going over every banality the world had so far produced. That was bad enough, but, now before he could take Vescinda to task for *her* treachery, he was in the sorry position of having to beg her pardon.

It occurred to him to wonder how the devil Vescinda—and

apparently the entire Blakely household—had become aware of his commitment to dine away. He supposed ruefully that the answer lay in the slightly crumpled letter he was still holding. He broke the seal, recognizing at a glance the same flowing hand he had seen in the letter which had tricked him into coming to Dorsetshire. Her message was brief. She had managed to fob off Lady Wildborne with the tale that she'd been aware of his plans from the outset and hoped that he would be good enough not to disabuse her of that notion.

He was considerably incensed by the implication that he might do otherwise, and even more so to learn that the wretched Wildborne girl had had the audacity to tell her mother that *he* had begged a place at their table! He was so caught up in a fiendish plan to rid the world of the entire female population that he had drained off almost a full glass of the wine, which had been hurried into his room, before it struck him that it was unquestionably the vilest balderdash ever to come in his way—sabotaged, no doubt, by the indignant butler below! It occurred to him that he had, after all, only stipulated that *something* to drink be brought to him, and, to the surprise of the footman who had carried in the tray, his lordship collapsed onto the bed in a fit of laughing. Things had gotten just that bad.

10

VESCINDA HAD RETREATED to the quietude of her bedchamber, hoping to put the situation into proper perspective, and resolved to direct her thoughts along more reasonable lines. Just when she was congratulating herself on having made creditable work of this, the sound of Sherworth's chaise, springing off to the Wiidborne's, caused such a violence of feeling that she alarmed herself into an unaccustomed headache. Only a determination not to give rise to the humiliating theories, already budding in the minds of the household, forced her down at the appointed hour for dinner.

When at last she was able to rise from a meal that she had eaten with neither interest nor appetite, her temples were throbbing with the effort to appear cheerful and content with her company. She followed her aunt out of the dining room, leaving Lord Bancroft to sit in solitary state over his port. As they made their way up the stairs, she commented pleasantly on the progress of the house, but, the moment they were behind the closed doors of the drawing room, Chloe waved aside such idle remarks.

"There's no point to tippytoe round the issue," she said. "There's just no accounting for the fancies a man will take, more often than not for a female whom you or I wouldn't suppose to have the power to attach an imbecile! The deuce of it is that she managed to get her hooks into him in London, or you may be sure she wouldn't be having it all her own way now. Why, there isn't a doubt that if he had made your acquaintance first—"

"Aunt Chloe," Vescinda interrupted as gently as she could. "You mistake. I don't pretend to understand his—his fancy for Liza, but

106

he might have pursued it with my goodwill had he not seen fit to abuse my hospitality and make a mockery of my efforts to entertain him. There *can* be no excuse for the discourteous—no—the *insulting* course he has run today. I am as certain of that as I am determined that he shall have no opportunity to place me in such a humiliating position again."

"Can't say I blame you," sighed Chloe, who had known all along it would come to this. "What do you mean to do? Turn him out of the house?"

"Hardly," replied Vescinda in a tone that hinted she had already entertained this thought. "Among the many reasons that make such a course ineligible is the fact that it is not my house. It is Papa's. But there is an advantage in that fact. In the strictest sense, there can be no thought of *my* having a gentleman guest. So, Sherworth, too, belongs to Papa." She rose, according her aunt's amused gasp of approval a speaking nod. "Yes, I mean to wash my hands of him. And—I am sorry to say, for it imposes the problem on you—to abandon all duties which bring me in his way." As she spoke, she moved over to the boulle cabinet where she had left her reticule. She searched through its contents, finally producing a ring of keys. Taking these to her aunt, she said, "You, ma'am, are now mistress of this establishment—in *all* its capacities—including the dubious privilege of planning meals and entertainments for your rag-mannered stepbrother."

Chloe chuckled. "Oh, I'll deal with him right enough. But what of you? Are you off on an extended holiday?"

Vescinda seated herself again. "Certainly the simplest and most preferable solution. But precluded, I fear, by the absence of my companion. Oh—I daresay it wouldn't do for me to leave the district in any case. But my object shall certainly be to keep from the house as much as possible. I shall continue to see to the estate and, for the remainder of each day, visit with friends in the neighborhood. Unfortunately, I can think of no grounds that will permit me to avoid dining here—not without raising every brow in the county. However, I am reasonably sure that I shall find myself entirely too weary to sit up in the drawing room afterwards."

Chloe applauded this plan. "Well, that will pay him out."

"No—I doubt that," said Vescinda seriously. "On the contrary, I think it is precisely what he has hoped I would do. He tried in every way imaginable to alienate me when he first arrived. But I wouldn't be put off—persevering, you see," she added, with a mirthless laugh, "in what I conceived to be my duty. Evidently he reached the conclusion that, unless I could be taken off my guard, he would not succeed in setting up my back. I can only suppose that he deliberately lulled me into believing he was sanguine before delivering these final blows."

Chloe looked doubtful. "It don't seem like him. Such round-aboutation."

"Indeed, it seems unlike *anyone* in possession of his faculties!" Vescinda agreed, her own expression becoming perplexed. But she shrugged away her thoughts and said, "Perhaps there is another explanation. I can think of none. At all events, I do not seek revenge. Only to put an end to his persecution of me. And *that*, I am persauded, can only be achieved by having nothing more to do with him."

Since Chloe seemed unable to offer a better explanation for Sherworth's abusive behavior, a brief silence fell, which Vescinda finally broke by introducing a discussion designed to familiarize her aunt with the daily routine that would fall to her lot. With that much settled, she decided to give in to her headache and excuse herself.

She was passing over the landing on the way to her bedchamber just as her father was completing his painful ascent from the dining hall. He stopped suddenly, rounding on her, "What's this nonsense about Sherworth?" he demanded. "You, at least, have never made it an object to cut up my peace!"

Vescinda, pardonably startled, assured her father, "I—I think I can promise you that I shan't do so now."

Lord Bancroft looked at her from under scowling brows. "There's tattle running round the house that you may be going to fall into a decline."

"Dear God!"

"Well, I won't have it! Things are deuced uncomfortable around here as it is, without you turning into a watering pot like your mother. Ah—er—a good woman, in many ways, you understand, but more than her share of sensibility. What with vapors and spasms and blubbering, it was enough to send a man to an early grave."

Vescinda forbore to point out that he had thus far survived his wife by fifteen years.

"The whole business—sadly mismanaged," he went on. "Trust a pack of females! I'll go bail neither of them thought to warn you that there wasn't a farthing's hope of bringing Sherworth up to scratch! Still, you've got eyes in your head, haven't you? Not at all like you to be casting stones against the wind! Marriage ain't his style of things! Forget him! Plenty of fish in the sea. Handsome girl—handsome *dowry,* by God! No need to be wearing the willow, just because one buck don't choose to throw the handkerchief!"

"Papa, Papa," Vescinda exclaimed, between amusement and dismay, "I promise you, I have been aware of Lord Sherworth's views on matrimony from the outset, and I have not so much as considered him in that light."

"Eh? Then why the devil have you gone down into the dumps because he's off dangling after Wildborne's chit? Well," he relented, "daresay it's natural you'd be a trifle piqued. Though it's no reflection on you. None whatsoever. Merely not the thing to seduce *you* while a guest of mine!" Suddenly struck, he exclaimed, "And, by God, it's well that he remembered it! Or I'd have that damned grandmother of yours treating me to a lifetime of clapperjaw because *her* stepson gave you a slip on the shoulder! What's this?—oh—well—I say, that's all right then," he said approvingly, when Vescinda removed the hands she had thrown up to her face and he was able to see that her shaking was caused, not by tears, but by an attack of laughter.

"Dear Papa," she said, smiling up at him, "it is precisely what I have been needing. One of your scolds."

Vescinda continued up to her chamber then. Much of her tension had found release in laughter, but her thoughts were heavy with the embarrassing events of the day. She was still seated with a book yet unopened in her lap when Sherworth's postilions halted his chaise, below her window, and set him down at the entrance steps.

Sherworth's thoughts were quite as heavy as her own as he waited for Rigsby to admit him. Upon hearing that Vescinda was once again installed in her bedchamber, he set his jaw but made no comment. It went against the grain with him to be delayed in any course he'd set, and he hated to have unpleasantness hanging over his head. On the other hand, after passing a disagreeable day and a positively agonizing evening, he couldn't be altogether sorry that a confrontation with an outraged hostess must be postponed until morning.

Morning, however, failed to produce the indignant young lady of his imaginings. Waiting in the breakfast room, Sherworth instinctively braced himself when the door opened at the time she usually made her appearance, but it proved only to be Rigsby, bringing in a fresh pot of coffee. Sherworth waved aside the butler's offer to pour, saying that he would await Miss Bancroft. Upon being informed that Miss Bancroft had already left the house, he looked back blankly, then frowned toward the garden.

"For a walk?"

"No, my lord, she ordered her mare," replied Rigsby, feeling all the strangeness of having lived through this scene before.

Sherworth dismissed him curtly and remained at the mantel for a full hour, thinking that Vescinda would yet return to assume her place behind the coffee cups. Finally he poured out his own, found it little better than tepid, returned the cup none too gently to its saucer, and stalked out of the room. For the next three hours he roamed the sprawling house at random, needing to spend his natural energy. He would have liked to take out a horse himself, but he supposed that, in such vast and unfamiliar country, the odds were against his being able to run Vescinda to earth.

When luncheon was being set out in the dining hall and there was still no sign of her, he was tempted to ride over to the Coach and Horse and see if she might be found at her little table on the porch. Even as the thought occurred, he dismissed it, for a suspicion that Vescinda's absence was a deliberate effort to avoid him was fast becoming a conviction. It was the one place, among her usual haunts, where he might be expected to look for her, and that, in the circumstances, made it the most unlikely spot for her to be. His patience had already been sorely tried, and now, with this new complexion on the matter, his temper began to rise. After searching about the house, he discovered that the front windows of the drawing room commanded a view of all possible approaches to the stableyard. He stationed himself there, resolved to prevent her gaining the no-man's-land of her bedchamber before he'd had his say.

This excellent plan had unfortunate results. Shortly after he'd begun his vigil, he found himself neatly cornered by Miss Wildborne. He made an energetic effort to send her packing, pointing out that the ladies of the house were either absent or in a far-removed wing. Strong hints at the impropriety of her remaining in the room with him under such conditions went quite unheeded. Sherworth was at last forced to steel himself, as best he might, to endure her grating voice for what he hoped would be the accepted thirty-minute call. Miss Wildborne, however, rendered almost giddy by an opportunity that was as inexplicable as it was golden, rose above her slight regard for such fine points of etiquette and gave herself over to his lordship's entertainment for a trifle less than three hours.

Once Miss Wildborne had mercifully taken herself home to dinner, Sherworth had yet to endure another hour and a half at the drawing room window before his efforts were rewarded by a glimpse of Vescinda's mare trotting along a path leading out of the wood. He waited just long enough to be assured that she was heading toward the stableyard and then stormed out of the room and down the stairs. During his earlier search of the house, he had discovered the yellow saloon, and, though it lacked scope as a vantage point, he had marked it down as the most convenient place for a private interview. He found Rigsby hovering in the entrance hall and ordered him to fetch a bottle of madeira, adding, "In here! I want it within two minutes, and it had better be fit to drink, or you'll be the worse for it."

Rigsby, quite unperturbed, acknowledged these instructions with a bow and turned to set about their execution. The footman had reported Sherworth's strange reception of last night's wine, which, of course, Rigsby knew to have been sadly adulterated. He had been prepared to defend his "error" to the master if the young gentleman had been mean enough to report the incident, but, since he had evidently accepted his forfeit for having insulted the mistress, Rigsby considered their brief conflict to have been honorably resolved. Naturally he knew, without the saying, that such a man would not permit himself to be victimized a second time.

He delivered a glass and a decanter of Lord Bancroft's finest madeira to the yellow saloon well within the prescribed time, but was a little hesitant about Sherworth's next command.

"Your mistress is approaching the house at this minute. I intend to have private speech with her, and it's damnably near to dinnertime. I want you to take yourself off. I shall see that she's admitted."

After brief deliberation, Rigsby decided to comply. There could be no denying that the mistress had been playing bopeep in order to avoid just such a conversation, but, on the other hand, his lordship had likely learned his lesson by now, and Rigsby had his own reasons for wishing the young pair to make up their differences before dinner.

Consequently, when the large double doors were flung open to her, instead of finding the benevolent Rigsby, Vescinda was confronted by a furious scowl. Understandably surprised to find Lord Sherworth acting porter at her front door—Lord Sherworth, looking wild and fierce and like a stallion ready to strike—she froze into an exquisite statue, all in dove gray except for a billowing crimson feather, which spilled down from her hat and nestled over one ear.

"Where in hell have you been?" he rasped out.

Vescinda raised her brows in a way that seldom failed to bring even the most unruly of young men to order. It had absolutely no effect upon his lordship, who was plainly waiting, and none too patiently, for an answer. She said, in a cool voice, "I am not accustomed to explaining my movements, sir."

"Oh, aren't you just? Well, you'll explain this day's work! Do you want to *walk* into this room?"

There was, of course, no mistaking the implied alternative. Vescinda tossed her crop onto a nearby table, collected the long train of her skirt and stepped past him into the saloon he had indicated.

Following her in, he closed the door firmly, and stood before her, glaring down. "You may begin by explaining this little game you've been playing today."

"I don't play childish games with grown men, Lord Sherworth."

"Oh, no, my girl! That's coming it a trifle *too* strong!"

Vescinda met his accusing gaze for a moment, then said quietly, "I can think of no good reason to stand here and be cross-questioned when it's plain that you have no thought of believing anything I say."

With this she moved around him to go, but, before she had taken two steps, a viselike grip snatched her just above the elbow and spun her back. She dropped her train. Her arms flew up instinctively, and were caught round each wrist, breaking the impact as she fell against him. He held her like that, helpless, her head flung back, her breast heaving against his, as her breath came in short gasps. She was conscious of nothing but fierce blue eyes burning down into hers. Then the expression in those eyes changed, and the thought came to her—it came from a great distance—that he was going to kiss her. Her brain seemed to have gone numb. She remained like that, his eyes holding hers hypnotically. Then, not a moment too soon, her thoughts rallied. He had released her wrists; his hands were sliding up her arms to take her in an embrace. She choked an inarticulate protest and wrenched herself away. The hands, which had been so caressing, closed sharply on each shoulder and held her fast again.

If ever she had chafed under her intense chaperonage, if ever she had wondered of what real use it was, she saw its value now. There could be some doubt as to whether even the presence of a forbidding duenna would have had the power to curb Lord Sherworth's outrageous conduct, but it would have been a wondrous help in keeping *her* from dealing so inefficiently with the situation. Never in her life had she been permitted to be alone in a room with a man. And now, without notice or warning, she was actually being encouraged to cavort with this one—this one, who could not be managed by any means known to the civilized world! And once again he was a breath away from kissing her!

"Lord Sherworth!" she said sharply, as sharply as he had ever heard her speak.

It had its effect. The heat in his eyes cooled. His hold slackened. At length his arms dropped to his sides. He was looking a little amazed—at himself?—at her?

She was still badly shaken. She turned away, pressing her gloved fingers hard against the surface of a table for support. Glancing down, she saw the decanter. She extended a hand, found it unsteady and withdrew it again.

Sherworth caught the movement. "Is it wine that you want?" he asked, striding round to the opposite side of the small table. She didn't reply or even glance up to acknowledge his question, but he uncorked the decanter and began to pour. "There is only one glass. Will you take mine?"

She accepted the glass he held out to her, sipped twice and returned it to the table. Sherworth waited, a decided look of longing in his eyes. Finally, he asked, "Is that all you mean to drink?"

When she nodded, he snatched up the glass gratefully and

dashed off the remaining contents in one swallow, then said in a constrained tone, "I'm sorry. I—"

She lifted her hand in a gesture that bade him not trouble himself. "There is only one thing I would ask of you, Lord Sherworth, that you be good enough to return to London—or Brighton—or wherever it is that you'd prefer to be. I—I realize I have no right to turn you out of my father's house, but—"

"Oh, if it comes to that," he interrupted gruffly, "you're in a prime position to have him do it for you. Even, if it would please you, to have him call me out."

"No, sir," she flashed, "with my father still unable to sit without a pillow, no, it would *not* please me to see him embroiled in another duel!"

Her tone had held no trace of humor, but Sherworth couldn't help smiling at her words. "Well, evidently you're not conversant with the finer points of dueling, or you'd know that in my position I couldn't return his fire—not within the bounds of honor. Or do you suppose me to be incapable of acting with honor?"

"I have no doubt, when dealing with other *men,* that you are scrupulous upon the matter. I assure you, however, that I have no wish to see you shot. I wish merely to be spared further association with you."

She started to go, but he reached for her. She stiffened and flashed him a look mixed of incredulity and accusation.

"Oh, damn it!" he snapped. "I just want you to hear me out before you hide yourself away again. I can only suppose you're trying to brazen out your part in this affair, and I think you should know that Miss Wildborne peached on you yesterday."

Vescinda's eyes narrowed. She might have guessed that it had been Liza up to her tricks! She hadn't a notion what lies she had foisted upon his willing ears, but she replied in an icy tone, "Did she? Then all the more reason you should be anxious to quit this place and my society. I cannot think what has kept you this long."

"Among other things, you're forgetting the party."

"Oh, the party! Yes, we were to enjoy your guidance on proper conduct," she returned, glancing at her reddened wrist. "Do you know, my lord, I think I should prefer to muddle through without that. I quite realize that you consider my father ramshackle past reclaim, but I will tell you, if upon occasion he has contrived to make a fool of himself, he has *never* made one of me! Now, sir, unless I am permitted to go from this room, I shall be forced to dine in my riding clothes! But I shan't move from this spot until you assure me that I may do so unmolested."

"Famous! Having had *your* say, you flick away my complaints like a speck of dust, and want to scour off—and you don't mind using your curst female weapons to help you do it! Well it won't fadge. If that's what it takes to have five minutes speech with you, then so be it! You will remain as you are, or you will be very much molested!"

Vescinda compressed her lips and stood fast.

He nodded a grim approval of her decision. "To begin with, I want you to understand that I was extremely sorry—for your sake, as well as my own—when I was reminded by your butler that I had engaged myself to dine at the Wildbornes'. The error arose, not in that I forgot *your* dinner, but hers! I accepted—yes, *accepted*—that stupid invitation solely to rid your house of her yesterday morning, partly to spare *you* the embarrassment of having your treachery unfolded in her presence, and partly because I was too furious to trust myself much longer. There was no doubting her accusations, yet I came near to bursting a vessel in an effort to keep her from knowing that I had believed one word of them—again to spare you embarrassment! Then, yes, I left in a rage, and I stayed in a rage for most the day, trying all the while to find excuses for you! But did you once consider that *I* might have suffered discomfort on your account? No, all you could think to do was to hide yourself away so there could be no opportunity for me to defend my actions or take you to task for yours. And now, ma'am, again, without caring so much as a fig for the cause of my actions tonight—without even allowing the possibility that they may have been in part justified— you order me from your home! Rather shabby work from a lady of your obvious boldness! But I'll go. And gladly! You may depend upon being rid of me by morning!"

He stalked off to the door, saying over his shoulder, "*Now,* you may go and change your damned dress!"

11

SHERWORTH ARRIVED IN the drawing room just a few minutes before the dinner gong. Only Chloe and Lord Bancroft were gathered there. When Chloe rose to head down, Sherworth stepped forward and detained her, saying, "Can't you wait for Vescinda? I kept her talking, but I don't think she'll be very much longer."

"So, that's it!" said Chloe. "Might have known you'd contrive to corner her. She's not late. No doubt you know better than I why she's sent word that she has the headache."

Sherworth made a sour face and offered his arm impatiently. "Then let us go down by all means. You needn't look so concerned. I can promise you that her 'headache' will be gone by morning."

"And what am I to collect from that?" asked Chloe.

"Merely that I shall be cutting my stick."

"Going?" Chloe halted, jerking his arm.

"Don't alarm yourself. I have our hostess's permission. To be precise, it is at her—er—suggestion," he said, tugging her along.

"So, she's turned you out after all," Chloe said meditatively, lapsing then into silence until they reached the dining hall.

As they stepped into the large oak paneled room, Sherworth looked about him curiously. There was a decided air of festivity about the place. The chandeliers were more brightly lit; the table had been elaborately decorated; an ornate sideboard was stacked with packages artistically wrapped in silver paper and tied up with colored string; and, near to Lord Bancroft's place, stood a wine cooler boasting no less than half a dozen bottles of champagne. Its

116

presence alone at an informal table was worthy of note. Champagne had become so expensive since the war with France that many wealthy families had never so much as tasted it.

No sooner was Sherworth seated than the question in his mind was answered. Lord Bancroft boomed to his butler, "Well, man, it's here, and it's chilled—we may as well drink it. Yes, yes, open away." He glanced up. "Ah, Sherworth! Here's a treat for you. I laid this down—can't recall the exact date—the year before they took Louis's head. Excellent stuff! It's my little gel's birthday, but she stayed in the sun too long—or some such thing—and won't be down. But we'll drink her health all the same."

Sherworth's features were rigid as he lifted the glass Rigsby had filled for him. When he had drunk the toast, he rose, circling the long table to take a place beside Chloe, and asked in a harsh undervoice, "Why the devil wasn't I informed it was her birthday?"

"Now don't ride rusty with me, Sherworth. The fact is, you *were* informed. I heard Mama tell you myself. Oh—I *meant* to remind you, but you've been busy, chasing after the Wildborne hussy these past two days, and I've had my hands full here. Come to think of it, I haven't seen you until a few minutes ago. Well, why all the fuss? You aren't telling me you'd have behaved differently if you'd known it was her *birthday*, are you?"

"Unfortunately, we are no longer in a position to know," he said through gritted teeth. "But, damn it, I would certainly have provided myself with a gift for her."

"Oh, well, if that's all that's bothering you. It has all been settled. My mother sent everything down. She had an extremely dashing gown made up for the girl to wear at our ball. And, in behalf of Bancroft, she purchased a ruby necklace. There was no time for me to arrange anything—leaving all in a scramble as I did—so I had her order the matching set of earrings for me."

"And what of me?—the matching bracelet?" he enquired acidly.

"Oh, Sherworth, hold your tongue," whispered Chloe, glancing at the footman who had stepped up to serve the first of many elaborate dishes. "You know you can't give her jewelry. Mama sent a little music box. It's trumpery, of course, but as much as is proper for you to give. Well, I don't mean to say it isn't a perfectly fine gift. It's a small enameled box on ornate legs. Quite pretty. And it works well. Not that it signifies now—though perhaps you could leave it with a civil note."

When the servant stepped back to his post against the wall, she said in a low, urgent voice, "Listen, Sherworth, there's no need for you to be making a great piece of work over this business when you get back to town. The girl is extremely well-mannered, and, if she did something as uncivil as ordering you from the house, it could only be that she was wholly overset. And—well, I, for one, am glad to see you out of this. I've rather taken a liking to her."

Sherworth laid down his fork with menacing precision. "Madam, can you tell me how it comes about that in this veritable *nest* of female connivance, *I* am consistantly cast as the villian?"

Chloe choked on a filet of turbot which she had just conveyed to her mouth. Looking extremely conscious as she recovered, she drained off her wine and waved her glass at the butler.

Sherworth eyed her speculatively, but, seeing that Lord Bancroft's notice had been aroused, he waited until they were alone together, in the drawing room later that night, to pursue the matter with his stepsister. "Your rather dramatic reaction at dinner made it plain that you've been aware for sometime that your niece has been playing a deep game."

"No, no. I mean—I don't know what *you* mean."

"I mean that you have known all along that the facts set down in her letter were a pack of lies."

"No such thing! Sherworth, no, really. Every word the unvarnished truth!" His skeptical reception of her declaration made her add nervously: "Oh, drat! I daresay there can be no harm in telling you the whole at this juncture."

Sherworth listened with a variety of emotions as she explained the sleight of hand which had been used on him regarding Vescinda's letter. When she paused, he said solemnly, "Then, all along, it was Mama getting me into line and not— But *why?*— Oh, yes, of course. I was right in the first place. Matchmaking!"

"Yes. Except you thought my niece was a party to it. Not so! *She* supposed we'd come to bully her out of her plan to watch over the place until young Freddy can manage to get himself through Oxford. Well, can't deny that's true, too. Regardless of anything else, Mama *had* wanted that scheme put to rout."

Sherworth stared thoughtfully for a moment, then cast his mind back over the various conversations he had had with Vescinda, wondering if it *could* have been nothing but a misunderstanding between them. At last, he requested Chloe to recite the exact context of Vescinda's letter. When she had done so, he shook his head grimly.

"Yes," she nodded, "a sad mistake from start to finish. Can't think yet how Mama could have been so off in her reckoning. It strikes me, if she'd had some notion of bringing about a march between the two of you, she ought never to have drilled the girl into becoming such a high stickler." She paused, aware of having said something to arrest Sherworth's attention. Supposing that he hadn't put sense to her words, she tried to elucidate, "I just meant that a girl who's been instilled with such niceties of principle is bound to take exception to one of *your* stamp." Seeing that there was still an odd expression in his eyes, and fearing now that she had offended him, she went on hastily, "I'm not saying that you ain't the thing. Only that *she* is unusually fastidious. And, of course, I knew *you* wouldn't be interested in such a reserved and cool-blooded girl, whose every thought and act is governed by an—an *exhausting* regard for propriety."

He remained quiet for a moment, stroking his upper lip with the knuckle of his forefinger. "I find much to wonder at that a girl, stuck out here and continually dosed with the Bancroft influence, has managed to develop and maintain these qualities."

"Oh, well, of course Mama herself passed nearly all the time you were away at school down here. And I doubt the girl has been out from under Lady Elena's eye these fourteen years."

"Ah, of course, Lady Elena! Who might that be, and what has become of her?"

"One of Yaxley's daughters. Perhaps you don't recall. It was in 'ninety-eight—something to do with 'change, I think. Well, one way or another, the family fortune was knocked into horsenails. He died soon after and left the two girls without sixpence to scratch with. But Lady Sarah—the beauty of the two—managed to make a fairly creditable marriage in spite of it. Mama had been a friend to Lady Yaxley and knew the girls well. She knew that Lady Elena's pride would be bristling at the thought of battening on her new sister's husband, or of becoming a pensioner of Yaxley's heir. So she offered her the position of governess and companion to Louisa's girl. The child wasn't even out of the nursery at the time, but it worked to everyone's advantage. Lady Elena was able to hold onto her pride without going out into a life of drudgery and snubs. She has always been more of a member of the family here. Mama, on the other hand, was assured that, when Vescinda came of an age to require a governess, she would have the benefit of one whose own background and rearing were of the highest."

"And where is this examplar at the moment?"

"Oh, I arrived to find her champing at the bit because Lady Sarah is soon to be confined. The girl has no need of a chaperone while I am in the house, so we packed her off to visit her sister."

Sherworth nodded, thinking sardonically that it had been all most convenient—or very well arranged. For, had she remained, the Lady Elena might well have found herself unable to jeopardize fourteen years of careful surveillance by casting her charge adrift, as Chloe had been doing.

After a few minutes he rose, saying he thought he would follow his host's example and turn in.

And so, very early the next morning, Vescinda, standing at her chamber window, was able to watch his tall sporting carriage dissolve into the parkland trees. She remained, waiting until what appeared to be a miniature curricle, drawn by a pair of toy horses, came once more into view. Another moment, and it passed through the lodge gates, turned into the lane leading to Charmouth and disappeared for good.

At least a dozen times throughout an almost sleepless night, she had bordered on the edge of sending a message, begging him to disregard her uncivil words and to reconsider his decision to return to town. Each time she had found herself unable to do it, either from an unwillingness to lay herself open to a snub, or from a reanimated conviction that his departure was, all in all, for the best. She deplored the weakness that had betrayed her into such rudeness, but she was honest enough to admit that no miracle had suddenly imbued her with the strength and wisdom to assure that a similar incident wouldn't result, if Lord Sherworth were to remain. She realized, however, that she had been hopelessly foolish to become so overset by his aggressive behavior. Calmer reflection told her that there really hadn't been the least difficulty in depressing Sherworth's advances, once she had recovered her *own* senses. She no longer feared that he would forcibly take advantage of her. She supposed, in all truth, she never had feared that. But his unruly ways had a tendency to break down barriers—barriers that were essential to her dignity and self-esteem.

Besides, there were other good and sufficient reasons for wishing him gone. If there were circumstances she could forgive him, there were others quite capable of bringing the heat of anger to her cheeks. A little more of Lord Sherworth's society, and she'd be no better than a brawling fish wife. She was maddened each time she recalled that he had attached such weight to whatever impalpable tale Liza had poured into his ears that it had required an entire *day* for him to recover his temper. Was her credit not as good as Liza Wildborne's? Would it not have been as easy to believe in her innocence as in her guilt? Apart from the dreadful humiliation his gullibility had caused her, there was the unforgivable injustice of it. No, she rather thought that, if that was Lord Sherworth's notion of friendship, it was a far better thing to be rid of him.

She went downstairs then, and not long after rose listlessly from an unsatisfactory breakfast to take her conflicting thoughts for an airing in the garden. It sent shudders through her each time she thought of her grandmother. How often had the countess said that a well-trained lady should be able to deal with anyone from a king to a dustman? Certainly Lord Sherworth could not be denied a place within *those* bounds. And far worse than having failed so miserably in her duties as a hostess was knowing that her grandmother was extremely fond of the gentleman whom *she* had just expelled from her home.

Vescinda was still belaboring these depressing thoughts several hours later, as she wandered aimlessly through the shrubbery, when, rounding a bend in the path, she came face to face with the author of all her distress. She stopped short and exclaimed in amazement: "You!"

"Yes," agreed Sherworth, looking her over as if he were meeting her for the first time. He smiled disarmingly. "I've been in a quandary, wondering how I might persuade you to hear me. I owe you—oh, a dozen apologies." He took a step forward, his expression now earnest. "Vescinda, it really is important that you listen."

"I will listen," she said quietly.

She didn't know whether second thoughts had caused him to break his journey and turn back or if he had merely pretended to go in order to draw her out of her chamber, but, after the first shock of seeing him, she had been conscious of a great sense of relief. She had been given a second chance, and she must do better this time. She asked politely if he would like to come into the house.

He nodded, offering his arm, but, after only a step or two, he halted and exclaimed harshly, "*NO!* Is there nowhere else? Deeper into the garden? The woods? Anywhere where it will be impossible to find us!" He laughed at her look of astonishment. "Yes, that does sound shocking, doesn't it? But I only meant that it's about this time the blond harpy makes her intrusion. She cornered me for three hours yesterday, driving me to the edge of violence with her prittle-prattle. And today I have even stronger reason for wishing to strangle her."

A smile crept unbidden into Vescinda's eyes. "I see. I should be grateful then that today, at least, you are not wishing to strangle *me.*"

"You're in sad want of instruction, my girl, if you think *that* is what I was trying to do."

She gave a soft little laugh. "Come," she said, turning, "we shall walk to the lake."

Sherworth, already a little baffled by Vescinda's unexpected amiability, was even more taken aback by her calm reception of a remark he had realized, too late, had been most ill-judged. But now, unable to resist, he said, "Naturally I'm grateful—though, I own, a trifle surprised—that you aren't afraid to go off with me to a secluded place."

She glanced up at him as they walked along. "Oh—no—I doubt you're planning to get up to that sort of thing today."

"No," he agreed, but added provocatively, "but then, I wasn't *planning* to get up to that sort of thing last night. Of course, it *was* largely your fault. I did tell you, I believe, that you're an extremely tempting morsel. And you must allow that you didn't struggle or cut up at me for some time. There was just a moment there when I was quite sure that you *wanted* me to kiss you."

If he had expected confusion or an indignant disclaimer, he was disappointed. Vescinda replied simply, "Yes, I'm sorry. You are quite right. I was largely at fault."

Sherworth stopped her abruptly and turned her to face him. "Look here, are you saying that you *did* want me to kiss you?"

Vescinda couldn't help laughing at his incensed tone. "Now, take care, my lord. You mustn't let me cause you to fall into error again. It was—as you said—for 'just a moment there.' Does that surprise you? I don't know why it should. I'm sure you don't need me to tell you that you're a most attractive creature. And—well, naturally, I've been curious for some time as to what it would be like to be kissed. I see nothing to wonder at—having been taken off my guard, as I was—that I should have known a moment of temptation." Drawing herself gently out of his grasp and beginning to walk on, she added in sweet retaliation, "So, you see, you're a bit of a tempting morsel yourself."

Sherworth let her go, but stood fast. He found her enchanting, but a complete enigma. He hadn't been particularly overwhelmed by what Chloe had told him of her background. He had realized, as soon as his temper had calmed sufficiently to observe her dispassionately, that Vescinda was far from the romping hoyden he had been envisioning. And he had seen for himself, shortly after they had reached their understanding, that the cant expressions she used—often imperfectly—did not always fall easily from her lips. He had guessed that she was amusing herself by exaggerating her situation, but it had amused him far too much to hear her doing it for him to wish to call her on it. What he hadn't guessed, of course, was that she had been reared in the image of a pattern card, or that she'd been accustomed to extensive chaperonage. Rather, he had supposed her to have enjoyed an excessive amount of freedom and, having had little but the example of her Bancroft relations, to have known a deal *less* of the proprieties than the average gently bred girl.

Since he had been permitted to labor under this misconception, Chloe's words had shown him that, if Vescinda were innocent of perpetrating the hoax that had brought him to Dorsetshire, she had nonetheless been cutting a sham since his arrival. He had met this realization without rancor; it had been his own rude comments that had set her course. Actually, he'd found himself wishing he had known the truth during the time he'd had the "fastidious" Miss Bancroft deep in a discussion of Lady Hamilton's foibles.

Today, the diverting opportunity afforded by Vescinda's masquerade had tempted him to introduce the subject of his attempted kiss. But her reply—hardly the admission of a "reserved and cool-blooded girl, whose every thought and act was governed by an exhausting regard for propriety!"—had left his mind reeling with questions. There had seemed entirely too much frankness in her response for one bent on drawing a long bow! But what then? *Was* she merely playing out the hand he had mistakenly dealt her? Or was she sincerely complying with his request for informality? Or was she simply being herself—the real self that existed beneath all the rules and restrictions she'd been taught? He vowed that, if he did nothing else before quitting Dorsetshire, he'd learn the answer to that! And in the meantime, he expected to be thoroughly amused, trying to discover at just what point this somewhat unusual "high-stickler's" lively sense of humor would desert her in favor of all those years of rigid training.

Overtaking Vescinda, who was a few strides ahead, he asked, "Has anyone ever told you, Vescinda, that you are a trifle unpredictable?"

"Am I?" she smiled. "I daresay it comes with the petticoat. But what was it you wished to tell me?"

"Never mind that for a moment. I have a more urgent need to discover if I understood correctly. Can you really have meant that you've never been *kissed?* How can it be that Lord Bancroft's beautiful daughter has attained your years and never been kissed? The local bucks must be a parcel of slow tops."

"I—well, sir, even Lord Bancroft's daughter knows that one is expected to marry where one kisses."

"And who told you that, pray?"

"Why, I believe it was Grandmama who first mentioned it. Oh, goodness," she chuckled, "I have just recalled the actual incident. I was thirteen—possibly fourteen—and walking through our wood. All at once I came upon one of our dairymaids, *crushed* in an embrace with a young laborer. Naturally, I startled them. Indeed, they startled *me* as well! Alice, who is much of an age with me, broke free, blushing furiously. Actually, we were *both* blushing furiously and could only stare at one another. I found my voice first and mumbled an apology. But that suddenly struck me as excessively humorous. I mean that I should have felt compelled to apologize when, of course, I had the right to be there and they had not. Then, hearing me laugh, Alice's blush vanished, and she smiled. Oh, I shall never forget it—a smile which was positively eloquent of a shared understanding. But, of course, I didn't understand—not beyond a certain knowledge that that kiss had somehow filled Alice with a—with a *sublime* happiness."

Sherworth stopped and turned her toward him again. "But, my dear girl, you must not be kept in suspense a moment longer!"

"Ah, you are very good," she laughed, "but, like Alice, you are free to scatter your kisses among as many as may take your fancy. Whereas I must keep mine for just one."

"Was that Mama's counsel upon the matter?" he asked, taking her hand and tucking it in his arm as they continued down the path. She nodded, the smile still lingering in her eyes, and he remarked, "A romantic thought, no doubt, but the truth, I fear, is that—barring a mandate for discretion—you are quite as free as your dairymaid. No one can know how many you have kissed before you marry, and no one will care a fig for how many you kiss after."

"No, truly, is that what most fashionable men feel?" she asked, her smile fading. "I mean that sort of stupid indifference—not caring if their wives are unfaithful?"

"Perhaps not so much an indifference as a feeling that what cannot be cured must be endured."

"Oh, how *can* you think like that?" Vescinda demanded hotly. "As though all women were alike! Could you really just—just *accept* such conduct in your wife?"

"On the contrary, if I were foolish enough to marry, I should doubtless end on the scaffold for having murdered her, *and* whomever she was getting up to her tricks with."

"Oh, I'm so glad," she said, smiling again.

He choked on a laugh. "Lord, but you say the damnedest things!"

"Oh—!" she laughed back. "That did sound a bit tottyish. But what I meant was that I'm glad you feel that way, for it means there must be a great many others who do, too. I shouldn't at all like a complacent husband. Even if it were an arranged marriage—even if he didn't love me—I should want to feel a sense of—of belonging. And I should wish him to take pride in my conduct and depend upon me *not* to make him appear foolish by getting up to such tricks. And now you are staring at me as though I must have escaped from Bedlam. Well, never mind, no doubt I am a trifle— lacking in the upper works. Tell me what you wished to say."

He seemed as though he would comment, but thought better of it. He continued regarding her in an absorbed way, then recovered himself and replied with a sudden smile, "Oh!— Well, mainly, I wanted to tell you what Miss Wildborne said that caused me to behave so abominably."

"Yes, I will own to some curiosity about *that*."

A slight brittleness had crept into her tone, and he said, "Now don't start to ride grub. I trust that, when you are acquainted with the details, you'll agree that I was somewhat justified."

Vescinda kept her eyes on the path before her and said stiffly,

"My lord, I am prepared—without hearing another word—to overlook the entire incident, but I should warn you that *nothing* could make me agree that you were justified in believing unsubstantiated lies of me."

"Oh, but she didn't lie. What she told me is perfectly true."

This time Vescinda called the halt and looked up at him challengingly. He laughed and said, "Very intriguing—that green fire which sometimes lights in your eyes. But unwarranted upon this occasion because, as I recall, the essence of her message was that you had no intention of marrying Freddy."

"I should think not, indeed!" returned Vescinda, her eyes grown wide.

Encouraging her to stroll on, he relented, "I think, lovely Vescinda, that I had better tell you from the beginning."

They were almost at the lake when he had completed his story, and Vescinda, greatly entertained, confessed, "Yes, you were quite right. I excuse you of all blame. Dear me, but you have been sorely imposed upon in this business." She added hastily, "Of course, Grandmama meant it only for a joke. She couldn't know, after all, that Liza would get hold of it. Though, why my father should have discussed it with her, or even how he came to know—"

"Alas, now I must destroy all my credit with you and admit that I am undoubtedly at fault there." He told her of his meeting with Freddy in Silver Street, supposing it to have been the grapevine by which the news of his misapprehension had traveled, through Lord Bancroft, to Miss Wildborne.

Vescinda was too much distressed at hearing of Freddy's activities to have further interest in the misunderstanding. It had been with design that Sherworth had made her aware of the rackety life her cousin was leading. It was the first and most logical step toward showing her the futility of her efforts in his behalf. But, after walking along in silence and watching her lovely brow furrowed with concern, he grew impatient with the damper that he himself had cast over their amusement.

At last the path emerged into a clearing and there, glistening before them, was the lake from which Vescinda's home had taken its name. They both stopped automatically to gaze out over the prospect, but it was plain that Vescinda's mind was envisaging something far less agreeable. Sherworth turned her gently toward him and took her chin in his hand. "Come now, we can't have this blighting our day. We shall deal with Freddy presently."

"We? But why should you concern yourself?"

"Because, if it is a matter of concern to you, Mama would wish it of me. However, there is nothing that either of us can do until he arrives—and, if he manages to take all the pleasure from the days intervening, I shall be sorely tempted to deal too harshly with him."

"No, don't do that. I thank you for your offer, but I doubt that anything you said would weigh with him. I have some influence. Perhaps I shall be able to talk him round. But you are right. There is nothing to be gained by giving over to a fit of the dismals in the meantime." Since he continued to keep hold of her chin, she smiled questioningly. "Well, why do you stare?"

"I think, lovely Vescinda, that you did not sleep well."

"Hagged to death, am I?" she laughed, turning out of his hold. "No, I did not sleep well. I was plagued most of the night because I had been so uncivil to you."

"Were you, poor girl? Should you like to return home and have a nap?"

"Certainly not. I should rather you tell me where you went this morning—since it is plain that you *didn't* return to town."

"Ah, yes. And so I shall, but first we must find a place to sit."

"I fear that will present a bit of a problem. There are rustic seats on the other side of the lake, but they are in view of the road. If Liza is hunting you in earnest, she could sight you there. On the other hand—and even at the risk of sounding missish—I must tell you that I have no intention of returning to the house with both of us covered in grass stains."

Sherworth ran a quick eye over her white muslin gown, gave a thought to his own white doeskin breeches and agreed that some discretion would be advisable. "However," he said, "I have a solution. My coat, you will perceive, is nearly the same shade as that darker grass. We shall both sit on it, making use of that rock for a backrest."

Vescinda looked at him doubtfully. "Are you quite sure you wish to sacrifice that magnificent coat to such a cause?"

"I trust it will come to no permanent harm. We shall place it face up."

Matters, however, did not proceed with the anticipated simplicity. Sherworth found it necessary to enlist Vescinda's aid in removing his form-molded coat. This was a slow and tedious operation which she likened to trying to peel an unripened orange.

At last he took the coat from her, spread it on the grass and handed her down onto the place he'd made for her before the rock. Unfortunately, when he tried to take his place beside her, on its narrow surface, they found themselves forced to lean away from one another at an uncomfortably sharp angle.

"It's all the fault of your great Corinthian shoulders," Vescinda observed. "I daresay it would present an odd appearance, but don't you think we should contrive better if we were to sit back to back?"

"No. Here, see if you don't fare better *beneath* the shoulder."

Finding herself tucked under his arm and asked to say whether that wasn't better, Vescinda was at least able to agree that it was more *comfortable*. She couldn't help thinking, however, that, now, instead, they were presenting an extremely improper appearance. Finally consoled by the reflection that, unless Miss Wildborne enlisted Sir Harold's hounds to assist in the search for Lord Sherworth, there was little danger of being seen in such a posture, she was free to consider the unusual intimacy of her situation. She became a trifle embarrassed and ill-at-ease. She had never lounged in a man's embrace, and it was strangely disquieting. She could feel his breath on her forehead, and she could hear his heart beating within his breast—or was it her own? She stiffened instinctively.

But it was no part of Sherworth's plan to make matters easier for her. Giving her shoulder a squeeze, he leaned forward. "Are you quite certain, Vescinda, that you wouldn't like me to end your suspense and introduce you to the delights enjoyed by your dairymaid?"

"Quite. I don't wish to appear immodest, but I have had ample opportunity to end my suspense any time these many years."

"Oh? Has there been no one to see that you kept the line then?"

"That is not to the point. I daresay anyone wishing to partake of a stolen kiss might contrive it. *I* have always placed an importance on reserving the experience for the right time *and* the right person."

"But how can you know that this is not the right time or that I am not just the person?"

"Easily. The right person will be the man I wish to marry, and the right time will be when *he* wishes to marry me. Now, sir, since we will agree that you don't qualify on either count—and since it is becoming evident that you and I are destined to find ourselves in these rather unconventional circumstances—I am going to ask your word on the matter."

He laughed. "Very well. But you must keep your—'solemn promise,' I believe you called it. I shall agree not to rob you of your first kiss, but you must hold up your end and stop making me feel I have hold of a trapped hare."

Vescinda agreed, and Sherworth was moved, by the slightly nervous smile she gave as she wriggled into a more conformable position, to reward her by dropping a kiss onto her forehead.

"Oh!" she gasped, struggling unsuccessfully to sit up. "Oh, and—and after just *promising!*"

"What? That? Merely an unclelike kiss. You'll not tell me *that* was what you witnessed on that memorable day in your wood!"

Vescinda could tell him nothing because she had gone off into a peal of laughter. When she had recovered sufficiently, she cried, "And I thought you meant not to acknowledge the relationship! Oh, my, I wonder if you know how outrageous you are."

The incident had done much to banish her constraint. In a few minutes, she was completely composed and leaning against his side, her head resting comfortably on his breast. Except to think dreamily that it was extremely soothing, she paid no heed when he began to idly stroke her hair, but reminded him, stifling a little yawn, that he was to tell what he had been up to that morning. She was too relaxed to show much surprise when he announced that he had gone no farther afield than Bridport and only asked sleepily what had taken him there.

"Because we are going to turn back the calendar tonight and celebrate your birthday—a far grander celebration than the one I spoiled for you last night. I have obtained a turtle and delivered it to Mrs. Rigsby—who, to my infinite relief, knew precisely what to do with it. And I have secured a dozen or so of champagne—but, alas, nothing dating from before they took Louis's head."

"Did my father say that?" asked Vescinda with a ripple of laughter. But she was touched by his efforts to make things up to her, and added, "Naturally I should enjoy a party, of all things, but you needn't have incurred the expense of champagne. Papa prides himself on his cellars. I'm sure he has a deal put by."

"No doubt, but I wanted this to be my party."

She tilted her head to smile up at him. "How very kind you can be."

Sometime during her ensuing reflections on the inconsistency of his character, the effects of her wakeful night stole over her, and

Vescinda fell peacefully asleep. She awoke several hours later, momentarily confused at finding herself cradled in a strong pair of arms. Somehow she had turned right around and was hugging him like a great cuddly toy. She rolled her head back drowsily and found Sherworth smiling down at her. She returned his smile spontaneously.

"I told you, you were wanting a nap."

"Yes, well it seems I have had one. Have I slept long?"

"I'd gauge it to be between two and three hours."

"Oh, dear, such dull work for you. Why didn't you awaken me?"

"Impossible. To my understanding, Sleeping Beauty must only be awakened with a kiss, and I was bound by a promise."

"You'd have done well to have given me a good shake," she replied. Considering this as she settled back into what seemed an extremely pleasant and cozy nest, she added, "I'm glad you didn't, though. I feel marvelously rested."

Soon the cobwebs of sleep began to drift away, and she said, "We should get back. I expect you will be quite safe from Liza now."

12

IMMEDIATELY UPON REACHING the house, Vescinda slipped up to her bedchamber, fearing that Sherworth's efforts to restore her hair to a respectable state might have fallen wide of the mark. Sherworth, still in his shirtsleeves, lingered below to help himself from one of the decanters kept conveniently available during Lord Bancroft's occupancy.

He was cornered there by Chloe, who exclaimed, "Sherworth! I thought you were returning to town! What does this mean? What are you doing here?—half naked?—and—and with a turtle?"

He continued to pour his wine with maddening care, then tested its bouquet before replying. "The turtle, as I'm persuaded you've already discovered, is for our dinner. As for myself, I've altered my plans and shall be remaining for the duration of the party."

"But why? What point is there in continuing to torture the poor girl—driving her from her home with your antics? We agreed that Mama was trying to make cheese out of chalk with this scheme of hers—" She broke off, her face becoming ludicrous with dismay. "Oh, Sherworth, *no*—no, no, you *can't* have taken it into your head that Mama *expects* you to marry her! Oh, I can promise you it's no such thing! She's excessively fond of her granddaughter and wouldn't wish such a fate—er—I mean— Well, you know what you are when you do something against the grain. No, no, Mama might have nurtured the hope that the girl would somehow manage to fix your interest, but I *know*—why, she said as much!—that there would be no difficulty in finding any number of eligible suitors!"

131

"Chloe, spare yourself—and me—these flights. I'll allow that, in a desperate circumstance, I might have accommodated Mama in such a way—if the girl had ruined herself, or been left penniless— or if there had been any other reason to bar her becoming creditably established. But in Vescinda's case, such an act would be so unnecessary as to be stupid! I'm staying because I've wronged her— through no fault of my own, I might add—and I intend to make it up to her. One of the ways I can do that is by not placing her in another humiliating situation! Evidently you haven't thought the matter through, but what the devil do you suppose would be said if I were to duck this party after having come here expressly for it?"

Chloe couldn't deny the justice of this view. Sherworth's elder sister, who had bitterly resented her father's remarriage to the countess, had been trying for years to make mischief. The countess's reputation had remained so flawless, her position in society so secure, that Katherine had never found the means to do much harm, but an assault on Vescinda could perhaps cause the countess more hurt than a direct attack. Of course, Vescinda was as unlikely to become embroiled in a scandal as the countess, but word of Sherworth's having sheared off from a plot to trap him into marriage with the countess's granddaughter would have made a highly satisfactory tale.

Chloe was glad to see Sherworth thinking so sensibly and said that, if he would, now, only keep a guard on his wicked temper, they might swim through the business without a hitch.

"Unless one of you ladies has further bamboozling tricks in store for me, I can see no reason for my temper to come into play," he replied in a way that made Chloe bethink herself of something she had left undone in another part of the house.

Vescinda did not appear until dinnertime. When she did, it was to dazzle Sherworth with an exquisite gown of Pomona-green crepe, spangled and raised at the front hem to expose a pair of lovely feet, which were bare except for golden sandals. A long train trailed behind her, and on her wrist were three bands of gold, matching a larger one placed artistically round the knot of dusky hair piled high upon her head. The green of her eyes had never been more pronounced, and Sherworth couldn't help thinking that, presented with this vision, any artist worthy of his calling must rush from the room for his paints and brushes.

Sherworth honored the occasion by effecting a compromise with complete formality. He had exchanged his Hessian boots for soft shoes, but instead of satin knee breeches, he wore ankle-length stockinette pantaloons, and had arranged his neck cloth in the dashing, but more casual, mailcoach style.

The dining hall could scarcely have been made more gala than the night before, but, tonight, the long windows giving onto the terrace revealed several festoons of colored lanterns, which, when the late summer light had faded, could be set alight with the dozens of candles already waiting within them.

Seeing this exciting display, Vescinda exclaimed with delight and took a moment to walk over to the window to examine the colorful array more closely. "How perfectly lovely," she said to Sherworth, who had followed her over. "This must be your doing, for I know we have nothing like it. Wherever did you find them?"

"I waylaid them enroute to an outdoor festivity in Lyme Regis," he confessed without contrition. When she bit her lip to stifle a protesting laugh, he added dismissively, "I left them half the lot. They shall do."

By the time they returned to the table, Lord Bancroft had already sampled the wine and called out, "Very tolerable stuff, Sherworth. Very tolerable, indeed—for something got locally and in the light of day!" He waved his consent for Rigsby to pour all around and lifted his glass. "Well, puss, we're glad to have you with us tonight to toast your—your—"

Vescinda came to his rescue with a rippling laugh. "I am turned twenty, Papa."

"Ah, yes, twenty. The time gets away." He flourished his glass higher still. "To your twentieth birthday and your very good health."

When Sherworth had set down his glass, he said softly to Vescinda, "Now *you* must drink. I expect to hear the rafters ringing with your giggles tonight."

"I do not giggle," she informed him with dignity, as she sipped her wine.

"You will once you've drunk enough champagne," he smiled.

Chloe and Lord Bancroft entered into another of their heated debates, leaving Sherworth and Vescinda able to converse as they chose during the remainder of the meal. The side table was still stacked with the sparkling packages, and Sherworth had planned for Vescinda to open her presents before the ladies withdrew. But the last course was barely over when, suddenly, Lord Bancroft leaped to his feet, shouting, "Damme, woman! We shall just see!" Looking down the table, he announced, "Ain't staying for port! Sorry, Sherworth, but this—this *female* is trying to tell *me* of billiards! The wine shall be brought to the billiard room. Come!" he commanded of the company at large.

Chloe was already on her feet and followed swiftly in his wake, but Sherworth waited for Vescinda to finish the Rhenish cream she had been eating. She laid down her fork, amusement brimming in her eyes. "Shall you dislike it? I mean, rising from your dinner to oversee a contest. You needn't, you know. I shall leave you to have your port in peace if you wish it."

"What? I wouldn't miss this for the world. In fact, I wish you will get a spring in your step."

They reached the billiard room just as Rigsby arrived, laboring under a tray bearing the remainder of Sherworth's champagne, several bottles of port, and a jug of beer, which Chloe insisted she must have if she were to play billiards. After placing these on a table, Rigsby assisted the master out of his coat and the game began.

Chloe, from having spent years in a military installation where the only refreshment for months on end was home-brewed beer, and the only entertainment for forty miles was a billiard table, had become quite a dab. She took the lead and held it from the beginning. Lord Bancroft, many years and many many more bottles ago, had once been renowned for his prowess at the table, but he was plainly going to be no match for her tonight. What he lacked in skill, however, he more than surpassed in tenacity. Upon the completion of each game, after much blustering and protesting, he insisted that another be played. His frequent trips to the port did as little to improve his temper as his score, and Vescinda was twice forced to feign a mild coughing spell when Chloe, bringing off a particularly difficult and telling shot, caused her opponent to produce the snorting sounds of a bull.

After a few hours of this, Sherworth whispered to Vescinda, "Shall we slip away and open your presents?"

She hesitated before replying to this improprietous suggestion, as much from habit as anything. She was forced to laugh at herself as it occurred that she could do little that was *more* improprietous than napping in his arms, as she had that afternoon. She smiled and said, "Yes, let's do. I doubt of our being missed here, and I own I have been feeling a trifle ill-used to have been wrested from all those exciting packages."

Handing her their glasses, Sherworth tucked an unopened bottle of champagne under each arm. At the dining hall, he brought over a package and set it on the table before Vescinda, then deftly opened one of the bottles and filled both of their glasses.

Vescinda looked up from her unwrapping. "I think that will have to be the last for me. I am ever so slightly feeling what I've had already."

"Capital!" he approved, smiling at her exclamation of pleasure as she threw off the silver paper and revealed a prancing stallion entirely executed out of ropeends and knots.

"Oh, what a handsome fellow. Where did you find anything so clever?"

"Where they make the Bridport daggers," he returned, still smiling.

"Bridport, do you mean? But Bridport daggers—I have never heard of them."

"I daresay you haven't," he laughed. "Down here they think of themselves as making rope, but there are certain factions in London who refer to a hanging as having been stabbed with a Bridport dagger."

Vescinda shuddered and murmured a little sound of dismay, but, glancing down affectionately at her gift, she said, "Well, I'm glad that this rope was put to better use. Thank you. Indeed, I have never seen anything so charming in any of the shops."

"I came upon a sailor who was making it for his daughter."

She asked, with a slightly pained laugh, "My lord, do you always just take what you want?"

"No, I buy it," he replied, moving over to the sideboard and gathering up three more packages. Carrying them to her, he said drily, "I wanted you to have mine first because it could only be anticlimactic after these."

"I haven't a notion what these may contain, but you are quite out there. I shall treasure this always," Vescinda said in unmistakable sincerity. "People who have known me a very long time have never hit upon anything of such meaningness and—and so *darling*," she laughed, holding the jaunty little stallion in his natural position.

When the wrappings had been removed from the largest of the packages, it revealed a bandbox designating, in flourishing letters, the name and direction of one of London's most fashionable mantua-makers. Vescinda moved it aside, saying, "Since this obviously contains garments purchased by Grandmama, I shall wait and open it in my chamber. I shouldn't wish to put you to the blush."

"Oh, I doubt you could. I have patronized that particular shop on numerous occasions myself."

"I might have known," she chuckled, taking a little of the wine he pressed on her and turning her attention to one of the smaller packages.

When both the ruby necklace and earrings were exposed, Sherworth joined Vescinda in admiration of them, but said that they should have been emeralds. "You should wear nothing but green. You are positively ravishing in that gown."

"Thank you. But then I could never wear my beautiful rubies."

The lanterns had been lighted on the terrace, and Sherworth offered his hand. "Come, shall we go out now?"

She agreed at once, starting to rise, but, as her gaze rested on the sideboard, she slid back into her seat. "But there is another package. May I not have it too?"

"Oh, you may have it," he said negligently. "It is something Mama sent up to represent my gift to you."

Not looking at the small box he handed her, she kept her eyes fixed on his and said softly, "Thank you."

"Come, bring it along," he said brusquely, taking up the champagne and heading for the door.

Vescinda hastily removed the paper and left it behind on the table. She joined him on the terrace, announcing, "Oh, a music box! I was curious to see just what Grandmama would consider proper for you to give me." Sherworth showed no interest, until she lifted the lid and declared, "Oh, it is playing a waltz! It must be the very latest thing. How dashing of her."

"And how fortunate!" he exclaimed. "Now we can dance—or don't you waltz?"

"Well, I do, but not in this gown. I should become hopelessly tangled in the first turn and no doubt end in the shrubbery. Had I but known there would be dancing at this party, sir, I should have come suitably attired."

Sherworth looked impatient. "Nonsense. Can't you fling the train over your arm as you do with your riding habit?"

"Well—*no,*" she explained, her voice catching on a laugh. "The front is not long, you see, and, if I did that, I should have my legs exposed up to the knee—at the very least."

"Oh, well, if that's all, there need be nothing to concern you. Lady Jersey was just telling me—" He broke off to ask, "You know who she is, don't you?"

"The Regent's former mistress? Is hers to be the word that rules our conduct?"

He laughed. "No, no, you're thinking of Frances, the dowager countess. I am referring to Sally, who is near to my age and far, far too young to suit Prinny's predilection for the elderly."

"Ah, yes, I have it now. She is one of the patronesses of Almack's."

"That's it."

"And so you will tell me that one of London's highest sticklers deems it quite the thing for young females to romp about with their skirts hitched up to their thighs."

Sherworth gave a shout of laughter. "Shocking girl! Don't you realize that ladies are not supposed to know that they *have* thighs? No, I shan't tell you that. Actually she was complaining bitterly because that is what has been occurring at her precious Almack's since the waltz was introduced there last spring. Oh, not *hitched* up, but swirling up. She tells me the ladies have begun to purchase ornate garters since they are now continuously on display."

Vescinda finished off her champagne, set the glass down on a rock ledge which ran round the building and walked out under the lanterns. "Yes, but *she* does not approve of this."

He shrugged. "I mentioned it only to assure you that it *is* being done—and in the holiest of sanctums. Besides, why set Sally up as your model? There are six other patronesses, many who *do* approve. Nothing against, her, of course, but compared to some of the others, Sally is almost a mere mushroom—the granddaughter of a banker. What is more, her own parents set the town on its ear by being married over the anvil in Gretna Green."

"Oh—! Oh, is *she* the one?" Vescinda asked excitedly, taking the glass he had refilled for her. "Elena has told me of it, and I always thought it the most diverting and romantical of tales. I—"

"Elena?" Sherworth cut in on her.

"Yes, a very dear friend. Well, she *was* my governess, but I have been out of the schoolroom for some time now. But never mind that. What I found so amusing was that most wealthy bankers are usually making a grand fuss because they *wish* their daughters to marry into the nobility. But, when this Mr. Child's daughter was so obliging as to fall madly in love with an earl of ancient lineage, he was ready to go to any length to keep them apart."

"An exception, to be sure," Sherworth smiled. "Actually, the higher the rank, the less satisfactory for his purposes. He placed far more value on the continuation of his own name than in bringing a nobleman into his family."

"Yes, and naturally one could scarcely expect the poor earl to change *his* name, even for such a vast fortune. But that is what I found so impressive—that both of them, knowing they would be quite cut out of that fortune, chose to elope. Oh, of course, it was most improper, but rather dashing all the same, racing up the North Road, her papa's outriders in pursuit—and the bridegroom shooting from his carriage to ward them off!"

"He shot the horse out from under one of them," Sherworth informed her mischievously.

"No—! Oh, now you've destroyed all the romance for me," Vescinda complained reproachfully.

"I didn't know you were such a romantic, Vescinda."

"No, how should you, indeed," she said, sipping from her newly filled glass.

Sherworth, gleaming down at her, said smoothly, "Then, if that be true, you cannot refuse to waltz with me under the stars and these fairy lights."

She raised her eyes to his. "Oh, I should like to, truly, I should, but—"

"Then you must. After all, you can't be concerned for the plainness of your garters, for I noticed that your toes are bare. And besides, there is no one going to see your legs—however much of them are exposed! *I* shan't, more's the pity, for I shall have you in my arms."

The intriguing muscle in Vescinda's cheek pulled at her smile, making Sherworth suddenly feel a trifle heady. "Very true!" she exclaimed. "You are most clever! Ah, but I think you have been trying to get me foxed. Take this away," she adjured, handing him her glass. "And we shall indeed dance—until the candles gutter in their sockets if you like! You may be sure I shall like it excessively, for I have never waltzed with a man. Oh, my dancing master," she shrugged.

"A caper merchant will outshine my poor efforts," he said, taking her glass and his and carrying them to the rock ledge.

"Oh, no, no. You shall cast him completely into the shade, because you are tall and—and not *womanish*."

"I hope I'm not that," he laughed, propping his shoulders against the wall.

"You are not," she twinkled. "Not even a little. Well, why do you stay there?"

"To give you an opportunity to get your gown under control."

"Aha, but not *that* clever, my dear Sherworth! I don't mean to do so while you are yet ten feet away. You will first take me in your arms as agreed."

The last of the lanterns had plinked out before Vescinda dropped her gown and stepped out of Sherworth's arms for the last time that night.

During the next three days, she found herself in those arms, from one cause or another, most of the time. When they rode, he lifted her from the saddle, in his most improper way, each time they planned to alight, and, in much the same way, he helped her down from the heights of his curricle when they drove out. When he was advising her on matters in the estate room, he would pull her unceremoniously onto his knee in order to share his view of a paper he was holding, and, when they were walking over the fields, to inspect her father's estate, he would whisk her up at odd intervals to convey her over muddied ground.

At first, the unprecedented experience of feeling his arm pressing against her thighs, as he proceeded to carry her, shocked her into uttering an inarticulate protest. Sherworth, willfully misunder-standing, said that she wouldn't find the going quite so rough if she would lend a little assistance, by hanging on and helping to distribute her weight. "You don't exactly ride a feather, you know," he informed her outrageously.

Vescinda's eyes widened, but, as her mouth opened to take issue with this piece of effrontery, she burst out laughing and, instead, threw her arm up round his neck.

Not content with these forms of familiarity, more often than not, he led her about by the hand, even going so far as to slip his arm round her waist when he wished her to halt and take notice of something. And, through it all, he continued to beseige her with his "unclelike" kisses. In fact he deviled her unmercifully, leaving little undone that might put her to the blush or force her to go against the canons of propriety.

His persecution had been so pronounced, and had been so carefully timed to moments when they were alone, that Vescinda became convinced that he had somehow discovered that she was not the underbred creature he had expected to find in Lord Bancroft's daughter. She knew it behooved her to put an end to her charade, once it was plain that Sherworth was no longer deceived, but she knew as well that it would mean the end of so much that was comfortable and amusing. There would be nothing to justify the license she had been permitting Sherworth. She would have to conduct herself properly and insist that he do the same. Their talks would have to be confined, their jokes, guarded and abridged, even his foolish, harmless, little kisses stopped.

So she had said nothing. It was the end of the week—the day the remaining guests were due to arrive—and still she had done nothing to disrupt their game. They were breakfasting in the woods, in an effort to avoid Miss Wildborne, who had become wise to their habit of slipping out in advance of her call and had descended triumphantly upon them, in the breakfast room, on the previous day. Vescinda had braced herself for an all-day visit, which was precisely what should have transpired had Sherworth not surprised both ladies by glancing at the clock early in the afternoon and announcing that it was time for Vescinda's daily driving lesson. Miss Wildborne was effectively precluded, by the limited seating of a curricle, from joining them in this activity, but Sherworth was equally powerless to prevent her inveigling an invitation to dinner. Consequently, after an all-too-brief respite, her company had once again to be endured until tea. It was then that Sherworth evolved the scheme of quitting the house shortly after rising on the following morning, in order to preserve what he designated bitterly as their last day of peace.

Vescinda had readily agreed, and so, just slightly before ten on this day, they had galloped, with saddle bags bulging, along a little-used path in Lord Bancroft's wood. A site near a brook was chosen. Charger was tied with a long rope beside a lush clearing, and Twilight, who could be depended upon to come when called, was allowed to roam free.

Vescinda sat on a leafy patch of ground, frowning as she sorted through the ambitious amount of food and drink Mrs. Rigsby had packed into the saddle bags. Suddenly, Sherworth, perched on a fallen log beside her, leaned forward and lightly touched his lips to her brow. She glanced up, her intent look melting into a smile. More than any of the rest, these unexpected salutes had been a constant wonder to her. She knew that he had begun it as a means of tormenting her, but there were times—quite often, when she came to think about it—when she had failed to catch that all-too-familiar gleam in his deep-blue eyes. She was left to suppose—what other explanation could there be?—that he had been sincerely moved by a surge of affection. And so it appeared to be upon this occasion.

She held his gaze with her searching smile and said, "It has occurred to me that neither my father, nor Freddy, nor my cousin Robert, who was killed recently in America, has ever kissed me—or even so much as patted my hand—that I can recall. You must be unusually affectionate for a man. Or, at least— Are you?"

"Has it not occurred to you that it might not be a matter of sex, but one of family trait? Perhaps *none* of the Bancrofts, including yourself, possesses an affectionate nature."

"Are you roasting me, or do you truly believe that?"

Sherworth had come to know Vescinda well enough to believe no such thing, but he replied with a slightly wounded air, "Well, I can't help but wonder. Can you cite one instance when you have been moved by affection to kiss *me?* Er—of course, it could be simply that your affections have never been aroused where I—"

"You *are* roasting me. For you must know that ladies may never kiss gentlemen."

"Do I?"

"Well, I should have thought— It is my understanding that gentlemen, even husbands, dislike it excessively."

"Which gentleman told you so?" he asked drily.

"Well, none, of course. Have you—did your *chères amies* kiss you?" Vescinda asked, rooting once again through the overstuffed saddle bags.

"Certainly! Could hardly keep from it!"

An involuntary gurgle of laughter escaped her, as she murmured, "Incorrigible! Well, then, did you never find it annoying, or—or did you not take them in aversion for displaying that kind of forwardness?"

"Never. I liked it." Allowing a moment of the ensuing silence to pass, he asked, "Can you find nothing in there? I'm as hungry as a June cow."

"The difficulty is that I can find too much, and I don't like to unwrap everything and spread it before you on the *ground*." She passed him some ham put up into a sandwich, saying, "I think you must be right! I am referring to your *implication*. Obviously the system of having unmarried women instruct girls in what men do and do not like is a stupid one."

Polishing off a good sized bite of his sandwich, he agreed. "True. I am eminently more qualified to advise you on such points. Is there anything else you would like to know?"

"Well, if something should occur," she smiled, handing him a jar of ale, "I shan't hesitate to ask you, for I can think of no improper or indelicate subject into which you have not already led me. All the same," she sighed, "enlightenment on these matters would be of little use. For, whether it be fact or fallacy, every governess tells every girl the same things, and it has all been reiterated so many times and for so long that any variation would be considered highly improper." She sipped some coffee from a second jar and made a face. "This is barely warm. You are better off with the ale. I am fond of picnics in general, but not, I think, for breakfast—unless, of course, one were well rigged-out and could have a fire."

"If you didn't have such noisome neighbors, it wouldn't have been necessary."

"Oh, how shockingly unjust! When it is you, who are creating the problem! I assure you, when she was used to visit *me,* she did not stay all day and all night! Goodness, I would have come away with no breakfast at all in preference to another such day as you put me through yesterday!"

"*I?*"

"Yes, I was in the liveliest dread that at any moment you would cause me to laugh in her face."

"What? Are you so afraid of her?"

"Yes, my dear Sherworth, I am. She is as spiteful as she can stare and would lose no time in hatching up the most uncomfortable reprisal."

"But this isn't like you! The redoubtable girl who just galloped by my side to this spot?"

"What would you have me do? Females, you know, are barred from the tidy means by which gentlemen deal with insult. I cannot call her out and shoot her or run her through with a small sword. Or—or even tip her a settler! To engage Liza in a *lady's* battle, one must be prepared to be the subject of a dozen scandalous rumors—and that besides whatever *other* vindictive trick she might think to play off!"

"Sounds like Katherine," he observed, taking a swallow of ale.

"To a point, perhaps. Not so clever, I think, but in her way worse. From what I hear of Lady Oxbrook, she would never sacrifice her own dignity just to rob you of yours. Liza would!"

Riding along a few hours later, Sherworth said, "I collect there are ample provisions in those saddle bags to support us for a se'enight if we chose to stay out, but I have been thinking—with the guests arriving in a few hours, there will be no future opportunity—how would it be if we partook of a last luncheon at your Coach and Horse?"

Although this scheme had Vescinda's wholehearted approval, she hesitated. It would mean showing the world, or at least that portion of it in and around Charmouth, that she had been out riding with Sherworth without her groom in attendance. But the thought that returning for Archer would most likely land them smack in Liza Wildborne's clutches decided the matter for her. "Yes, let's," she said, thinking, as she turned Twilight in the direction of Charmouth, that, with so little time left to them, she should prefer to hope that her credit was good enough to carry her through this slight lapse.

13

THE MAILCOACH HAD already swept through Charmouth by the
time Vescinda and Sherworth reached the Coach and Horse. They
rode their horses directly to the stables and walked around to their
table. Sherworth insisted on the same fare that had been served
them on the first occasion, so there'd been nothing to do but nod to
the innkeeper when he stepped out onto the porch.

"We mustn't let the time get away from us today," Vescinda
said, as she drank the last of her cider.

Sherworth nodded. "Does the harpy dine with us again tonight?"

"Yes," Vescinda replied, not pretending to misunderstand, "but
that should at least spare you her presence when we return."

As she glanced out toward the bay, her attention fell on a young
gentleman, apparently lingering in the roadway for the express
purpose of catching her eye.

Her friendly wave was all the encouragement he required to
hurry over to the porch rail. He was as tall and as powerfully built
as Sherworth, but there was not the same look of agility or air of
fashion about his bearing. Vescinda performed the introductions,
and, although Mr. Davis bowed civilly and said everything that was
proper, his manner made it plain that, if he'd had the means to
make Sherworth disappear without a trace, he would have acted
without compunction.

At first only amused, Sherworth became steadily more impatient
as it began to appear that Mr. Davis intended to devour what was
left of the day by the simple device of relating every minor affliction

suffered by his family and then falling upon each trivial occurrence to have taken place in the neighborhood over the last decade. Sherworth eased himself into the conversation, first demanding absurd details of the slight complaint suffered by the young man's mother, and then forcing the unfortunate Mr. Davis to elaborate, in a ludicrous way, upon several mundane happenings, managing in the interim to fluster him into at least two embarrassing disclosures. Twice Vescinda attempted to intervene, but Sherworth refused to heed her and kept Mr. Davis entirely too busy to notice. Only after he judged to a nicety that 'the blond Adonis in the hideous waistcoat' (as he later stigmatized him to Vescinda) was sufficiently uncomfortable to welcome an opportunity to take his leave, did the rapid volley of questions abate.

As anticipated, Mr. Davis pleaded an errand at the chemist's and was well on his way when Vescinda called out to him. She walked the length of the porch and met him just out of Sherworth's hearing. No more than a minute was involved, but it was plain that she had worked miracles with Mr. Davis's lacerated feelings.

She rather thought, however, as she resumed her seat, that, if Sherworth's thunderous look was any indication, she wouldn't find the task of smoothing his ruffled feathers so easily managed. Was he jealous, she wondered, or merely enraged at having had his will crossed? She observed him calmly for a moment and then said, "Well, sir, you are looking as if you would like to murder me. I collect this sudden display of wrath is because I couldn't let poor Mr. Davis go off under the cloud of such a mortifying experience. I cannot suppose that, if he'd been small and puny, your sense of honor would have permitted you to—to *mill him down!* What you apparently don't realize is that a simple country gentleman such as he is just as unequally matched in the sophisticated battle of wits you forced upon him. What could the poor fellow do when you would—when you would—"

"It's called kittle-pitchering," supplied Sherworth helpfully. "Or at least a variation of it. Would you rather I'd planted him a facer?"

"No, but I have no doubt Mr. Davis would have." Reaching across the table and laying her hand over his, she smiled. "Come now, let us not be tiffing over Mr. Davis. I know you would not wish to be unkind, and there is no harm done. I invited him to join one of the riding parties, and he has already forgotten the other business."

Sherworth stared for a moment and then laughed. "And was that piece of magnanimity to spare my conscience or Davis's pride?"

"Both," she laughed back.

They returned to Blakely by the rear path and were greeted at the stable by an undergroom who informed them, in some excitement, that there had been a carriage accident and that Archer was busy seeing to the injured horses. He was unable to give particulars, but ventured that they would know more at the house, where the victims had been carried.

Vescinda cast an anxious glance at the stable and gathered up her skirt. Running to keep up with Sherworth's long strides, she followed him to the house. They stepped through the front door and into a state of pandemonium. Just inside the entrance hall, Mrs. Redding was ordering a scullery servant back into the kitchen to procure feathers from Mrs. Rigsby. It was her evident intention to make use of these to revive the young housemaid stretched unconscious at her feet. The stone floor and the grand stairway, which had been scrubbed to spotlessness only the day before, were covered with mud and bore evidence that a dozen or so hobbed boots had marched through. In the next instant, a footman, bounding toward the stairs, skidded in the mud and collided with the harassed housekeeper.

Vescinda rushed forward and helped to steady her. "Mrs. Redding, whatever has occurred?"

It was the footman who answered. "It's Master Freddy! He was carried in on a gate a few minutes since."

Vescinda was conscious of a strong supporting arm slipping round her waist just as Mrs. Redding took up the tale. Pointing an accusing finger at the unconscious girl, she said, "And this peagoose waited just long enough to set up the cry that he was dead before fainting clean away!"

Vescinda's color drained, but her voice was steady. "Is he seriously injured?" she asked, looking from her housekeeper to the footman. "Joseph, do you know?" she implored. But, hearing footfalls on the stair, she turned her attention hopefully toward her aunt, who had just started to descend.

Chloe informed a general audience as she came down, "Well, he ain't dead. Corpses don't utter oaths so poetically."

Almost immediately, a second footman appeared at the balcony and called down, "Mr. Rigsby says as— Oh, Miss Vescinda! Don't be in a fret, miss. His lor'ship's groom is above and says that Master Freddy ain't busted but one arm—for all he's bruised from one end to other. Overturned his high-perch, making the turn in here," he added, anticipating the next question.

Vescinda wilted a little from the relief and felt Sherworth's arm tighten. Without thinking, she covered the hand that held her with her own, as though to keep it firmly in place. "Thank you, John. And Freddy's groom? Has he been injured?"

"Ricked his ankle, jumping clear. Don't worrit, Miss Vescinda, your own Archer and the master's groom is seeing to the horses. An' a stable boy's gone for the doctor, an' others have gone to get the farm wagon and phaeton off the roadway. Was the farm chaps as brought Master Freddy to the house. They still be here, making a fair mess of the floors."

At this point, the scullery servant, a girl of no more than thirteen, ran back into the hall, strewing feathers in her wake and explaining, in an excited voice, that Mrs. Rigsby, who'd been fond of the poor dead gentleman, was in no fit state to think of feathers. She proudly produced two cupped hands, brimming with soft down, and announced, "But I snabbled 'em from that nasty goose what does chase ever'body and nips us regular in the bum!"

Sherworth choked on a laugh, and John in the gallery, bethinking himself of his original errand, called down, "Mr. Rigsby says as how Nelly is to be carted off somewhere as Miss Vescinda wouldn't wish her to be laying about the hall when them Lunnoner's comes in."

Sherworth began to shake again. Vescinda pinched his hand and whispered, before turning out of his hold, "Hush, abominable creature, or you'll set me off."

The acrid smell of burning feathers assailed her nostrils as she returned her attention to the drama in the hall. Joseph, evidently wishing to lose no time in adhering to his senior's orders, had taken the unfortunate Nelly by each wrist and was sliding her across the stone floor toward the kitchen. The enterprising scullery maid followed along, pressing singed feathers to her colleague's nose.

"Oh, do not *drag* her," Vescinda exclaimed.

Chloe, who had become oblivious to all but energetic plans with Mrs. Redding to restore the house, looked up at this outcry. She said with amusement, as she watched the young footman bundle the girl up into his powerful arms, "I see now—what with all your relatives having to be carried into the house, and your staff having to be toted about within—why you must needs keep such giants for footmen—" She broke off to shout to the scullery servant, "Girl, girl! Stop strewing those feathers about! Lord, what will we have next?"

Vescinda shook her head in a hopeless gesture and turned to Sherworth. "I must go to Mrs. Rigsby. If she truly believes Freddy to be dead, she must be in an agony of mind."

"And has no doubt ruined our dinner," Sherworth added helpfully.

When Vescinda returned to the hall, everyone but Sherworth, who was just coming in from outside, had disappeared. She made a slight gesture to him and started up the stairs.

"Hold on," he said, coming to her. "Where do you go now?"

"Why, to Freddy."

"I was afraid that was what you had in mind. No, my girl," he said, ushering her toward a high-backed chair in the main hall. "Cousin or no cousin, you will not visit an unbreeched man in his bedchambers—at least not until he has been properly rigged out and sobered up."

"Unbreeched? But they said it was his *arm* that had been broken!"

"Yes, but you can take it from me that whenever a man has the misfortune to injure himself in *any* way, the first thing everyone thinks to do is to add to his misery by robbing him of his breeches! How else do you suppose they were able to state that he was bruised *from one end to other?* Besides, I have it from Wiley that he is as drunk as David's sow and is mumbling such inventive phrases as would put *me* to the blush."

"Oh, dear, they *must* be bad," she said mischievously. "Very well, I shan't visit Freddy until he has recovered himself, but then I must—"

"You must sit a while and drink this wine I have poured for you," he said, pushing her into the chair and picking up a glass from the table beside it and holding it out to her.

"My dear, dear Sherworth, you are very good, and I appreciate your concern, but I cannot sit about sipping wine in the midst of a calamity. After I see about Freddy's horses—"

"I knew that would be your next concern and have already been to the stables," he interrupted. "Neither animal has sustained a permanent injury. One will most likely bear a scar from the cut on his knee; the other has only a sprain. Archer has treated them swiftly and expertly. I have also regaled the farm lads with several coachwheels and bid them refresh themselves at the nearest alehouse, explaining that everyone here is in too much of a pucker to extend the proper hospitality. Mrs. Redding is organizing a cleaning party, and Chloe has set out to restore order among the other servants. So, you see, there is nothing for you to do but—"

"But change my dress before the guests arrive."

"True. And so you shall when you have drunk this wine. You've been too caught up to realize it, but you've sustained a bit of a shock, and it *will* tell if you don't repose yourself a little before taking on an entire house party."

She took the glass he held out to her, smiling. "You will cause me to become spoiled and helpless if you cosset me in this way."

"You could do with a little cosseting. You've had too much on your—" He broke off to listen.

Suddenly, a male voice sounded near the main entrance. "What's this? Door flung open and nobody about! I'll be damned! Looks as if they've been holding a cock fight! Judging the feathers, I'd say the gray got the worst of it."

The owner of the voice appeared in the entrance hall. The position and height of Vescinda's chair hid her from sight, but he spied Sherworth and exclaimed, "Ho! Sherworth! You rascally devil, what sort of hell have you diddled us into?" He glanced over his shoulder: "Come along, Bobus. This is the place—God help us!"

In that instant, Sherworth's hand had shot out, pressing Vescinda's shoulder, adjuring her to keep hidden. He walked forward to greet Lord Edward, a tall, dashing blade with golden hair and blue eyes. "We've had an accident here, Ned. It will be best if you and Bobus go right on up to your chambers—"

"*Accident?* More like a turn up, I'd say."

"Yes, yes, but come along, Ned," coaxed Sherworth, trying to guide him toward the stairs. "There's a good fellow. Off to your chambers, and everything will be right as a trivet when you come down again."

"By Jove! *Is* it Sherworth? When did you become so sweet-tempered? Won't be for long, by God! We came by way of Brighton, and Worlington's been dangling after that high flyer of yours. And *she's* in a devil of a pucker at not having word from you since the note you scrawled off in London!"

"Never mind that. Just come—"

At this point, Mr. Bobus Wilkes, a sturdily built young man of medium height, joined them and added his mite. "Hallo, Sher. Think you ought to know that one of Bancroft's relatives told your Miss Stratton that Bancroft's daughter is a regular out-and-outer. Very put out, Miss Stratton is, old boy."

"Nothing to concern yourself about—"

"Oh, *no?*" Lord Edward broke in. "Charged me to tell you that, if you're too busy dancing attendance on your fine lady to remember what is to be with a *woman,* she might just accept a carte blanche from Worlington."

"Better take care, dear boy," warned Mr. Wilkes solicitously. "As prime a piece as ever I've clapped eyes on. Wouldn't do to let her slip the collar for want of a letter."

Sherworth's exasperation led him to laugh. "If it will ease your mind, I'll get off an express in the morning. Now, *will* you go up to your chambers!"

"Well, where the devil are they?" demanded Lord Edward, reasonably.

"My stepsister is somewhere on the first floor. Ask her!"

"By God, don't they keep servants in this damned place? Now, Sherworth, no need to come the ugly," he said hastily, going to the stairs. "I mean, *I* don't mind, it's just my valet ain't accustomed to such shabby arrangements."

Sherworth watched them out of sight and then returned to Vescinda.

It would not have been wonderful to suppose that a delicately nurtured damsel had been suffering a fair degree of mortification, but Sherworth's knowledge of Vescinda had led him only to fear that her lively sense of humor might cause her to betray her presence. He was certainly not prepared to find those brilliant green eyes blazing at him in undisguised fury, as she demanded, "Why did you constrain me to stay hidden here? I can assure you, my lord, that the details of your intrigues are of no interest to me!"

"Vescinda, for God's sake! After what had already passed, I thought it would be embarrassing for you both if Ned became aware that you had heard! I'm sorry for the nonsense that followed, but since your presence wasn't detected, no harm has come of it.

Actually, I thought to find you in whoops. We've joked about such—"

"Oh, yes, 'Lord Bancroft's ill-bred daughter!' Well, sir, I think you have discovered by now that Dorsetshire is not, after all, some little uncivilized corner of the world, that I have been provided with the guidance and instruction usual in one of my birth, and that, despite the disgust in which you hold my family, I have managed to grasp and retain the principles of breeding and good conduct! I agreed to the ribald atmosphere you find so necessary because it was my duty to keep you comfortable and entertained during your enforced stay, but only, you will recall, until the start of the party. Well, the party has begun! The game is over. In future, I shall expect you to conduct yourself in keeping with your presence in a gentleman's home, and to treat me with the respect due to his daughter. If you find yourself unequal to this task, let me recommend you to spare yourself the expense of an express and to lose no time in returning to your—your 'high flyer' in Brighton! And, while you're about it, sir, you may inform your Miss Stratton that, while few women know how to be a lady, *all* ladies know how to be a woman!"

She swept away, leaving Sherworth looking bewildered and a little hurt. She was experiencing a good deal of confusion herself, and, by the time she had gained the gallery, she was wondering how she could have spoken so unreasonably and with so little restraint. Upon reaching her bedchamber, she was forced to admit that the only explanation for her extraordinary conduct was that she had succumbed to a fit of jealousy, which was as unlike her as it was ridiculous. This led her to recall previous instances when an emotion all too similar had threatened her control, most notably, the day when she had believed Sherworth to have deserted her in favor of Liza Wildborne.

Such a disillusioning enlightenment into her own character was depressing enough, but it occurred to her that, at the same time as she had been making her impassioned speech in defense of her good breeding and training, she had been violating one of the foremost rules of both. Even ladies who might be supposed to have the right to feel that sort of jealousy—and she certainly had not—did not abuse gentlemen over 'the inevitable mistress.' Not only had she behaved with unspeakable impropriety, she had exposed herself most foolishly! For what else could it mean, but that she had allowed herself to become so accustomed to Sherworth's exclusive attentions that the mere thought that another had claim to those attentions had sent her into a jealous rage?

Only a few hours ago she had been regretting that the arrival of the guests must put an end to these carefree days, to the closeness, the casual intimacy she had been enjoying with Sherworth, that it would, in fact, force her to keep him, like the others, at a respectable distance. Now that she could see the danger of breaking such rules, it was well indeed that there should be no further opportunity for the sort of days that had just passed, no further opportunity for whatever madness that had taken possession of her to flourish!

When Vescinda came down again, beautifully gowned and prepared to receive her guests, she went directly to Sherworth, who was still standing in the hall, his surroundings much improved by the efficiency and diligence of the party of servants who had swept and scrubbed away all traces of mud and feathers. She apologized for her outburst, excusing herself on the grounds of having been overset by Freddy's accident and by the embarrassment of having had guests find her home in such disorder. Her voice was soft, her words pleasant, her tone perfectly polite. Yet there was a reserve in her manner, a coolness in her eyes that Sherworth had not witnessed in many a day.

As time passed and the guests began to arrive and assemble, and the party got into full swing, he was to wonder if the girl he thought he'd known had ever really existed. She was the same kind and thoughtful hostess, with the same unaffected and smoothly perfect manners, but, as he watched her dealing with each guest in his or her turn, he became aware of something new. At least he was made to wonder if it were new. It wasn't that she lost herself in a social mask or, in any way, projected something false or unreal, but, in some indefinable way, Vescinda seemed to become what each person wanted her to be.

Plumpish, faded, warmhearted Milissa was soon repeating a thousand times, the way she did when anything impressed her, that the countess's granddaughter was a dear, quiet, and gentle girl, who seemed to feel just as she ought. Milissa's daughters, however, found something quite different in Vescinda. Mary, Sherworth's favorite niece, a bit of a rebel with a determination not to be ruled by her sentiments, saw in her a kindred spirit, and a close friendship seemed to develop, between them, almost immediately. And young, effusive Kathy, still a year away from her first Season, had never met an 'older lady' who so well knew the difficulty of always minding one's tongue or curbing impetuous acts.

The formidable and self-consequential Katherine, although shown all the respect due a countess, was left to feel she had not sufficiently impressed the cool, self-possessed young lady who had greeted her with such a lack of consciousness. Yet, her ladyship's daughter, Charlotte, sadly lacking in confidence—in fact, a frightened mouse—was somehow never aware of that agonizing feeling of shyness when talking with one so able to understand, the way Miss Bancroft was, the terrors of confronting so many varied and overpowering personalities under one roof.

Sherworth couldn't help thinking that it all lent a rankling degree of credit to Vescinda's claim that she had merely adjusted her conduct and conversation with him in order to make him feel at home. On the other hand, he was somewhat mollified, as he considered her treatment of the gentlemen of the party. Though naturally each had made it plain that he too would have enjoyed a warmer and less formal relationship with Lord Bancroft's beautiful daughter, Vescinda showed not the smallest sign that she considered it any part of her duty, as hostess, to accommodate any of them in this way. On the contrary, she had an inexplicable though extremely effective way of making a man recall himself if he ventured, by word or act, a trifle beyond the line—and it was a strict and unwavering line that she drew! Of that, Sherworth was heartily glad, for he certainly hadn't chosen the gentlemen with an eye to what dependence could be reposed on their keeping a proper distance, and the matter had been causing him no small amount of concern for several days now. He knew, of course, that Sir Richard would neither insult nor harm her—out of affection and respect for the countess, if nothing else. And poor Bobus Wilkes was like putty in the hands of most any female. But, if there had been the least inkling that Vescinda would turn out to be the stunner that she was, he wouldn't have invited Lord Edward or Caversham within miles of the place.

He soon saw, however, that Lord Caversham, a corseted, scented dandy, would be no problem. He had followed his usual pattern of first trying to discomfit Vescinda with a cutting wit (learned imperfectly from Beau Brummell), but Vescinda had bowled him out in the preliminaries. Having no taste for females his match or more, he was thereafter content to reserve his crude flirtations for Miss Wildborne.

But Sherworth was grimly aware that Lord Edward would be quite another matter. Even the Princess Charlotte would not be spared Ned's special brand of gallantry if he judged her chaperone to be cajolable and her guardian complacent. Apart from finding it an agreeable sport himself, Lord Edward was convinced that all ladies secretly enjoyed improper advances. Vescinda's deft handling of him had so far kept him at bay, but Chloe's inexperience and Lord Bancroft's indifference made her a prime target. Sherworth was sure that Lord Edward would find his ground and become more and more familiar, and, sooner or later, he would kiss her if he could.

It became a matter of stern determination to Sherworth that Vescinda's first kiss not be taken from her in circumstances other than she had described. To that end, he devoted most of his time to watching over her whenever his amorous friend was at hand. By the end of the second day, however, he became aware of a perverse sense of irritation. Vescinda was apparently in no danger of having her valued first kiss wrested from her, nor, so it seemed, did she stand in need of his protection. Each time Lord Edward attempted a new stratagem, she countered it with a serviceable defense.

Sherworth began to feel foolish, like an overanxious dog following his mistress about in the misguided belief that he was guarding her from an unknown peril. Certainly he found no pleasure in her company! That was not to say that she didn't entertain and charm him as she did all the gentlemen. Actually, he thought bitterly, she divided her time between them with the precision of a well-made clock. But even when she chose to favor him, there was nothing of the girl who had laughed so delightfully and thrown her arm up round his neck and allowed him to carry her over muddied fields. There were no delicious gleams when he would try to tease her, no confiding tones in her conversation. In fact, if she remembered ever having met him before, *he* could see no sign of it. Gracious and polite, indeed, but Sherworth liked being considered the same as everyone else as little as any man; in fact, being totally unaccustomed to it, he liked it less.

And no more did he like feeling thoroughly unnecessary. Even his services as deputy host had proved to be unwanted. At first

Sherworth had put no great faith in Chloe's claim that she had been slowly raising Lord Bancroft up from himself, but it transpired that she had in fact worked miracles. He was playing his part with a goodwill and a surprising regard for good conduct. If his manners on occasion were a trifle frayed about the edges, there was certainly nothing in them to disgust.

It might have been supposed that Lord Bancroft's newfound respectability would provide a great many opportunities for two people who had been privy to the transformation to share a joke, if by no other means than a speaking glance across the room. But Vescinda made no attempt to catch Sherworth's eye, as she was used to do, nor was there ever a responding twinkle when he would try to catch hers. Alternating between vexation, umbrage, and boredom, he decided to come to grips with the situation, and, when next Vescinda granted him his innings, he took her arm and said, "Let us walk out onto the terrace."

"Quite impossible," she replied lightly.

"Not in the least impossible," he returned, tightening his hold on her elbow. "We have only to step this way."

"I trust you don't mean to drag me from the room," Vescinda said, the smile still on her lips, but a sharp warning in her eyes as she resisted his efforts to guide her away.

"The devil!" he hissed in a harsh undervoice. "Not a se'enight ago, I held you in my arms and danced the night long with you on that very spot. Now you make a piece of work about a few minutes' conversation."

"Your intellect is too good for you not to perceive the difference. *Then,* there was no one to observe such a breach of propriety. What is more, I should be accused of displaying a partiality—and justifiably—unless I agreed to step out of the room with each of the others."

"*Of course,* you will not step out of the room with the others!" he exploded. "Damn it, Vescinda, it's not the same thing!"

"My dear Sherworth, in what way could it be thought different? Like the rest, you are a young, unmarried man with libertine propensities and a loose interpretation of proper conduct."

He said in a stiff voice, "I had supposed the difference to lie in the relationship that—"

She broke in laughing, "No, no, that was very well as a joke, but we have no *true* relationship. Ours qualifies merely as a *connection*—

and that not of a nature to protect us from the gossip that would arise if we were to slip away together. Truly, I am sorry that you should be so bored. I know that you don't voluntarily put yourself in the way of females where these things must be considered, and, while no harm could come of it, I did my possible to make it up to you. However, you cannot expect me to *ruin* myself in such a cause! Besides, it wouldn't be fair. *All* of the gentlemen have been forced or tricked into coming here, and your desire to get up a flirtation is no greater than the others'."

She had judged his motives to a nicety, but Sherworth was piqued by her obvious indifference to a pastime he had supposed to be of equal enjoyment to them both, and said, "There *are* other reasons to seek privacy. As it happens, I wish to converse with you on a matter of importance."

Vescinda's eyes flew up to meet his, but quickly lowered again. She waited until she could be sure her voice would not betray the slight breathlessness she was feeling and asked, "May I know the nature of this important subject?"

"Yes. It concerns your cousin."

She smoothed her long gloves over her arms. "Freddy?" was all she could manage.

"Yes, as he concerns this nonsensical plan you have for hiding yourself away for another three years. It *was* to look into that that I was sent here."

"'To rescue me from my own folly,' I believe you said," she returned hollowly. Then drawing a resolute breath, she added briskly, "Well, I'm sorry, but I fear that in the eyes of those who concern themselves with such things, *that* would not justify our having a tête-à-tête on the terrace. Even I must wonder why, when you have had a full se'enight in which to perform this duty, you should have waited until a party was in progress."

"Then wonder no more!" he snapped. "It was Mama's express wish that I wait until Freddy had arrived before taking up the issue."

"I see. Then I will of course hear you, but you will have to arrange for my aunt to be present at the interview."

"The devil!"

"Yes, this is all very tiresome for you. However, the only alternative I can offer is to tell you that such a discussion will accomplish nothing." She glanced about her. "We have been talking too long. I must circulate amongst the others."

Sherworth stood, frowning after her. It occurred to him that, with so much on his mind, he had clean forgotten that her determination to stand guard over young Bancroft's inheritance was a matter yet unresolved. After gazing thoughtfully at the ceiling for a few minutes, he walked purposefully over to Chloe and drew her unceremoniously away from a discussion she'd been having with his two sisters.

Once out of earshot of the others, he informed her impatiently, "I must settle this business about Vescinda's remaining on here after the party, but it's impossible to get more than five minutes' uninterrupted conversation with her, and she refuses to come away with me unless *you* are present."

Chloe nodded. "No doubt she's right. If Katherine saw you go off together, she'd have it that you'd seduced her. You know she would."

"Normally," he said frostily, "one might expect leniency amongst one's own family. Instead, we are more hidebound with rules and cautions here than at an Almack's assembly! Damn it, Mama is usually such a knowing one. If she'd harbored even the remotest hope of bringing off a match at this affair, why the devil did she saddle us with *Katherine*—making it effectively impossible for me to even *talk* to the girl?"

"Wondered that myself," confided Chloe. "But I don't think Mama's thoughts have been too steady on this subject. Still," she allowed, "I daresay it wouldn't have been easy to induce many females to attend such a party, and, without Katherine, I doubt she could have secured Milissa and the girls."

"Folly! All of it! Filling the place with rakes and shrews, and expecting me to solve this 'little problem' in the midst of all the hubbub!"

14

SHERWORTH WOULD HAVE liked to scoop up Vescinda and go immediately to one of the saloons, but Chloe wouldn't hear of it. They were getting up an impromtu dance, and she had exacted Lord Bancroft's promise to stand up with her. In a burst of unwonted punctilio, Sherworth reminded her that her role as chaperone made her ineligible to take part in the dancing, but all Chloe would say was, "Pooh! The girl is well up to snuff. Knows better than I how she should go on." So, in the end, he had to be content with her promise to schedule the interview after church, on the following day, when there would be no organized entertainment.

The time in between was not designed to appease one of an impatient disposition. With Freddy still confined to his room, Sherworth was obliged to participate in the dance. For, even with Lady Milissa and Lady Oxbrook abstaining—one to supply them music, on the pianoforte, and the other to supervise the proceedings—Miss Wildborne's presence brought the number of ladies planning to join in to a total of six. Unfortunately, before Sherworth had even become aware of the program, Vescinda's hand had been solicited for more dances than the night could possibly hold, and so it fell to him to stand up with each of his less interesting nieces: sixteen-year-old Kathy and boringly shy Charlotte. Having borne this with as good grace as might be expected in a man of his temperament, he had yet, upon the following morning, to sit through an endless sermon delivered in the droning accents of a country parson, and then to stand by while Vescinda's local suitors vied with the gentlemen of the party for a word with her after the services.

Finally, as they stepped back into the house, Vescinda favored him with her friendly smile and said, "I collect you mean to treat me to a lecture on the folly of my plans after all. Very well, let me just run up and put off my bonnet and gloves, and I shall join you in the bookroom. I think we shall be most private there."

Good to her word, Vescinda followed Chloe into the bookroom a few minutes later. She was still in the dress she had worn to church. It was appropriately simple, high-waisted with a narrow skirt and made of white jaconet muslin. There was no ornamentation on her gown or on her person, but, as she reposed herself in an attitude of polite attention, Sherworth was thinking that there were few ladies in England who wouldn't trade every jewel in their possession for the glow in her complexion, the sparkle in her expressive eyes, and the shimmering lights in her rich, deep-brown hair.

Waiting only for Chloe to be seated, he addressed himself to Vescinda, and, not mincing matters, declared: "I shall begin by telling you that, under no circumstances, are you going through with this stupid plan of yours."

Vescinda exclaimed with her delightful laugh, "Oh, no, no, no! You are supposed to solve the problem, not *bully* me."

"That *is* how he solves problems," Chloe informed her.

Ignoring his stepsister's remark, Sherworth replied, "The *problem,* as everyone delights in calling it, exists only in your mind. Good God, Vescinda, you have seen for yourself what a complete reveler your cousin has become!"

"Yes, yes, I have," she agreed sadly. "But the way to cure him of his bad habits is not to abandon him to them."

Sherworth refrained from venturing an opinion on her ability to cure a young hellion, who would, if nothing else, be entirely out of her reach. "My dear girl, as I understand it, you believe you must remain here until Freddy is able to come down and take the reins into his own hands. What if he fails to complete his education? Or what if, at the end of three years, he is merely disinclined to assume the responsibility of his uncle's estates? Shall you wait five years? Ten? The rest of your life?"

"No, no, of course, I will not. I must grant him *three* years, because that is what is required. But, if he fails to make use of them, or, if at the end of that period, he is unable to see where his interests lie, I shall feel myself free of obligation."

"And you will have wasted all that time."

"Naturally, I should not remain a moment if I could see into the future and *know* that would be the result. But we can none of us know what his attitudes may be when he grows a little older. I am persuaded, however, that they shan't be much improved if, in the meantime, his only prospects are let fall into ruin."

Sherworth hesitated briefly, then said, "Very well, we shall grant that Freddy must have his opportunity. Let us instead examine the matter from another view. Are you so sure the place will fall into ruin?"

"If you are thinking that Papa *must* concern himself once I go off, it is most unlikely. He has quite a large fortune invested in the funds and will not feel the pinch if the estate ceases to produce its proper income." Observing that Sherworth was frowning thoughtfully, she added, "But Papa's private fortune is not a prospect upon which *Freddy* can rely. It is not part of the entail and will come to me. Or are you thinking that I should make it over to him? That will not answer because it shall not—I pray—be forthcoming for a long, long time and will naturally pass directly into my husband's control."

"No, I wasn't thinking that," he smiled. "I was *supposing* that the place must be entailed and thinking that your father could be forced to hire an agent."

"What? Take my own father into court? Oh, I daresay you are thinking that that is for Freddy to do. No—impossible! Besides being terrified of Papa, he is dependent upon him for his allowance. At all events, I have already thought of trying if I could persuade Papa to hire an agent, but Mr. Tilsdale tells me that, with the entire family out of the county on a year-round basis, most agents would be tempted, by such indifference, to—what did he call it?— to crib the proceeds and deprive the tenants. Then, too, you do not understand West Country people. At least it is so with those in this district. They are suspicious of strangers and would become insecure without a Bancroft on the Bancroft estates. I mean, if the house were just to be shut up indefinitely. Then we should lose our good tenants—most of whom have been with us for generations— and—and, well, there are so many objections that it comes down to being a very risky plan."

Sherworth had seated himself opposite Vescinda and was leaning forward, his forearms resting on his knees. He smiled and took one of her hands. Chloe watched in unholy amusement, as her niece retrieved her hand as unobtrusively as possible, and could only wonder that her stepbrother hadn't learned by now that Vescinda wouldn't brook the sort of liberties he was accustomed to take for granted. She gave him credit at least for not flying into a miff.

His smile merely broadened as he said, "Very well, lovely Vescinda, I shan't press those points. Whether you have judged the matter correctly isn't an issue—only what will, or will not, permit you to feel at peace with it. Just one more question: If Freddy didn't exist, should you be teasing yourself about the place itself? I mean, would your fondness for Blakely make you unwilling to go off and leave it in the hands of an agent?"

She couldn't help responding to his teasing smile, and twinkling green eyes met roguish blue ones in a moment of silent communication. "I am almost afraid to answer," she chuckled, "knowing how much you dislike obstacles to be set in your path. I trust you don't mean to settle the matter by murdering my poor cousin." Her reply, however, was serious. "No, I should, of course, be sorry to learn of its deterioration, but I am not such a zany that I would jeopardize my future for the sake of a home that can never be mine."

"Then the *problem* is solved," said Sherworth, rising. "You will instruct your maid to pack for you, because you will be departing with us for London on Friday."

Chloe, who had been sitting in pensive silence, started at these words. "Daresay I missed something. How did you arrive at that?"

"Yes, if you please," said Vescinda. "I was quite convinced that we had reached what you would call point non plus."

"Bah! It is simplicity itself! Your father shall be persuaded to hire an agent. We shall set Mama onto him, if necessary. And, so that you may be easy, I shall see that a sum is placed in trust that will be adequate to restore Blakely to its present yield. The trust shall be paid, at the end of three years, should it be found that the agent has in fact cribbed the proceeds to the detriment of the estate, and, of course, only if Freddy has actually graduated from Oxford and is willing to take charge down here at that time."

Vescinda's hand had flown to her cheek where a not unattractive flush had risen. "No, oh, no! Dear God, I could never permit you to do such an extravagant thing!"

Such animation in her niece's manner was new to Chloe. She was moved to pat her hand. "No need to distress yourself about the proprieties. My mother *told* Sherworth that she was relying upon him to resolve the business. Said that, regardless of all else, you mustn't waste three years down here. Depend upon it, if she doesn't actually supply the sum in question, which she may very well do, she will arrange it so that no one shall be the wiser."

Vescinda stared blankly for a moment, then waved away this reassurance. "No, no. I could not allow *anyone* to assume the expenses of my father's estate merely to accommodate me in what, I am persuaded, you all consider a most nonsensical flight."

Sherworth was looking extremely annoyed, but he did not attempt to argue with her, nor, for that matter, did he have anything further to say on the subject. Yet, when Vescinda stepped out of the bookroom a few minutes later, she was far from the belief that he had viewed her protest as a happy release. On the contrary, she was much of the opinion that, unless she did indeed instruct Dorcas to pack for her, she might well find herself departing for London with nothing but what she stood up in. This thought did not much trouble her; she had always intended to go for a visit. And, although she had meant to wait until after the Little Season, so that there could be no temptation for her grandmother to exert herself in her behalf, she supposed it would be as well to make the journey now, while there was any number of male escorts readily to hand. Something of far greater moment teased her mind. Her aunt had supplied an explanation for Sherworth's extravagant solution to her problem—he had himself once said something along the same lines—but somehow she was left with the impression that he had not been acting for her grandmother when he'd described the means by which he meant to free her. Yet, if he *had* been speaking for himself, surely it could only mean that he wished to make her his wife! Apart from the impropriety of his extending such a sum in any *other* circumstance, it was most unlikely that it would occur to him to do so.

Vescinda was almost annoyed with him for having raised the question. It was one which she'd been careful not to entertain in the past, and she couldn't help thinking that she'd be wise not to do so now. He had warned her—in the most bludgeoning way—not to take any such notion into her head. She had thought him a most complete coxcomb and had been nothing but amused when she'd promised that she would not. Yet, when he had asked for a private interview, her nonsensical heart had leaped right into her throat. And, with the folly of *that* error still fresh in her mind, she was most foolishly toying with the idea again! She tried to put it from her mind, by telling herself that she was being fanciful, that if he'd had any thought of marriage he would have said so. It clearly behooved her to forget the entire incident, but no sooner had she resolved to do this than it occurred to her that perhaps he was in doubt as to whether she would *welcome* an offer from him. God knew she had done her best to convince him that she would not! She supposed it was entirely possible that his plan was to see if she became more receptive once the obstacle of Freddy had been removed.

That was all very well, she thought with unaccustomed irritability, but, with his intentions so vague and Lady Oxbrook watching her every move, how could he expect her to *provide* him with that sort of encouragement? She dared not give his odious sister the opportunity to spread it abroad that she had set her cap at him, particularly when it was all too possible that she had misjudged his feelings. Just when her annoyance had reached its height, she was forced to smile as the thought darted through her mind that, really, much must be forgiven him, for it could not be doubted that, in the area of proper courtship, the outrageous Earl of Sherworth had no experience whatsoever! The real problem was that she was allowing herself to be overcome by the same sort of impatience that characterized his behavior. Time would resolve the question, and in the meanwhile she could occupy herself with trying to discover if her great, wild stallion was indeed looking beyond mere flirtation, or if it was only a bout of wishful thinking on her part.

However, the contradictory disclosures made to her as the day progressed did nothing to lessen Vescinda's quandary. She went directly from the interview with Sherworth to join Freddy, who, despite many representations of the danger to his health, had insisted on coming down into company. She found him on the terrace, his arm dramatically caught up in a black silk sling, and his entire attention caught up in Sherworth's youngest niece. Apart from a trifle too much animation in his manner, he was behaving quite unexceptionally, and, since young Kathy was obviously enjoying his youthful gallantry, Vescinda was content to sit quietly by, providing chaparonage in an unobtrusive way, while her mind drifted between their artless conversation and her own thoughts. It was not long, however, before Lady Oxbrook loomed onto the scene and bore her niece inexorably away, barely troubling to conceal the fact that she considered Mr. Bancroft a most undesirable association.

Their footfalls had scarcely faded when Freddy observed, with a disgusted shake of his head, "A regular horse's godmother, that one."

Vescinda noted with relief that Lady Oxbrook was safely out of range and replied with a stifled laugh, "Yes, but whatever that may be, I beg you will not mention it within Sherworth's hearing."

"Lord, *he* don't care. Don't like her above half, himself. It's probably the only thing we'd be likely to agree on. Devilish fine girl though, that niece of his."

"Yes, she is very pretty, but do remember that she is not out yet."

"Oh, *out*. For that matter, neither are you, but that don't stop all these bucks from angling after you with a silver hook."

"Freddy," Vescinda begged, becoming alarmed. "Oh, do not even *think* of behaving improperly to Sherworth's niece!"

"Oh, the devil! Sherworth this and Sherworth that! You've said little else to me since I arrived. You'd better mind you don't end up in Kensington."

This cryptic utterance caused Vescinda to stare fixedly at him, wondering if perhaps a fever had begun to come on. At last she laughed. "I daresay that makes sense to you, but I cannot begin to understand why I should wish to go to Kensington."

"Well, I hope you *won't* wish it. It's where Sherworth houses his convenients. Has a place there, *and*, just to put you on your guard, there ain't anybody residing there at the present!"

Vescinda thought caustically that, unless someone named Worlington managed to steal Miss Stratton in the meantime, that little omission would shortly be made right. She said dampeningly, "Don't be a goose. You know Sherworth would not suggest such a thing to me."

"Well, I hadn't thought he would. Supposed you not to be in his style, but he's been looking devilishly besotted."

She glanced up. "I don't know why you should say that."

"For one thing, I saw him following you into the house when you got back from church. Looked as though he'd have liked to drag you to the nearest hedge."

"Oh, *Freddy,* that is not the same thing," she said despairingly.

"I reckon it is to Sherworth. Keeps himself well out of anything that smacks of a more permanent entanglement."

Vescinda murmured a mechanical protest, but her thoughts had flown away. She would have liked to demand an account of his conversation with Miss Stratton. She knew the relative, mentioned by Mr. Wilkes, who had described her to Sherworth's mistress, could be none other than Freddy, but she could not admit to having overheard that particular conversation.

Since she had determined not to take her roisterous cousin to task for his misdeeds in London until he was more recovered from his accident, and the temptation to do so was proving almost overwhelming, Vescinda soon excused herself and went back into the house. Lord Edward must have been lying in wait for her, because just as she entered the yellow saloon through the door giving onto the terrace, he was slipping in by way of the door that led from the entrance hall. It was scarcely a minute before Vescinda emerged into the hall, alone and unruffled, and found Sherworth bearing down upon her with a look of mingled apprehension and menace.

"What has he done to you?" he demanded, glaring over her shoulder at the innocent door.

Vescinda took his arm as though he had come with no greater purpose than to escort her, and said calmly, "He has done nothing to me. Come, we shall look in on Papa and Lord Caversham, who suppose no one knows they are irreligeously playing piquet in the blue saloon."

Her serenity had its effect. He turned grimly and began to walk with her, observing, with a perverse satisfaction, "I might have realized that you would have no need for *my* assistance."

She glanced thoughtfully at him, then smiled. "Ah, but you have been of the greatest assistance to me. Actually, I have imposed upon you in the most infamous way, because I find that the only means of curbing Lord Edward's ardor are quite beyond my power."

"But you said—" He broke off, causing her to halt. "I saw him rush out of the dining hall and slip into that room in such a havey-cavey way that I made sure he was after you." He looked searchingly at her and asked gently, the calm in his voice betrayed only by the tensing muscles in his arm, "Did he ruin your first kiss for you, Vescinda?"

She shook her head. "No, but he was certainly determined to try. None of my most effective set-downs seemed to weigh with him. He even had the effrontery to inform me that I needn't fear for my father's displeasure, because he was convinced that we might have run off together three days ago, and Papa would not know of it yet. I was beginning to think myself at a stand, when I recalled that he had seemed a little afraid of you—you know, on the day he arrived, and you began to lose patience with him. So I warned him that, if he kissed me, I would desire you to tip him a settler."

Sherworth gave a shout of laughter and looked so much as though he would take her in a great hug that she whispered urgently, "Mind what you are about, or *you* shall land me in the suds."

Sherworth nodded, the amusement lingering in his eyes. "Ah, yes, you so reminded me of a girl who once lived here that I almost embraced the formidable Miss Bancroft. Did you really say that to him, Vescinda?" he asked with a chuckle.

She did not answer right away; her thoughts had arrested on his first remark. The sound of footfalls on the stair brought her to herself, and she bade him walk along again. "No, not quite that," she replied in response to his question. "I told him that, if he supposed I had no other protector, he would shortly find himself having to answer to Lord Sherworth." Watching him from under her lashes, she added, "Of course, I made it plain that you were acting purely on my grandmother's account."

It seemed as though he would say nothing, but at last he spoke. "No doubt that was for the best. Ned is a sad rattle and might otherwise have spread it about that he had been caught poaching on my private preserves."

And if that little piece of artfulness has told me anything at all, it was not what I wished to know, Vescinda said to herself a short while later, as she strolled away from Sherworth in answer to Lady Oxbrook's beckoning gesture.

Lady Oxbrook's purpose in summoning Vescinda to her side was evidently to increase such doubts as were already forming. She congratulated her for the good sense she had thus far shown in not rising to the bait of one whom Lady Oxbrook knew only too well to be merely trifling. After expanding upon this theme briefly and warning Vescinda to continue with the levelheadedness she had shown in setting Sherworth at a distance, she moved regally off. No sooner had she stepped out of earshot than Mary, who had been seated nearby, ostensibly scanning the pages of a recent number of the *Ladies' Monthly Museum,* came over to Vescinda, a speculative expression in her deep-blue eyes, which, like her rich chestnut hair, were so like Sherworth's own.

She said, without a hint of consciousness, "No doubt you will say that I was eavesdropping—"

"My dear Mary," Vescinda laughed, "I shouldn't dream of saying that. Were you?"

"I daresay I was," Mary laughed back. "At least, I couldn't help overhearing my aunt hinting you away from my Uncle Sher, and that made me too entirely curious to shut my ears. I haven't a guess how you may feel about him, and I don't suppose you'll tell me, but, if I know my Aunt Katherine—and unhappily I know her only too well, I'd say she'd be more inclined to encourage you to set your cap at him—if, that is, she truly believed he was merely trifling."

Vescinda hesitated, then replied with the same frankness. "Yes, I have been warned that Lady Oxbrook would be only too pleased to make use of me to embarrass Grandmama. But how could she presume to know what Sherworth's sentiments may be? She cannot be in his confidence, after all."

"Hardly," said Mary disdainfully. "But she keeps a malicious eye on him, and I'll warrant she knows him fairly well."

If Mary harbored the belief that she too knew him fairly well, that belief was badly shaken in the next moment, when Miss Wildborne tripped up to them and demanded that they wish her happy. "Just as I foretold," she announced triumphantly, "I am soon to be the Countess of Sherworth!"

Mary's astonished eyes flew to Vescinda, who, except for a slight paleness, appeared to have received the startling news with unimpaired calm. After only the slightest pause, she said, "Why, yes, Liza, indeed I shall, if Sherworth has offered for you."

"Oh, well, he hasn't yet, but he means to. I have just learned that there is a wager between him and Lord Caversham—an extremely *large* sum to go to the man who wins my hand."

"And was it Lord Caversham who told you of this wager?" Vescinda asked.

"No, of course not! Caversham is clever enough to realize that he would be completely cut out if I were assured of Sherworth's intentions. I overheard Mr. Wilkes telling Lord Edward of it."

"But, Liza, only consider—it could be a mistake. If Sherworth has given you no sign—"

"Oh," Miss Wildborne tittered. "I daresay this *does* quite dash *your* aspirations. Well, I'm sorry if his *appearing* to have a partiality for you has raised false expectations, but, as I have told you often and often, you simply don't understand these things. Depend upon it, he has been trying to pique me. That, and—as my father would tell you—'A good sportsman does not follow his quarry too closely.'"

Mary, bristling in defense of her friend, said mendaciously, "Miss Wildborne, I think you should know that only moments ago I had the impertinence to ask, and Vescinda assured me, that she *has* no expectations where my uncle is concerned."

But Miss Wildborne only smiled in a way that made Mary yearn to box her ears and flitted away again.

"She does have a way with her," Vescinda remarked, her eyes brimming with amusement at Mary's shock and indignation.

"Insufferable! I vow I don't know how you managed to hold yourself. Is she as mad as Bedlam, or can her shocking tale *possibly* be true?"

A worried furrow returned to Vescinda's brow. "Oh, I could not be more certain that Sherworth hasn't the smallest intention of offering for her. As to the wager, I cannot say. It *may* be all a mistake, but I very much fear it was some form of joke."

This estimation of the affair was confirmed in a conversation with Sir Richard later that evening. Possibly because he was Sherworth's closest friend, or perhaps it was the affection in which he held her grandmother, but, of all the gentlemen guests, Vescinda was most at her ease with Sir Richard. So, after chatting with him for a short while, she glanced over to where Sherworth stood, drumming his fingers in boredom on the mantel shelf, and remarked lightly, "I very much fear that Sherworth will lose both his money and Miss Wildborne to Lord Caversham if he doesn't bestir himself a little."

"Ah, told you of that, did he?" replied Sir Richard, mistaking her source. "It genuinely tickled Lady Sher, the way we brought off Caversham with *that* little hookee walker."

Vescinda afforded this communication as much of a smile as she could muster. In other circumstances, she might have thought it quite as amusing as her grandmother had, but now, thanks to the indiscretion of one or more of the gentlemen, Miss Wildborne had become aware of it, and the repercussions of her fury could very well turn their little joke into something extremely disagreeable. She glanced again at Sherworth and thought of telling him that Miss Wildborne had learned of his disreputable wager. However, short of actually offering to marry her, a remedy which Vescinda was by no means prepared to advocate, there was really very little he could do to make use of her warning.

The evening wore to a close with everyone a trifle restless from the day's inactivity. The talk was all of the riding expedition that was scheduled for the next morning. It was agreed that an early start was called for and settled that they should all meet for a sustaining breakfast at nine.

However, when Sherworth entered the breakfast room at the appointed hour, he found several vacant seats, most notably, Vescinda's and Lord Edward's. Chloe launched immediately into a recital of the menu and recommended him to try the anchovy toast, but Mary, meeting his eyes in silent understanding, said at the first opportunity, "A local gentleman who is to ride with us has brought over his new hunter. Just after Ves went out to try his paces, Lord Ned decided to have a look at—"

She trailed off, for Sherworth was already on his way, leaving Lady Oxbrook to comment acidly that it was quite a novel experience to see Sherworth concerned with the *defense* of innocent females.

Mary and young Kathy exchanged looks of despair, as their mother, without really attending, supported Lady Oxbrook's observation.

Sherworth crunched swiftly along the gravel path to the stable, but drew up short at the sight of Vescinda galloping a well-ribbed-up hunter straight at a tall fence. He let out his breath as she came easily over it, and continued walking, a look of admiration softening the sternness of his features. As he rounded the bend, he saw Lord Edward standing a few feet from a gentleman whom he had no trouble recognizing as Mr. Davis. He thought acidly that they looked like a pair of blond gladiators, poised to pounce on Vescinda as soon as she came within bounds.

She brought the hunter sidling up beside Mr. Davis, her lovely face alive with exhilaration. She was apparently extolling the virtues of the animal, whose glossy neck she patted as she spoke, when Lord Edward slipped between the horse and his owner and reached up as if to take Vescinda by the waist. Mr. Davis, in a swift action, clamped a strong hand on his shoulder and sent him staggering backwards, advising him that *that* was not the way to assist Miss Bancroft from a horse. At the same time, as if to demonstrate his point, he held up his right hand for Vescinda to take as a support as she dismounted.

Vescinda accepted his hand and sprang lightly down, but said chillingly, "I shall take it as a favor if neither of you are so foolish as to enlarge upon this incident. You will both excuse me now, if you please. I must see to something in the stables."

Sherworth, almost up with them, veered off to the right with the intention of intercepting her, but Lord Edward detained him, complaining, as he watched Mr. Davis lead his horse over to a post where a groom waited to remove the ladies saddle, "The devil! Who is that curst clodpole? I think he's broken my shoulder. Has a grip like the jaw of a bear!"

Equally annoyed with both gentlemen, Sherworth merely recommended him to have his man see to his injury and pushed his way past, lengthening his stride in order to overtake Vescinda.

15

At the sound of footsteps quickening behind her, Vescinda turned, an expression of annoyance on her countenance. When she saw that it was Sherworth, however, she took on an aspect of concern and asked, "Ought not you to remain with them in the event Lord Edward takes it into his head to issue a challenge, or whatever foolish thing—"

"Does Davis have the right to interfere in matters concerning you?" he broke in.

"None that I have granted him, but—"

"Then, since you hadn't yet raised an objection, Ned was well within his rights to demand satisfaction. The bumpkin may count himself fortunate that Ned—as you have already discerned—is not disposed toward fighting."

"Oh, it is all so absurd! But nevertheless I think it may be Lord Edward's good fortune that matters have gone no farther. George Davis—besides being as strong as a bull—is accounted a masterly shot. Everyone remarks it."

Sherworth made an impatient gesture. "Enough of them both! Come, walk with me. I trust we may have a little privacy *here* without raising a breeze."

"For a little while," she agreed, falling into step with him. "What is it you wish to discuss?"

"I don't wish to *discuss* anything. I wish to *tell* you how elegant, how dashing, how maddeningly beautiful you are in that habit."

"Oh—well, if you mean to converse along *those* lines, you may be sure of my fullest attention," Vescinda returned, her eyes laughing up at him from under a long, green ostrich feather that curled round a small black beaver riding hat, trimmed with gold cordon and tassles *à la militaire*. Today she had quite deliberately worn the emerald green creation her maid had suggested shortly after Sherworth's arrival. She let him guide her to a bench and seated herself in compliance to a slight wave of his hand.

Sherworth placed a booted foot on the edge of the bench beside her, resting one arm on his knee. He seemed about to comment when his attention was caught by the sight of Archer taking up the saddle that had been removed from Mr. Davis's hunter and setting it atop a tall, lean bay. Looking down at Vescinda in some concern, he asked, "Isn't that your saddle? Has Twilight come to harm?"

"Oh, no, she is well," Vescinda assured him. Then, recalling his reference to the "formidable Miss Bancroft," she paused, and, instead of fobbing him off with the explanation she had prepared for those who might enquire after her mare, she said, "Archer has advised me to ride Elmer because Midnight is to be of the party."

Sherworth nodded his understanding in an offhand way, causing a smile to flicker across Vescinda's lips, as she thought of how wonderfully unaware he was that she had just made a flagrant sacrifice of proper delicacy. After a moment she went on. "At all events we may expect to have a time of it today. Even when Midnight isn't feeling particularly amorous, he has a tendency to herd the mares away from the rest of the party."

Now this did shock him. "Good God, is he so ill-mannered? I thought the harpy could at least ride."

"Oh, Liza is a superb horsewoman! However, Midnight is a trifle strong for her, and she cannot always keep him from behaving like the dashing stallion that he is."

"You sound as if you approve."

"If you are speaking of Liza, then, no, naturally I cannot approve of everyone being made uncomfortable because she insists on bringing him into such a situation just to puff off her consequence. But if you are referring to Midnight, I cannot think *approve* an apt term. He is a stallion. Ought I to admire him less because he displays the spirit of one? You may be sure that I don't wish to see that spirit driven out of him, simply to make it possible for Liza to manage him as though he were—as though he were *Elmer!* But I could, however, wish to see him in the hands of someone capable of maintaining control *without* changing him."

"And you think you could be that person," said Sherworth, smiling down at her.

"I'm not sure," she replied with a slight frown. "I daresay not."

"But you'd like to try."

"Oh, yes, I'd like to try. Ah," she exclaimed, tilting her head as the shrill protests of a stallion sounded in the distance. "There he is now. I've asked Liza to keep him well away from the stables—or he will be wishing to make a morning call." Laughing at the sound of a responsive whinny, she added, "And who can blame him, when Twilight will flirt so outrageously?"

Sherworth said, with more affection than reproof, "You *ought* to have insisted that she keep him well away from the party altogether."

"Yes, well, I did suggest it, but I should have had as much success had I told the ocean to stop rolling for a day."

He just shook his head and remarked, "I shouldn't have thought you could spare Twilight and still be able to mount this group of ours."

"No. But Mr. Davis is coming to our rescue. He has returned home to fetch an extra hack of his own."

"You've discussed this with that fellow?" demanded Sherworth, his expression turning at once to one of censure.

Vescinda just managed to catch herself before replying and, instead, asked, "Oh, do you think it so improper to mention such things to a gentleman?"

"You *know* that it is," he retorted.

"Oh, dear," she said contritely, "then I daresay I must beg pardon for having sullied *your* ears—but, you know, you *did* ask." She burst out laughing at his look of menace. "Yes, yes," she gasped, "you will tell me that it is *not* the same thing! And, indeed, I must have caught the trick of such original thinking, because I shouldn't dream of broaching such a subject with Mr. Davis. For one thing, he would most assuredly go off in a swoon if I did." Wiping her eyes, she added, "It was Archer who attended to it."

Sherworth advised her, with his most dangerous smile, that only their public surroundings prevented him from dealing with her as she deserved.

"Oh, I was depending upon *that*," she replied with a responsive twinkle. Rising, she said, "And now we must end this agreeable dispute, for I hear the others coming down from the house. Will you intercept them and explain that there shall be a slight delay while we await Mr. Davis? I must step into the stable and console poor Twilight with a few lumps of sugar."

Vescinda had just reached the stable entrance when a cry was set up behind her. Suddenly, there were loud hoofbeats mingled with screams and shouts. She turned, startled, dropping the long train of her riding habit, and saw Midnight, bearing his unwilling mistress, galloping toward her. In an effort to clear the doorway, she moved too swiftly. Her skirts coiled like a snake round her legs, bringing her down in a whirlpool of emerald green. Trying not to panic further, she made rapid calculations. Impossible to crawl with her legs in such a tangle—! The stallion would jump clear!—No!—The overhead—! Better to be trod on once than tumbled between his legs—!

She flattened herself, steeling her mind against the inevitable pain and shock, yet unable to tear her eyes from the horrifying vision bearing down on her. She could hear the sound of running boots. People were scattering in all directions. No!—Boots coming *closer!*—It was Sherworth—! Oh, *no!*—No, he mustn't run in front of him—! She struggled up onto her elbows. *Oh, my dear, don't!*

He didn't. He rammed his shoulder against the stallion's in a terrific impact, knocking him onto one haunch. The huge animal was up again with amazing agility. Sherworth, with the same agility, found his balance and was snatching for the bit. He caught hold, just as the stallion reared, ears laid flat in rage. Sherworth was jerked into the air, swinging to the side only just in time to avoid the powerful legs striking out at him. As he was impelled violently to the ground again, he threw his whole weight against the bit, forcing the great head down. Large eyes rolled to the whites with hate, and long, ivory teeth twisted viciously to reach him. Down and down he worked the head, lower and lower, giving several savage jerks at the bit, and finally bringing his fist like a sledge across the flaring nostrils.

Stunned by the blow, the stallion ceased resistance for an instant, then shrieked his fury, his great body buckling and writhing in an effort to wrench himself free. But Sherworth managed with gritting determination to keep the muzzle a few inches from the ground, until at last Sir Richard lent his weight to the frothing bit.

All at once, Vescinda found herself being dragged by one of the stable boys to one side of the door, where he left her in a heap just inside the stable. She didn't try to rise but squirmed into a position to see out.

Sherworth and Sir Richard continued to render the furious stallion ineffectual by keeping his nose pressed to the ground, while Miss Wildborne's groom, who had arrived, puffing, on the scene, took her off. Archer and Wiley ran over with ropes, which they fastened swiftly to the animal's muscular neck. Then, as they stepped back, one to the right and one to the left, several stable boys dashed in to lend hands to the ropes. There were shouts to stand clear. Sherworth and Sir Richard released the bit and jumped back, leaving no less than a half dozen men—three ranged on each side—one team defending the other as they seesawed the raging and unwilling stallion away from the stable.

Laboring for breath, Sherworth looked wildly around, finally fixing on Vescinda, half-sitting, half-lying, where she'd been left. He ran into the stable and dropped onto his knees beside her, extending both hands.

She clasped them convulsively and cried, "Oh, God, oh *dearest* God! You might have been killed—fighting him that way!"

He tore his hands free and pulled her against him, holding her as though she would be snatched from him. His whole frame heaved, as he drew in long painful gasps, but he whispered hoarsely, "Almost too late—Vescinda—my poor girl—I—"

"No, no," she soothed, "you were in good time. Hush, now. You must get your breath."

Mary came first into the stable and found Vescinda still locked in Sherworth's arms, and, on her face, an expression Mary had never before seen there. She wondered for a moment if she should step out again, but her practical side reminded her that interruption for the pair was imminent, and that Vescinda would most assuredly prefer not to be discovered by Lady Oxbrook, while she was so obviously lost to her surroundings. Lady Charlotte had just hurried up to the door, bearing a small vinaigrette. Mary snatched it from her cousin without preamble and thrust it under Vescinda's nose. Vescinda blinked and coughed, then looked up in bewilderment.

Mary sharpened her voice to convey a deeper message. "You were not yourself. I daresay my aunt would have given you an even stronger dose. She is just coming."

Intelligence registered on Vescinda's countenance. She closed her eyes in silent acknowledgment of Mary's warning, then shifted slightly within Sherworth's arms and said gently, "The others are coming now. I must get up."

He loosened his hold and raised his head to stare at her. His breath was coming easier, though still in short, rapid gasps. He seemed to be thoroughly disgusted by the disturbance, and there was a recalcitrant look in the set of his strong, square jaw.

Vescinda smoothed back the hair that had tumbled down onto his damp forehead and said coaxingly: "Come now, help me up, so that I can greet your sisters with some degree of dignity."

"Damn my sisters!" he hissed. But he rose to his feet, pulling Vescinda up by both hands.

Mary and Lady Charlotte began immediately to pick the bits of straw from the back of Vescinda's habit, while she shook out her skirts and dusted off her front, as best she could. She then adjusted her hat, which had been knocked askew, only to find that her grand ostrich feather had cracked and was now drooping ludicrously in front of her face.

Sherworth snapped it off and handed it to her, and Vescinda took note, for the first time, of his appearance. His doeskin breeches and once gleaming top boots were covered in dust, and the white of his shirt gaped through a long gash where the shoulder of his mulberry coat had given way.

"We look a most disreputable pair," she said, hatching up a wan smile.

"Come," he ordered gruffly. "There is no need for you to stay here and entertain Katherine with the tale. You'll want your maid to see to you, and then an hour or two of quiet."

"But the ride—I must show them the way."

"You will not be riding today," he returned in a tone that invited no debate.

He took her by the elbow and guided her out of the stable, where they encountered Lady Oxbrook and Lady Milissa. Sweeping Vescinda past them, he replied, in her stead, that, no, she was not injured, but she had suffered a shock and was in no case to be standing about gabbling.

Vescinda could only be grateful to be spared having to enter into polite conversation with Sherworth's sisters, but, thinking to lighten his mood, she called his high-handedness into account. "Are you aware of how shockingly uncivil you have caused me to be?" she asked, struggling not to succumb to the amusement, which Mary, who was hurrying along beside them, was so thoroughly indulging.

"You won't say you had a hankering to stand there and be cross-questioned by that bitch," he snapped.

Mary flashed an anxious look in her direction, but Vescinda merely agreed with great affability. "No, I'm quite sure I shouldn't say *that*."

A smile broke through Sherworth's tense expression, and he drew her a little closer as they walked along.

As the house came into view, however, his temper was back in high flame. Just to the side of the carriage sweep, the stallion stood, still guarded by several grooms and stable hands. With them was Miss Wildborne, her own temper very much in evidence.

Bidding Vescinda and Mary to go up the steps to the house, Sherworth marched over to the group. He strode back, after what could not have been more than a few terse sentences, with Miss Wildborne hot on his heels.

"Vescinda," she demanded, as she scrambled up the steps, "are you going to permit this—*this*—?"

Sherworth turned so sharply that Miss Wildborne almost tumbled backwards down the stairs. He spoke through clenched teeth. "Vescinda has no knowledge of the matter—and *less* power to prevent it! So you may spare her your screeches and starts." Addressing Vescinda, he continued in less rancourous tones, "So you will be aware, I have just informed Miss Wildborne that I am going up for my pistols, and that, if I find that animal on the premises when I return, or at anytime in the future, I will put a bullet through him."

Vescinda did not permit her countenance to display so much as a shadow of emotion, but Miss Wildborne, her face suffused in red, fairly exploded. "You are a vicious fiend!" she shrieked. "Only moments ago, you almost knocked my horse on top of me, and might have killed *me!*"

Sherworth made no reply, but his expression made it plain that, had the risk even occurred to him, it wouldn't have made a jot of difference.

Vescinda's soft, calm voice broke through the electricity. "Liza, you were in no way injured in the incident at the stables, but, if you continue to jump about on the stairs in this agitated way, you may very well break your neck. I think you will do better to use this time to return Midnight to his own stable, where he can be made comfortable. I'm sure that none of us—Lord Sherworth included—wishes to see your horse harmed, and it requires only that you behave sensibly now to prevent it."

Miss Wildborne turned in a flurry of sapphire blue skirts and flounced down the steps, somehow managing to gain the ground on her feet.

Giving Sherworth a reassuring smile, Vescinda went with him and Mary into the house, where she lent herself to the task of soothing the alarm of everyone she encountered on the way to her bedchamber.

As they passed through the gallery, Mary asked, "Do you want my support, or are you wishing me at Jericho?"

"No, do come," Vescinda replied. "You may pour the tea they are sending up. As shaky as I am, I should likely scald myself."

"Are you?" Mary asked with interest. "You don't appear to be."

"Don't I? I feel as if every nerve in my body were trembling."

Once inside her chamber, Vescinda threw off her hat and pressed her hands to her cheeks, just standing that way for a moment. Mary removed her own rather plain riding hat and placed it on the mantel shelf, then began to unfasten Vescinda's habit.

She was supplanted almost immediately as Dorcas, followed by a train of maids bearing cans of hot water, rushed in, white with the shock of learning what had nearly befallen her mistress, and blessing Sherworth in every other sentence. While the bath was set out and filled in the adjoining dressing room, Dorcas stripped Vescinda of her dusty riding clothes.

Becoming steadily more conscious of a growing fatigue, Vescinda could only repeat that she had emerged quite unharmed and agree, with slightly more energy, that Lord Sherworth was indeed a man in a million. She allowed herself to be led off to the hot bath, and reappeared twenty minutes later, swathed in a dove gray satin wrapper. Her dark tresses, brushed and rubbed back to their usual luster, fell loosely about her shoulders. She smiled at Mary, who was making an interested study of the toy horse that had been

Sherworth's gift. Noting gratefully that the tea had arrived, she slipped into her bed.

Dorcas gathered up the dusty habit and boots, issuing sounds of distress all the while, then went off to begin the lengthy task of restoring them to their original state, while Mary prepared two cups of tea and brought them over to a table beside Vescinda's bed.

Vescinda pulled up the coverlet and sank back against a stack of pillows, sighing. "Thank you, dear Mary," she said, as she accepted one of the cups. "I am not usually such a poor honey, but each time I think of what should have been Sherworth's fate had he been unable to hold that *powerful* animal, I feel a trifle faint."

Since she showed no disposition to discuss the matter further, Mary did not attempt to draw her out. When they had finished their tea, she patted Vescinda's hand and rose, saying that she would leave her to rest.

Only moments after the door had closed behind her, the exhaustion brought on by the morning's near catastrophe claimed Vescinda in a fitful sleep. She did not awaken until midafternoon, when there came a scratching at the door. This proved to be a pair of young maids, bearing luncheon trays for two. A little refreshed by her nap, Vescinda could even be tempted by the delicacies being set out on a small table near the window. She was pleased by the arrangement, for she had no desire to go down among the guests just yet, but she was at a loss to know who her intended companion was to be. The maids were unable to satisfy her curiosity and left her shortly to try and puzzle it out for herself. She doubted that even Sherworth's impatience of propriety would lead him to arrange an intimate luncheon in her *bedchamber,* and no more likely candidate presented itself to her imagination.

She was not made to wonder long, however, for in a few minutes Chloe sailed into the room, full of apologies for disturbing her rest and assuring her at the same time that she would be better for a good meal.

Vescinda said at once that she found the notion charming and disposed herself in a small gilt chair opposite her aunt, but, just as she was about to raise her fork, a completely unlooked-for announcement caused her to suspend all action. "I came up to tell you that I'm going to marry your father," Chloe said, helping herself to some ham.

Vescinda overcame the impulse to voice her shock. After waiting to be sure that more was not forthcoming, she said with concern, "Aunt Chloe, I must know if this is something you *wish* to do."

Chloe surprised her again, by throwing back her head and enjoying a hearty laugh. "Oh, I'm safely past getting into the kind of fix that could *force* me to marry him."

Vescinda's color heightened slightly, as she said earnestly, "I *assure* you I didn't mean to imply any such thing! I thought perhaps you might feel that you must do this for me."

"Oh, well, I won't deny it was your circumstances and a few of the things you pointed out to Sherworth that set me to thinking. And *that* set me to teasing Bancroft about his neglect of the place. For one thing, having probed into every crack and corner of it, I've grown attached to the great old barn. So I brought him to realize that he hadn't disliked his stay here as much as he'd been determined to, and that got *him* to thinking.

"Told me he'd been happy here in his youth, but that he had learned to hate it after his marriage. I'm sure it's no surprise to you that my sister wasn't up to dealing with such a passionate and hot-headed blade. Any more than—well, never mind that," she said, glancing at Vescinda. "The long and the short of it is that they made each other generally miserable, and he took to dreading the time spent down here—because it offered so little opportunity for what he likes to call diversion. And then, after Louisa died, it seems bad memories kept him away, and he just got in the habit of avoiding the place—avoiding everything in the sane and sober world, for that matter! Oh, I don't fool myself that he'll ever be more than he is, but, so long as I can continue to defeat him at billiards, I have a hold on him that will keep him somewhat in line."

Vescinda's countenance had lightened during this speech. "Oh, Aunt Chloe, I think you are pleased by the notion, and, if that is so, I couldn't be more delighted. It—it is just so surprising. Well, I know you've been getting on better with Papa, but you had such a strong dislike of living in the country."

"Thought I would. That's because I like to keep busy. But it's different when you're perishing at someone's country seat as a guest. Here there's the house to run. And, once I'm Lady Bancroft, I'll be entertaining and making calls and holding public days. Oh, but don't get it into your head that we mean to stay the year-round here! We've made it up between us that we shall open up Bancroft House for the London Season, and then drop in on Brighton before coming back this way. Yes, and we may even keep Christmas with Mama at Whitowers."

Vescinda began to laugh. "I've just thought! Papa shall have Grandmama for a mother-in-law again."

Chloe's eyes crinkled. "He didn't remember *that* until after he'd lost his head and proposed! Stone sober at the time, too," she added, not without a degree of pride.

She then applied herself to her plate, saying, after she'd swallowed a mouthful of cold chicken. "We'll be making the announcement tonight at dinner, but I wanted to let you in on it beforehand. For one thing, didn't want to spoil your reputation for keeping control by causing you to choke on your soup."

"Indeed, I am grateful for that," Vescinda smiled, "and even more so for the additional time it affords me. I have so much to arrange—notes to send, sorting and packing, with—goodness, little more than three days in which to do it! Oh, and one of them to be spent at Lyme! And then there's the ball tomorrow night—"

"That puts me in mind of something," said Chloe, breaking in. "There's the trifling matter of a marriage ceremony before I can remain on here alone. I shall have to remove with you to London on Friday. There's a problem, though. A day must be spent with the man of business down here—you know, so that Bancroft can reacquaint himself with his affairs. But the notice being so short, this Tilsdale fellow cannot come to us. So, we shall just have to journey to Bridport and fit ourselves around his other appointments. We mean to do it while everyone is at Lyme Regis—owing that it's the only time left when there won't be any entertaining to be done here. No need for you to worry, though. Katherine and Milissa will be of the seaside party, and you'll have ample chaperonage in them."

Vescinda, who had long since realized that her dear aunt's form of chaperonage was just barely suitable for appearance's sake, smiled politely and said that she was sure they could manage for one day without her.

She listened then, with great pleasure and relief to Chloe's plans for the future, and, when luncheon was over, passed the remainder of the afternoon, except for a brief visit with Freddy, in a whirlwind of activity. She was not seen in company until shortly before dinner, when she came into the drawing room wearing a gown of green satin cloth shot with white, and ornamented round the bosom and waist with a rich white trimming—aptly named frost work— which had become all the rage during the last year.

She was instantly thronged with solicitous enquiries, which she acknowledged politely as she moved steadily to where Sherworth was standing off to himself. She made no attempt to camouflage her purpose, having decided that it must be considered reasonable in her to single out the man who had, only that morning, risked his life to rescue her from serious injury. And, when Sherworth took her hand in an urgent gesture, she allowed him to keep it clasped between both of his until dinner was announced, paying no heed, except to wonder with slight amusement if the great wild creature had any notion of the concession she was making.

As they chatted quietly, she noticed that he was holding his right shoulder a little stiffly, but he fobbed off her attempts to question him about it, and, instead, complimented her on her gown.

"Thank you," she said, smiling up at him. "I owe it all to you that I wasn't obliged to come down swathed in bandages."

"Vescinda," he broke in roughly, "I cannot talk of that."

"No," she agreed on a note of understanding, and instantly turned to a lighter subject.

She went down to dinner on his arm and took a place beside him at the table, where she divided her conversation between him and Mr. Wilkes until Lord Bancroft startled the company with the announcement of his engagement. A buzz of excited tones filled the room, the reactions split equally between shock and high amusement. All but Sherworth's. He was looking unmistakably disturbed. A mortifying thought came unbidden to Vescinda's mind as she sat silently observing his grim profile. At length, she questioned him, forcing a note of raillery into her tone. "Can it be that you object to your stepsister marrying into the ramshackled Bancroft family? You are plainly displeased, my dear Sherworth."

"You knew of this?" he asked, the remnants of a frown still on his countenance.

"My aunt broke it to me this afternoon. For which I am heartily grateful, because I have made good use of the time in a desperate round of packing."

"Your packing ought to have begun when I informed you that you would be going with us to London."

"Well, in all truth," she laughed, "I did have Dorcas pack enough for a *visit,* fearing that you would abduct me. But, now, of course, I shall be making my *home* with Grandmama."

"Then you are satisfied with this arrangement, as far as it concerns your plans?"

"Oh, yes, indeed. Aunt Chloe will see to it that the place is kept up, and she promises that Papa shall keep a closer eye on Freddy's progress in future. And, since he controls the purse strings, I have no doubt of his being heeded! Then, too, something Aunt Chloe said gave me to think. The Bancroft men have always had the habit of drowning their grief in excess. I have had a talk with Freddy, and I feel that much of his bad behavior might stem from his mother and brother having both died within a year of one another—that he felt suddenly cut adrift—as though life was too capricious to be taken seriously. Oh, I don't mean that he has not always been a trifle wild, but witness, even Papa was not completely past reclaiming!"

Sherworth's expression softened. "Very well, green-eyed beauty, we shall toast the happy couple. By the by, I have told you, haven't I, that you should always wear that color?"

16

NOTHING IN THE way of special entertainment was planned for the following day, so that those who wished might repose themselves for the ball. With the exception of a few of the gentlemen, who got up an archery match on the west lawn, everyone passed the hours in languid idleness or, like Vescinda, busily engaged in personal pursuits.

She had had breakfast brought to her chamber on a tray and ate it amid mountains of things waiting to be discarded or packed. A pile of hot-pressed paper and wafers reposed on her writing table, a nagging reminder of the many notes she must dash off to acquaintances she would be unable to take leave of personally. Yet, despite the rapidly diminishing time in which she might hope to attend to all these things, she was continually having to drag her thoughts back from an all-consuming brown study, in order to concentrate them on the project before her. The celebration that had erupted from the announcement of her father's betrothal had kept her too occupied to heed the vague sense of disappointment growing behind her gaiety, but, later, as she had lain wakeful in her bed, she'd realized that she had gone down to dinner more than half expecting Sherworth to take steps toward settling matters between them. That he had not, that, upon reflection, it became plain that he had actually been avoiding all comments concerning her future, had set forth a train of highly disquieting conjectures.

As she pushed aside the remnants of her breakfast, Vescinda stared vacantly into the gaping trunk that lay at her feet, and wondered for the hundredth time if it were possible for Sherworth to remain fixed in his determination not to marry, after coming to love her so deeply. That he did love her, she could no longer doubt, not because he had rescued her from Midnight—she was reasonably certain he'd have made a push to save anyone from being trampled by a horse—but because of what had followed. The way he had looked at her, the intensity of his embrace, both betokened a strong and lasting passion. Yet, that same event also made it no longer possible for her to soothe herself that his reticence sprang from a doubt as to her sentiments; only a fool could suppose that she had been displaying mere gratitude in those desperate moments in the stable. With that much settled, however, she was left with nothing but to ask herself all over again if he could conceivably remain silent, knowing that, as soon as she reached London, she would be expected to set about establishing herself in the only way open to females of her station. *Could* he watch her go to another rather than wed her himself? She would not have thought him capable of it, but, as she riffled through her wardrobe, she was forced to admit that, her yearning love notwithstanding, she had really not known him all that long.

During the course of her many tasks, a glimmer of hope peeped through her depression when Vescinda began to ponder Sherworth's curious reaction to her father's betrothal. At last she felt she had hit upon an explanation that suited all the facts: Her great, impatient darling must have been planning to discuss his own engagement with her father, and had been understandably vexed at finding himself forestalled. Naturally she could only honor him for the nicety of manner that had caused him to refrain from stealing the glory away from the happy couple in the midst of their own celebration, but, at the same time, she felt an overwhelming desire to box his ears for choosing that, of all moments, to curb his impatience and, with an unwonted regard for propriety, await permission to address her. She thought warmly that he might at least have told her quietly of his intentions.

Although considerably heartened, Vescinda was now seized by an unaccustomed, but tormenting, sense of impatience herself and found it as difficult as ever to apply her mind to her mundane project. The day wore on, until at last it was time for her to dress for the ball and then to go down to greet the neighboring guests who had been distinguished by an invitation to dinner.

Sherworth was in the hall below as Vescinda began her descent down the grand staircase. He glanced up, and the smile froze on his face. Vescinda's gown was of a white, filmy gauze, so soft and fine that it seemed to melt into her exquisite form, displaying every inch of her long, beautiful legs. The waist was fitted fashionably high, but, with each graceful step she took, the material clung for a tantalizing instant to her natural waist, revealing the full curve of a shapely hip. The bodice was cut just low enough to hint at the gentle rise of a firm bosom swelling beneath soft gathers of gauze. And, as she came closer, flickering candles from chandeliers blazing their promise of a gala evening teased his eye with glimpses of creamy pink beneath the diaphanous fabric. His breath caught in his throat.

When she reached him, he expostulated in a harsh undervoice, "Good God, you can't wear that! It's the most improper thing I've ever seen!"

Fortunately for Vescinda's enjoyment of the evening, his appreciation of her appearance had been blatant enough for her to meet these words with nothing but amusement. "I think perhaps you must have been a very selfish little boy," she twinkled. "Yes, and an untruthful one, too. For, if this is the most improper thing *you* have ever seen, then the tales told of you have been sadly exaggerated."

Ignoring this sally, he went on accusingly, "That slip or underpart—or whatever you call it—is almost the same color as your skin. One would swear you were naked beneath those few wisps of gauze!"

"Fiddle! *You* wouldn't swear it, for you can see perfectly well that I am not."

"Well, damn it, it's too dashing by half for you to wear amid a parcel of yokels! You'll have the eyes out of their heads the night long!"

"Well—yes, I fear you may be right about that," she relented with a tiny frown. "I own I did think it a bit much for a country ball, myself, but it cannot be *improper,* for it is the gown Grandmama sent to me for my birthday—with the explicit wish that I wear it tonight!"

"With the explicit wish to drive me to distraction," he retorted.

Something flickered behind Vescinda's eyes, and she asked slowly, "Do you think that was her reason? So, it *has* been a matchmaker's plot, and you were right all along—oh, not in supposing that I requested Grandmama to send you to me." The wayward muscle caught in her cheek, making her smile extremely mischievous "But, then, she once sent a puppy I hadn't asked for, and I became excessively fond of it."

Sherworth's expression remained stormy, and she laughed softly. "Well, I can see you don't mean to come down off your high ropes, but what am I to do? It's much, much too late for me to think of changing. Yes, even now, I can hear a carriage pulling up. I must go and take my place beside Aunt Chloe. Are you not even going to ask me to save you a dance?"

"*All* of your waltzes," he rapped out.

"Oh, but there will be no waltzes—at least not for me. I mayn't waltz in public until I am approved by one of the holy seven at Almack's, you see."

"What a stupid, asinine world!" he exploded. "You may set the house on its ear by wearing that gown, but you may not waltz! I'll take you into supper."

"Oh, I am *truly* sorry," exclaimed Vescinda in genuine dismay, "but I am promised to Mr. Davis for supper."

After a brief, deafening silence, Sherworth turned sharply on his heel and stalked away, leaving Vescinda unreasonably vexed with Mr. Davis for his relentless foresight.

Dinner was a tediously formal affair, and those who had at first thought themselves privileged to find Lord Sherworth next to them made the unhappy discovery that a surly earl was a far less gratifying table companion than a commoner of good disposition.

When at last the gentlemen of the party filed out of the dining hall, the remaining guests, invited for the ball only, began to appear at the large entrance doors. Twenty minutes later, the ball was opened as Lord Bancroft led Lady Oxbrook onto the floor, neither of them particularly pleased with the partner whom form and precedence had imposed upon them.

Vescinda would have been enthusiastically solicited for every dance had she worn a plain, stuff gown, but, looking as she did like an exquisite Grecian statue come to life, the enthusiasm swelled to fervor, and the rush to her side threatened riot.

Of course, not all of the gentlemen present were so engaged. Miss Wildborne had her own court. Most prominent among them was Lord Caversham, who had been receiving sudden and marked encouragement. And there was the usual smattering of dandified young gentlemen, who were far too preoccupied with the fold of their own or other gentlemen's neckcloths to notice mere feminine attire. Then there were those who were athletically inclined and still at an age of hero-worship. They had arrived hoping for nothing so much as an opportunity to exchange a few words with one of the bang-up Corinthians who had come down from London. Their attention remained fixed on Sherworth and Sir Richard, with occasional speculative glances aimed at Lord Edward or Mr. Wilkes.

Freddy, of course, looked upon his gorgeous cousin more in the light of a sister, and, beyond grinning occasionally at the stir Vescinda was causing among the rural community, he spent his time having, as he would have phrased it, high gig, flirting with Mary's younger sister and reuniting himself with former playfellows who had since bloomed into young ladyhood.

Naturally, it was not to be expected that Lord Bancroft, a busy and gracious host throughout, would take more than a cursory interest in his daughter, but the gentleman most noticeably absent from the cluster that formed round Vescinda after each dance was Sherworth. Throughout the evening, he divided his attention between a mace—displayed amid a collection of ancient armament on the oak-paneled wall—and Mr. Davis, who was carefully guarding Vescinda from the slightest display of high spirits that might arise among the younger gentlemen as they vied for her attentions. Having nurtured a fear that Vescinda would come to grief while wearing such a sophisticated gown in company with a pack of unwhelped puppies, Sherworth might have been supposed to feel grateful for Mr. Davis's careful vigilance. He was, in fact, raging, as much at the confident manner in which Vescinda's country squire had set himself up as her natural protector, as at the way he was so unquestionably accepted in that role.

It was not until nearly the end of the ball that Mr. Davis permitted his attention to waver from Vescinda for the first time. He left her as a waltz was striking up and stepped over to address a few words to Lord Bancroft. Sherworth watched this maneuver through narrowed eyes, and, when Mr. Davis returned to Vescinda and proceeded, after a brief exchange, to guide her away from the company, he pushed his shoulders from the wall. Setting down the glass a diligent footman had filled no less than a dozen times throughout the evening, he began to thread his way through the crowded room.

Vescinda had preceded her escort into the yellow saloon, but the door had not quite closed behind them when Sherworth thrust it wide and strode in after them. Mr. Davis, at first taken aback by the violent intrusion, squared himself up and said indignantly, "I've his lordship's permission to speak privately with Miss Bancroft."

Turning to guide Vescinda out of the room, Sherworth snapped, "I don't give a damn if you have the King's writ. She's not closeting up with you."

A sudden shuffling behind him caused Sherworth to spin round sharply. He found the outraged Mr. Davis only inches away, instructing him to mind his language in Miss Bancroft's presence. "What's more, my lord," continued that incensed gentleman, "you'll take yourself off from what doesn't concern you. You've no right to interfere here."

Vescinda's voice broke in urgently. "Mr. Davis, listen to me! I *wish* to go with Lord Sherworth!"

At these unexpected words, Mr. Davis hesitated, but then his features took on a stubborn aspect, and he said, "Those were not your wishes before he intruded himself. Your father said I might address you, and you agreed to hear me. *He* has no say in the matter! No right!" he reiterated, his clenched fists proclaiming his intentions if Sherworth made a further attempt to remove the lovely bone of contention from the room.

Sherworth released Vescinda and gently urged her toward the door, saying quietly, "Go back to the ball, Vescinda. Davis and I shall discuss this between ourselves."

Knowing precisely what form that discussion would take and in what condition she might expect to find both powerful men at its conclusion, Vescinda thrust her hand determinedly under Sherworth's arm and said calmly, "Indeed I shall, but I beg you will escort me." To Mr. Davis, she added, "You mistake, George. Lord Sherworth has every right. He is—my uncle."

This announcement had a more lasting effect upon Mr. Davis. His hands dropped limply to his sides, and his handsome features collapsed into a dumbstruck expression. The effect upon Sherworth, however, was not so auspicious. He looked furious and was obviously within an ames ace of disclaiming, when Vescinda laid her other hand over his arm in an imploring gesture. "I *beg* of you to come along now," she whispered. "It would cause a shocking scene if you two were to brawl with the house full of people."

Sherworth let a long breath escape through his nostrils and walked rapidly out of the room. Vescinda managed to keep hold of him until he halted abruptly at the steps leading down to the great hall. There, he rounded on her and rasped in a low steely voice, "Could you not have spared me the humiliation of saying such a *stupid* thing?"

He jerked his arm free and stalked off toward the back of the house. Vescinda would not have followed him in any case, but, as her eyes scanned the company, she saw that their little scene had been observed by both Mary and Lady Oxbrook, one looking toward her in deep concern, the other, in contemptuous amusement. Each began to converge on her from opposite directions.

Lady Oxbrook reached her first, saying with a sympathetic smile, "I see that my brother has been indulging another of his childish rages. Don't heed him, my dear. He has no right to interfere with you. I will own that I, too, thought it a trifle irregular for you to go off with a young man, but Chloe informs me that he had your father's permission to make you an offer." She added drily, "I can think of nothing to recommend the match, but evidently Lord Bancroft sees it differently. At all events, if only Sherworth would trouble to secure the facts before indulging in these foolish displays of unwanted heroism, he would not make a figure of himself quite so often."

Mary had arrived in time to hear the greater part of this speech and had a decidedly militant look in her eye. Vescinda greeted her with an almost imperceptible shake of her head and returned her attention to Lady Oxbrook. "I am afraid, ma'am, that the fault is mine. My grandmother bade Lord Sherworth keep watch over me during this party, because she, too, does not always agree with my father's decisions. I should have sought your brother's advice before going off with Mr. Davis, and, of course, I see now that he was quite right to insist that a private meeting be put off until there could be no one to speculate on our purpose."

Vescinda had the satisfaction of seeing Lady Oxbrook bite back an automatic condemnation of her brother's logic. Having already admitted to thinking the incident irregular, herself, she was neatly cornered into a grudging concession that perhaps Sherworth's motive—if not his method—held merit.

Mary looked from her aunt's retreating figure back to Vescinda, her eyes wide with admiration. "A truly masterful job of rolling her up!" she acclaimed. "I vow, Grandmama Countess couldn't have done it better." She added reflectively, "And I don't suppose it really matters that she hates you now, because she'd have done her best to ruin you in any case. Where has Sherworth gone?"

"I rather suspect that he is shut up in the bookroom, rehearsing my iniquities because I thwarted an excellent opportunity for him to knock Mr. Davis down."

Mary couldn't help laughing. "He surely is a handsome thing— Mr. Davis, I mean."

"Yes, he is."

"But you don't care for him?"

"I am fond of him. We were playfellows. But I don't wish to marry him—which I have made abundantly plain these many years. Unfortunately, like many gentlemen, he suffers from a mulish streak and has made it into a challenge."

"I never gave it much thought," Mary smiled, "but it must be fatiguing to be a reigning belle."

"Oh, no, that accolade belongs to Liza Wildborne, but I will own to a fervent wish to pass a few peaceful moments well away from anyone wearing breeches!"

Even as she spoke, however, Vescinda realized that her statement was untrue. There was very definitely one creature, so attired, whom she would have given much to confront. While she continued to take her place in the dances, outwardly as placid as ever, she was seething with the wish to take issue with Sherworth. It seemed incredible that she could have looked forward so to her first ball, only to find it such a great nuisance. Everything had contrived to keep her from the one person she longed most to be with. Before the affair had even begun, jealousy and possessiveness had caused Sherworth to fly up into the boughs. She had no quarrel with that, certainly, and she might have smoothed things over in a minute, but not so much as a minute had been granted her. And, now, another and more foolish incident had caused him to go completely out of reach. She was almost beside herself with impatience, for it meant that she would have to pass yet another night without knowing if it would have been her own dear Sherworth proposing to her had not George Davis been so *very* much in the way.

It was almost two hours before the last of the guests had taken their leave or collected their bedroom candles and retired. The house party had shown no inclination to linger below, knowing there would barely be time to recruit their energy before the carriages and horses would be at the door to convey them to Lyme Regis for a day by the seaside and another evening of dancing.

Glancing into the empty hall, Chloe said to her niece, "Gad, I'd almost forgotten how it looked when it wasn't bursting at the walls with people!" She added with a yawn, "Well, if you're reasonably sure there's no one collapsed behind the sofas, I fancy we may go up."

Vescinda agreed, and was about to take up her candle when Chloe remarked: "I haven't seen Sherworth for over an hour. He must have escaped to his chamber sometime during the dancing."

Vescinda suddenly found herself entertaining a thought that had no place in the mind of a well-brought-up young lady. Nodding an agreement to her aunt's surmise, she said, "Go along, Aunt Chloe. I think I'll search out a book to read, until the excitement of the ball wears off."

Vescinda opened the door to the bookroom and let out her breath as her eyes fell on Sherworth, pacing about the room, a brandy glass in his hand. She saw, with some concern, however, that he had been drinking rather heavily. His chestnut-brown locks, which had been so painstakingly arranged in a semblance of disorder, were now tumbled down upon his forehead in genuine disarray—the result no doubt of having dropped his head carelessly into his hands, as he sometimes did when he was exasperated or extremely amused. It was obvious, however, that he had been anything but amused during his sequestration in the bookroom.

The expression of displeasure he'd been wearing gave way to one of condemnation, as he glanced over and saw her. "What the devil are you doing here without a duenna?" he demanded a trifle thickly.

"Everyone has gone up to bed," she replied calmly. "Since you have complained more than once of the lack of opportunities to be private with me, I had scarcely expected to hear such a rebuke on *your* lips. At all events, I am here, and I think it high time we put an end to this nonsense. Do you intend to make a career of running off all my suitors and leaving me to end my days as a spinster?"

His mind evidently fixed on his grievance, he ignored this home question and accused, "You made a damned cake of me, telling that jolterhead I was your uncle."

"Fiddle. One would suppose it was a disgraceful thing to be. But I should be grateful if you would tell me what I *ought* to have said when he was quite reasonably questioning your right to order my movements."

"You ought to have left the room as I bid."

Once again Vescinda was aware of a strong desire to box his ears. She wondered if he was simply too fuddled—she knew it was not his habit to indulge in strong drink—or if he was being deliberately obtuse. One thing was certain, however. He had a crow to pluck, and there was no hope of introducing any other subject until it had been plucked clean. She drew a resolute breath and said: "I think you should know that I shall *never* do as you bid, when it means leaving you to risk your life—particularly for such a trifling cause."

"*Trifling?* Trifling cause?" he expostulated. He slammed down his glass, causing the honey-colored liquid to swirl and eddy to the rim. "He had your father's permission to address you! Don't you realize he would have felt perfectly within his rights to *kiss* you?"

"He might have felt within his rights to *try* to kiss me."

"Try! If that great, hulking looby had decided to kiss you, he *would* have kissed you! How the devil do you imagine *you* could have stopped him?"

"Simply by telling him that I did not wish to be kissed."

"Oh, would you just? You think you can go about in that gown, driving a man half mad, and then merely say that you don't *wish* to be kissed!"

The thought of Mr. Davis becoming so impassioned, through any cause, drew an irrepressible laugh, to which, in his present mood, Sherworth took instant exception. Catching her by both wrists, he pulled her roughly to him. "And do you think you could prevent me so easily?"

The conversation having at last taken a turn along the lines she had intended, the tenseness Vescinda had been experiencing vanished, and she was able to smile mischievously. "Oh, far easier, for I have *your* promise."

But Sherworth's next reaction was not so satisfactory. He appeared at first disconcerted, then chagrined, as he said, "Yes, I remember—the right man and the right time."

His step was a little unsteady as he released her and turned away. Vescinda studied his profile, a tiny crease between her brow, as she thought despairingly. Oh, it must be the drink. It wasn't at all like him to take such an unpretentious view of his position. Her own impatience aside, she couldn't leave matters on *that* note. She moved toward him and laid her hand on his lapel. "Yes, and I think this would be a very good time."

It took what seemed an interminable time for him to grasp the invitation in her words. Finally, his eyes widened for an instant, and he caught her in a fierce embrace. Vescinda slid her arms up round his neck and raised her face to receive his kiss. Her pulses were racing, and she was feeling quite breathless. Again, there was a long pause as their eyes met. Then, all at once, he pressed her face against his shoulder and groaned, "Oh, damn, this isn't fair! I— Vescinda, you shouldn't even *be* here with the house all abed and me half-seas over!"

Vescinda stiffened with mortification. It came home to her with a blinding clarity that she had misread the entire situation. His exception to her gown had not been engendered by a feeling of possessiveness; it had been resentment! He had felt—he had said as much—that it was a contrivance designed to tempt him into an action he was unwilling to take. He desired her, and, yes, he cared for her, but he did not want to *marry* her! She realized suddenly that it had been *this* opposing force that had been warring within him all along. And foolishly—most foolishly—she had cast this possibility aside in favor of one better suited to her wishes. And now, as a result, she had submitted herself to a frightful humiliation and him to a most unfair situation. He was aware of the terms she had placed on her kiss, and he had given his word not to violate them. She became panicky, thinking that there was at least one humiliation she must spare herself. She must not allow him to succumb to temptation and then feel obliged to marry her.

She tried to break free of a hold, which, despite his words, had not slackened. She said gently, but with an urgency in her tone, "Sherworth—my dear—you must let me go. You are right. It was wrong—madness—for me to have come here. I understand, truly."

He didn't release her, but he leaned back to look down at her. "No," he said huskily, "I don't think you do. You mustn't—"

"But I do. *Trust* that I do! It was my own folly—but thanks to your good sense, no harm has come of it. But you must let me go now. We—we shall forget this, and—"

All at once he pressed his finger to her lips, cutting off her speech, as he cocked his head to listen. A servant was speaking to someone in the hall. "Damn her!" he half-hissed, half-whispered. "It's Katherine!" Pulling Vescinda by the hand to the window, he commanded, in the same harsh undervoice, "Bolt this after me! Do not fail!"

In the next instant he had flung the casement open and disappeared into the moon-soaked shrubbery. Vescinda pulled the window to and threw the bolt in unthinking obedience. Then, as she collected her wits, she snatched a book from a nearby shelf, praying it would not prove to be set down in Latin or some other improbable text. She had no sooner stepped into the hall than she came upon Lady Oxbrook, obviously on her way to that very room. She was looking extremely vexed—no doubt because the helpful servant had unwittingly betrayed her presence.

She made an effort to conceal her anger, but spoke in admonitory accents. "Miss Bancroft, I had waited to have a few words with Chloe, regarding tomorrow's expedition, and learned that you had remained below. It was most imprudent in her—and in you, my dear. Did you forget that my brother came in this very direction during his distempered freak?"

"No, ma'am, I did not forget," replied Vescinda in perfect honesty. "However, it was not until my aunt had said that she thought he had already gone up to his chamber that I begged permission to fetch a book."

Although Lady Oxbrook's tone had implied that her presence on the scene was in the nature of a rescue, her intelligent eyes held a hint of suspicion as they made a careful survey of Vescinda's appearance. "I see," she said at last. "I trust such has proved the case?"

"I haven't a guess where he is, ma'am," returned Vescinda, again in all truth.

But Lady Oxbrook was evidently determined to leave no stone unturned, and, bidding Vescinda goodnight, said that the notion of some late night reading appealed to her and that she, too, would look in on the bookroom.

Vescinda was in no doubt as to what Lady Oxbrook meant to seek in the bookroom, and she lent a silent prayer of thanks that Sherworth, despite his befuddled state, had had the presence of mind to remind her to bolt the window behind him. Whatever his spiteful sister might suspect, she would find no proof. The brandy, though a telltale sign that a gentleman had made use of the room, could easily have been abandoned there hours before, and, by her own admission of having noticed her brother taking that direction earlier, she was effectively forestalled from making something of it. Still, as Vescinda ascended the stairs, she couldn't help wondering if she were worthy of her blessed escape. That, after a lifetime of meticulous care, she should suddenly cast her bonnet over a windmill, while Lady Oxbrook was under the same roof, was foolish past permission and seemed almost deserving of a punitive consequence.

She closed the door of her bedchamber behind her, but made no move to prepare herself for bed. Sleep was never farther from her. She wandered over to the window embrasure and sank down, and there she remained, gazing out at the moon hanging over the park, wondering if Sherworth was roaming out there somewhere beneath its pale glow, and dreading the moment when she would have to face him again. The scene between them had been quite enough to make their next encounter awkward, but she was further mortified to think that her imprudence had been the cause of his having to flee through a window like a common thief.

Although the hours until morning bore on ponderously, the moment to take her place in one of the carriages departing for Lyme Regis seemed to arrive with terrifying swiftness, and, long before she felt herself equal to an encounter with Sherworth, she was once again descending the stairs, cheerfully attired for a day by the seaside in crisp white and sky blue, her eyes as heavy as her mood.

She had delayed until the last possible minute, hoping to find Sherworth already joined with the group assembled for departure in the entrance hall. This goal was not realized. He had taken up a post in the first-floor gallery. However, speech with him was mercifully reduced to only a few whispered sentences, since Lady Milissa and her youngest daughter, coming late, forced them to move along and into the hearing of those waiting at the foot of the stairs.

He came up to her, exclaiming in an undervoice: "For God's sake, Vescinda, why didn't you come down sooner? I've been waiting almost an hour!"

She laid her hand on his arm and continued to walk, though more slowly. "We cannot talk now. I daresay everyone is eager to be off. I—I'm sorry you waited to no purpose, but, you see, I was hoping to avoid conversation—at least for a while. I find it necessarily embarrassing." She looked up, a wavering smile on her lips. "I think perhaps we were both a trifle bosky. You—you would be doing me a great kindness if you would put the entire episode out of your mind."

"No! Confound it, I am trying to tell you that you misunderstood! You are supposing that I didn't want to kiss you. There is nothing in the world I wanted more! Vescinda, I—oh, the devil, who is that?"

"Never mind. We must not delay in any case. I was in no doubt as to how much you wanted to kiss me, and that is why I can only honor you your forbearance. Hush now, they must not hear us whispering!"

Sherworth, looking like he might explode, seemed about to speak in spite of her warning, but he yielded to the strong appeal in her eyes and continued down the stairs, grunting acknowledgments to the commonplaces she addressed to him for the benefit of their audience.

17

THE GENTLEMEN, WITH the exception of Freddy Bancroft, rode beside the four carriages that made up the seaside party, and, less than half an hour later, Vescinda's coachman led the cavalcade through the charming town of Lyme Regis and halted at the Three Cups, where a private parlor and two chambers had been engaged for the day. After partaking of a light luncheon, most of the ladies expressed a wish to explore the quaint shops, and Lord Caversham, Sir Richard, and Freddy volunteered as escorts for this expedition, leaving Sherworth, Lord Edward, and Mr. Wilkes to adjourn, with a sigh of relief, to the taproom.

Almost an hour later, as Vescinda gazed listlessly at the display in one of the many bow windows that characterized the little seaside village, Mary hurried over to her, taking her arm and urging, "Pray come along with me, Ves. I wish to walk on the thing they call the Cobb, and my mother has said I mustn't go alone."

"No, of course you must not," Vescinda replied absently, her mind not fully recalled from her various unhappy reflections.

"Then, let us go now. I don't wish to have Kathy or Charlotte tagging along, and they will if they learn where we are to go."

Considerably fatigued by a sleepless night, Vescinda could raise no enthusiasm for the project, but she supposed that strolling with Mary on the Cobb, an ancient structure built as a breakwater sometime in or before the fourteenth century, would prove no more exhausting than being pulled in and out of shops by one of the other well-rested members of the party. She submitted to the tugging on her arm and allowed herself to be guided down Bridge Street toward the walk that led along the sea cliffs to the harbor.

Mary let out her breath. She had been carefully waiting to approach Vescinda during a moment when Lady Oxbrook was safely inside one of the shops and had been in the liveliest dread that her aunt would emerge again to notice their direction. However, once across Buddle Bridge, the slight curve in the street screened them from those ever watchful eyes, and she was able to congratulate herself on a job well done.

Unfortunately, there had been another pair of eyes, which Mary had failed to take into account. They belonged to Miss Wildborne, and they had been watching her off-behavior with the greatest curiosity and interest.

It had been Miss Wildborne's practice of late to keep Sherworth under close observation—no longer in an effort to fix his interest, but in the hope of discovering a way to be up with him for the double insult he had served her. She had learned, through the simple expedient of eavesdropping, that he had paid off Lord Caversham with an unflattering degree of goodwill. Since he had done so without having made the least push to attach her, she was left to the only conclusion possible. He had been making May-game of her with a sham bet. To her way of thinking, this affront was equaled only by his high-handed and humiliating handling of the incident involving her stallion. So it was not to be expected that she would let pass any opportunity to avenge herself. Although she had seen nothing promising in Sherworth's coming by a short while ago to engage his eldest niece in a few minutes of private speech, she'd found it fascinatingly suspicious that, a little later, Mary should be leading Vescinda off and plainly taking care to conceal her direction from the ladies who were chaperoning the party.

Miss Wildborne had given one of her thin smiles, knowing from long experience that, where people were engaged in secret business, there was usually the means to cause those people considerable discomfort. At first, she had reveled in the delightful possibility of being able to catch her old rival in the same net as Sherworth, but it soon came home to her that this aspect of the situation boded ill for the entire project. Unfortunately, if the rig Sherworth was running were improper enough to be of any use, it would scarcely prosper if he was expecting such a prude as Vescinda to take part in it. Still, Miss Wildborne reasoned optimistically, there could be no denying that Sherworth was a highly practiced rake. There was every hope that Vescinda might find herself in his web before she knew what she was about. So, in the happy anticipation of being able to show Sherworth to the world as the dishonorable blackguard that he was, while at the same time watching Vescinda become helplessly embroiled in the *worst* kind of scandal, Miss Wildborne disbursed her escort on an April fool's errand and took up a steady, but unobtrusive, pursuit of the two young ladies.

Meanwhile, Vescinda and Mary had reached the path leading to the Cobb and had already covered the short distance past the buildings that straggled along it on the outskirts of town. There was little for over a hundred yards but fields to the right and the sea to the left. The walk, however, was crowded with visitors taking the sea air, and the pace was necessarily slow. Soon they came upon one or two cottages, and shortly they were in the hamlet of the Cobb. Here, Mary startled Vescinda by suddenly pulling her out of the string of promenaders and tapping on the door of a color-washed shack just this side of the bonding yards.

"Mary, what are you about?" demanded Vescinda with widened eyes. "This is a store building of some sort!"

The words were scarcely out of her mouth when the door was flung open by a dashing gentleman in a well-fitted bottle-green coat. "Come in quickly!" he bid.

"Sherworth!" Vescinda exclaimed. "But how is this?"

"Come in, before you're noticed," he urged, then replied, as Mary swept past him into the building, "I greased a lobsterman in the fist to let me have the use of it for an hour."

Vescinda stood in the doorway, wondering miserably why he hadn't just bespoken a room at an inn, so she could have met her ruin in comfort and without the smell of stale fish. A brief glance at the entreaty in his eyes, however, and she followed Mary into the pungent old building.

"Good girl," Sherworth applauded. "I know it's a trifle revolting, but it's the only place I could find that was along a logical walk for you to take and yet out of sight of the shops and inns."

Mary spoke up. "And you needn't fear we shall have my Aunt Katherine down upon us, for I made certain she didn't see us go off. What is more, when she questions us later, I shall swear that you were never out of my sight."

"And *shall* I be out of your sight?" Vescinda asked, trying to conceal the depths of her dismay.

"For just a few minutes," Sherworth intervened. "Don't tease yourself. You may take it from me that Katherine is no enemy to a convenient lie. Oh, I know you can't like this, but, damn it, I'll reduce this town to sticks and splinters if I don't talk to you soon!"

"There!" Mary laughed. "Console yourself with the knowledge that you are saving Lyme Regis from imminent destruction." Dusting off a barrel with her handkerchief, she indicated that she required Sherworth's assistance to use it as a seat.

He plumped her unceremoniously on top of the barrel and bore Vescinda off to a smaller storeroom a few paces away. No sooner had he closed the door behind them than he reached out to take her in his arms.

"No! No, you must not!" Vescinda gasped, drawing back in alarm.

Chagrined by the fright in her tone, he exclaimed, "Well, of all the— You change your sentiments mighty fast, my girl. You weren't so averse to snuggling in my arms last night!"

Pressing two elegantly gloved fingers to his lips, Vescinda gasped again, "Mary shall *hear* you!" Then, choking on an involuntary laugh, she shook her head in reproach and removed her fingers, saying quietly, "My 'improper' gown of last night was too soft to crush, but an embrace in starched muslin, and I shall have the devil to pay. So you see, great, wild creature, I have not changed my sentiments, only my dress."

The tenseness around his mouth and eyes relaxed, but he continued to stand stiffly. Finally he demanded in comic exasperation, "Well, give me *something* to hold."

Vescinda wisely provided him with both of her hands and said: "You are a dear goose to worry about me so, but truly there is no need. I feel a bit foolish about—about *everything* that occurred last night, but I shall come about. I should be best pleased if we could put the whole nonsensical business behind us and go on being good friends."

"If you think I could be anywhere near you and be no more than a friend, you don't know me as I thought you did."

Vescinda had passed several miserable hours wondering if she could bear that herself, but the thought that he was about to tell her that he couldn't see her again filled her with something akin to panic. Trying to hide her wretchedness behind a bantering tone, she said, "Dear me, you don't wish to be my uncle; you don't wish to be my husband; and you don't wish to be my friend. Have you brought me here to suggest that I take up residence in Kensington?"

"So, they've told you of that, have they?" he asked grimly. "Well, I won't give you a thorough shaking, because I think you're joking. I brought you here to tell you that I wish very much to be your husband."

Vescinda dropped her eyes. "I had hoped you wouldn't do this. It is the most embarrassing of all. You explained at the outset that you had no wish to be married. You don't owe me this kind of—of—"

"Vescinda, my love, you are glaringly abroad." Taking her hands and laying them against his chest and holding them there with his own, he said, "It's true that I once said that, but it has been several days now since I have been able to think of anything but how much I yearn to install you as mistress of Whitowers, to show you off to my dozens of relatives at Christmas, to be with you by *our* ornamental lake. And, then, in the spring, to see you in Berkeley Square, turning tedious social functions into a delight—" He broke off, the softness in his eyes vanishing as he continued in a menacing tone, "Most of all, by God, when next you appear in such a gown as you wore last night, I want it thoroughly understood that you belong to me!"

Almost overcome by relief and happiness, Vescinda collapsed against him with something between a laugh and a sob. Sherworth, who had been fairly vibrating with his own restraint, seized upon the situation, crushing her closer still and doing further damage by knocking her bonnet half off and brushing his lips over her silken hair as he whispered, "Mine—all mine."

Vescinda replied softly, "Yes."

For several moments neither of them seemed willing to move or to speak. At length, Vescinda implored, "Oh, my dear one, are you quite *certain* that you wish to be married?"

His voice catching on a weak laugh, he replied, "Well, unless you can think of any other way I can have you all to myself for the rest of my life, I'm going to insist on it."

"Yet, even as late as last night you were in some doubt."

"I was in no doubt about that."

"But why else would you scruple to kiss me?" she asked, pushing herself back a little to look up at him.

"What I was trying to tell you, with all the inadequacy at my disposal, was that I didn't trust myself in the situation—you, in that maddening gown—everyone asleep—myself, three-parts foxed."

"Oh, Adrian, what *are* you about? If you don't know that you would never stoop to forcing yourself in that way, *I* do!"

"I wasn't thinking of force."

"What—? You—you were afraid you might *seduce* me?" she gasped with incredulity. Seeing that he was taking umbrage, she tried to bite back the laughter trembling on her lips. "Adrian, p-pray don't look so. I didn't mean to cast aspersions on your powers of seduction, I—I am sure they are great, but, my dear, they would have to be very great indeed to cause me to so far forget myself in a room that was accessible to no less than *twenty* people! And don't, *now,* be looking as though you would like to put that to the touch!"

"Oh, no, I shan't—*now.*"

"Wretch," she laughed as she slid her arms up around his neck and hugged her cheek to his lapel.

He held her that way for a moment, then tucked his hand down to find her chin. She let him raise her face, but, as he bent to kiss her, she became distressed and exclaimed, "Oh! Oh, no—not *here*—pray?"

"Not up to your notion of romance, eh?" he asked, amused.

Her eyes traveled to take in their dingy surroundings, and she broke into a slightly embarrassed laugh. "Am I being perfectly nonsensical?"

"No, but you're being perfectly enchanting, and, if I'm not to kiss you, we must go *now!*"

"Yes, yes, we must in any case," she said, smiling gratefully. "So that Mary may swear *truthfully* that I was not out of her sight above a few minutes. Only the most fanciful gossip could make much of that."

Sherworth drew her to him again. "Vescinda, really, you mustn't tease yourself with that. Mary's life would have been an agony to her if she hadn't learned to draw the long bow with Katherine."

"Yes, I can understand that, and I shouldn't cavil if it were only Lady Oxbrook. But it might be Lady Milissa who questions her, and, while we may have to throw a little dust in her eyes, I can't cause Mary to *lie* to her."

"Oh," he waved this away. "Milissa is no more than Katherine's puppet."

"Dearest, she *is* more. She is Mary's mother. In any event," she said, wriggling her nose, "let us go. This place is the outside of enough!"

As soon as they emerged, Mary sprang down from the barrel, demanding, "I must know at once. Shall you insist that I call you *Aunt* Ves?"

"Good heavens, that aspect hadn't occurred to me!" Vescinda exclaimed, choking on a laugh. In an aside to Sherworth, she confessed, "Yes, I can see now that it *is* a trifle lowering."

Mary turned to Sherworth. "But I am to congratulate you, surely."

"If it is in order to congratulate a man who has surrendered his freedom without so much as a kiss, I daresay you may."

"Truly? Not even one?" said Mary. "And she looks so marvelously disreputable."

Vescinda smiled. "I'm sure he'd also like to tell you that, after bidding him to take care not to crumple my gown, I cast myself on his chest and caused my own undoing."

She pulled off the sky-blue gloves, a perfect match to her kid sandals, and made futile efforts at the creases in her pretty walking dress of white jaconet muslin. Matters were worse than she had imagined. She tugged the once-charming bonnet of white willow shavings all the way off. The blue flowers hung drunkenly from the matching ribband round the crown. Much worse!

Mary, watching this between amusement and dismay, came forward. "If you will stoop a little, I shall engage to put you into better repair."

"Oh, yes, thank you," Vescinda said, availing herself of Sherworth's arm for balance.

"You had better know, however, that there is not the least hope of restoring you to your original state of flawless respectability," remarked Mary, setting about her task with a thoughtful frown. After a moment, she said, "Ves, I'll stand buff if you really wish it, but I haven't a notion how we shall explain your returning from a stroll with me in such a condition. Don't you think we ought to own to having met Sherworth? Perhaps there won't be too great a kick up once we explain that you have become betrothed."

"Oh, worse," assured Vescinda, her mind already grappling with the problem. "To say that we are betrothed would only add one more piece of misconduct to the affair, besides creating a deal of undesirable conjecture. Not being of age, I cannot properly receive an offer—far less accept one—without my father's consent. What is more," she went on, "the greatest difficulty should come in trying to explain *where* this offer, which caused me to become so disordered, was made! Certainly I should be thought abominably fast to have been embracing in public, and, from there, the alternatives become steadily more outrageous. In fact, to dispel the very natural conclusion that we used an inn for the purpose, we should have to describe *this* sordid little establishment. . . . And, of course, no one is likely to *believe* that we set up a clandestine meeting in an improper place, solely for the purpose of making and receiving a proposal of marriage! Not when my father would have happily given us permission to be private anytime this past se'enight. There would seem to be no reason to have arranged such an unexceptionable thing in so havey-cavey a manner."

"No, I see," said Mary, deftly pinning a curl in place. She glanced up at Sherworth. *"Did* you have a reason for arranging such an unexceptionable thing in so havey-cavey a manner?"

"Well, yes, he did, poor fellow," Vescinda intervened, laughing. "But *that* explanation would only sink me further into disgrace. Are you anywhere near finished? To add to all else, I think I am becoming permanently bent."

Mary completed her makeshift repairs to Vescinda's hair with a final pat and indicated she might rise. "Perhaps that is our solution," she offered as she analyzed Vescinda's bonnet, trying to recall the smart angle at which it had originally reposed. "If you hobbled back, we could say you'd been run down by a carriage."

Vescinda smiled appreciatively. "Ah, but to lend credit to that tale, I should have to wallow about on the floor, and we should then have to explain how it is that I am carrying about the aura of a not-precisely-fresh lobster."

Sherworth, who had been watching the ministrations to his love's dusky curls, slipped an arm around her waist and dropped a kiss onto her forehead.

Vescinda colored slightly, and Mary, stifling a laugh, said, "I think, dear Uncle, you had better tell me, *before* I replace this bonnet, if you are likely to be overcome by further whims of that nature."

Evidently not wishing to commit himself on this point, Sherworth merely smiled down at Vescinda and said, "Surely you females are making more of a hobble of this than need be. Can't you just nip off to the inn and have one of the chambermaids iron your gown?"

"Good heavens!" exclaimed Vescinda.

"No," agreed Mary with a twinkle. "It wouldn't do at all for her to be found skulking about an inn in her petticoat."

"Oh, the devil," returned Sherworth. "We've bespoken two chambers, one expressly for the ladies to use for dressing."

"Yes, love," soothed Vescinda, "but *we* are not permitted to go to ours without a chaperone, and, most assuredly, we are not expected to be dressing in it until it is time to change for the ball tonight—and besides, there is my hair and my bonnet and, most likely, an exalted look in my eye. However should I explain all that?"

He smiled. "For all you've said, I think we should simply resort to the truth. After all, it is really only Katherine, who will try to make anything of it, and a fig for her gossip! Soon—*very* soon, if I have anything to say—you'll be the Countess of Sherworth, and I assure you that no one will cut you because it got out that you once spent five minutes alone with me before the knot was tied! And, as far as I can see, the only thing that can be construed from a few paltry wrinkles in your gown is that you were certainly *wearing* it at the time!"

"How wonderfully uncomplicated, the male mind," smiled Vescinda, allowing Mary to set her bonnet in place. "In the meantime, however, I am merely the unmarried Miss Bancroft, who is sadly vulnerable to scandal and whose duty it is to deliver herself to you with her reputation intact. Besides, think of your own reputation. Surely you don't want it said that you were caught by one of the oldest feminine wiles known to man!"

"What—?"

"Why, yes," Vescinda laughed. "Did you expect a round tale would be told? Unquestionably it would be a veiled account—too entirely painful to be put into words—but quite complete enough for it to be understood that I tricked you into compromising me, and then coerced your own niece into acting as a witness to my undoing! Oh and, naturally, I should be held to have made wicked use of your relationship to my grandmother in order to *force* your sense of honor! Why, you'd never be able to hold your head up in White's again!"

Sherworth had begun to look angry, but at that he laughed. "No, and certainly not if it got out that I was so neatly rolled up over nothing but a few minutes' conversation! Very well, I'll not have such things said of you. All I can see to do—and really, now that I come to think of it, I like the notion excessively—is to take you home. Mary shall tell them that you had the headache."

"You are half right, my love. I must indeed have the headache and go home—but alone. You are forgetting that Aunt Chloe and Papa are gone from the house and will be away until late this evening. If you turn up missing, too, we shall have come full circle back to the same tangle." She laid her hand on Sherworth's arm and replied to his muttered oath. "Yes, I should have liked it of all things, but it cannot be. Mary and I must contrive to slip out of here unnoticed, and, since she shall say that we went to the Cobb, I think it best that we go there now and wait for you to send my coachman to fetch me."

When Vescinda was judged respectable enough to pass unnoticed in a crowd, Sherworth took up his beaver hat and headed for the door. Pausing there, he turned to ask, "Is there a sinister reason why I may not return to the Cobb and wait with you while your horses are being put to?"

"None. I wish you will," she said warmly.

"Right," he said, going out. "A tap on the door will mean all's snug."

Vescinda and Mary, stood, holding their breath, not daring to speak. In a moment, the anxiously awaited tap sounded. They shot out into the passing crowd and adjusted their pace to that of young ladies enjoying a casual stroll. The lobsterman, who had been keeping an eye on his property from a nearby porch, turned to his companion: "Lor', that swell had *two* of 'em in there and didn't take half the time he paid fer."

Fortunately, only this indifferent gentleman was able to associate Vescinda with the disreputable shack. Miss Wildborne, who had been heartily disappointed at seeing her pass by both inns (certainly the logical place for an assignation), had continued to dog her cautiously along the walk, but, like Vescinda, she was at home to a peg in Lyme Regis and knew every turning of the place. Once the town was left behind, there had seemed no other possibility but that Vescinda and Mary were making for the Cobb. There were, of course, a few cottages along the way, but they had all been hired out long before the season.

From time to time, as the path curved, Miss Wildborne had been able to spot her quarry ahead in the steady stream of people, but there had seemed nothing to be gained by maintaining a careful watch. So, she had allowed her attention to wander until reaching a vantage point near the entrance to the Cobb. There she had positioned herself, waiting to see which way they meant to go.

There had been many repairs and improvements made to the massive jetty over the last six hundred years. The most recent of these had been to increase its height to sixteen feet above the waters which it molded into a beautiful and practical little bay. The builders had not disturbed the paved level of the original structure but had merely added another, higher one, so that, in calm seas, visitors could walk safely on either what was now called the Old Cobb, or above, on the new. Miss Wildborne was waiting to see which of these Vescinda would choose.

Soon, however, a frown began to gather on her brow, for she was sure that the couple who had been walking just behind Vescinda were at that moment stepping onto the Cobb. This perplexing development seemed to indicate that, somehow, Vescinda and Mary had managed to vanish into thin air. Shaking her head as though to rid it of a wild and unreal conjecture, Miss Wildborne scanned the area once more. In the end, however, she was forced to assume that she had misjudged the distance and that Vescinda must have gained the entrance sooner than expected. Nevertheless, a thoughtful frown lingered on her brow, as Miss Wildborne hurried along, lacking any very clear idea what it could be, but tingling with the sense that something untoward was afoot.

The Cobb was over two hundred yards long, so Miss Wildborne was not surprised that she was unable to pick out Vescinda and Mary from among the many other gaily dressed ladies sauntering along its separate levels. She was resigned that there was nothing for it but to set out herself, searching both levels thoroughly. It was not until she had returned, discouraged from this unrewarding task, that she saw them—just arriving! She stood, watching them, her countenance extremely suspicious, as she wondered where they could have been for all that time, and what they were up to now. It was plain that they did not intend a walk, for after coming only a short way they stopped, pretending—in Miss Wildborne's opinion—to admire the view. It was a simple pursuit and certainly innocent enough, but Miss Wildborne felt that tingle of excitement returning, and she wished for all she was worth that she might know what they were saying. Then, suddenly recalling her surroundings, she almost shrieked with delight and began moving rapidly, away from the objects of her interest, to the opposite end of the Cobb.

The semicircular form of the structure caused an acoustical peculiarity, similar to that of the Whispering Gallery of St. Paul's Cathedral, in that it concentrated at one point the sounds produced in another. Miss Wildborne had entertained herself for many hours as a child, experimenting with the effects of this phenomenon. She realized, of course, that Vescinda, too, was familiar with it, but even she herself had not recalled those youthful adventures until need had brought it to mind. And, although there was the possibility that Mary might call it to Vescinda's attention by mentioning the sounds of muffled voices in her ears, it was more probable that, like most strangers not familiar with the curiosity, Mary would simply suppose it to be the echoed sounds of people walking above her on the upper level, and say nothing at all. In either case, there was little to fear, for so long as Vescinda was unaware of the presence of anyone wishing to single out her conversation, she would not trouble to watch her words.

Miss Wildborne bustled along, her ears on the cock. If Vescinda were in what they were used to call a good listening post—and her position at one end of the arc boded favorably—Miss Wildborne needed only to find the corresponding place at the opposite end. Then, after accustoming her ears to the general din, she would be able to sort out Vescinda's and Mary's voices and, thereafter, concentrate on them until she had shut out all else. Unfortunately, since voices traveled both ways, Miss Wildborne was forced to consider the danger of someone attempting to engage her in conversation.

It was no small concern. Any young girl walking about in such an assorted crowd, with neither a companion nor an escort, was bound to draw the wrong kind of attention to herself, and Miss Wildborne, an exceptionally beautiful specimen, had already endured several bold looks and rude comments. Those, however, had been made in passing, while she was on the move, but, when she would be standing still looking for all the world as though she were inviting such notice, these comments could be pinpointed directly into Vescinda's hearing. Lady Wildborne would have been prostrated if she knew that her daughter was exposing herself to such vulgar interest and abuse, but Miss Wildborne was concerned only that such concentrated speech might betray her presence to Vescinda or, at the very least, cause her to move away to a less advantageous position. However, always single-minded and forever optimistic when in pursuit of revenge, Miss Wildborne continued in a relentless search for the right spot, and in a very short while a slow, unpleasant smile crept over her flawless features.

18

Since neither Vescinda nor Mary was in the habit of slipping in and out of buildings in a hugger-mugger fashion, they were entirely too unnerved to speak of their adventure for a space of time after reaching the Cobb. Contrary to Miss Wildborne's opinion, however, it was hardly necessary for them to pretend a pleasure in the view, for it was one of the finest in the land. The closer aspect showed the surf dotted with brightly painted bathing machines drawn by large placid horses in colored harness and the sandy beach covered with dozens of holiday makers. Farther off, toward Charmouth, were the steep, wild cliffs that made this area the most spectacular of the entire Dorset coast.

After a few minutes in the calming effect of the gentle sea breeze, Vescinda pointed toward them, telling Mary, "Those great cliffs there are riddled with the remains of creatures that lived thousands of decades ago, and only two years since, a young girl living here in Broad Street—also named Mary—caused a great stir by discovering a giant one called an—an Ickysomething-or-other. They carted it off—to a museum, I daresay—and pieced it together. Shocking to think such an enormous thing once resided in the neighborhood."

"Well, let's hope there are none of them clinging to life," returned Mary. "I have already *one* dragon to deal with. Aunt Katherine is no doubt breathing fire at this very minute."

Vescinda's expression immediately became concerned. "Oh, Mary, you were more than a little rash to take this on. If your part in the affair should become known, I fear the least you'll be in for is a hearty trimming."

Mary shrugged. "Oh, no one should be too very shocked that *I* have behaved rebelliously. Besides, Aunt Katherine would use as much energy to conceal my indiscretions as she would to publish yours. Still, I am not without regrets. I want you to know that I *did* hesitate when Sherworth desired me to bring you secretly to a *lobstering shack!* But then he said that you two had had a misunderstanding, with no chance to put it right, and—well, when he told me that he wished to make you an offer, I'm afraid I thought it terribly romantic. It just never occurred to me that you wouldn't be able to breathe a word of it until he could see your father."

"Oh, it's *that* which is so vexing!" Vescinda exclaimed. "If I were of a superstitious turn, I should be regarding such an ill-timed chain of events as an evil omen. To *think* that we should come to this pass on the one day when my father—after ignoring them for twenty years—has decided to look into his affairs!"

Gazing out across the sun-glistened sea, she added a little wistfully, "I should have so liked to dance with Adrian at the ball tonight. The rooms here are the most romantic imaginable." She sighed, "But what instead? The most glorious moment of my life must needs be swept away as though it were a mere trifle—No, worse!—treated as a shabby incident!"

"Yes, it is a great deal too bad," Mary said sympathetically. "I should have done better to leave be."

"Oh, pray, do not think it! Indeed, you make me ashamed to be repining. If you but knew how unhappy I was *before* speaking to Adrian! Besides, it was wholly my own folly that caused everything to go awry. If I hadn't hurled myself into his arms like a perfect ninny, we might have walked back, and no one the wiser." She paused, considering this, and said, "Though, I think I am as well to be going home. *Had* we brought it off, I should have been obliged to go on pretending that Adrian is no more to me than any of the others. Yes, that should have been excessively uncomfortable. I wonder even if I should have managed it."

Mary cast her a sidelong look and said, "You are a trifle surprising when one gets to know you. I should have said there wasn't much could penetrate your reserve."

"Well, I like to think that as a rule I keep myself in hand,"

Vescinda laughed. "Unfortunately, I have enjoyed little success in matters involving your abominable uncle. Indeed, I find it a little frightening that he—that anyone—should have the unfailing power to turn me silly. But, of course, I have never been in love before. Perhaps I shall grow accustomed. I trust so. It is a bit lowering to think I shall end by going through life making a spectacle of myself."

"Oh, well," Mary laughed, "I should scarcely call a brief hug, at the moment of your betrothal, making a spectacle of yourself."

"But you don't know the half," returned Vescinda with a twinkle. "And I *think,* since you couldn't have failed to overhear Adrian's outburst in that horrid shack, that I had better explain his mysterious reference to 'last night' lest your imagination provide you with a more interesting version."

"Oh, a little earlier I might have begged you to leave me to my imaginings, but, with Sherworth complaining that he hasn't yet received so much as a kiss, I'm sure the truth has *got* to be more interesting."

"I think I can promise you that," Vescinda replied with a rueful smile and gave a brief account of her visit to the bookroom and the adventure that resulted from it.

Mary couldn't help smiling at the description of Sherworth's flight through the window, but she seethed at her aunt's meddling. When Vescinda finished, she said, "Well, this at least explains why Sherworth went to such lengths to speak to you with the least possible delay. He must have been miserable, thinking that with every minute that passed you were feeling hurt and embarrassed— and all to no purpose!"

Vescinda had been staring down at her hands, which were resting on the stone barrier. She smoothed the soft kid across the back of one, and exclaimed suddenly: "Oh, I do wish I had not stopped him kissing me! At moments like this, one needs reassurance, not a lot of foolish, romantical notions that ought to have been left behind in the schoolroom! I am teased by a sense of unreality about it all, and I know Adrian must feel it even more. No sooner do I consent to become his wife than I tell him I must go out of his reach for hours and hours!"

"Ves, this is the merest irritation of nerves. He is disappointed naturally, but he *does* understand."

Vescinda nodded and fell silent. Yes, she supposed he understood. *She* understood, but that did little to ease an almost aching need to be with him. She wanted to *feel* that she belonged to him, not that he was someone to be avoided on pain of her reputation! She told herself again that she was being unreasonable, that only an hour ago her future had been hopelessly black. She had believed Sherworth didn't want to marry her, would probably never want to marry her, and there she had stood on the threshold of the long awaited move to London, a move that had but one purpose: to provide a stopping place until she was married. There was no longer even the excuse of Freddy's affairs to warrant a delay. Her grandmother would have taken the business in hand and, because she was "fortunately" circumstanced, with a consequential sponsor, a handsome dowry, good birth and a desirable appearance, she would have found herself expected to choose between any number of eligible offers before the year was out.

Yet, even though, on balance, things had turned out happily, she was prey to a strange discontent, conscious of a growing uneasiness. She wondered if she could possibly be sensing something Sherworth was feeling—remorse perhaps. Could he, with the heat of the moment past, have begun to regret the surrender of his cherished freedom? Or was he, like herself, feeling a trifle ill-used?—he with every right and reason. Such a great step for him, and what had he to show for it but a girl who could think of nothing better to do than to refuse to kiss him and send him off immediately on an errand!

Trying to give her thoughts another direction, she glanced out over the bay and said to Mary, "It has turned into a lovely day for the outing."

"Yes, yes," said Mary impatiently, "but I can't discuss the weather just now, because I'm losing my mind! Twice now someone has whispered obscenities in my ear, yet when I turn, no one is near!"

From looking pardonably startled, Vescinda went off into a peal of laughter. "Oh, Mary, *dearest* Mary, if I survive this day, I shall owe it all to you."

"Thank you, but I wasn't joking."

"No, I know you weren't. I heard someone too. My thoughts were otherwhere, or I should have explained it to you. The voice sounds closer than it is because of the curved structure."

"Oh," said Mary, looking about her apprehensively. "Do you

think it was that poor specimen with the bag of apples? Among other things, he had the impudence to ask if I'd like a green gown—I think that means a tumble in the grass. What did he suggest to you?"

Still laughing, Vescinda said, "Something along those lines, but you don't understand. He was not speaking to us. It is an echo from—oh, five or six hundred feet away. No doubt a holiday tripper conversing with his doxy."

"Oh. Well, it's a relief to know I'm not suffering from hallucinations—vulgar ones at that!" She glanced again over her shoulder and said, "Ah, here is Sherworth just coming."

Vescinda's eyes lit in a smile, but she said hurriedly, "I think we shall not mention the voice."

"No, or he will likely want to scour the—what is this thing, a pier?—for the culprit who dared to sully your ears. Not, I have noticed, that he hesitates to do so himself."

"Ah, but that is not the same thing," returned Vescinda, quoting her love with an inward chuckle.

He joined them, announcing that Vescinda's coach would be along all too soon.

"Well, then," said Mary, "while I remain here and admire the place where my namesake found the Ickysomething-or-other, why don't you two stroll a little and take advantage of the time you have left."

Sherworth favored his niece with an appraising frown, then turned to Vescinda. "Do *you* know what the devil she's talking about?"

She nodded. "But I shall tell you when time is not so precious. However, we cannot leave her to stand alone. One of these country beaux might run off with her."

"We'll step only a few feet off, and I shall engage to see that doesn't happen," replied Sherworth, taking Vescinda by the elbow.

Miss Wildborne, several hundred feet away, had all she could do to keep from informing them that, if no one had attempted to run off with *her,* they would certainly not take Mary Milton! But that was only a minor point on her mounting list of irritations. She had got the headache from straining to keep abreast of their conversation, and she had been driven almost to distraction, trying to ward off several highly offensive overtures, while keeping as mute as mumchance, lest Vescinda recognize her voice. Moreover, what pleasure there had been in learning that Vescinda had landed herself in a proper coil had been thoroughly cut up by the mortifying intelligence that she had succeeded in snatching one of England's greatest marital prizes right from under Miss Wildborne's outraged nose. It had been a near-run thing, trying to decide who, between them, she hated most, but she'd settled on Sherworth when he'd insisted on dragging Vescinda out of earshot.

A moment later, however, she was agreeably surprised to hear his voice intrude upon her murderous reflections with almost startling clarity: "Vescinda, you're looking a trifle pulled—no, it's more than that—blue-deviled."

"Well, if you will keep robbing me of my sleep," she protested.

"I could wring Katherine's neck!" he said violently. Looking down into her face, he added, "But that doesn't account for your looking as gloomy as a Good Friday sermon."

"Oh—not that, surely. I—I am sorry that things must be as they are, but—" She glanced up expectantly as she saw Sherworth signal to Mary.

"Yes," he confirmed gloomily, "your coach is arrived. Why must everyone be most efficient just when—" He broke off and shook his head in disgust.

"If you told him I was ill—"

He nodded. "I had to assure him it was only the mildest of headaches to stop him *running*. Oh, well, I'd be the last one to wonder at his loving you when he has known you all your life." Glancing up impatiently, he said, "There is no time— Tell me, at least. You *are* happy? I mean about—"

Closing her fingers on his arm, she whispered, "Oh, yes, so very much." Then, trying to rally his spirits (and her own), she laughed lightly and exclaimed, "Why, indeed, how could I not be happy when I have won my dear wild stallion?"

"Your *what?*" he choked.

Coloring slightly, she explained, "That has been my secret name for you."

She had hoped to lighten his mood, but she was a trifle surprised to see him throw back his head and positively roar. At last he managed to say, "Well, my lovely goose, you had better keep it a secret because a *stallion* is a cant term for a man who is paid or kept by a woman for *secret* services!"

"Oh, for heaven's sake," Vescinda exclaimed, but she added in a considering tone, "though I doubt anyone could suspect a man of your fortune to be putting himself to so much trouble for what little I could manage out of my pin money."

"Oh, I don't know. How much *could* you manage?"

They reunited with Mary a moment later, both laughing and giving at least the outward appearance of good spirits. At the coach, Sherworth motioned to the footman to remain in his place, and handed Vescinda into its luxurious interior himself. When she was comfortably settled against the crimson squabs, he let up the steps, closed the door and, taking her hand through the window, held it while she took her leave of Mary. When she returned her attention to him, their eyes met and held briefly before she said softly, "I shall pass the time dreaming of ornamental lakes and Christmas."

Thomas Coachman, receiving the signal to get underway, found himself sorely torn between a reluctance to separate what all but a regular knock in the cradle could see was a pair of lovers, and the strong desire the reach the ears of his fellow servants with a minimum of delay. It had not been his privilege to be the bearer of interesting news about the family since Lord Bancroft had had to be searched for along the roads with lanterns, having mysteriously disappeared from his coach after a convivial evening at the George in Charmouth.

On their way to rejoin the rest of the party, Sherworth rehearsed Mary in the story she was to tell: "Remember now, when Vescinda took ill, you left her to await you on the assembly room steps while you found someone to fetch her coachman from the inn. But, learning that he had gone to visit a crony at the other end of town—that part is true, by the by—you sent a message into the taproom for me. I agreed to hunt him down for you, but Vescinda, not wishing to draw attention to herself by remaining so near the entrance to the inn, walked with you to the Cobb, to await her coach there. Of course, I returned to the Cobb in order to escort *you* back to the bevy. Right?"

"Right."

When they came upon the irate chaperones, just this side of the custom house in Bridge Street, Sherworth remained with Mary, lending support until the sharp admonitions of his elder sister and the whining complaints of her junior had begun to dwindle into pointless repetition. At this juncture, preferring to be alone with his thoughts, he repaired to the Lion, a short distance up Broad Street from the inn where his companions were regaling the hours. He remained there, consoling himself with what the tapster recommended as the finest Sir John Barleycorn in town, until it was time to change his dress. He had yet to endure a festive dinner at the Three Cups and, afterwards, the gala benefit ball across the way.

His party remained fixed in the charming assembly rooms until the last tune ended, all of them most favorably impressed with their company and their surroundings. Although the exterior of the building was unpretentious, Vescinda had not exaggerated in her praise of the ballroom. The glass chandeliers were lovely, the painted panels extremely pleasing, but most appealing to one of a romantic turn was the line of windows from which the dancers could see nothing but the moonbright sky and the shimmering sea rhythmically producing rolling threads of silver light.

Sherworth, nonetheless, was on thorns the whole night, wanting nothing so much as for the musicians to lay down their violins and put an end to his impatience to get underway. As it happened, he might have spared himself the anxiety, for, when they arrived back at Blakely shortly before midnight, it was to find that its master, in keeping with his erratic behavior of late, had retired hours earlier. Actually, the entire household, relieved of the necessity to provide for the house party, had been quick to take advantage of a most welcome opportunity—coming as it did at the end of three weeks of hectic activity—to enjoy an evening of simple peace. Even Chloe had lingered, after her return from Bridport, only to make arrangements to leave a cold supper for the seaside party in the charge of the night porter before brushing off to her bedchamber, where she surrounded herself with pillows and snacks and slipped happily between the pages of an adventurous novel.

Vescinda, also in her bedchamber, though not so comfortably disposed, heard the returning carriages with mixed feelings. It was an event that she had once eagerly awaited, but now, aware that her father had retired with instructions that he was not to be disturbed, she could see little profit in joining a party where, after being embarrassed by solicitous enquiries about her supposed illness, she would be obliged to sit up for hours, engaged in trifling discourse. Considering the agitation of her mind, she far preferred to remain safely in the isolation of her chamber until she would be able to meet privately with Sherworth. She could not be sure, however, that he would enter into her sentiments on this point. She passed rapidly from the conviction that he, too, would find it uncomfortable to sit about, attempting to conceal his feelings, to a nagging fear that he would look upon her failure to appear as a sort of callous indifference. Yet, no sooner had she steeled herself to go down than the thought occurred that, after such an anxious day, he was likely to be in as much need of rest as she had been and that her presence at the party would only serve to keep him kicking his heels below, deprived of his sleep, yet gaining no particular benefit from her company.

Still a prey to her conflict, she paced over to the window, but even that was unsatisfactory. The great laughing moon that had been her only companion throughout the long evening had ducked behind a cloud, leaving the prospect shrouded in dark impenetrable shadows. She sighed, told herself that it was nonsensical to make such a piece of work over a few hours, and, throwing off her elegant dressing gown, walked back and dropped listlessly onto her bed.

The next morning, Mary located Sherworth pacing in the bookroom. He showed no disposition to talk, only muttering once, "You'd think, since the silly b—buzzard went up at a wholly unprecedented hour, he would come *down* a little earlier!"

Although it was apparent that he wished for no reply, Mary settled in a chair, thinking he might be glad of company before his vigil came to an end. However, it was not long until he was offered another form of diversion, when Rigsby came in to inform him that Archer was in the estate room and wishful of a word with his lordship.

Sherworth headed out immediately, his brow furrowed. He found Vescinda's groom twirling his hat on one finger, his tanned countenance thoughtful, but his sharp eyes alert to trouble.

"Oh, your lordship," said Archer, obviously relieved to share his perplexity. "I've come about the stallion. He's here again—and the Wildborne girl with him! Would have seen you about it in any case, but the thing that's got me in a wood is that she *asked* me to tell you! Says that you'd best see her first, before—if you'll pardon me, sir—before you do something stupid."

Sherworth's eyes blazed. "She'll know about 'stupid' before I'm done. Is that mare still at heat?"

"Ay, but all's safe enough. The black's locked away in the

stallion quarters. Funny thing is, it was *her* told me to settle him there! She can be a bit cockish, if you take my meaning, sir."

"Yes, and she can also be a bit of a dog's wife, if you take mine!" returned Sherworth, storming out of the room.

Miss Wildborne was waiting in the stableyard, perched on the mounting block and flicking her riding crop against the swinging toe of her boot. She was wearing her sapphire blue velvet habit, despite the warmish weather. When she glanced up, there was a sneer to match Sherworth's own marring the lines of her classically perfect mouth. "So prompt, my lord! Should I thank you for this condescension?"

"No. You should get on with whatever it is you have to say."

"Very well. I sent Archer to you because I thought you ought to know that, if you shoot Midnight, you shall have to answer to Vescinda because he now belongs to her—that is, he does unless she's been lying again."

"Damn you! Are you here with more of your fetches?"

"I shan't trouble to ask you to curb your profanities, but since the King's English is not good enough for you, you will have to explain what you mean by *fetches.*"

"*Deceptions,* Miss Wildborne. You should learn *all* the ways to say deceptions."

"Indeed? Am I to collect, by that, that you believe me to have lied to you in the past? I have yet to learn that Vescinda does in fact plan to marry Freddy Bancroft! Indeed, I should be delighted if it were so, because that would mean that *you* could not have offered for her, and then, of course, I may take my stallion back."

This naturally startled him. What the stallion had to do with anything was baffling in itself, but how to account for her knowledge of his offer left him momentarily bereft of speech. He schooled his countenance to a look of contempt, while he searched his mind for a reasonable explanation. It had been agreed to tell no one until he had spoken to Lord Bancroft. He could only suppose that someone—one of the servants—must have guessed how it was and *assumed* that he had proposed. Deciding to let that pass while he dealt with the other matter, he said levelly, "You imply that the ownership of the stallion is tied up in whom Vescinda marries."

"Oh, no," Miss Wildborne returned in an offhand voice. "She had no thought of actually marrying you when we made the wager. Midnight became hers when you offered for her yesterday."

After only the slightest hesitation, he asked, "And how can you be so sure that I *did* offer for her yesterday?"

"Oh, I can't," she said, a watchful look in her eye. "I have only Vescinda's word that you did. But, of course, she must know that it needs only for you to deny it." After a slight pause, she went on, "She slipped into my bedchamber last night to boast of what a perfect milch cow you had been—putty in her hands, she said—and dear God, if what she tells me is true, you must have been indeed! I am obliged to give her an additional fifty pounds for bringing you to point without having to endure so much as one kiss! Oh, yes," Miss Wildborne smiled as he stiffened, "she poured out the whole, so excited as she was to have won her stallion—her 'dear, wild stallion,' as she likes to call him." Raising her hand to supress a titter, she added, "Yes, she told me that in her excitement she almost gave herself away by rapturizing of it to you! Ah, but I was assured that you were an agreeable dupe—so besotted that you were easily fobbed off with a rubbishing tale that it was a pet name she had for *you*."

Miss Wildborne, watching him from under lashes, saw that his eyes were no longer focused on her, nor on anything that could be seen in the stableyard. She was sure that he was looking back, and that his thoughts were far from pleasant. Her thin smile flashed for an instant, as she prepared to twist the knife. "Well, I must say that either you *are* besotted or as mad as Bedlam. *Can* it be that your eagerness drove you to make your offer in a *lobstering shack?* Dear me, Vescinda was quite on her high ropes about that! Of course, if her fantastical tale is to be believed, she resorted to a rather shocking shift herself—I mean, catching you alone after the ball and trying to *trap* you into a proposal! She was quite willing *then* to have sacrificed the fifty pounds. Evidently, however, you need to become intoxicated to recall that you were at least *bred* a gentleman, for I understand that you refused even to kiss her—not *even* when *she* went so far as to suggest it. Odd behavior, indeed, for Miss Bancroft of Blakely! But I daresay she was becoming desperate. It was necessary, you see, to receive your offer *before* the party was over, and I fancy she would stick at nothing where Midnight is concerned. She has envied me him since—"

Sherworth broke in abruptly. "You have reason for telling me all this. What is it?"

Miss Wildborne hesitated, before saying carefully, "Oh, I don't mind owning that, if your interest didn't happen to run with mine, I shouldn't dream of giving you this opportunity to save face." Seeing his lip curl, she added hastily, "As it is, we can both benefit from your crying off. You may keep your pride, and I may keep my stallion."

"Cry off!" he repeated, a note of perturbation coupling with a suspicious stare. "Why do you say that, when you have already told me that it was never her intention to marry me?"

Miss Wildborne, annoyed as much with herself as with him, made a recover. "Oh, well, if you're willing for a Smithfield bargain, you may have her," she snapped. "She has since decided— now that she no longer has the estates to worry about and is *free* to marry—that the odds are against her making a *better* match."

He continued to watch her with slightly narrowed eyes. "That still doesn't explain why you spoke of crying off. A minute ago you indicated that it didn't signify whether or not I married her—that the wager was won unless I repudiated having made the offer. Does that stallion belong to Vescinda at this moment, or does it not? Answer me!"

"Yes," Miss Wildborne hissed. "Yes, if you're willing for the world to know you've been Vescinda's plaything—that—that you've fallen in love with a girl who holds you beneath contempt and wants you only for your rank and fortune. Do you intend to give over to that, my lord?"

"I think you know me well enough to be very *sure* I won't give over to that," he returned harshly.

19

VESCINDA WAS AT her dressing table when a maidservant, big with news, was admitted by Dorcas. The girl, giving a curtsey, conveyed Lord Sherworth's compliments and his request that Miss Vescinda join him in the drawing room at her earliest convenience. Having performed this office with all the decorum of a highly polished servant, she relapsed into a state of idiocy and stood gaping at her mistress with an expectant grin.

Dorcas drove her from the room, abusing her roundly for her unbecoming display of curiosity, quite conveniently forgetting that she herself had been guilty of posing no fewer than a score of comments, with the blatant object of drawing a confidence that would either confirm or deny Thomas Coachman's impudent announcement. When she had firmly shut the door behind the young servant, she turned and looked her mistress challengingly in the eye.

"No, Dorcas!" Vescinda said with a little laugh. "It is useless to attempt to bully me, for I cannot very well inform you of an event that has not yet taken place." She gave her old maid an impulsive hug. "I must go. Lord Sherworth has an impatient nature, you know, and, when he says 'at your convenience,' he expects me to realize that it is the merest civil whisker."

Vescinda gathered up more than was seemly of her soft pomona green skirts and sailed down the flight of stairs. When she threw open the door to the drawing room, her eyes fell on Sherworth, standing by the window, twitching a pair of leather gloves. In her barely surpressed excitement, she failed to notice the glint of steel in his eyes, and her own lit with happiness as she closed the door behind her and hurried into the room. Coming up to him, she said, smiling a little shyly, "At last." But as she raised her arms, intending to place them round his neck, he caught both her wrists and held her at bay.

She blinked, a mixture of hurt and surprise banished her smile. She looked down at those strong fingers clamped round her wrists as if to assure herself that she was not imagining it. Foolishly, knowing it was impossible, she asked, "Is—is it that you have been drinking?"

He didn't answer. He just held her that way, staring long and hard, as though he searched for something that had hitherto escaped his notice. At last he dropped her arms and moved away, saying in a dull, empty voice, "No, merely awakened from a dream."

Aware of a weak, sinking feeling, Vescinda thought that, if he had been awakened from a dream, just as surely she had been pitchforked into a nightmare. Her pride, if nothing else, had been dealt a cruel blow, yet the desolation in his tone filled her with the need to reach out to him once more. "Adrian, pray do not set me at a distance. Tell me what it is. Perhaps—"

He raised a hand, warding off her attempts to come to him. "Spare yourself—and me! Your game is played." Vescinda halted, but could only stare blankly, and he added bitingly, "You may leave your stage. I have just come from the stable!"

Her eyes flew open at this meaningless announcement, but the look he returned was so filled with hatred that she could scarcely believe he was the same man who had parted from her with so much tenderness only yesterday. Fighting for command over her voice, she managed at last, "And what did you find at the stable to make you look at me with such—to look *so?*"

He gave a laugh so wholly devoid of humor that it might have been mistaken for a cry of pain. "What did I find? For one thing I found the proceeds of your wager, and, as might be expected, I was treated to the details of the May-game you've been making of me."

Vescinda's eyes flashed with sudden comprehension, but they became as impenetrable as jadestone before she spoke. "I think you mean, rather, that you found Liza Wildborne?"

"Oh, *that,* of course! Didn't you realize that she would never surrender her stallion to you while there was still a card left to play? And you, beautiful deceiver, made her a present of that card! How imprudent—how *stupidly* rash of you not to have waited until my neck was *all* the way into the noose before crowing in Miss Wildborne's treacherous ear! You might have guessed she would be aware of your father's matutinal habits. While I was champing at the bit, waiting for permission to speak to you, she loped off to fetch her stallion—*knowing,* of course, that *its* presence on the property would assure her my attention! But she has offered me a not altogether contemptible bargain. She suggests that we club together, so that she can keep her horse and I can keep what, if anything, remains of my pride— Tell me, how *would* you prove that you had—*'brought me to point,'* if I deny ever having made you an offer? Mary did not actually *hear* me make it—and even if she had, knowing what use you are making of me, I doubt she'd swear home for you anyway."

"Did you agree to this bargain?" Vescinda asked in measured accents.

"What do you think?" he goaded maliciously.

"I hope you shall never know what I think. Kindly do me the courtesy of answering my question."

"No! No, I didn't agree. You may be easy," he added with a sneer. "The animal is yours! But don't suppose I foiled her plot for *your* gratification. I was damned well not going to let her have the pleasure of hacking me to pieces *and* walking away with her stallion as well. And I am so determined on this, that if she tries to hedge off, you may refer all doubters to me. Oh, yes, and be sure to collect your fifty pounds, vixen. I *want* it to cost her as dearly as possible."

Vescinda's anger had turned to cold rage. She asked icily, "And did she tell you what *that* was for?"

Sherworth's lip curled. "Can you imagine she would let such an opportunity go by the boards? But, by God, I don't see why I should be the only one to come away with nothing!" Suddenly he gripped her roughly just below the shoulders and bent to kiss her. Vescinda stood coldly rigid, and, just as suddenly, he thrust her from him. "No!" he rasped through clenched teeth. "I forget that you're not above employing the methods of a common strumpet to gain your ends—*and* that you still have use for my rank and fortune. No—keep your kisses for the poor chub who gets you!"

Stung past endurance, Vescinda gasped, "Damn you!"

He gave a singularly mirthless laugh. "I was told you had not altogether escaped your father's influence. Yes, by all means, fly your true colors. You'll get nothing more from me."

Of everything he had said, nothing had cut so deeply as his obvious willingness to see her go to another man—*"the poor chub who gets you."* The words stabbed at her heart. Sherworth had shown himself to be an unusually possessive lover—and not a whit more than Vescinda required in order to trust her heart to him. Nothing else was needed to show her that, whatever love he'd felt for her, if love indeed it had been, was dead past reviving. Her mind searched wildly for a handhold on dignity, and she managed to shield her pain behind attack. "You needn't despair, my lord. Perhaps you shan't have to go away with nothing after all. Perhaps, even now, you are succeeding in steeping me in scandal. I don't think you can have overlooked that in the circumstances I should have supposed you had gained my father's permission for this private interview." Glancing out the window, she caught her lip between her teeth for an instant, then said briskly, "At all events, I see that your carriage has been brought round, and since you have had ample opportunity to say all that is necessary—all that shall ever be necessary—I shall take my leave of you."

Vescinda came out of the room, feeling all the instincts of a wounded animal. She wanted a place to hide, somewhere safe and dark and secure from the watchful eyes of other creatures. But, once more, Lord Sherworth had placed her in the uncomfortable position of having to enlist the aid of her butler in a personally embarrassing situation.

Rigsby, aware that Sherworth was in the habit of driving Vescinda's bays, was also aware that, on *this* morning, his lordship had ordered his own job horses put to. Suspecting that all might not be quite plummy, he had been lingering nearby in case his support should be needed.

Vescinda did not betray by word or manner that she had come from anything but a civil exchange when she bade him follow her into the little room Chloe had been using as a temporary office, but, once inside, she wondered for an agonizing moment if she had overjudged herself. She could actually feel the blood draining from her face, and there was a fearful sensation in the pit of her stomach. She caught at the corner of the table for support, trying to call up every ounce of willpower she possessed. She was just barely conscious of a sense of relief because Rigsby was too occupied, arranging things on her aunt's desk, to notice her lapse. She forced herself to concentrate on his busy hands, watching as if, for all the world, it were the most fascinating thing she had ever witnessed. Soon her brain stopped its awful floating and began to drift slowly back on course. The nausea ebbed to manageable proportions, and she was able to turn her thoughts to the problem at hand. When she spoke, however, her voice sounded vaguely unfamiliar. "Rigsby, I don't know how many of the servants are aware—Lord Sherworth is impatient, you see—" She was forced to break off. She had the wild feeling that she was going to start laughing and never stop. Taking hold, she began again. "His lordship is impatient of the conventions at times. He sent for me without thinking, and I went to him not realizing—not aware of the circumstances. It could be—if the guests were to learn of—"

Rigsby, for the first time in a faultless career, interrupted his mistress and spoke in a tone he had not used since she'd discarded the colored sashes from her dresses. "Now, Miss Vescinda, it's no wonder you're pale and a trifle out of sorts, when you wouldn't come down and have your breakfast. You may be sure that none of your guests have been so foolish. They've, all of them, been below at table this hour past. That is to say, excepting his lordship, of course, who, I collect has been called away on urgent business. I daresay, not wishing to disturb the others at their meal, he sent for you to come down to the hall in order that he might inform you of the circumstance. Now, if you'll just sit quiet a while, I'll fetch you up some tea, and see if it doesn't have you right as a trivet before the cat can lick her ear."

He held a chair for her, which she accepted wearily. "Thank you, Rigsby, but the servants— Rebecca came to my chamber and—"

"Now, Miss Vescinda, there's no need to be troubling your head over the silly gibble gabbling of *that* foolish girl. And if there be any tittle-tattle going forward in any other quarter, it will cease on the instant!"

"My dear Rigsby," was all she murmured, causing her butler to turn away abruptly and go out of the room without responding.

Vescinda remained as she was, quiet and unmoving. Had it been left to Rigsby, she would have been granted whatever time she needed to recover herself, for no power on earth could have wrung the secret of her whereabouts from him. But Mary, aware that something untoward had occurred and on the lookout for her, had chanced to see the butler coming out of this room.

She burst in unceremoniously, demanding, "Ves, what is *happening?* I have just passed Sherworth in the hall, and he is going away—and he meant not to say a word to anyone! Lord, he will set the company on its ears, taking French leave of them in this way! I don't understand how this can be! One minute he was waiting eagerly for your father to come down, and the next— Oh, forgive me if this is impertinent, but I feel so much a part of it all, and now everything is flying to pieces! And I know it *must* be all a stupid mistake. Can you not tell me? Perhaps I shall be able to stop him. He has gone for a word with Fairfield."

For a minute, Vescinda could only stare blankly. Then something mechanical enabled her to say politely, "No, certainly not impertinent." Her thoughts, a long way off, began to marshal themselves. At first, she could only add vaguely, "Naturally you want to help—" After another brief pause, she looked out at Mary for the first time through intelligent eyes, and, although her tone had a wooden quality, she said in a voice that was perfectly steady, "It would accomplish nothing to stop him. You are quite right—it has all been a stupid mistake."

Before Mary could protest, Vescinda hurried from the room, saying in a businesslike manner, "You must excuse me, Mary, I have just recalled something that will not wait."

Vescinda reached the stables a few minutes later and found precisely the scene she had anticipated. Miss Wildborne had waited just long enough for Sherworth's carriage to pass off the Blakely property before demanding that her stallion be brought out to her. And Archer, his ears still ringing with Lord Sherworth's amazing explanation, was making a spirited resistance.

Miss Wildborne was noisily engaged in giving Archer an excellent portrayal of a termagant in full vigor when his sudden expression of dismay caused her to look round sharply. At first, the sight of Vescinda approaching caused her face to crumble ludicrously, but it took only an instant for her to remember that there was really nothing to fear from a girl who would rather lose all she owned than to risk the slightest scandal or noise. She had also very accurately sized up Archer's sudden look of apprehension. He had realized, of course, that his mistress would intervene to settle the matter in the most conciliatory way possible.

With this comfortable conclusion, she demanded of Vescinda the moment she was within tongueshot: "Will you kindly inform this—this *fool* that Lord Sherworth has no right to issue orders regarding my stallion."

"Your stallion, Liza? Can you have forgotten that he is my stallion now—the proceeds of my wager?"

Miss Wildborne almost reeled. It had certainly not been within her calculations that Sherworth would confer with a girl he believed had treated him so shabbily. Deciding to brazen it out, however, she shrugged, "Well, you know that I never meant for you to keep him."

Vescinda lifted her brows and, turning to her groom, asked, "Am I mistaken, Archer? Are not the stakes in a wager considered a debt of honor?"

Archer's face broke out in a grin of relief. "Yes, miss, they are," he asserted.

"Oh, Vescinda, must you always waste time playing the fool? You know perfectly well that there has been no wager."

"Nonsense, there must have been a wager in order for you to bring Midnight here and say that I had won him."

"Oh, *will* you stop this! Naturally it was nothing but a joke."

Vescinda turned again to her groom. "Archer, have you heard anyone laughing?"

"*No,* miss, I have not," she was assured unhesitatingly.

"There, you see, Liza? It cannot have been a joke because no one laughed."

Suddenly Vescinda's tone changed to one of crisp authority as she addressed her groom for the third time. "The stallion belongs to me, Archer. He is to be kept locked up and guarded until he can be conveyed to London with my other horses. In the meantime, you will deal with any attempt to remove him from my possession in whatever way you deem necessary."

Miss Wildborne gasped, "Vescinda, are you actually giving him permission to behave in this insolent manner?—to—to withhold my stallion from me *forcibly?*"

For the first time, Miss Wildborne began to know genuine fear, as Vescinda stared back at her through eyes that belied the chill in her tone as she replied, "Yes, Liza, I am. Since you know better than anyone how dearly I have paid for this animal, it should come as no surprise to you that I mean to stick at nothing to keep him."

"Well, you shan't keep him!" Miss Wildborne all but screamed.

"Do you think not?" Vescinda returned coolly. "You should know perhaps that Lord Sherworth has promised to testify as to the exact terms of the wager—as described to him by the stallion's former owner."

With that, she lifted her skirts out of the dust and began to walk back to the house. She had not gone far when Miss Wildborne, recovering from her shock, hurried after her, calling to her to wait. Vescinda did not wait, nor did she slacken her pace, and Miss Wildborne was obliged to run to come up with her.

"Vescinda; you cannot mean that!" she adjured, scrambling along beside. "Your nerves are disordered at the moment, but you know that you would not wish to air such an issue in a public court!" She paused, but was afforded no reply. She would have liked to say that she did not believe that Lord Sherworth would expose himself to such an embarrassing scene either, but she had her own reasons for believing that *he* would be capable of anything. It went against the grain, but she perceived that it clearly behooved her to proceed at this point with overtures of peace.

She exclaimed in a wheedling tone: "Oh, fie on you! You know, of course, that I would never bring suit against *you*. Come now, Vescinda, won't you cry friends? You are making more of this than need be. You cannot have been thinking when you spoke of what Midnight has cost you. Why, if you simply permit me to take him away, Sherworth will see in a trice that it was all a hum, and all will be made right! There! See how foolish you have been to fly into a grand fuss over nothing? *Silly*, I never meant for you to *lose* him—I merely wanted to give Sherworth a set-down for having made a hoaxing bet about *me*. I shall write him if you like, and, by the time you reach London, everything will be made up between you."

Still there was no response from Vescinda. She just kept moving relentlessly toward the house, and Miss Wildborne's voice took on an exasperated whine. "Vescinda, you are not usually so stupid. Don't you see that if you keep Midnight, Sherworth will remain convinced that you have been playing fast and loose with him?" She was white and nearly hysterical when she fired off her last desperate appeal. "And the *talk!* Have you thought of that? Such a thing is bound to get out. Vescinda, you would not want it thought that you had participated in anything as improper as a *wager*—and of *such* a nature!"

Finally, and only when they had reached the front steps, Vescinda halted and said, "You can be amazingly dense at times, Liza. Therefore I shall speak so plainly that even you cannot fail to understand. If you wish to sue or spread scandal, do so. It may be true that I am more easily distressed by such things, but I am not more easily ruined—and it takes two to make a wager! If you are banking on my reserve, don't! If you make it necessary, I shall fight you in every court in the land—or, in the last drawing room either of us is ever permitted to enter! So, if you don't wish to end your days in social obscurity, you will put it about that you have *sold* Midnight to me—but, regardless of what you do, do *not* call at Blakely while I am here, nor in Green Street when I am there, nor at any home I may ever have in the future, because you will be turned away at the door. And, if perchance the various butlers are too nice and fail to keep you out, I shall personally throw you down the stairs!"

20

TWO DAYS LATER, Vescinda was gazing out at the frantic activities of a busy London Street. Her journey was nearly over, as her father's coach turned into Park Lane at a little past ten. The last light of day was slipping away behind the grand mansions of Mayfair, and, though the lamplighters had done their work hours since, everything was obscured in the impenetrable murk that lingered between night and day. It seemed in keeping with the depression that had settled on Vescinda during her recent passage through Kensington. Had she been in charge of the journey, she would have ordered her coachman miles off his course just to avoid it, for she was resolved that her grandmother be given no hint of the bitter outcome to her well-intended scheme. Sherworth, she had decided resentfully, could be depended upon to keep a still tongue in his head simply to prevent her learning what an unprincipled hussy she had for a granddaughter.

Vescinda turned away from the sight of Hyde Park as they rattled past the Grosvenor Gate. It seemed impossible that she would ever again look with pleasure upon anything associated with horses and riding. But this was not the time to dwell upon such thoughts, she told herself. She must think only of happy things. She cast about in her mind for a happy thing. There was a scant selection beyond the pleasure of being with her dearest grandmother again. Yet that at least was real, and it was a breath away from fulfillment.

They drew up. The team, still fresh, stamped and fidgeted, protesting their sudden idleness. Chloe and Lord Bancroft, jerked from the hypnotic languor of a long journey, instantly fell into argument. Vescinda glanced beside her to where Freddy was sleeping, unaware of the rustling sounds of arrival. She decided not to disturb him. It was a little way yet to the lodging district of St. James where he kept rooms.

The footman opened the door and let down the steps. Leaving her companions, Vescinda alighted. The town smells and the oppressive air did more than all the efforts of her will to take her back to the earlier, carefree days when, at eighteen, she had arrived, full of hope and excitement, for her first London Season. She waved aside the footman's offer to summon someone from the house and hurried up the few steps, taking the brass knocker in her own gloved hand.

Longly was on the scene in an instant. The Dorsetshire party was long overdue. The countess's coach, which had conveyed the personal servants and most of the luggage, had arrived some time ago. Chloe's Millie and Dorcas had had time to partake of two cups of tea, enjoy an hour's rest, and completely unpack for their ladies.

As Longly bowed and smiled a welcome, he noticed that the lovely young girl he had admitted not two years ago had blossomed into a most elegant young lady. The smile she returned was warm but apologetic as she sidestepped him and rushed up the stairs, untying the strings of her bonnet as she went. Longly knew, in the mysterious way most butlers know the plans of their employers, that this was the young lady intended for Master Adrian, and, watching the skirts of a dark-blue carriage costume swirling in the rhythm of a well-paced trot up the stairs, he gave his silent approval to the match.

The countess had come to the head of the stairs and was immediately engulfed in a great hug. "Grandmama, oh, Grandmama!"

Returning the embrace with equal enthusiasm, the countess exclaimed: "Ah, my dear, if I didn't know your father is never tempted to drive himself, I should have been in a high fidget—you are so long behind the others!"

Vescinda heard herself laughing and was surprised. She'd wondered only yesterday if she would ever laugh again. She said with a false gaiety, "Oh, but they had not to wait until nearly one in the afternoon to depart, nor to halt twice to be fortified against the ordeal of travel."

"Well, never mind. You are here—and in a great beauty, I see—" The Countess broke off, a slight frown forming on her gentle brow. "Though, perhaps you have not been getting as much rest as you should—?"

Conscious of her grandmother's searching look, Vescinda glanced away, as though to take in her surroundings. "No, I daresay not," she replied casually.

"Well, I fancy it was to be expected at your first party after so much mourning, poor girl," returned the countess, matching Vescinda's offhand manner as she guided her into the drawing room with an arm about her waist. "Dorcas is waiting to undress you, so you shall go up in a minute and get right into bed. But first, can you tell me the grand secret? Both maids are behaving as though they are under orders not to respond to inquisitive old ladies."

"But surely none have come in their way!" Vescinda laughed, pressing her cheek against her grandmother's. "No, the secret is not mine to tell either. I only pray you won't dislike it *too* much."

"So that's it! Certainly I shan't dislike it! If for no other reason than it means you are not come merely for a visit, but to stay."

"*Grandmama!* You will have me marked down as a talesman! How *could* you have guessed from that? *Have* you guessed? Oh, you are the most complete hand! You were *expecting* it!"

"Well, they have always irritated one another to a point of fascination, and it has been my experience that if two people of similar background and passions have the power to attract each other by any means, one need only isolate them from their usual distractions to expect a logical conclusion."

Plainly her cunning grandmother had been hoping to effect two such matches with her formula, and just as plainly was she waiting for some mention of the other. But Vescinda was not yet up to light comment on that subject, so she feigned ignorance, saying instead, "So! That was the object of your elaborate scheme! You intended my poor aunt to rescue me from—to solve my problem."

"Well—naturally, I realized it would have that result. Why, yes, my dear, I think we can say that the means to solve your problem so nicely supplied the opportunity to solve Chloe's that it was well worth a try. But where can she be?"

"She is below, shocking darling, in a fearful argument with Papa as to how best to break the unwelcome news to *you*."

"Is she?" the Countess chuckled. "Yet, my complaint has never been with his merits as a son-in-law—only as the father of my grandchild. Now that it is happily out of his power to present me with further worries of that nature, I have not the least objection. He can be an amusing rattle and will keep Chloe out of the mopes. She has been at sixes and sevens ever since losing her colonel—and nothing to occupy her but town scandal! Well, with two great houses to manage and a husband who would drive a less pragmatical woman to collapse, she will be kept busy enough now."

"Oh, indeed, yes. She is full as can hold with plans. And though it cannot have been an object with you, it has had a most beneficial effect on Papa, too."

"No, I can't say it entered my mind to attempt to reclaim his character, but I can understand how it should be so. While his revel routs and pretty young light skirts enable him to forget his middle age for an hour or so, Chloe makes it possible for him to reminisce about the dashing days of his youth round the clock. And," she added drily, "since I make no doubt he will avail himself liberally of both, he should be as merry as a grig."

Vescinda nodded sadly. "Yes, I fear it will be so. But Aunt Chloe is aware of it and doesn't seem to mind—" Suddenly, she exclaimed in a hushed, imploring tone, "Oh, Grandmama, I hear her coming now!"

"And you think it will be a great disappointment to her if I am not surprised by her exciting news," the countess smiled. "Do not fret, my dear. I may even put her to some effort to bring me round to the match. Now, take yourself off to your chamber—you must be exhausted—and I shall be up shortly to drink tea with you once you are tucked into bed."

Vescinda felt an absurd stinging at the back of her eyes, but she managed to say, "As you were used to do when I was a little girl."

A few minutes later, she found herself trembling on the edge of tears again, so touched was she to find that her bedchamber had been kept with the few innovations she made toward its decoration so long ago. When she had got command of herself again, she sighed and tossed her smart traveling bonnet onto the bed, grateful, at least, to have brushed through the first interview with the countess so well.

Could she but have known it, she had no sooner left the room than her grandmother uttered, in a mixture of concern and exasperation, "Oh, what in heaven's name can he have done to drain the laughter from her eyes that way?"

However, she made no attempt to put that question to Vescinda when she rejoined her a short while later. She was well aware that, if her stepson were guilty of an unforgivable slight, no amount of coaxing would wring the story from Vescinda's lips. And, although the countess had considered the possibility of its being a case of unrequited love, in which event she certainly had no wish to break down the reserve Vescinda was fighting so hard to maintain, she thought it not at all likely. If nothing else, Sherworth's rather conspicuous absence argued in favor of its being more in the nature of a falling out, and one that had occurred only after strong feelings were engaged on both sides. This being so, she felt there was no reason to despair, but she would need more information before deciding how best to proceed. She didn't find it wonderful that Chloe had noticed nothing amiss. Chloe could only be sorry that her mother's hopes had failed to flourish. She was surprised to see that a fast friendship had seemed to spring up between the unsuited pair, but nothing, she had assured, of a warmer nature. Since the countess knew that only Lord Bancroft could rival Chloe's profound lack of perception, she hadn't troubled to make enquiries of him.

She decided that the surest means of gaining the information she desired was to see for herself how they went on together. So, immediately after kissing her unhappy granddaughter goodnight, she jotted off a note, insisting upon Sherworth's presence at a small dinner party to be held three nights hence.

The time in between was filled with plans for Chloe's wedding and shopping expeditions to update Vescinda's wardrobe and—although London was still thin of company—with Vescinda's developing a small court of admirers.

Each morning the countess's landaulet was brought round, and the three ladies set out for Bond Street, accompanied by an energetic footman who spent most of his time transporting packages from the various shops back to the carriage. Vescinda found that many new fashions had come into being. All the modistes and milliners were speaking of special designs for Regency caps, Regency mantles, Regency walking costumes and Regency ball dress. After hearing these things puffed off nearly everywhere she went, Vescinda finally asked, as the emerged from a shop owned by one of London's most exclusive mantua-makers: "But, Grand-mama, what *is* a Regency costume? I have seen nothing out of the way."

"No," the countess smiled. "They are merely fashions so-called in honor of the Prince Regent. Oh, the caps are of white—the Regent's color, you know. The other things are distinguished by no more than epaulets—even the ball gowns, imagine—and a change over to long sleeves."

"Oh," moaned Vescinda, "then I wish nothing to do with them. I daresay long sleeves might be a very welcome change in a few months' time, but just now I can't bear to think of it. I'm perfectly ready to *wilt* as it is."

She found there was also much fuss being made over a bonnet named for Princess Caroline. But, though it was extremely attractive, Vescinda thought it altogether too pink and was no more tempted by it. She was delighted, however, to learn that riding hats, the same shape as a gentleman's but made of plain straw and trimmed with a figured ribband had been adopted for walking dress. Madame L'Arlésienne set one at a rakish angle atop Vescinda's dark curls, and she wore it out of the shop on the first day. She was just directing Henry, the footman, to collect the box containing her old bonnet, when a high-perch phaeton drew up with a flourish before the shop. An impressive but haughty-looking gentleman, exquisitely attired, had been about to alight when he caught sight of her. After exchanging bows with her grandmother and her aunt, he slowly settled himself back into his seat, apparently intending to observe them from its lofty vantage point.

The three ladies crossed over Bond Street and entered Hookham's Library, where Vescinda was anxious to collect a supply of books that would hopefully replace the unhappy thoughts monopolizing her idle moments. She was scarcely settled within the fashionable lounge when the gentleman of the phaeton sauntered in. He stopped before a table near the door, idly flicking the pages of one of the books displayed there, his eyes all the while scanning the room. A moment later, he was drifting languidly in the direction of Vescinda's party. When he reached the countess, he said with as much pleasure as a lazy drawl would permit. "Lady Sherworth. It is good indeed to find a familiar face in this deserted town."

The countess smiled quizzingly. "And you would like me to make you known to one which is not so familiar. By all means. My dear," she called to Vescinda, "this is Lord Worlington—Worlington, my granddaughter, Miss Bancroft."

Something in Vescinda's memory exploded. *Worlington!*—the one Miss Stratton meant to have if Sherworth had continued with his neglect!

Lord Worlington made Vescinda a faultless bow, then, helping himself to a pinch of snuff, said suavely to the countess, "Yes, naturally, I had wished to make the acquaintance of your lovely granddaughter. Also, I thought you might be glad to have news of your stepson. I left him only hours ago in Brighton."

"Ah, so that is where he has got to? They have no word of him at Sherworth House, which, to be sure, is not at all wonderful, for they seldom do unless he is actually beneath the roof."

"Then I am happy to have been of service."

Vescinda returned to her survey of the shelves, thinking, Yes, happy to have been of service, *not* so happy, I fancy, to have had your prospects with Miss Stratton dashed at the eleventh hour. She paid no further heed to him as he continued in light discourse with her grandmother, but, when Chloe claimed the countess's attention, she found him at her side.

"I fear my conversation must have bored you, Miss Bancroft."

She smiled politely. "Not at all, my lord. It is rather that I have only just arrived in London and am still finding myself a trifle overwhelmed by having so many books at my disposal."

"Then, pray, go on with your browsing."

"Thank you, I should like to, if you are sure you do not mind."

"Not if you will allow me to converse with you now and then."

Vescinda assured him that she would like that and continued reading over the titles, chatting comfortably with him as they moved along the shelves. He was a pleasant enough companion, she thought. A man of practiced address, a little guarded in his manner and more than a little high in the instep, but for all that not offensive and certainly not boring. After a short while he relaxed as much as she supposed could ever be expected of him, and she was pleased enough to have her mind diverted—*challenged,* she could almost say—for he seemed to be interested in her reactions to a great many things and her opinion of a great many more.

She stretched to take a book from a higher shelf, but he forestalled her, reaching up effortlessly and lifting down all of its volumes for her. She smiled, "Thank you. They make it a trifle difficult for a female to extend her reading beyond the fifth shelf."

"Perhaps it is a plan to prevent ladies from riffling through the unsuitable material," he suggested. When his provocative gambit won him no response, his arrogant expression was softened by a slight smile. Raising his quizzing glass, he glanced casually at the title in his hand, reading, *Popular Essays on the Elementary Principles of the Human Mind.* He then leveled his glass briefly at Vescinda before saying, "I trust I needn't scruple to pass *this* edifying piece into your hands. Are you bookish, Miss Bancroft?"

"Yes, a little," she replied, taking one of the volumes from him and leafing through Miss Hamilton's introduction.

His smile lingered as he took down another heavy volume. "Then perhaps this dusty work will win your interest," he suggested, holding out a copy of *An Enquiry into the Duties of the Female Sex.*

Vescinda looked at it and laughed. "And who makes this enquiry?—a member of the *male* sex, I make no doubt."

"Just so," he replied, returning it to its place.

It was the first sign he had given that he might possess a sense of humor, and Vescinda regarded him for a moment out of the corner of her eye. She could scarcely credit that he would be trying to fix her interest upon such short acquaintance. Yet he seemed oddly pleased that she had failed to take him up on his efforts to lead her into an improper flirtation. It was also a trifle incredible that he should have recovered so quickly from his loss of Miss Stratton, but evidently *men* found it no hardship to transfer their interest all in a trice. She thought perhaps that this was an ability more to be admired than scorned and decided that she must try to do the same. Besides, there was a sort of irony that fate should have seen fit to throw together the castoffs of the couple in Brighton so precipitously. She wondered, with a humorless inward smile, if it could mean that they were intended to console one another. Well, why not? Her grandmother's easy reception of him, her willingness to leave them to talk alone, plainly signaled her approval of my Lord Worlington as an eligible *parti.*

Vescinda went on, interspersing her browsing with light conversation and making use of Worlington's offer to carry the books she had selected. Soon she was joined by two more gentlemen. Sir Richard, accompanied by a pleasant young man, came purposefully over to her. A warm smile of welcome lit in her eyes. "Sir Richard! Have you completed all your escort duties so soon?"

He chuckled. "Yes, but only because I managed to raise fears of a gathering storm, which effectively disabused their ladyships of the notion that it would be wise to break their journey a *third* night."

The countess, hearing his familiar inflections, had come out from behind a nearby shelf. "Richard, my dear boy, I have been hoping that neither of my stepdaughters would contrive to keep you lingering in the country."

Sir Richard welcomed her, laughing, "So! Here you are, Madam Gadallover! I called in Green Street only to discover you were already off on a lark. Then I chanced to spy the Sherworth lozenge wending its way up and down Bond Street, and, after making enquiries of your coachman and disrupting the day of two milliners and a mantua-maker, I have at last run you to earth. I am charged with messages for you all. Mary sends her best love to Miss Bancroft and prays that, if Mrs. Standish's wedding is not to be very, very soon, that you, Lady Sher, will invite her to stay with you, so that she may join Miss Bancroft in a search for the—the *inky-thingumbob,* which she suspects is lurking somewhere in London. Can you make sense of that?" he asked, turning to Vescinda. "She swore you would."

"Oh, perfectly," Vescinda laughed.

"By the by," said Sir Richard, recalling his companion. "Let me make Lord Tern known to you. Tern, this is Lady Sher's poor little antidote of a granddaughter from Dorsetshire. Sher and I were obliged to trot down there to assure she wouldn't be neglected at her own party."

Lord Tern looked first with shock, then with disapproval, at his friend, but neither the subject nor the object of Sir Richard's twit was at all abashed. Vescinda merely smiled, and the countess said with a chuckle, "Now Richard, own that *I* never said such a thing."

"No, I'll have to give you *that.* Oh, well, served us out heartily for daring to suppose your granddaughter could be one dash less beautiful than yourself. Come and have an ice at Gunter's with us. I have a great many more fustian messages to relay from Lady Milissa and Lady Oxbrook."

It would have been impossible to judge Vescinda's opinion of this scheme, until the countess had said that she thought it an excellent notion. Then, however, she sighed gratefully, exclaiming, "Oh, *indeed* it does! I am not at all accustomed to this horrid heat!"

Lord Worlington, who had been taking unobtrusive but careful note of Vescinda's reactions, stepped forward at this point, proffering his free arm. "Then, Miss Bancroft, you must bespeak these volumes and allow me to escort you there."

Sir Richard suggested drily, "Now that you think of it, Worlington, why don't you join us?"

"Good of you, Thale," returned Lord Worlington, ignoring both Sir Richard's irony and the right of either host to escort Vescinda to the fashionable ice parlor. "But I shall merely see Miss Bancroft to the door and be on my way."

The ladies returned home late in the afternoon. Sir Richard and Lord Tern had both accepted the countess's invitation to join her table for an informal dinner that evening. Although Vescinda was pleased by this, for already she had begun to think of Sir Richard as a dear friend—one, moreover, who had the power to divert her mind, she was not at all sorry, after the fatigue of shopping in the damp London heat, to have a few hours in which there was nothing to do but sit in complete idleness in her grandmother's drawing room.

The countess and Chloe were likewise grateful of this period of inactivity, and all three ladies were content, for a time, to rest there in comfortable silence. Chloe was the first to recover and said to Vescinda with a chuckle, "Well, you certainly made a conquest on your first day out. Worlington is a great prize, you know."

"Is he?" Vescinda asked, amused. "I know *he* thought so."

Chloe's eyes crinkled with laughter. "Oh, yes, he knows his worth well enough. Still, there's no denying he's a mighty eligible catch—a marquis, you know—and handsome in a snobbish sort of way, don't you think?"

Vescinda smiled. "He does rather look down that long aristocratic nose at one. But he forgets his worth at odd moments and can be quite agreeable company."

"So you liked him, did you?" said Chloe, adjusting her position to get down to business. "Actually, he ought to suit you to a nicety. He's a regular high-stickler and a great candleholder for propriety and family duty—and his disposition is cool. He would make a reasonable sort of husband, I should think."

"Complacent, do you mean," asked Vescinda pointedly, "the sort who makes a marriage of convenience *very* convenient?"

"Well, I can't say I know just what you mean by that. He wouldn't brook scandal or gossip, and I'm certain he'd expect his heir to be his own, but he's been raised in the old school. So, I'd be inclined to say that, so long as his wife minded her duties and was discreet in her dealings—which would be no chore for you, God knows—she'd be free to have any number of cicisbeos. And, once the succession was secure, I don't doubt he'd offer to turn a blind eye to lovers. But surely, *that's* not an object with you at this stage."

"Hardly," Vescinda laughed, adding with a gleam, "Not even once the succession is secure."

"Well, he appeared quite taken with you. You might just catch him," offered Chloe encouragingly.

Vescinda imprudently glanced at her grandmother and, catching her in the act of casting her eyes to the ceiling, gasped, "Oh, *Grandmama,* it is too bad of you to make me laugh!" She was then forced to palliate her aunt's confusion. "Grandmama is recalling that I was always used to say that Lord Worlington's generous attitude is precisely what I could not like. However," she went on, addressing the countess, "you must remember, as well, that I was quite young and perhaps a trifle too romantical in my notions. Now that I am turned twenty—dear me, almost at my last prayers! Well, I think, at all events, that it is time for me to abandon childish dreams of being loved to distraction and concentrate on finding just a suitable gentleman who would make a comfortable companion."

21

THE NEXT MORNING the shopping party split up. Chloe was set down in Curzon Street, where she wished to inspect Lord Bancroft's long-abandoned town house with an eye to seeing what would be needed in the way of refurbishing. Vescinda and the countess, taking advantage of her absence, went on to York Street, St. James's Square, to choose a wedding present in the form of a handsome set of dinnerware. They pored over sample patterns displayed on large tables amid tall sculptured pillars in the elegant warehouse of Messrs. Wedgwood and Byerly, but in the end decided to add nothing to the already elaborate Bancroft crest beyond two narrow lines of gold around the edges.

Next, they crossed the square to visit a fashionable linen-draper in Pall Mall and to laden Henry with several ells of cloth. That done, they were off to a glove shop, to have Vescinda's hand measured for the dozen pair of long white evening gloves that would be necessary to see her through the entertainments of the Little Season, and to purchase the same quantity of silk stockings in a nearby shop. It was time then to collect Chloe and to return home for a light nuncheon before undertaking a more time-consuming project at the stay-makers.

There had been fashion changes in that quarter, too. No longer were stays being made to force the bosom up to such "unnatural heights." Vescinda had had the significance of this innovation impressed upon her in the shop where she had bespoken three ball gowns on the previous day. The mantua-maker's young woman had ventured to hint during the fitting, that, owing to the new patterns calling for even lower necklines, miss would find herself coming right out over the top—unless, of course, miss decided upon having new stays made to correspond with the current fashions in gowns.

Vescinda had somehow maintained her gravity just long enough to clear the entrance of the shop, where she burst into laughter. "Merciful heavens!" she gasped. "Oh, Grandmama, I didn't dare to catch your eye, for fear I would offend the poor woman by laughing in her face. S-she made it sound for all the world as if it were some little consideration I might like to mull over!"

The countess was enjoying the joke as much as her granddaughter and said, "Perhaps she thought you just an old-fashioned girl. There was a brief period during my young days when they raised the stays and lowered the neckline quite on purpose. It was thought very fashionable and not at all improper to 'come right out over the top.'"

With nuncheon out of the way, they set out once more, and again Chloe parted company from her mother and niece, this time to have calling cards and writing paper printed up with her future name and style.

Since it had been agreed to make an early day of it, as soon as Vescinda had completed her business at the stay-maker's, the countess instructed her coachman to fetch Mrs. Standish from the stationers and return home. He nodded and began picking his way down Little Swallow Street. This route would not have recommended itself to a novice driver, for Mr. Nash's commission to create a grand new street was just in its beginning stages. Soon both Great and Little Swallow Streets would cease to exist, but, at the moment, they were badly torn up in some places, and heaped with the rubble of demolished buildings in others.

As they were guided over this precarious course by the expert hands of James Coachman, a high-perch phaeton, at first intending to cross over to Glasshouse Street, turned and fell in behind the countess's landaulet. Even when the broadness of Piccadilly was reached and the opportunity to pass round presented itself, its driver chose to keep the sober pace of the Sherworth equipage. It was not until the landaulet drew up before the stationer's that the phaeton moved ahead, and then only to come to a halt before them.

Henry jumped off the landaulet, darting into the shop to find Chloe, and Lord Worlington, once his groom had run to the near wheeler's head, climbed leisurely down from the phaeton and sauntered over to Vescinda's side of the open carriage. He bowed to both ladies, and, after exchanging civil greetings, addressed the countess. "I recalled your granddaughter's mentioning that she is unaccustomed to our hot weather and thought to offer an hour's drive in the cooler atmosphere of the park."

"By all means, Worlington, if she would like to go."

Turning to Vescinda, he raised his brows, and finding her hesitant, said, "Perhaps you have an aversion to a perch phaeton?"

"No, none at all," said Vescinda, coming to a decision. "I should like very much to go with you. Thank you."

Lord Worlington helped Vescinda into his phaeton, and they continued down Piccadilly and turned into Hyde Park. Once on the carriageway, he dropped his hands, letting his team fall into a brisk trot. His manner did not lose its stiffness as easily as it had the day before, and, during the first part of the drive, he seemed a trifle preoccupied. Vescinda found no fault with this; she was much inclined to go off wool-gathering herself. So she answered pleasantly when he addressed her and left him to his thoughts when he did not. One of his questions, however, which at first she had supposed to be only polite commonplace, developed into a topic commanding her whole attention. After being assured that it was indeed true that her father was soon to be wed, Worlington asked if she believed his marriage was likely to bring about a change in his habits. She had to check an impulse to laugh and give a joking rejoinder. It would seem she had fallen into a few bad habits herself! She certainly knew better than to suppose a "high-stickler" would be pleased to hear a young lady laughing at her father's vagrancies. It occurred to her suddenly that neither would a high-stickler encourage a young lady to discuss her parent in such a way unless there were a serious problem at hand. With little doubt as to what that problem must be, she was at once startled and incensed. She could readily understand that someone who was very starched-up in his notions about family honor and duty might reasonably view the infractions of a father-in-law with as much abhorrence as if they had occurred within his own household, but why then, in heaven's name, single out Lord Bancroft's daughter? It would seem that, if Lord Worlington were looking about him for a wife and knew himself to be put off by such fustian, he might as easily—and far more sensibly—have sheered off the moment he had learned her name. In her case, no harm had come of his thoughtless conduct. She was not in the least let down by failing to come up to his exacting standards—so long as her grandmother would be satisfied that she had made a good match, it didn't matter greatly to her whom she married—but it did indeed say something of his character if he went about encouraging girls, only to raise objections that had been known to him from the outset.

She replied coolly, "My lord, I should think, being a man, you would be a better judge of that than I."

There was a long pause before he said, "Certainly he will not give up his pleasures. I wondered, merely, if he would be likely to exercise a greater discretion than he has in the past."

"I should recommend you to put your question to him, except I doubt he would be willing to answer."

"Miss Bancroft, I have no wish to offend you. Does my interest seem so unusual? Your father's activities have inspired a good deal of gossip in the past, and much of it of an embarrassing nature. Has it not been unpleasant for you?"

"Perhaps if I were *his* parent, I should have blushed for him, but I have always supposed that persons of sense would realize that I could have no possible influence over the way he conducts himself."

The marquis hesitated before saying, "Unfortunately, the world is not primarily made up of people of sense."

"Then I must count myself as fortunate, to have a natural shield against those without it."

He turned sharply to look at her, at first in a good deal of shock, but then his lips began to tremble on the edge of a smile, and he returned once more to his thoughts.

Vescinda raised her face to the rushing air, as he quickened the pace of his horses. The fact that he had been able to smile at the heavy set-down she had given him had put her back in charity with him. She supposed that, if he could ever bring himself to come down off his high ropes, he would be an agreeable young man. His manner bespoke a greater maturity, but she judged him to be not much above four and twenty. At all events, since she greatly admired both his taste in horses and his ability to handle them well, she was thoroughly enjoying her brief escape into greenery and tall trees.

She was content for some time to keep the silence he had established, but, when he took the exit from the park and turned onto the post road, she exclaimed, "Why, it never occurred to me, but, by coming this way, one gains the pike road without paying the toll at Hyde Park Corner!"

This time Lord Worlington actually laughed. "Yes, but I hope you aren't supposing that was my object. I thought you would prefer coming through the park."

"Oh, indeed. It is only that it struck me as rather a flaw in the system. Can you doubt that there are many travelers who *do* come this way with just that object in mind?"

"No, but, as public conveyances are not permitted in the park, I trust the loss is not too great."

"Likely not, but, in that case, it is only those who can best afford to pay who are provided with the means to evade it."

Glancing at her in amusement, he asked, "Do such things trouble you a good deal, Miss Bancroft?"

"No, but they interest me," she laughed, "—a little. I daresay I shan't think of it again, but at the time one does wonder why anyone has gone to such effort to create so inefficient an arrangement. They might easily have put the gate here."

"You must not hesitate to tell me if you would prefer me to pay the toll on our return," he said, still smiling.

"No, oh, no," she laughed again. "Besides, *we* are not traveling." It suddenly occurred to her, however, that what they were doing was clipping along the Kensington Road and heading for the one place in England she least wished to go. She asked, a shade too urgently, "Now that I think of it, why *have* you got on the pike road?"

"I hope you aren't suspecting me now of attempting to abduct you," he smiled. "It's merely that I wished to fill the drive with as much variety as possible. I had thought to skirt round Kensington gardens, but I'm beginning to regret the impulse. You might catch a glimpse of the Princess—and, if ever there was a case of a great effort to create an inefficient arrangement, I'm afraid *she* epitomizes it."

Vescinda smiled, but said, "Poor woman. Do you think—"

She broke off because, in the next instant, she caught sight of something far more disturbing than the unfortunate Princess Caroline. Spanking toward them from the opposite direction was the black and silver curricle she knew so well. Due to the combined speed of the two vehicles, it was not a minute before Sherworth, tooling a showy pair of match-blacks, was in plain view. Lord Worlington raised his whip handle in salute, but Sherworth's only acknowledgment of the meeting was to show them a scowling countenance as he shot past.

The marquis was quite unruffled and merely remarked indifferently that Sherworth was looking like God's revenge against murder. But to Vescinda, the sight of him had been a galvanic shock piercing through her system, a heart beating at an erratic and desperate pace, and the return of a sweeping misery which, until that moment, she had believed had abated into the dull ache that would always be with her. She worked frantically for a command over her emotions, reminding herself that this encounter had been nothing—a bagatelle!

Knowing that their mutual relationship to the countess would throw her into constant association with him (far more *intimate* association than a mere passing on the road) had been the most daunting aspect of her journey to London. But there had been little choice—none at all without betraying the true state of affairs. And so she had worked at preparing her mind and had believed herself finally indurated against the inevitability of meeting him. She tried to calm herself with the thought that her overreaction had been only the result of coming upon him so unexpectedly. But she dismissed this idea, asking herself in a mixture of pain and scorn in what more likely place might she *expect* to find him? He had undoubtedly just come from installing Miss Stratton in her new home. For a foolishly, shockingly, wicked moment, Vescinda found herself envying an unknown woman of questionable character and unsavory reputation. Then, in the form of a mixed blessing, another problem took possession of her thoughts. If Sherworth were returned from Brighton, he would receive the countess's invitation to come to dinner the next night—and that *scowl!* It was plain that his contempt for her had diminished not a jot. It was entirely possible that he might suppose her quite capable of having tried to enlist the countess as an ally against him. And, if he came in glaring at her in that way and leaving no doubt as to how matters stood between them, it would ruin everything she had done to spare the countess the strain and unhappiness of trying to maintain a neutrality between two whom she loved so much. She decided that there was nothing for it but to try to get word to him. If his loyalties were frail in all *other* quarters, at least where his stepmother was concerned, he would do whatever was necessary to assure her peace of mind.

Turning to Worlington, she said, "My lord, the sight of Sherworth has recalled me to something I must do for my grandmother that cannot be put off. I know there is a postman who comes by to collect the mail in London. Can you tell me at what time that is?"

"Yes, he should be there near to five of the clock. You will hear the bell he rings as he walks through the streets. May I suggest, however, that, if your letter is written, I can assure of its getting off by driving you to one of the post offices?"

"Thank you, you are very good, but, no, it has not been written. Shall I be back in Green Street in good time, do you think?"

"I shall engage to see that you are," he replied imperturbably.

Lord Worlington was good to his word. It wanted ten minutes to four when he stopped his team before the countess's house. His groom was at the wheeler's head before the last hoof was planted firmly on the cobbles. After he had assisted Vescinda to make the precarious descent from the phaeton, he escorted her to the door, saying calmly, "I shall be speaking to your father, Miss Bancroft— not regards to his future, but yours."

Vescinda's mind was full of the difficult letter she must compose, but, at that, she paused. Displaying neither gratification nor indifference, she returned, "Isn't that a trifle precipitous? You know very little of me, after all."

"Enough, I think. I was drawn, by your bearing and air, to pursue you into Hookham's. There, I was extremely impressed by your conduct and manners. Oh, not," he said, producing an ornate snuff box and flicking up its lid with one expert hand, "that you *possess* these things, but that they are so much a part of you that they can be most impressive, without being overpowering to the spirit or senses. In short, you are eminently suited to the position I have to offer. You will understand, I have no doubt, that that must be a first consideration with me."

He had said all this, not with his original hauteur, but in a simple matter-of-fact way, while helping himself to a pinch of snuff. In much the same tone, he continued, "I must marry, of course, but I have shrunk from taking the step because it has so far appeared that, in order to satisfy the requirements of my position, I must forfeit a natural preference to have an attractive and entertaining wife." Returning his snuff box to his pocket, he took her hand. "With you, Miss Bancroft, I could look forward not only to the very agreeable prospect of having to sacrifice nothing, but, on the contrary, to the extreme good fortune of adding beauty, intellect—er—a most *practical* outlook, and—perhaps most valuable of all—the opportunity to share your shield against the necessity to suffer fools."

Vescinda smiled. Not a romantic speech, but certainly amusing and excessively flattering. Actually it was no more coolly practical than she had expressed herself to her grandmother only the day before, rather like getting up a table for whist. One looked for a skillful and amiable partner, then dealt the cards, depending, to some extent, on luck for a successful game. Still— But she had no time to think of that. She must see about her letter to Sherworth. After thanking the marquis, she added, "I know you will understand that it *is* precipitous for me to comment further on the matter."

The next evening, as Vescinda applied the finishing touches to her toilet before going down to the countess's dinner party, she was slightly agitated and more than a little vexed. She had dashed out her note to Sherworth the day before, sending it off in good time. The postman had promised her that it would reach its direction by late morning this day, yet there had been no reassuring reply. Now, in only moments, she must go below without so much as a clue as to whether Sherworth was in agreement with her plan to put on a good face for the sake of the countess, or if he was planning to set the party on its ears by cutting her dead!

His lack of consideration in failing to respond argued against all hope, but there was, of course, another explanation. Naturally, if he had passed the night at Kensington, he might not have received her letter in *time* to send a reply. This possibility, so far from causing her to view his lapse with a lenient eye, only served to sink him further into her black books, and the evidence supporting its likelihood was just one more thing that had kept her on the fine edge of tears for most of the day.

That morning, Vescinda had paid a second visit to Madame L'Arlésienne's and, while the countess was discussing designs with madame, had wandered into an adjacent room, where she was soon struck by the unusual beauty of a redheaded lady who had just come in. A brief conversation between this person and the shop girl, however, brought it sharply home to Vescinda that she had been.

quite at fault in supposing the Titian beauty to be a *lady*. Her arrival had evidently been expected, for she'd been hurried directly into a stall that was set apart from the room in which Vescinda browsed by a tier of shelves. While this effectively removed her from Vescinda's vision, it had no effect whatsoever upon her hearing. Clearly, the stunning woman had been addressed as Miss *Stratton;* clearly she had been informed that his lordship had come by and left instructions that the bills for whatever Miss Stratton might wish to order were to be sent to him; and *clearly* Miss Stratton had been advised of his lordship's express desire that she take a *green* hat, one which he had personally selected for her because he liked her so particularly in that color! Vescinda had almost ground her teeth. Apparently he liked *everyone* in green—the lady he had planned to make his wife—his current mistress! It was all one to Lord Sherworth, so long as she wore *green!*

Though heartily frustrated by the restrictions of such a status, Vescinda reminded herself that *she* was a lady, and refrained from shredding everything she possessed of that color to pieces when she returned home later in the afternoon. Her only outlet had been to order Dorcas, in a brusquer tone than she was wont to use, that she would wear *blue* down to dinner that evening.

Still seething from the memory of that experience, Vescinda glanced at the clock that sat atop the high drawers in the corner of her room and saw that it wanted only two minutes until seven. The countess had desired her to come down half an hour before the guests were due. She rose hurriedly, fastening on a pearl earring as she did, and was on her way in the next minute. As she stepped into the drawing room, every ounce of control was required to check an impulse to falter. For there, alone with her grandmother, sitting next to the empty fireplace, was Sherworth.

The countess smiled. "Ah, Vescinda, my dear! I asked Adrian to come a little early because I thought you might like the opportunity to renew your acquaintance before the others arrive."

"Why, yes," agreed Vescinda, as though she thought this a grand notion. She held out her hand and started toward Sherworth, who was rising and, for all she knew, coming to strangle her. Fortunately, he smiled, taking her hand warmly and guiding her to the red damask chair he had vacated. Evidently he had not received her message until being forced home to don his evening clothes. He was dressed smartly and correctly in white knee breeches and blue coat. She knew he preferred less formal wear, but there could be no denying that he lent an air to his present costume. And he was making excellent work of his role, looking at her with such pleasure and admiration that anyone might have sworn he held her in genuine regard.

When he had seen her seated and taken a place on a nearby sofa, he asked, with that tormenting smile of his, what she had been doing, leaving Vescinda to reflect bitterly that he was indeed wise to keep to that, for it certainly wouldn't do for him to describe what *he* had been doing. She maintained a perfect calm, however, as she recounted several of her experiences since arriving in London.

Once they were comfortably launched in conversation, the countess rose, explaining that there were still a few details she wished to run over with Longly. As soon as she had gone, Sherworth said confidingly, "I'm sorry, but there wasn't time to send a reply to your letter. I didn't find it until this evening."

"I collected as much," replied Vescinda, reminded of one of her grievances.

"I was relieved to learn that my failure to call sooner hadn't already raised her suspicions."

"No doubt it did, but then she discovered that you had gone directly to Brighton," returned Vescinda, ticking off a second point against him.

"Did she, by God?" he laughed unwisely. "It's positively uncanny the way she—Oh, but I daresay I know the source in this case. How did you make Worlington's acquaintance, Vescinda?"

"He came into Hookham's Library while we were there. Grandmama introduced us."

"I see—and off for a drive with him slap bang," he said grimly. After swaying on the edge of adding something, he lightened his tone and turned the subject. "Richard tells me he is to take you riding in the park tomorrow. I hope your woman was able to get your beautiful green habit back in good trim. I've never seen you in anything more becoming."

It was like waving a red flag before a nervous and angry bull. Vescinda said crisply, "Sherworth, you must conserve these efforts to be agreeable for when my grandmother is by to benefit from them."

The color deepened beneath Sherworth's tanned features. For a moment, one might have supposed him to look a trifle hurt, but then he began to smolder, finally flaring up, as he said, "Yes, of course. How stupid of me to forget. My regard and opinions can be of no further interest to you now that you've won your prize."

Vescinda's eyes flashed, but she knew herself to be at fault. After a brief pause, she said a little stiffly. "I beg pardon for flying out at you. I think you were well intended, but it will be very much more comfortable for us both if we don't dwell on the past."

Unfortunately Sherworth was no longer interested in comfort. His barely suppressed jealousy and pique, once unleashed, could not be called tamely to heel. "Yes," he agreed through clenched teeth. "Let us, by all means, look to the future. I see you've now set your cap at Worlington. No doubt you've already calculated the odds on bringing *him* up to scratch. Not at all good, I should say. But evidently it's the challenge that puts you on your mettle."

"Sherworth, I must beg you not to do this to me," Vescinda said tautly. "Moments from now, we shall be before company, obliged to carry off an entire evening with the appearance of mutual regard and friendship. For your own sake as well as mine, do not make it more difficult than need be."

"Oh, don't have a care for *me*. And, as for you—" he broke off to laugh harshly. "My dear, you are a Siddons, a tragic loss to the theatre! Why, you should be able to carry off such a paltry piece of playacting without a thought! But, come now, having learned the rules of the game, I am anxious for a little sport myself. I've decided to back Worlington. And, as it happens, I, too, have a black stallion in my stable. Oh, nothing to compare with yours, but I'm confident enough to throw in the pair you saw me driving yesterday. How will that be? Surely well worth your while to—"

He broke off, suddenly becoming alert. Vescinda had pulled open the drawer in a table beside her chair and withdrawn from it the long sharp knife the countess kept there to cut open the pages of a new book. Paying no heed to him, she bent over, turned up the bottom of her gown slightly and, inserting the blade between the fold of its hem, severed the threads. She replaced the knife, and stood up. "Pray excuse me, if you please. It appears my hem has come undone, and I must see to it before the other guests arrive."

A short while later, the countess remarked, as she settled herself opposite her stepson, "It is indeed surprising. Dorcas is usually so careful of Vescinda's things that it is hard to imagine her allowing her mistress to come away with a torn hem."

Sherworth closed the subject firmly by muttering that the best of them would let you down. The countess made no further attempt to draw him out. Within minutes of seeing them together, she had realized that they were making a united effort to pull the wool over her eyes. For the time being, she could think of no better plan than that they should be left to cope with all the complications of such a diverting common goal.

At dinner, Vescinda was seated between her father and Sir Richard. Sherworth was opposite, well within tongueshot, but barred by table etiquette from conversing with her. The countess, one of his partners, made few demands upon him. So he was left with ample leisure to follow the cheerful bantering that was taking place across the table between Vescinda and Sir Richard. While he was far from pleased with this entertainment, given a choice, Sherworth would have gladly endured many more hours of it in preference to what he was privileged to overhear when Lord Bancroft claimed his daughter's ear and boomed jovially, "Damme, little gal, looks like you'll be snapt up even before you can be fired off! Had two of 'em round, begging permission to pay their addresses."

"Two?" repeated Vescinda in surprise. "I knew of one—"

"Young Worlington and Tern."

"Lord Tern! But I can't have said above ten words to him!"

"Well, if you want my advice, you'll say only one more—*no*. Nothing against the lad, but the devil may dance in his pockets. By the time *Old* Tern stuck his spoon in the wall, he'd managed to bring an abbey to an anthill—and piled up a mountain of debt into the bargain. Worlington, of course, is swimming in lard, but a damned sight too stiff rumped for my taste. Still there's no telling about females, and I don't fool myself that *I* shall have anything to say when it comes to point. Told them they may dangle after you with my goodwill, but it's your grandmother they'd have to turn up sweet. Well," he added generously, "she'll know what will best suit you, and you may depend upon it, she won't let you buy a pig in a poke."

Vescinda laughed and turned the subject, but, alone in her bedchamber several hours later, she considered her father's words carefully. Like most girls of her station, Vescinda had faced the fact that life offered her virtually no alternative but to marry. She had seen as well that, unless fortune smiled on her, she might one day find herself forced to forgo a natural preference for a lovematch. She had accepted these things along with the many other restrictions and benefits of her birth and had decided long ago on one point. She would choose a loveless marriage rather than risk her heart—or another's—in a marriage where love was not equal. She had come to London knowing that such a marriage was now the only course open to her, and she saw no reason to delay. She felt lost and confused. She wanted to put temptation and doubt behind her, to have her life settled.

Drawing a gold-colored dressing gown over her night dress, she hurried out into the passage and over to the countess's chamber. She found her grandmother's dresser just setting a pretty night cap in place. "Grandmama, I thought, if you are not too tired, we might talk for a few minutes."

The countess was only too pleased, and, after dismissing her abigail, submitted to Vescinda's insistence that she make herself comfortable in her large four poster, then waited placidly for her granddaughter to set a chair near the bed.

Vescinda smiled affectionately, taking her grandmother's hand in hers. "This time, dearest, I shall talk *you* off to slumber. I—has Papa told you that Lords Worlington and Tern have spoken to him?" The countess nodded, just the slightest twinkle coming into her eyes as Vescinda went on, "Have you no advice for me? Papa has assured me that you won't let me buy a pig in a poke."

"I daresay I shall have a great deal, but tell me your thoughts on the matter, love."

"Well, since Papa tells me that Lord Tern is—what he calls *dished up*—it has occurred to me that perhaps my dowry could be of help in bringing him about. It would be nice to feel of use—to do some good."

"Indeed, that is always gratifying," agreed the countess, settling herself for an entertaining discussion.

"Oh, well, you are roasting me, but it truly *is*. On the other hand, if he is *too* dished up, he may have lost his estates and would have no use for me in that regard. And it isn't likely that he can afford to do much entertaining. In short, it wouldn't be the kind of position you have been at such pains to prepare me for. I daresay you should like to see me make the most of all those years of training."

"Well, yes, my dear. And particularly if we are going to choose a husband as one does a new hat. I should be a trifle disappointed, but most willing, to wave aside all those years of training if you were here to tell me that you had fallen in love with a young man whose social position will never require your skills and accomplishments. Since that is not so, I strongly advise you to consider this point as well. A lady has little enough to fill her life. In your case, I have noticed no artistic leanings. So, allowing, of course, for children and pets, if one eliminates love, there is only duty, fashion, and social achievements. If you marry a man whose consequence is too modest, you will find your duties are too light for your abilities and your social sphere is not challenging enough. To be always functioning so far below one's own potential, whatever that may be, is defeating to the spirit. You would become bored and begin to develop eccentricities." She paused and smiled. "Next, I should find you, like the Duchess of York, filling your stables with horses that no one may use, turning monkeys and parrots and whatever else she keeps—not to mention *forty* dogs—loose in the house, and insisting that your guests defer to the whims and fancies of these creatures."

Bubbling with laughter, Vescinda said, "No, no, I promise I shan't do that—but, dear me, I should adore to visit Oatlands and *see* it. How vastly amusing it must be."

"Oh, it is—once one overcomes a foolish annoyance at having a kangeroon, or whatever they are called, hopping onto one's lap and quite thoroughly destroying one's new Brussels-lace gown."

Vescinda went off in whoops, and the countess shook her head sadly. "Only see how the notion appeals to you already."

It was a few minutes before Vescinda could command her voice. "Oh, Grandmama, how good it is to be with you again," she gasped, wiping her eyes. "But you must tell me, darling, how you account for Her Grace going on in that way? Surely a royal duchess cannot find herself without challenging duties."

"No, but hers are nowhere near what she's been prepared for. York, like his brother, will not go on as he should. He stays in town with his mistress, she out there at Weybridge with no husband, no children, and entirely too many principles to take a lover— What I am trying to point out, my dear, is that ideally a woman wants both the love of a man and the position in life for which she's best suited, but that it is insupportable to have neither."

"Yes," said Vescinda, turning away for a moment. "Well, then! Worlington it shall be! I can assure you that *he* plans to make full use of my training. It was that, mind, which attached him! He dotes on my manners and has become so enamored of my conduct that he is going to overlook my parental handicap."

"Good God, did he say so?" asked the countess, amused.

"Well—*very* elegantly. But I must be fair. He was most charming and paid me a great many compliments. And he was careful to assure me that my suitability alone would not have won him over. Not if he had not found me attractive and—and, what was it?—oh, yes—and entertaining. Though how he could have been entertained when he passed almost the entire drive in a brown study, trying to decide if his credit was good enough to overcome making a connection of Papa—"

The countess had thrown the back of her wrist up over her eyes. When she had emerged, she said, "Oh, my dear—and he offers yet another advantage! If you will but marry him, there will be no end of the stuff to keep us in jokes."

Trying not to laugh, Vescinda exclaimed, "Oh, Grandmama, I oughtn't to make sport of him in this way. He was not nearly so silly as I have painted him. And—really, we cannot fault him for being concerned about Papa. He *does* get into outrageous scrapes. I should be sensible of the honor he does me in offering for me in spite of that!"

The countess patted her hand. "Very well. You have asked me to advise you, and so I shall. It is a dictum of mine that every girl should have at least one spring Season before leaping into a loveless marriage. Why, who knows, you might find someone in even more urgent need of your dowry than poor Tern! It is even possible that you shall find love. Yes, I know you have decided that isn't likely. We shan't discuss it. But neither shall we make important decisions while your mind is still so unsettled from all the changes and excitement of the last few weeks. We shall take advantage of the Little Season, because it will soon be upon us, but shan't regard anything that may result from it. Instead, we shall rest up and then go out to Whitowers for the Christmas month, where you shall enjoy some time in the country. After that, we shall tuck ourselves up for a cozy winter and emerge again in the spring—but on no account shall we consider *comfortable* husbands a moment before June!"

22

THE NEXT MORNING Vescinda had returned from her ride and was in her chamber, revising a list of things left to purchase, when a housemaid came to her door. The girl was plainly enjoying a high state of excitement, but, unlike her colleague in Dorsetshire, she managed to complete her message with no lapse in her deportment. "His lor'ship is below in the drawing room, with permission to address you privately, Miss Vescinda."

She curtsied and rushed away, leaving Vescinda to wonder which lordship it was. Not that it signified. She would do as her grandmother had advised and put them both off. At first it had seemed foolish to wait. Six months would make her no better able to love another than she was at the moment. Yet, in some ways, her grandmother's plan, with the exception of spending Christmas month at Whitowers, brought a measure of peace. Glancing into the mirror in a mechanical way, Vescinda clamped a thin gold bracelet round her wrist. She would thank "his lor'ship" and send him away, and then get on with the business of putting the pieces of her life back together.

When she stepped into the drawing room, however, she experienced all the shock of having one fragment of that life flung back at her to be lived all over again. There before her was that great broad back and, when he turned, those wild blue eyes almost taking her breath away. She gasped, "You!"

Sherworth faltered, slightly taken aback by her reaction. "I— didn't they tell you I had called?"

"No—well, she merely said 'his lordship,'" replied Vescinda, a little off her balance, too.

Sherworth's mouth clamped shut, and the muscle in his jaw stiffened. "And you were hoping it was Worlington."

"I wasn't *hoping* anything. It simply didn't occur that it might be you." Suddenly her eyes narrowed. "And now that I think of it, how did *you* secure permission for a private interview? Or haven't you permission?"

His smile was a little conscious when he answered. "Yes, this time I have permission. I stopped off to see your father last night, and I spoke to Mama this morning."

"My father?" Vescinda repeated, feeling her legs begin to weaken. "You cannot mean—"

"That is what I mean," Sherworth said a little stiffly. He appeared to be laboring under a great effort, as though he spoke almost against his will. "I've come to offer for you—to offer you a proposition."

"A *proposition!*"

Again his smile went slightly awry. "A perfectly respectable proposition. It is, of course, marriage that I have in mind."

"Are you quite certain that it is not a perfectly *un*respectable plan to torment me further?" demanded Vescinda, becoming angry.

"Vescinda, I am completely in earnest," he said gruffly. "I am asking you to marry me—to consider—"

"Why?"

"I—" He broke off to take a turn around the room, his hands clamped together behind his back. He stopped a short distance off and turned abruptly. "I've given the matter considerable thought and believe it to be the best solution for everyone."

Vescinda had to wait to exhale a sharp breath before saying, "For *everyone?* Who, pray, is everyone, and in what way is this—this *solution* best?"

"You—me—Mama. I know that, on first consideration, it would appear that you couldn't do better than to accept Worlington—oh, by the by, I owe you an apology and my thanks. No doubt you knew already that you had me outdistanced in the matter of that wager I offered you."

There had been no sarcasm in his tone when he had produced this afterthought. Just acceptance. The sort of casual remark one sporting buck might make to another in acknowledgment of fair play. For some reason, Vescinda found this more unnerving, more overwhelmingly insulting, than the heated accusations he had flung at her previously. She did not comment, however, for he had gone right on to outdo himself.

"I must give him the higher title, of course," he allowed liberally. "But there are other aspects to consequence. As an instance, you would be only the third marchioness, whereby, if you took me, you'd be the seventh countess—" He broke off again, forced, evidently, to laugh at himself as much as anything. But he continued manfully. "I will own that even a mere *first* marchioness gets in to dinner before a seventh countess, but our family is an ancient one, of noble heritage as far back as it can be traced. Whereas Worlington's honors sprang from military achievements less than a century ago. Many people place a great importance on such things," he finished lamely.

Turning to finance, he found himself on surer ground. "Well, there can be no denying that my fortune is by far the greater. And *that* is coming to figure more and more. Good God, mere mushrooms, with enough of the ready, are in some cases courted as if they were dukes! Title alone is nothing anymore if one wishes to cut a real dash in the world!" He paused to pace again before concluding. "I realize that you will inherit from your father, but you said yourself that that would be a long time in coming. On the whole, I think you would not be the loser to accept me. Most of all, there is Mama to consider! You must know that she wished for this match when she sent me to Dorsetshire. Actually, she must have been planning it for a long time. Surely you wouldn't wish to cut up all her hopes merely for one step up in the peerage!"

Vescinda had been listening in fascination. Even Worlington hadn't been so glaringly crass. Of course, being a marquis, he had not been obliged to enumerate the advantages of a *lower* rank. Yet there was one thing she felt she must grant the Earl of Sherworth. He *did* seem vaguely aware that he was being outrageous. She knew she oughtn't stay, but she couldn't resist asking, "You have explained the benefits to me and to my grandmother. How does this *solution* serve you?"

He turned away, saying, in an offhand manner as he walked over to the window, "Oh, we've agreed, haven't we, that it's as much an object with me to please Mama? And—well, though I've avoided the issue, there can be no denying that I *am* in need of a wife. I have four homes, all in sad want of a mistress, Sherworth House the worst of the lot." At this juncture, he was evidently reminded of an uncomfortable experience, for he added, with bitter feeling, "I'm sure I could get better meals and drier sheets in any hedge tavern!"

Vescinda's marvelous sense of humor was quite wanting, for not so much as a smile touched her lips. "Ah, yes, and you mustn't forget that there is no one to call on your dependents and tenants in the country and that you are obliged to impose upon Grandmama to hostess your family parties and public days. And, *naturally,*" she added, her own tone scathing, "you will want an heir to carry on this ancient family of yours."

He spun around. "That has never been an object with me. If you would hesitate on that score, you need not. There need be nothing of that."

Vescinda had supposed herself beyond further insult, but to hear that great passionate creature suggesting such a thing—and so *eagerly!* It struck her suddenly, making her fury complete, that such an arrangement would impose no hardship on *him,* after all, not with Miss Stratton only a stone's throw away!

Green fire flashed in her eyes, but there was a calm, arctic chill in her voice as she asked, "Shall I murmur the proper phrases, citing the honor you do me and so forth, or shall I be as blunt and as rude as you and say that I don't *like* your proposition? Yes, that is more in your style! Good day, my lord!"

"Vescinda, wait!" he called after her, but he was too far into the room to have any hope of impeding her brisk exit.

The countess, encountering her granddaughter in the upper passage, asked in some surprise, "My dear, have they not told you that Adrian is awaiting you?"

"Yes, I have seen him."

The countess followed Vescinda into her chamber but emerged again in a few minutes, shaking her head in exasperation. After making her way down the stairs, she paused for a moment, unnecessarily rearranging the flowers in a bowl just outside the drawing room doors. Finally she went in. "Adrian, for goodness' sake, what *are* you about?"

Sherworth had been sitting, glaring down at the tassels on his gleaming Hessian boots. He rose, throwing up his hands in a gesture of hopeless disgust.

"My dear," she said, more tolerantly, "you told me that you

wished to marry Vescinda. What could you have said to give her the fixed idea that your offer was primarily to accommodate me? Good heavens, even if such a thing were true, can you be such a goosecap as to suppose that confessing it would gain favor?"

She sat down in one of the chairs by the hearth, but Sherworth remained on his feet, pacing for short, abrupt distances. At last he exclaimed, "Evidently I *am* just such a goosecap. I *did* think it would gain favor—her favor. I wanted to make my offer as agreeable to her as possible—to give her reasons to prefer it over Worlington's. Good God, how's a man to compete with such an offer? It never occurred to me that *he* was hanging out for a wife!"

"There are many who would be amazed to learn the same of you. But *I* should not find it remarkable if every man in England wanted to make Vescinda his wife. She is everything I might have hoped and more. But what has that to say to anything? It isn't like you to quail before competition. To be sure, I have always thought you *more* than confident where the ladies were concerned."

"A coxcomb, to be precise," he offered.

She couldn't help laughing a little. "Well, no more than is reasonable, my dear. But what is this fiddle-faddle? If I am not mistaken, Worlington also offered a carte blanche to your light-o'-love, yet *her* preference remained fixed on you."

"Oh, it's not at all the same thing," he snapped impatiently. "What could it signify to Miss Stratton? There's no precedence amongst mistresses! They get into dinner the best way they can, and it's first come, first served! Damned bobbery!" he muttered.

"And what has persuaded you that my granddaughter cares for nothing but this bobbery?"

"I meant her no insult," he assured with more haste than truth. "It's generally known that most females are born tuft-hunters."

"I shall be more generous and agree that *many* of them seek titles indiscriminately, but I should think that if you care enough for Vescinda to wish to marry her it is because you find her different from the sort of girl you have always held in contempt."

"I thought—well, of course, in many ways she is."

"I see. I wonder what you shall think if Vescinda refuses Worlington's offer as well."

"Why should she?—good God! If you tell me next that Devonshire is dangling after her, I'll just toss myself in the Thames and be done!"

"No, no, His Grace has not yet made her acquaintance," the

countess laughed, shaking her head. "Oh, dear, this would be most amusing if it weren't causing you both such unhappiness. No, don't curl your lip at me. I said both, and I mean it. When a girl of Vescinda's warm and romantic nature begins to speak of comfortable husbands, one can only conclude that she is wearing the willow. I did allow a *slight* possibility of its being Richard, but when I left her alone with him for a few minutes, she didn't find it necessary to disengage her hem."

"If you construe *that* to mean she has a *tendre* for me, you're glaringly abroad," he lashed out, his temper exacerbated by the memory of that incident.

"Am I, indeed? I can't help wondering then—being you are quite satisfied that she doesn't care a straw for you—why you should be so eager to make her your wife."

"Oh, can't you just? Well, I'll tell you this. I'd give all I own *not* to love her! But I can't—no, damn it, I *won't*—see her go to anyone else, though the odds favor my utter ruin!"

"*Ruin?* Adrian, for heaven's sake."

"Yes, ruin! I fancy the *least* I may expect is to be hung for murder. You needn't tell *me* of her warm and romantic nature! But she doesn't care a groat for *me*, so it's Lombard Street to a china orange she'll make a buck's face of me before we're done, and there's not the smallest hope I won't kill the first b-beggar who—"

"Adrian, Adrian! You are permitting your passions *and* your imagination to run off with you! Goodness, anyone would think I had Circe above in the gold bedchamber, instead of my sweet child! Now, ring for a little wine—*I* shall have some, too—and do, pray, try for a little calm reflection! You might have seen for yourself—over the Freddy business—that, if Vescinda has a fault with loyalty and scruples, it is in having too much and too many!" She paused as a notion struck her, then added shrewdly, "Why, even now, I doubt anything would prevail upon her to tell me what it is you have done to her."

"What *I* have done to *her!* If that don't beat the Dutch!"

"Well, Adrian, I should have staked everything that there wasn't a man in the world who could attest, with such assurity, to Vescinda's *warm* nature. If she has shown it to you and now refuses to marry you, what am I to think?"

"You might try thinking she had a *reason* to show it to me, which no longer exists!" he snapped back.

The countess had known that her only hope of learning what had created such a coil would be, not from Vescinda but from her less-reserved stepson during one of his passions. "Pooh! How can I think anything so nonsensica!? What reason could there be when, not ten minutes since, she snapped her fingers at your title *and* your fortune?"

But Sherworth, feeling the thin ice beneath him, stalked off for another turn around the room. Calmed sufficiently, he said, "We'll leave that, Mama. Even *I* have some scruples."

"Why, you have a great many, my dear, but you are overset and have revealed just enough that it would be better to tell me the whole than to leave me to imagine something worse."

"There is no need for either! I assure you that she has done nothing to disgrace you."

"There now, see!" She twinkled. "Already I am much relieved. But it is too bad of you to take hold just as I was getting at the root of the problem."

He said, with grim appreciation, "Lord, after more than twenty years, I *should* be up with your tricks. Yet, God knows you catch me napping often enough!"

"But, my love, if neither of you will tell me what has caused this misunderstanding, how am I to help?"

He sat down opposite her, his hands pressed hard on each of his knees. "You do believe that, don't you, Mama—that it must be a misunderstanding—that Vescinda is incapable of anything the least bit deceitful? I thought so once, and even now, when I know it's madness, I find myself half believing it still."

"Then it is a case of your mind telling you one thing and your heart another."

"Yes, no doubt that's it. But I'm *not* mad, Mama, and my mind can find no answer to please my heart."

The countess suggested that perhaps *she* could, but Sherworth remained adamant in his refusal to render details; though, upon further questioning, he did admit that, while the incident had by no means given him a disgust of Vescinda, it had left him disillusioned. He added, however, that it was no doubt the result of having allowed himself to expect too much.

This magnanimity, far from reassuring the countess, cast her into the gloomiest foreboding. She said, concern clouding her merry gray eyes, "Adrian, if this—this incident is something that you feel you cannot forgive her, Vescinda is very right—and very wise, too—to refuse to marry you. It would be impossible for either of you ever to be happy."

Privately, she suspected that it was he who had put himself outside Vescinda's forgiveness, but the same unfortunate truth applied.

Sherworth had attended her words carefully, giving more than his usual consideration before replying. "I wouldn't be forever pinching at her, if that's what you mean," he said, rising again. "I realize, however, that I've given her no reason to believe that."

That evening, when Vescinda came down to join her aunt and grandmother before dinner, she was not surprised to find Sherworth there, looking very dashing in a claret-colored coat. She had made up her mind that she would do well to expect to see him *whenever* she entered the drawing room. And, when she came to think of it, if things were at rack and manger in Berkeley Square, it wasn't wonderful that he would prefer to take his meals in Green Street. One might suppose, she thought rancorously, that he would have taken himself to Kensington, but evidently arranging for meals was not within the province of a high-flying mistress. For *that* he wanted a wife!

Dinner was informal. Vescinda thought that in other circumstances it might have been pleasantly intimate. Her grandmother had caused several leaves to be removed from the table, and they sat in a cozy square round it. There was no way for her to avoid conversing with Sherworth, but he was at least extending himself to be agreeable—the generous might even say entertaining.

Chloe, unaware that a proposal of marriage had been made and refused that morning, treated her two slightly tense table companions no differently than she had been used to do in Dorsetshire, and the countess, though perfectly aware, was equally unselfconscious in her behavior toward them.

The party was made up of light conversation and familylike joking. Vescinda had never seen Sherworth with his stepmother in such warm and casual circumstances, and it was evoking a tenderness in her which she would have preferred never to have known. She tried to dissipate its effects by remembering that, if he hadn't ruined everything, she might have been looking forward to a lifetime of this sort of happiness, that this charming evening might have been real, not affected and brought about only by straining every nerve she possessed.

When the countess signaled for the ladies to withdraw, Sherworth forestalled Vescinda's efforts to rise by laying his hand on her arm and saying, with a disarming smile, "Don't leave me to sit all alone over my port."

Vescinda widened her eyes at this extraordinary request, but the countess intervened to say, "Yes, he's shockingly unconventional, isn't he? But I know you are no stranger to such antics. Do stay, my dear. There is no one to decry our lapses."

She would have preferred not to remain alone with him, but it would have seemed churlish to refuse once her grandmother had given her consent. She settled back in her chair and waited quietly while the covers were removed. She was extremely tense and annoyed, but she almost laughed in spite of herself at the shocked look on Longly's face, when he came in to find that a lady had stayed behind for port. She reclaimed something of her character by refusing his disapproving offer to provide her with a glass.

When they were alone, she looked at Sherworth and said with asperity, "I wish you would not do this to me."

"Oh, it was only the surprise. He'll forget all about it in a minute," he returned, dismissing the problem.

"I don't ask it for *Longly's* peace of mind," she exclaimed indignantly.

"Vescinda, I cannot leave things as they stand. I didn't mean the things I said this morning! I said them—oh, I don't know—partly to spare my pride and partly because I truly *did* believe that, in the circumstances, an arrangement might be more acceptable to you."

"Did you?" she asked scathingly, drawing away the hand he tried to grasp and placing it in her lap. "Then spare your pride now by believing that, 'in the circumstances,' nothing you have to offer will be acceptable to me."

"I—Vescinda, give me your hand to hold."

"I shall do no such thing!" she gasped. "And—and don't you *dare* to do what you're thinking," she warned, seeing that he meant to dive his hand into her lap and help himself.

"Vescinda, don't set your mind against me," he begged. "I *want* to marry you. I want it more than anything in the world. If you're thinking I mean to be forever ripping up at you over that other business—my word on it—I'll never mention it again. I hadn't meant to goad you last night. I came hoping we might start afresh, hoping I might win your affection, but—well, I was still smarting from the wound, and—"

"And now, one day later, you are quite recovered," she interrupted. "Prepared even, I make no doubt, to view the entire episode as just one of the little paw paw tricks I get up to when I'm bored."

"I'm prepared to forgive it completely, if that's what you mean."

"Yes! Oh, *yes,* that is *precisely* what I mean! And you will be very indulgent of this flaw in my character—until the next time!"

"Good God, what next time? I don't expect you would do such a thing again!"

"Don't you? But how can you be certain? Perhaps not the *same* thing, but— Is there nothing here but port?"

"No, but I'll fetch whatever you would like," he said, starting to rise.

She waved him back to his seat. "No, never mind. I shan't be staying."

"Then take a little of this," he said, holding out his glass. "Go on, a sip won't hurt you."

"No, it's not at all necessary. I shall—Sherworth, you will have that all down the front of me!—I—oh, for heaven's sake, give it to me!"

"There," he smiled after she had drunk some, "isn't that good?"

"Very—bracing," she said, making a face and returning his glass to him. She took a moment, swallowing once or twice, then said, "There is no point in brangling over the issues. I find it inconceivable that you should wish to—that you could possibly want such a *vixen*—such an unprincipled *strumpet*—to be your wife. If nothing else, it argues a sad want of particularity, and makes one wonder if—if you would *know a hawk from a handsaw!*"

"Vescinda, I *love* you."

She hesitated, but evidently he had no more to add. Rising, she said in an indifferent tone. "Do you? Then you have a remarkable ability to do it without holding me in the slightest esteem. It's my opinion, however, that you know nothing of such matters."

He was on his feet. "Vescinda, you can't just walk away," he cried, taking hold of her arm. "You must hear me, I—"

"I *have* heard you, and you have said nothing of the mildest interest to me."

"Don't you care at all that I love you?" he demanded, beginning to fire up.

"I don't know if you believe it. I cannot! At all events, it doesn't signify. You see, I intend to be much more discriminating in choosing a husband than you have been in choosing a wife."

He grasped her roughly just below the shoulders. "What is it that you want, damn it?"

"First of all, I want not to be mauled about in this high-handed and improper fashion," she returned, her own temper rising. "Next, I want you to understand that nothing, *nothing*, could persuade me to give myself to a man who would throw me away— oh, *more* than that—consign me to the arms of 'some poor chub' every time there is flimsy evidence raised against me."

"Flimsy, by God! *Flimsy?* The—the devil!" he ejaculated, glaring down at her in astonishment.

"Oh, your pardon," Vescinda said, meeting his glare un-flinchingly. "I was forgetting your unimpeachable source! You— you might despise *her,* but you trust her so implicitly that you hadn't even the need to ask *me,* whom you profess to love, if the despicable things she said of me were true!"

"Ask you?" he said blankly. "Good God! Can you possibly mean to brazen this thing out? She could only have learned it from your own lips! And—and, confound it, the damned animal is actually in your possession at this very moment! Did you think I wouldn't *know* that? Wiley and Archer have become friends, you know. They drink together at the Running Footman, in the very mews where your horses are stabled! Wiley has *seen* him!"

"Then there is nothing more to say."

"You could say that you're sorry, that you made the wager before you came to care for me, that you couldn't resist getting your own back at the Wildborne for chousing you in that breeding transac-tion—or even that you *haven't* come to care for me, but that you will marry me and let me try to win your affection."

"No," she replied coolly. "I can say none of those things. But I shall say this: I do not intend to discuss this matter with you again. You have taken advantage of me tonight, but this is the last time. I am expected to make this my home until I marry, and I shall *attempt* to do so, but no longer under this handicap. Each time I find myself alone in a room with you, I shall walk out. If you try to corner me as you did tonight, I shall explain the situation to

Grandmama, and if you attempt physical force to restrain me, I shall do the only thing I can do to get free of you. I shall scream, sir, and don't think I won't! Now, we shall begin this new program on the instant. Take your hands from me, Sherworth, and permit me to pass!"

Dropping his hands to his sides, he asked miserably, "Vescinda, what in the name of God have I done to make you hate me this much?"

"I—I don't hate you. I hate what you are doing to me," she said, moving to the door.

"But *what?* Vescinda, what am I doing to do you besides begging you to let me love you? *Tell* me! At *least* give me that!"

She had pulled open the door. She paused and said, choking on a sob, "You are *hurting* me past bearing, and I cannot stand up under it any longer. If you do care at all, leave me be! It is impossible. I couldn't *live* like this. The world is full of spiteful, jealous people who may wish to hurt you—me—both of us! Even now, without the excuse of shock, you cannot even *conceive* of my innocence in so vile an act. You are incapable of trusting me! You do not love me *enough!* I need more, *much* more!—or I need no love at all. You— you can offer me neither. I *beg* of you, let me be!"

23

THREE DAYS LATER, Sherworth marched past Longly, demanding that the countess be sent to him the moment she was free. He charged into the gold saloon on the entrance floor and slammed the door behind him. He hadn't long to wait. In less than ten minutes, the countess hurried in. "Ah, Adrian, I am glad that you have come, and that you have decided to wait down here. I've been wishing to speak to you privately."

"Mama, I don't want to cause a scene in your home."

"No, dear, I beg you will not."

"But I must speak with Vescinda, and she is making it impossible. Every time I get near her, she bings out of the room. Naturally, I could hold her back, but she threatens to scream. I don't know if she actually *would* scream, but—"

"But she might. My dear, you must not risk it. If nothing else, it is apt to cause Longly to go off in an attack. Besides, I can assure you that it wouldn't answer. If you caused Vescinda to do something so outrageous, you would only succeed in sinking yourself further into her black books. You must understand, she has been rigidly trained to guard her dignity. It has become almost second nature to her. Vescinda is not a coward or a weak-willed girl. If she is avoiding you, it is because she regards you as a serious threat to that dignity— Adrian, as much as it pains me, I must beg you to give over."

"Mama!"

"I know, I know. That must seem very hard to you. But your courtship has taken on more the elements of a persecution. I am afraid that you will drive her to take more drastic measures to avoid you. Perhaps, after a while—when there has been time for calmer reflections—"

"Mama, you don't understand!"

"No, dear."

Striding over to the fireplace, he gripped the mantel in both hands. "I'm not sure I do, either. Somehow—past my comprehension—there *has* been a misunderstanding. I have said all the wrong things!"

"Adrian, we agreed on the last occasion that you had said all the wrong things. I made it possible for you to speak with her again, and you succeeded only in making matters much, much worse."

She moved over to a chair, but only to use its back for support. "Adrian, you must heed what I am about to say. Vescinda arrived here in less command of herself than I have ever known her to be. I said nothing, but waited for time to ease her agitation. At last, she began to come about—oh, not a tithe of her former self, but *taking hold*. I was not greatly worried, because Vescinda is not a foolish girl and because she was willing to place herself in my hands, to trust me to guide her, until she could find her ground. But she will not trust me much longer if I continue to conspire with you against her. For reasons which I am sure she has weighed carefully, Vescinda has concluded that a greater unhappiness lay in uniting with you than in turning you away. She is neither a child nor a dimwit. Her judgment has always been sound. It is time for us both to accept that decision! If she has been betrayed by wounded sensibilities, time will alter her thinking. We must hope and pray for that, but, if it does not prove to be the case, she must be left to pursue her future as she thinks best. Above all, we must, neither of us, turn this, her home, into a place she must abandon in order to have peace. She has already begun to talk of returning to Dorsetshire—of a gentleman there who had offered for her—of the possibility of having been too hasty in her refusal of him."

"Davis!"

"Ah, you know of it. Yes, an amiable young man, but you won't, I trust, accuse me of being a—'a tuft-hunter' if I tell you that such an alliance is far removed from what I wished for her. I do not insist on a title or great wealth, but I cannot have her driven off to a loveless marriage with an obscure country squire, merely to place herself outside your reach!"

Sherworth, still gripping the mantel, fired over his shoulder, "Then assure her that she would be wasting her time! A few miles and the likes of Davis won't keep her from me."

The countess's expression of concern deepened as she watched the muscles of his back and shoulders straining against the seams of his formcut coat, and the knuckles of his large hands whiten from the intensity of his grip on the shelf.

After a moment, she said quietly, "I beg you will not sink us all in a scandal. Whomever Vescinda marries, or even agrees to marry, must be regarded as her natural protector. You cannot thrust yourself between a man and his wife, Adrian. Vescinda would never thank you for it, not even if she loves you to the limit of her capacity."

He spoke almost to himself. "No, I know she wouldn't." Then he turned, his demeanor controlled, but his ruggedly handsome features set in a look of studied determination. "That is why she *must* marry me."

He came away from the mantel to stand facing her, his booted legs planted wide apart, his wrist caught in one hand behind his back. "Mama, there is little I wouldn't do for you, but," he shook his head, "not this. I don't want to cause a scandal. I don't want to hurt anyone. I simply want the woman I love to be my wife. I wanted her when I believed she didn't care for me. How much more do you suppose I want her, knowing that she does?"

After a brief hesitation, he went on. "There's something you don't know. I won't go into detail, but that Wildborne bitch— your pardon, Mama, I can call her no better—has done me over in a way that I cannot yet even fathom, and it has caused me to hurt and insult Vescinda abominably. Each time I've spoken with her since, I've compounded my folly. Perhaps she can never forgive my—my lack of faith, but I believe that, once she understands the circumstances, she will. But I can't make her listen without kicking up a dust. I am asking for your assistance one more time, but if you don't give it, I'll tell her anyway I can."

The countess's expression was inscrutable as she heard his ultimatum. After submitting him to an appraising gaze, she said, "I shall offer you terms. You used the words 'one more time.' I shall hold you to it. In exchange for my assistance, I want your word—not only as a gentleman, but on whatever affection you hold for me—that, if you fail to win Vescinda over this time, you will never again approach her with this matter *nor* do anything to cause her embarrassment if she should choose another."

He stood without movement or sound, resembling one of the many dozen bronze statues that were strewn throughout London. At last he said tautly, "You've got it. But I must have time to speak my piece."

"Yes, that shall be the most difficult. It is no matter to get her *into* a room with you, but to keep her there—and I mean, of course, without submitting her to the indignity of a wrestler's lock."

"Perhaps if you told her what I have said, *why* I must speak with her."

"No, my dear. I don't know if I *could* persuade her, now that you have so thoroughly set up her back, but I should prefer not to try. You must plead your own case. Very well, great bully, go away now, and I shall send word to tell you what I have contrived. But, Adrian, do, pray, try this time to say the *right* things."

The countess dropped into the chair and remained sitting there for some time, her lips pursed thoughtfully, slight furrows on her lovely brow. Finally she rang for her butler, desiring that pen and paper be brought to her. Dashing off a note, she hastily affixed a wafer. Her page boy was then summoned and instructed to seek out Sir Richard, wherever in London he might be, and to await a reply.

In less than an hour, the page returned, not with a reply, but with Sir Richard himself. He followed young Buttons (so named because of his livery) into the gold saloon, exclaiming cheerfully, "Always at your service, Lady Sher. What deviltry are you getting up now?"

The countess kept him closeted for nearly half an hour before taking him above to join Vescinda, who was engaged in providing Chloe with lists of reminders and suggestions for the care and management of Blakely.

Sir Richard had several thoroughly useless, but mildly amusing, additions for their list, and soon the mood in the drawing room was light and comfortable. It was then that he was struck by an excellent notion. All three ladies must be his guests for dinner that very evening.

Chloe, whom the countess knew well had plans to attend a

function with Lord Bancroft, refused, but Vescinda accepted graciously, as soon as she saw that her grandmother was in favor of the plan. Ten or fifteen minutes later, Sir Richard took his leave, claiming that he was off to bespeak the best dinner in town and would call for his ladies promptly at half after seven.

When Vescinda came down at the appointed time, she was surprised, in spite of herself, to find Sherworth waiting with Sir Richard. She wondered immediately if his presence were by accident or design. He was not in formal evening wear, but there was nothing in that. Her grandmother was lenient about such matters when it was a family party. The informality of his attire not withstanding, Vescinda thought he looked as elegant as she had ever seen him. He was dressed in a coat of black superfine, cut away squarely just above the waist and worn open, over a snowy white waistcoat. His neckcloth was tied in her favorite mailcoach style, and his finely knitted pantaloons, of the softest dove gray, melted into Hessian boots that were polished to a mirror finish and were distinguished by the absence of the usual tassels.

Vescinda supposed it was possible that he wasn't of the party, but had merely dropped in unaware that they were engaged for the evening. Sir Richard, however, put that theory to rout, by announcing in the next instant, "I was afraid my poor address wouldn't be sufficient to entertain *two* such fascinating ladies. So I asked old Sher to come along and lend support."

Vescinda strongly suspected that "old Sher" had invited himself because, acting a trifle too promptly on his cue, he stepped forward, offering his arm and saying smoothly, "Since it is well known that Richard has a *tendre* for Mama, perhaps you will allow me?"

Only the absence of her ready smile betrayed that Vescinda was anything but pleased with the arrangement. She laid her hand lightly on his arm without comment or hesitation. A short while later, the Sherworth town coach set them down before the Clarendon Hotel. The large double doors were thrown open by a porter in resplendent livery, and they were met without delay by a dapper French maitre d'hôtel, who took them unobtrusively through a passage skirting the public dining room to the private parlor engaged for the party.

Just as they reached the exquisitely appointed chamber, the countess, motioning for Sherworth and Vescinda to precede her, murmured that she had spied an acquaintance and would be along directly. Sherworth guided Vescinda into the room. He refused the proffered ministrations of the maître d'hôtel and held her chair for her himself. Then, taking a place opposite her, he set about trying to make her return his smile. But Vescinda would not be drawn. She wanted only the swift return of the others and kept her eyes fixed on her own white-gloved hands.

Soon the maître d'hôtel came in again, to explain that, alas, Comtesse Sherworth, having recalled an urgent matter at home, had been forced to claim the escort of the other gentleman in order to return there. He was perfectly able to appreciate mademoiselle's sudden look of distress. Naturally, she would be imagining that such delicate cuisine must be spoiled quite beyond recognition if delayed for such a cause. He was pleased to relieve her of this very reasonable concern, for her most excellent *grandmère*, fully sensible of the horrors of such an event, had been explicit in her instructions that dinner must indeed be served according to schedule. When, instead of being mollified, mademoiselle began to look censorious, he perceived in an instant that, with eyes so *éperdu* and a mouth so *provoquant*, here was obviously a lady able to enter into his own sentiments, and she would naturally be thinking it an unforgivable *sottise* that the other members of her party should miss such a delectable repast for so stupid a reason. He was, therefore, happy to share what placation there was in the intelligence that *Madame la Comtesse* did, at least, expect to return in good time for the second course. He did honor to his ravishing and fiery-eyed sympathizer by uncorking a bottle of champagne with his own hands. When it had been tested and poured, he left it conveniently to Sherworth's side and bowed himself out, saying that their waiter would begin serving in five or ten minutes.

No sooner had the door closed behind him, than Vescinda sprang from her chair. Sherworth, rising too, started toward her, but she put up her hand, saying bitterly, "Oh, you needn't trouble, I am effectively trapped. You must know I cannot be seen walking out of a private dining parlor without a chaperone, unless I wish to make a byword of myself! I am too entirely vexed to sit quietly just now. Do you drink your wine, Sherworth, and leave me be!" she ordered with a wave of curt dismissal.

She moved out to the center of the room and stopped, still holding her train, undecided whether to stand or walk or return to her seat. Sherworth had remained where she'd halted him, his face grim and tense. His eyes, however, had followed her spirited but graceful movements with automatic appreciation, and he breathed, "By God, you're beautiful!"

This only recalled Vescinda to another thing that had her nearly in a tearing passion. With the news that they were to dine out, she had told Dorcas to lay out her florentine silk of willow green, believing *he* would not be present to see her in it. She exclaimed, "Oh, I simply cannot believe my grandmother would *do* this to me!"

"I'm afraid I held a gun to her head."

"*That* I can believe! Well, you may be sure of one thing, this is positively the last time you will play off such tricks."

"Yes, it is," he asserted, causing her to look up sharply in suspicion. "You see," he went on, "she made me bargain dearly for her assistance tonight. I am never to approach you with this matter again."

After briefly considering his words, Vescinda said, "Yes, I should have agreed to *those* terms, had I been asked. Why *wasn't* I asked?"

"Because she couldn't be certain that you would agree. And, if you hadn't, she knew I'd make good my plan—which was to get you in a Cornish hug and let you scream your heart out until I'd emptied my budget. She thought you would find this more dignified."

Vescinda looked away quickly. Abominable of him to make her laugh at such a time. When she looked back, he was at her side, whispering, "Don't scream, Vescinda. I love you so very much."

Her blood seemed to surge through her system in a wild erratic path. She thought he was going to kiss her. She raised both hands as though to ward him off, but he merely laid an arm across her bare shoulders and guided her back to her chair. She went without protest, thinking that if she were to keep her concentration it would be better to have the table safely between them. There was something in his manner, something that had been missing in their recent interviews, but *so* reminiscent of the way he had been before all the trouble.

He held her chair again, until she was seated, then returned to his own, raising his glass in a gesture that invited her to taste her wine. Having already decided on precisely this course, she was able to comply to his complete satisfaction. Sipping a little of the fine vintage and drawing a long breath, she said over her glass, "I've twice told you that you have said everything that could possibly signify. Why do you persist in causing me this distress? My decision wasn't a happy one, but it is quite irrevocable."

"Is it, Vescinda? I pray you are wrong. I've staked everything on the hope that the one thing I haven't said will make it possible for you to forgive me. You see, just as I've been unable to conceive of your innocence, you have apparently been unable to allow the smallest excuse for my folly." His tone became more emotional as he went on. "You must realize that it *wasn't* flimsy evidence. Rather it was such a piece of perfection that, even now, only blind faith convinces me that it was in fact all a hoax. And, for the life of me, I can't begin to guess how it was done."

Vescinda set down her glass after taking another sip. Her annoyance was reanimated by the memory of what she must always regard as the most dreadful moment of her life. She fired back, "Can you possibly be so dense that you can't see how she could have known you had proposed? I can tell you! It was *painfully* easy. The household was alive with talk of it! Everyone *else* had guessed. Why should not she? And, if she lent credit to her tale by citing Lyme Regis, *you* might have guessed that the tattle could only have originated with my coachman."

"Vescinda, Vescinda, had it been no more than that, I should have sent her packing. My beautiful girl, my precious love, you must believe that I wasn't so easily persuaded to swallow something that came as close to unmanning me as anything I have ever faced! I loved you then no less than I do now! The shock and hurt was beyond anything I can describe to you. You must know that I would have grasped at *any* explanation that might have spared me that! I swear to you, there were things that defied even reasonable doubt! For an example, do you recall my mention of a side bet for fifty pounds?"

Vescinda frowned. It had been so minor a point compared to everything else that it had slipped her mind. She could recall his biting instructions to collect her fifty pounds. She had asked, but he hadn't said what it was for. Flushing at the recollection, she realized that he had made it perfectly possible to guess with any thought at all. Well, he had also made rational thought quite impossible at the time.

Glancing up, she found him waiting expectantly. She demanded, "Are you thinking I told her *that?*"

"No, no, of course not. But it's urgent that you remember that it was mentioned then. I—you see, I'm afraid I won't be able to convince you that there were things beyond the obvious, that my character has fallen so completely in your eyes that you might suspect me of inventing them now, merely to support my defense."

Vescinda exclaimed with self-reproach, "Oh, no. Ad—Sherworth, I never meant you to think I would suspect you of being deliberately dishonest. Pray, do not think it! I will believe anything you tell me of the events which took place."

He smiled ruefully. "But you don't intend to believe that I love you, is that it?"

Vescinda let her eyes fall to her fingers, which were toying with the stem of her wine glass. Sherworth didn't press his question, however, because at the moment the door flew open to admit a wiry little waiter and his two assistants, as they carried in the first course of their dinner.

The waiter's eyes lit first with surprise and delight, then narrowed in a silent condemnation of the efficiency of his superiors. He exclaimed, in accents mixed of wounded sensibilities and apology, *"Comte Sherworth!* They did not tell me it was you!"

Sherworth acknowledged him with an impatient gesture, returning his attention immediately to Vescinda, who slipped easily into light table talk, while the three Frenchmen performed fussing ceremonies over the several dishes they were serving.

Vescinda drank the remainder of the champagne in her glass, hoping it might settle her inner self, which was behaving at great variance to the appearance of calm she was presenting. When the waiter and his satellites swept from the room, she smiled down at the array of sumptuous viands, saying, "Well, Richard said that he meant to bespeak the best dinner in town."

"Richard—you call him that?" asked Sherworth accusingly.

"Grandmama said I might, because he is such a close friend of the family. I thought he was *your* closest friend."

"He *was*. What does he call you?"

"You are being absurd," said Vescinda, trying not to respond to the teasing gleam in those maddening blue eyes. Thinking to divert him by reminding him of his treachery, she added, "Obviously, however, he was head and shoulders in this plot to entrap me. So I may not permit him to call me *anything* in future."

"Don't be too hard on him. His part was merely to extend the invitation. I arranged the rest. Come now, you haven't commented on the side bet. *Can* you account for her knowing that?"

"Only to suppose it was a well-reasoned guess. She was used to twit me on my observance of proprieties."

"Quite unable to guess, however, what a delightful baggage you can be when it suits you," he quizzed.

A rush of pink tinged her cheeks, and she became unusually interested in the duckling prepared with a delicious cherry sauce. The truth of his words struck her, however. No, Liza would never have guessed that. No one ever seemed to. Worlington, for instance, would no doubt retract his offer on the grounds of fraud if he suspected that she delighted in being slightly outrageous now and then, or at least as human as everyone else. She glanced up and found him watching her with patient interest.

He smiled. "You've been wool-gathering, Vescinda."

"I was thinking that this is an excellent sauce," she replied. She *had* thought it, after all. He didn't pursue the subject, but the smile flirting in his eyes, when he recommended her to sample the *cochon de lait* quite robbed his tact of its gallantry. Vescinda took up her glass, which he'd refilled, thinking it was well that he wouldn't be permitted to wage this form of attack again. He truly was like a wild stallion—intriguing, exciting, and, at odd moments, gentle and affectionate. But, like an undisciplined stallion, with little cause and no warning he could also strike a cruelly wounding blow.

Sherworth broke in to chide her gently. "If you won't share your thoughts with me, Vescinda, I must insist upon having your attention. My life depends on these next *very* few minutes."

Her smile was a trifle weak when she said, "Not quite that, I think. Your life has always been uncommonly full. Still, I am sorry. I shall keep Grandmama's part of the bargain and hear you out."

"And without the least intention of altering your decision," he remarked grimly. But he went ahead, recounting his experience in the stableyard at Blakely, listing the information that had been at Miss Wildborne's disposal and explaining how she'd twisted it to fit her vicious story. He described, as best he could, his reactions each time she'd thrust her dagger deeper. There had been shock; there had been confusion, making it all the more difficult, because there had been *her* to deal with. She had, of course, laid her plans, trusting that he would deny the proposal in order to save his pride.

But she hadn't allowed that the intensity of his feelings would so far outweigh considerations of pride that striking back would be the only palliative for his pain.

Throughout it all, Vescinda listened in silence, finally putting aside her fork, forgetting completely the elaborate meal that lay before her. Only now and then did she reach out to sip from her wineglass. Her reactions varied with his narrative. One moment the color would drain from her face, the next she would flush red with mortification. When he had finished, she said unsteadily, "I—oh, Adrian, I'm so sorry you were made to suffer that."

His eyes lit with hope. He repositioned himself urgently, reaching across the table to lay his hand over hers. "Vescinda, how the devil did she do it? Do you keep a diary? It's the only thing I can arrive at, though I am almost certain you were in your chamber the entire time she was in the house."

Vescinda shook her head slowly. "No. Eavesdropping is the only thing that can account for it, and that, in the circumstances, is almost incredible."

"It *is* incredible! I daresay she might have been lurking near the bookroom on the night of the ball, but some of those things were said in the lobstering shack! Where could she have been to overhear? Surely, you aren't suggesting she might have been in the *barrel,* the one Mary was sitting on!"

Vescinda couldn't help laughing in spite of her wretchedness. "No, no, but I've been wracking my brain all the while you were talking, trying to retrace our movements on that day, and those things—both the incident in the bookroom and the lobstering shack—were discussed again on the Cobb. I'm terribly ashamed to say it, but she did indeed get most of her information from me. I was gabbling to Mary all the while we waited for you to rejoin us there." She noted his frown and added, "You are wondering how she could have overheard us. I cannot be certain, of course, but, allowing for the far more baffling fact that she somehow knew we were there in the first place, there are two ways she might have overheard our conversation. She might have simply stationed herself above us on the upper level and listened that way—though I should think it would have been difficult to pick out our words so precisely. And then, too, there should have been the risk that we would glance up and see her with her ear cocked over the rail. But there is another and even more fantastic method she might have

used," said Vescinda, going on to explain the acoustical pecu-
liarities of the Cobb.

"Those infernal echoes," Sherworth murmured, his thoughts far
away. He added, however, with the sharpness of suppressed
violence, "She had to have been dogging you."

Vescinda allowed this to be the only reasonable explanation, but
reminded him that they had not gone directly to the Cobb and that
no one had been lurking near the lobstering shack when he had
sounded the all clear for them to come out. "Really, it's hard to
account for it unless she was off somewhere with a *spying glass!*
Oh—and there is something else I cannot account for," she gasped,
turning pale. "The *things* she heard—all of them precisely the
ingredients for the sort of scandal broth Liza loves most to brew!
And she is actually here—in London—betrothed to Lord Caversham as you are no doubt aware! It is a thousand wonders that the
story is not already all over town! My God, think of the
repercussions when it *does* get about!"

"It hasn't, and it won't," he assured. "I took care to scotch that
little plan."

"But, how? Are you certain? I mean, short of strangling her,
how *could* you assure that she will hold her tongue?"

This time Sherworth's color deepened. "Truly, Vescinda, you
have nothing to fear from her on that head." Seeing that she was
looking far from convinced, he went on reluctantly. "It was no time
for half measures, you understand. I warned her that, if so much as
a hint of it came to my ears, I would devote the next decade to
passing it about the men's clubs that she had met me in your
hayloft." He shifted slightly and went on, drawing patterns in the
cloth with his finger as he spoke. "One would *suppose* that to be
enough to turn away any female blue, but—well, you know as well
as I do what a brazen, almost scandal-proof, little hussy she is. I
could actually see her weighing the consequences! So I added that,
if she supposed her beauty would catch her someone willing to
accept her as damaged goods, she'd be bowled out because—
because I am accounted something of a judge, and I'd take care that
anybody worth having would be convinced, past interest, that she
was so devilish incompetent that it hadn't been worth the climb up
the ladder! *That* went home, I promise you!"

Glancing up, he caught Vescinda's expression of shock. It was
gone in a flash, but she continued to look discomposed as she

slipped her hand out from under his. Sherworth was thrown into fury with himself. He might have known! He *had* known! He hadn't wanted to tell her that. Now she had drawn away, no doubt thinking him a complete rogue to have threatened *any* lady with such a reprisal, *and* an unprincipled cad to have repeated such a tale to her! But he hadn't been able to bear the distress in her eyes, and he'd known that her own experience with the Wildborne would have made it impossible for her to be fobbed off lightly. He'd wanted to bring her peace, but it seemed he had only succeeded in bringing her greater distress.

The servants had come in to clear the table, and he could say nothing. A panic began to rise. He realized that they were getting ready for the second course. The countess was due back. His time was nearly up. His only chance almost gone!

The instant the door swung shut behind the servants, Sherworth ejected from his chair. He dropped down beside Vescinda, resting on his heels and taking both her hands in his. Surprised by this abrupt action, Vescinda uttered an involuntary gasp, but she was given no opportunity to speak.

"Vescinda," he said urgently, "you don't understand. You said a while ago that my life has always been full. I thought so once, but I knew nothing of you—of love. There was nothing to repine. Nothing will ever be important to me again without you, and I've staked it all on tonight, on this last chance. I gave my word, not only as a gentleman, but on all the affection I hold for Mama, that I won't try to win you myself, nor interfere if you choose another. Vescinda, it's a pledge I cannot break. But it's one I cannot *keep*— not and see you again. Do you understand? I'll have to go off—far enough that there's no possibility of having even news of you! I'm afraid—I *know*—that, if I heard someone was to take you, not only would I break my word to the woman I love second-most in the world, I'd bring ruin on us all. I *couldn't* let it happen. I couldn't let anyone have you! I'd kill the bastard! It makes no odds what the world may think—what *you* may think. To me, you're mine! You belong to me, and you always will!"

A state of acute breathlessness held Vescinda speechless. She tore her eyes from his fervent gaze, hoping to compose herself, but she was given no opportunity for that either. With a stifled groan, Sherworth sprang to a standing position, pulling her up and out of her chair and into a crushing embrace. All the heat and passion and possessiveness of his words found new expression in his kiss. At first she felt weak, dizzy, as though she would faint if he didn't stop. But he didn't stop, and soon a strange kind of strength began to course through her. There seemed to be enough power coming into her limbs to cast him off, to break away. But she didn't want to cast him off; she didn't want to use her new power to break away. She wanted to draw him closer—but that wasn't possible. Surely that wasn't possible—

She found herself, in the next instant, back in her seat, acutely aware of a sense of loss, vaguely conscious of Sherworth moving away to the accompaniment of a volley of oaths. The daze lifted, and she saw that the waiter had come into the room, set a tray on the sideboard, and was darting out again. It had been he who had caused her to be abandoned so suddenly! She looked across at Sherworth, her breathing still a trifle out of control. He seemed to be experiencing the same difficulty. He poured a little wine into her glass and filled his own.

After drinking his off in one tilt, he said, in a voice not quite his own, "I seem only to sink myself deeper. Now, not only have I broken the promise I made you, I've spoiled your first kiss for you."

Vescinda began to feel a little giddy as she thought, *spoiled it?* She couldn't answer, however, because the waiter had come back into the room, but she smiled at her harassed lover over the rim of her glass as she sipped slowly, letting the bubbles nibble at her lips.

The effect of this upon Sherworth was both immediate and great. He brought the heels of both hands to the surface of the table, and his eyes flashed dangerously toward the waiter.

This amused Vescinda further, as she thought with a wonderful detachment that he was deciding whether to thrust the poor man back into the kitchen or cast him out of the window. The notion occurred, only to be ignored, that she really ought to say something prosaic and give his thoughts another direction.

Fortunately the busy little Frenchman was too engrossed in his art to feel at all threatened. He stepped round the table, bowing before Vescinda in a way that begged her attention. She glanced up, wishing him a million miles away. He was presenting her with an ornate serving dish. She supposed he desired her approval of something he had carried in from that sea of sauces in the kitchen, and, nodding her permission for him to raise the lid, she peered in, prepared to praise a particularly delectable concoction. She was momentarily struck dumb by what she saw. Reposing on a cushion of black velvet was a pretty little brooch set out in garnets. It had been borne in upon her some time ago that she was dining in one of London's most elegant and extravagant places, but she doubted even Clarendon's would dispense gems with its meals. The alternative possibility, however, was distressing in the extreme and almost as hard to believe. She should have thought Sherworth would know that it was beyond the line to give her jewelry, in any circumstances, and shockingly improper to make a public display of it. She didn't think for a minute that he had intended it as the insult it surely *was,* but she certainly couldn't accept such a thing. She hoped he would understand and not make matters worse by protesting. Schooling her countenance, she said with a slight smile and a dismissive tone, "Yes, it is very pretty, but I'm afraid you have mistaken the room. This cannot be for me."

"Mais oui, mademoiselle, la vôtre," the waiter assured, as though speaking to one who needed to be convinced of her good fortune.

Sherworth, in the meantime, had turned white with suspicion. He whipped the waiter's hand out of his line of vision to complete his horror. "No! Take it away, you jolterhead!"

"But Comte Sherworth, you said——"

"Away! Away! Before I give you the drubbing of your life. *It doesn't belong here!"*

The waiter, giving a shriek of comprehension, dropped the serving dish, spilling the brooch on the table. He fumbled frantically, retrieving the despised article only to drop it again.

Vescinda watched in awesome calm. The exchange of words and the alarmed behavior of the waiter had been all that was needed to convince her that the brooch had indeed been delivered at Sherworth's instructions. Evidently, before the scheme to entrap her had been devised, he had planned to regale Miss Stratton with this very dinner! The poor waiter had not mistaken the room, only the woman. Her burning thoughts were interrupted by the waiter, who was addressing her in hysterical French, apologizing and begging pardon and giving excuses that were almost as incomprehensible as they were absurd. She tried several times to reassure him, but he seemed to have forgotten all he ever knew of the English tongue. Vescinda certainly didn't hold him accountable, but now, more than ever, she wanted him to go away. She was on the edge of strong hysterics herself. Lapsing into French, she informed him in a flawless accent that she was only disappointed because she had thought he'd brought her more of those delicious mushrooms.

Sherworth's threats and her assurances had gone in vain, but at this his face lit with relief. If mademoiselle wished for mushrooms, she would have every one in the house. Mademoiselle told him firmly, however, that she wished for only a very *small* portion and hurried him off on his mission of atonement.

No sooner had he turned his back, than Vescinda's eyes blazed across at Sherworth. A passion, amorous in origin, rechanneled its energy into fury. When he leaped up to come to her, she was out of her chair and ranged on the other side of the table before he'd taken two steps. "You *dare*!" she hissed. "You dare to think you will use me like the harlot you'd meant to have here in my place! You—you *chartered* libertine! Don't dare to touch me—ever!"

"Damn! Oh *damnation!* Vescinda, you don't understand!"

"And stop saying that! I *do* understand! I understand that you are an odious, rakehelly blackguard, and I hate you! Do *you* understand? I *despise* you! I want never to see you again, as long as I live! Go! Go away! Go to China! To—to India! Go where you can keep a harem! That's what you want, you abominable—*abominable* loose fish!"

Sherworth tried again to reach her, but she moved lithely round the table in the opposite direction. At this moment, the door opened to admit the countess and her escort. Sir Richard succumbed instantly to a severe attack of coughing, but the countess, coming sedately into the room, said in a light admonitory tone, "Vescinda, my dear, it is not the thing to be chasing Adrian round the table." She addressed Sherworth in the same light tone, a lightness belied by the speaking look in her eyes. "Well, Adrian, I daresay you will like to get on with your meal."

24

IF A COMMON thought was shared by the little party, it was a profound relief when the coach drew up in Green Street an hour later. The crackling tension that had lain beneath their practiced civilities during an uncomfortable meal had reached its zenith during the short drive home. Only Sherworth had spared himself the effort of pretense. He waited now, in the same unrelenting silence he had maintained throughout, while Sir Richard alighted to help the countess from the elegant vehicle, and then stepped out himself. But there was a strong message in his wild blue eyes when he turned and offered his assistance to Vescinda, as pronounced as the warning pressure of his gloved hand over hers when she came down the coach steps, as plain as his intention when he made it impossible for her to reclaim her hand once she had reached the walkway.

She met his intense gaze steadily. His morose silence over the past hour had led her to believe that he intended to simplify the whole matter by thinking himself well out of a bad situation. But, instead, he was making it plain that he was determined still to speak with her—and all but demanding that she clear the way for him with her grandmother.

She walked on to join the countess at the door, her hand still imprisoned in his, her look of gravity covering a mixture of other emotions, distress, unhappiness, the remnants of her humiliation and anger. A tense anticipation held the little party silent for a moment. Then a quick pain running through her hand caused

Vescinda to flash a sharp look at Sherworth. But her decision had already been made.

She had wanted nothing so much as to be quietly alone with her misery and shame for a few hours. She dreaded what she must now say to him, but he had ended all doubt that it must be said. And, apart from being convinced that he would make a frightful scene right there in the street if she attempted to put him off, she was beginning, herself, to feel a wish to have it done and behind her.

She addressed the countess in a controlled voice, "Grandmama, if you have no objection, I should like a few private words with Sherworth."

"Why, certainly, my dear. Go on up to the drawing room, and Richard shall bear me company over a glass of wine down here."

The countess sighed and almost wilted onto Sir Richard's arm, as they watched Sherworth and Vescinda go hand and hand up the stairs.

Vescinda was not set free until the door of the drawing room had been firmly closed and Sherworth had taken a position with his back to it. She walked to the center of the room and dropped her shawl on a chair, then began to remove her long white evening gloves.

"In the circumstances, sir, I should have been willing to speak to you without this," she said, lightly massaging her hand as she turned to face him. "To begin with, I am *obliged* to beg your pardon. It was the height of impropriety to say such things of you."

Sherworth stared back in fascination. "Even if they're true?"

"Particularly if they are true," she replied, without a trace of humor. "Because it is extremely improper to even notice such things. I certainly know better. I have no defense other than to say I am extremely sorry."

"Amazing! Had you not told me this, I would have sworn that it was I who owed the apology. I wonder who the devil makes all these bizarre rules."

"I'll warrant *that* one was made by a man!" she answered a trifle hotly and had to wait a moment to command her tone. "Nevertheless, it is accepted by everyone. Compliance is expected."

"I see. Well, you may depend upon me to tell no one that you took a pet merely because you were served harlot's fare with your second course."

There was a slight choking sound, but she did not speak. Sherworth gave up his effort to lighten her mood and said curtly,

"So, with the obligatory apology thus made, we can return to the simple and more logical fact that you are still excessively disturbed over that damnable business at Clarendon's."

"Yes, yes, of course, I am. Could I be otherwise?" Seeing him take a tentative step forward and then cautiously resume his position, she said, "Sherworth, you needn't guard the door. I shall promise not to run away, but I wish you will sit quietly and hear what I have to say."

He went to her immediately. "Vescinda, if you will let me explain, you will see—"

"It isn't at all necessary," she interrupted. "I realize that it was an oversight of some sort. And it isn't what *you* did that concerns me. I—Sherworth, do, pray, go away. I can't think with you ready to pounce on me."

He sighed and moved over to stand by the mantel. "I'll keep my distance if that's what you want, and I'll try not to interrupt, but do try to remember that I, too, have something to say."

She walked a little as she spoke, saying almost to herself, "It truly didn't occur to me that you could possibly wish to go on with this. That you do places me in the unhappiest of situations. But I think perhaps you do not properly understand, that you are looking upon this as an isolated incident, relying upon my good breeding to see me through in the future. Oh," she added scornfully, "you would be quite right in thinking I have been thoroughly *trained* to deal with such things. Time without number I have had it drilled into me that a lady must first *accept* the inevitable mistress, and then completely forget that she exists! Oh, yes, I have certainly been *told* how to go on if I should hear her mentioned and how to behave if I should chance to see her—even that I might find myself in company with her at the same party. Because, as often as not, she will be the wife of some other gentleman in the room! I shan't pretend a liking for that part of my education, but I had supposed myself to be as capable as anyone else of acquitting myself properly. The pitiful thing is that I *should* be, if I were to marry Worlington."

"Now, just a minute. I said I wouldn't interrupt, but don't delude yourself that *he* has been leading the life of a monk."

"No, no," she said with an edge of temper. "You will recall that I have reason to *know* that he goes on very much the same as you. Even that he shares your taste in females!" She gave an annoyed whisk of her hand. "What signifies is that he is not like you in any other way. He keeps the rules. His conduct is compatible with my training. He would have his mistress just as any of you, but he would never cause in me a feeling of being threatened by her. My role would be quite defined. He wants me for his lady—"

"And I? What the devil do you think I want?"

"You want a woman. A woman to love and who will love you."

"Well, yes, of course," he agreed impatiently, but he paused, and a smile crept into his eyes. "And what of that? You once told me that all ladies know how to be a woman."

Vescinda looked at him sharply, then began to walk again. "Yes, and I told you at the same time that few women know how to be a lady. You—you keep me constantly behaving and feeling like a woman, and you see the proof of my words in the disastrous results tonight. It—it is what I have been trying to explain to you. As *your* wife, I *should* feel threatened by your mistress, just as I should feel an improper sense of possessiveness in the area I should be expected to share you with her. Already I have been conscious of a—a shameful sense of competition!" Her voice took on a note of agitation. "But don't you see, I *cannot* compete with her! I *am* burdened with these dozens of rules. I have been kept closely and prepared for one thing only, to be a gentleman's wife. Whereas, she enjoys an untrammeled existence, and her education has been centered on something *quite* different. I only wonder why it has not sunk in before now that a man must most naturally prefer a mistress to a wife."

He strode forward and clasped both her hands. "Vescinda, Vescinda, I want you for both my wife *and* my mistress, and I promise you, there could be no one to compete with you in either role!"

She exclaimed impatiently, "But you can't know that! For all either of us know, I could turn out to be—to be 'not worth the climb up the ladder'!"

Sherworth stared blankly, then went off in a helpless fit of laughing. Vescinda tried to pull her hands away, but he held her fast, saying through his laughter, "No, no, I'm sorry. It's just that I quite mistook your expression when I told you of that. I was afraid—very afraid—that you didn't *approve* of what I said to her!"

"Approve?" exclaimed Vescinda, still incensed by his amusement. "Of course I approve! I don't know what else you could have said to stop her. I am only glad that you thought of it. If you hadn't, she'd be busy lying her spiteful little head off, and everyone would be saying such things of *me!* Only not a hayloft, but a *lobstering shack!* Which somehow seems very much worse."

"Very much worse," he agreed through trembling lips. "But my adorable girl, my exquisite lady, my most *magnificent* woman, you mustn't concern yourself over that other. It never occurred to me that—" Sherworth broke off, finding himself in another dilemma. He took a deep breath and said, in a rallying tone, "Oh, come now, surely you know it's utter nonsense to tease yourself about such a thing."

"If I'd thought about it at all, I should have been comfortable in that conviction up to an hour ago. But I didn't know then that you are accounted a judge of such matters—or even that there was anything *to* judge! I'd always supposed it was purely a matter of one's feelings! How—how could I possibly guess that there is—that there is a question of *skill!*"

"Well, *of course,* there isn't!" Sherworth asserted, putting the first wrinkle in his mantle of honesty. "I merely said so to frighten the Wildborne. It is just as you say—except, of course, that a great many females are singularly lacking in feeling."

Vescinda was studying him, not fully convinced. So he decided on a frontal attack. "My darling goose, I promise you, there isn't the slightest cause for *you* to concern yourself. Never—*never,* in my entire career, have I encountered a look with *more* feeling than the one you cast my way at Clarendon's tonight."

Vescinda blushed and looked away, uttering a stifled protest. Sherworth pressed home his advantage. "Come, come, delightful baggage, own up! We've just agreed that I am accounted a judge of such matters. Would you have *me* believe I don't know a spirited filly when I see one?"

She smiled reluctantly through her embarrassment and drew her hands out of his grasp. "Very well, if you will have it, but this spirited filly caused a shocking scene tonight, and I beg you will heed what I am trying to tell you. It would be folly to think that I could let myself be treated as a woman, made always to feel as a woman, and then conduct myself as a lady when I am challenged in my woman's role. No! In such circumstances, there is no reason to hope I shouldn't go on making just such a spectacle of myself—if not worse! Tonight, when you kissed me—in a most improper way and in a most improper setting—and then, in the next instant, I found myself confronted with the evidence of your *other* woman, I went a little mad, and I had no thought at all for my precious training. I broke every rule, and I did it heedless of the consequences. For all I knew or cared, anyone might have come in and found me in the heights of that undignified outburst. It fills me with mortification that Grandmama and Richard saw as much as they did, and I don't think I need tell you that I look upon a future filled with that sort of thing with the utmost repugnance. I am sure, if you can bring yourself to believe what I am telling you, you will realize that you would be as miserable and find it just as humiliating as I!"

"Vescinda, I'm beginning to go a little mad myself. None of this signifies! I care only for one thing, for you to say that you will marry me!"

"Oh," she cried hopelessly, "of course! I *must* marry you, if you are still convinced that you want me."

He had started toward her again, but he stopped, somewhat at a loss. "Must? *Must* marry me? Now what is this? Another confounded rule? You call a man a chartered libertine and a rakehelly blackguard and you must marry him?" He frowned. "Or is it because I despoiled you with my kiss?"

Something between a laugh and a sob escaped Vescinda, and she brought the back of her hand to her lips. She stood for a moment, looking down and shaking her head slightly in denial. Then she walked over and into Sherworth's arms and pressed her face against his coat. "You haven't the least notion of how desperately I love you, have you? It's because I *daren't* marry anyone else, as long as you are still determined to have me. Far, far less than the disgrace of a jealous scene could I bear what you might cause me to do, if you went on saying the things you do, and looking at me *so,* and swooping down and kissing me as you did tonight. And you would! I have only to think of my crushed fingers to know you wouldn't keep your word to Grandmama." She was sobbing in earnest now. "And—and I am becoming such a wickedly weak-willed thing that I should probably be *glad* that you hadn't!"

"Vescinda," Sherworth said in a thick, slightly shaken voice, "if you are weeping for this mythical husband whom you believe I might have caused you to be unfaithful to, forget it. I promise you, no such thing would have occurred. Long before the marriage could have been consummated, you would have been a widow! And think how sad that should have been, for I should have been forced to flee the country. And, with England at war with most of the civilized world, I should have had to carry you to one of those uncomfortable islands, where we should have had to exist on coconuts and shellfish and— Oh, my precious love, *why* did you keep me all this time listening to grim warnings, when you must have known you couldn't frighten me away with such stuff?"

"I *didn't* know," she protested with a watery sniff. "I remember, if you don't, a long dissertation about how terrified you would be to have such a wife as Lady Hamilton, because she has been known to vent her feelings in public."

"Ooh, yes. How could the great similarity between you and the notorious Emma have escaped me? Well, if you will promise not to fall in love with any naval heroes or fill the newspapers with your indiscretions, I shall try to bear with the rest."

She chuckled and slipped her arms around him. "I trust you will recall how lightly you've taken all this, if ever you find yourself the victim of a public hair-combing. The *least* you may look for is numerous, long curtain lectures."

"Ah, yes! Getting back to that. My dearest love, even though it means flying in the face of convention, I feel I must apologize for what occurred tonight. In fact, I am going to be downright shabby and explain. There *was* no harlot—nor a female of any description—meant for your place tonight. I had no thought of going to Clarendon's until I received Mama's message."

Pulling back, Vescinda used her hands to push herself slightly away. She glared up at him through swimming eyes. "You aren't going to tell me that it wasn't you who ordered the brooch brought to the table, are you—*Comte Sherworth.*"

"How can I," he laughed, "when only tonight you expressed such touching faith in my honesty? No, the fault was entirely mine, but it was an arrangement from the past, one I had simply forgotten—and—well, I daresay it was the circumstance of your being there without a chaperon that caused Henri to suppose the unthinkable."

"To suppose that I was she, surely you must mean."

"No, lovable darling, there was no 'she'—no particular she."

Vescinda's eyes flew open. Pushing herself further back, she demanded incredulously, "Do you say that *anyone,* anyone at all, who sits next you there, is served garnets? That it is *automatical?*"

"No, no, certainly not!" he refuted, taking umbrage. "Only the dark-haired girls were served *garnets*—er—but you may be sure I mean to—"

"Good God, you truly *are* abominable, aren't you?"

"Well—yes, but pray don't feel you must disgrace yourself by saying so."

Vescinda went suddenly off in a peal of laughter, and threw her arms round his neck, and kissed him soundly.

"Oh, this is all very confusing," he complained. "I thought you told me that ladies were never to kiss gentlemen?"

"They're not, but you, my sad rip, are not precisely a gentleman. What was it you were going to say? Not, I hope, that you mean to collect your store of brooches from Henri! I beg you will not. It rather equalizes things to learn that you are also unfaithful to your mistress. Yes, by all means, have a great many, so many that you can't possibly keep their names straight. To begin with, I shan't be in a quake, wondering if you are falling in love with 'Miss Very Special,' and, secondly, it will go very much easier on you if I am not able to conjure up such a vivid picture of her as I did tonight! Oh, dear," she sighed, "at all events, I am at least relieved to learn you haven't such shocking taste as to give Miss Stratton garnets to wear with that head of hers."

Sherworth had been listening in high amusement, but at that last, he was taken aback. "What is this, now?" he demanded. "What can you know of Miss Stratton's head?"

"Everything! She brought it into the milliner's where I was shopping with Grandmama."

"Did she?" He laughed with what Vescinda considered entirely too careless an attitude.

"Yes," she flung back tersely, "and she used it to carry out the hat of your favorite color."

"*My* favorite color?"

"Green," said Vescinda, recommending him to recall his reputation for honesty.

"I do, I do, and I assure you that I place no blot on that reputation by saying that I have never had a partiality for green— ah—except, of course, where it concerns a pair of magnificent green eyes."

Vescinda twisted out of his arms impatiently and turned away.

"Oh!" she huffed. "It is most improper for me to be pursuing this!" She looked back over her shoulder, saying defensively, "Well, I warned you that the benefits of having a woman would deprive you of the comfort of having a lady."

"Yes, yes, you warned me," he agreed, taking her by the shoulders. "And since I didn't instantly cut my stick, we shall assume that I am well up to your worst. Come now, dear and beautiful hellcat, don't curb your tongue on my account."

She let him turn her and smiled up contritely as she worked her way into his arms again. "Oh, hellcat, indeed! Are you quite certain that you want such a wickedly jealous wife?"

"I feel it is a concession I must make, since you are going to have such a wickedly jealous husband," he said, folding her tightly against him.

She returned dismissively, "No one disapproves of jealous husbands. Besides I shan't mind that at all."

"Then I must try to match your magnanimity. But tell me what it is about green that has made you look yellow? I collect it has to do with a headdress Miss Stratton has been sporting about."

"You are trying to make me feel perfectly goosish about it, but I can tell you, I was extremely vexed because you have remarked it every time I have worn green."

"Have I? Very likely. It becomes you. And, most of all, I like the effect it has on your eyes."

"Yes. Well, perhaps you will understand, then, why I should have been a trifle put out to hear the shopgirl informing Miss Stratton that his lordship wished *particularly* to see her in a certain green hat."

"Oh, indeed. An unforgivable defection. Gad, it's gratifying to be the *victim* of an injustice for a change! My love, we must add two points to the wedding vows: I shall never believe anything Miss Wildborne tells me, and you will try to remember that I am not the only peer in London. The 'lordship' of your little horror story is Worlington. Miss Stratton has been under his protection for a se'enight."

"*Worlington?*" Vescinda exclaimed. "But—but how does this come about? You drove directly to Brighton from Dorset. Surely, it was reasonable to assume you went there to collect her!"

"Oh, yes, I went expressly for that purpose and arrived at the theatre just in time for her performance. However, I bowed out before she had even left the stage and locked myself away to get quietly drunk. I maintained that blissful state for two days, during which, I have a vague recollection of Worlington coming to my hotel and telling me that both he and Miss Stratton were anxious to know my intentions. I mumbled that I had none, that her hair was too red, her eyes were too blue, her laugh held no music, and her figure was all wrong—" He broke off and held Vescinda away from him. "Yes, *all* wrong!" he repeated, running his eyes over her. "Too much here—not enough there—"

Vescinda gave a scandalized gasp. "Mind yourself!" Then robbed the reproof of its conviction by flinging her arms around the neck of the offender and laughing with the simple delight of pure happiness.

Sherworth's only reply was to sweep her up into his arms and convey her to one of the chairs by the fireplace, where she passed the next several minutes comfortably in his lap and being thoroughly adored.

This scene was witnessed by the countess, when she entered at this point. She halted on the threshold, shaking her head and wondering what Chloe would think, to see her "high-stickler" of a niece nestled unconcernedly in the lap of one of London's notorious rakes, most of her once-flawless coiffure flowing down her back, and apparently content, after having lost one of her shoes, to share her lover's boot, for her bare toes were tucked in a most friendly fashion into the top of one of Sherworth's Hessians.

Advancing into the room, she remarked cheerfully, "Poor girl, I see you had to sit on him to get him to listen. But you will have to come down from there now, for I have ordered tea, and Longly, you know, is not accustomed to this sort of thing."

"Oh, dear, yes," Vescinda exclaimed, sitting upright. She put an exploratory hand up to her hair. "Goodness! A birch broom in a fit, to be sure! Is Richard still here?"

"Oh, indeed, and already calling me his dear *dow.*"

Vescinda stared blankly, then chuckled. "Oh, *dowager!* I hadn't thought of that. Shall you mind my usurping your title?"

"My dear, I shan't mind anything, if only you will both assure me that this tumultuous courtship is at an end."

"Oh, yes, his neck is all the way into the noose this time," Vescinda returned, giving a sharp little tug to Sherworth's crumpled cravat.

"Then I think it will be well if you dashed up to your chamber, where Dorcas is waiting to make hasty repairs. Your father is expected to squire Chloe home shortly and will be joining us. Not that we need concern ourselves over him—I doubt he would notice anything amiss if you drank your tea perched as you are—but we mustn't spring too much on your poor aunt all at once. The news of your betrothal shall be quite enough for Chloe to digest in one evening."

Vescinda twinkled lovingly at Sherworth and leaned forward to hunt for her Italian slipper. Watching her for a moment, the countess laughed, "Well, Adrian, if this is the cold, boring formality with which she conducts herself in a drawing room, what must we expect?"

Vescinda had never heard the old joke between them and looked up curiously. Sherworth took her hand in his and met the question in her eyes steadily, as he replied to his stepmother, "One thing you may expect—and my vow on it—is to see two dozen brooches and a house in Kensington go out of my life forever."

The countess exclaimed, "For goodness' sake, Vescinda, you mustn't start that again! I can hear your father's carriage drawing up already!" Seeing that her words went unheeded, she settled back in her favorite red damask wing chair and drew her footstool forward. "Shocking creatures, both of you. You will have to spend a great deal of time in the country, I think."